ALL NEW FOURTH EDITION
1987 GUN DIGEST HUNTING ANNUAL

Edited by
Robert S.L. Anderson

ABOUT OUR COVERS

The name "Parker" is legendary in the world of shotgunning. In fact, to many American shotgunners, the name "Parker" is synonymous with double-barreled (side-by-side) bird shooting.

Absent since the close of World War II, Parker doubles have become some of the most collectible firearms ever made. Knowing this, the Skeuse family introduced their line of Parker Reproduction shotguns about 3 years ago. First there was the 20 gauge, and now the 28 gauge.

On our front and back cover you'll see (to the left) an original Parker A-1 Special in 20 gauge. Few were made. As a result, a collectors' gun like the A-1 Special will set you back about $50,000. To the right of the A-1 Special you'll see a Parker Reproduction in 28 gauge. It's beautiful. And true to the original. How "true?" Parts interchange. Enough said.

Want more? See our New Products '87 column.

GUN DIGEST HUNTING ANNUAL STAFF

EDITOR
   Robert S.L. Anderson
SENIOR STAFF EDITOR
   Harold A. Murtz
ASSISTANT TO THE EDITORS
   Lilo Anderson
CONTRIBUTING EDITORS
   Edward A. Matunas
   Clay Harvey
   Layne Simpson
COVER PHOTOGRAPHY
   John Hanusin
MANAGING EDITOR
   Pamela J. Johnson
PUBLISHER
   Sheldon L. Factor

DBI BOOKS, INC.

PRESIDENT
   Charles T. Hartigan
VICE PRESIDENT & PUBLISHER
   Sheldon L. Factor
VICE PRESIDENT — SALES
   John G. Strauss
TREASURER
   Frank R. Serpone

ISBN 0-87349-003-7   ISSN 0739-4403

CONTENTS

CONTENTS

Depending on the source, being called a "trophy hunter" these days can be anything from a compliment to a castigation. It's the old "eye of the beholder" thing, but as is always the case, the less one knows about the subject, the more myopic the observing eye.

Just what is trophy hunting? Who does it? And why is it perceived so differently, not only by the non-hunting and anti-hunting factions, but among we hunters ourselves?

In the 25 years or so that I've been chasing game across five continents, I believe I've crossed trails with just about every kind of hunter there is. From the sub-Artic to the Namib desert, from Alaska to Zambia, I've shared camps with the rich and famous, with royalty, with the movers-and-shakers. For the most part though, it's been with ordinary guys; guys who wanted to be there, hunting what we were hunting, badly enough that it took no small sacrifice on their part, along with a huge chunk of their savings. Men who, without the moral support of their families back home, probably would not have made what they would otherwise consider a selfish decision. I've seen men who could afford to return to wherever it was we were, to hunt whatever it was we were hunting, every month for the rest of their lives, yet shot the first animal they saw. And I've seen men pass up a decent trophy on the final day of a hunt even though they knew full well this would be their *last* chance for that particular specie.

The Definition of "Trophy"

Before taking on the subject of trophy hunting and trophy hunters, perhaps we should first try to define "trophy," for it is our personal interpretation of that term that determines much of our attitude.

To the tree-hugger types, a "hunting trophy" suggests a macabre souvenir of the kill and has nothing whatever to do with the quality of the specimen. To them, a carcass or any part thereof is a "trophy," and our posing with it for a picture or having its horns, antlers, or head mounted, is no

After decades of big game hunting experience,
the author has worked over the positives
and the negatives of trophy hunting.
His conclusions are valid.

THE TROPHY HUNTER

by
JON R. SUNDRA

different from the barbaric rituals of displaying a severed head on a pike or a scalp dangling from a belt. It is proof of a kill, nothing more. To these people, killing an animal for meat is the most acceptable of what are all unacceptable reasons for hunting. We've all heard it: "Well, as long as you eat the meat and nothing goes to waste . . . but to just kill for a . . . a *trophy!*" It's an either-or situation for them. A trophy is somehow undigestable; only non-trophy animals are good to eat. Yet we should not be allowed to kill either, according to some.

Drivel, of course.

At this point I could cop out and tell you that a "trophy" can just as easily be a spike buck to one hunter, as it could be a record-book head to another, and that it just depends on one's perceptions and the circumstances under which that particular animal was taken.

Sounds good, doesn't it? And in certain contexts that sort of subjective, liberal interpretation would suffice. But there's another facet, too, that's just as important. There must also be some objective criteria by which we judge excellence. That's why we have organizations like the Boone & Crockett, Pope & Young, Roland Ward, the CIC and others who maintain records and scoring systems. While those standards may vary to some extent,

Over the long haul, a trophy hunter pays his dues many times over.

an animal qualifying for any of them would be a well-above average specimen—one that would impress anyone even vaguely familiar with the specie. Whether it was killed by a worthy hunter after an arduous stalk, or hit by a car and picked up on the side of the road, is irrelevant to its status as a trophy-class animal. Whether it's a *trophy,* however, is something else again.

To illustrate: one of the best whitetails I've ever taken, I shot from the porch of a cabin. It happened on a miserably wet day. After taking as much of a soaking that morning as I could endure, I returned to the cabin around 10:30 to dry out. While tending to a few strips of bacon, I happened to look out the window to see this nice 10-point emerge from the thicket into a little clearing some 80 yards from the cabin.

Yes, it's up on my wall now, and I'm proud of it . . . sort of. After all, I did have to be in the right place at the right time, to not spook the critter, and to make the shot when the time

One becomes a trophy hunter as conditions permit, says Sundra. When you hit the caribou migration just right, any hunter can afford to be highly selective.

came. Lots of people get a similar opportunity and blow it, so I'll take a small pat on the back. But in another sense, it's a hollow pride because I know the circumstances of that trophy's taking.

Another example of the trophy itself far overshadowing its taking was a beautiful 57-inch kudu. It was taken by a friend of mine from Chicago, Orville Brettman. We were among a party of eight encamped on the banks of the Umniati River in Zimbabwe. All of us had collected nice bulls ranging from 49 to 54 inches . . . all but this friend of mine who hadn't seen anything other than immature bulls and one ol' stud with a broken horn. On this, our last morning in camp, we had to be packed and ready by 10 AM for the long drive back to Herare and the flight home. The hunt was history. Resigned to the prospect of not having collected the one animal he wanted most, Orv stayed up late the previous night to keep a bottle of Cognac company. The following morning while most of us were getting our hearts started with our second and third cups of coffee, one of the trackers came shuffling up to the head Professional Hunter, Dave Masson, and pointed across the river. "Nhoro, bwana. Kuru." Big kudu.

Everyone scrambled for their binoculars and soon we were all gaping at what appeared to be a very good bull standing on a high bank above the river some 250 yards downstream.

"Where the hell's Orville?" Dave hissed. "Somebody get him. Tell him his kudu's waiting." Orv must have heard the commotion 'cause he emerged from his tent a few moments later in nothing but his white Fruit of the Looms, rifle in hand. I could feel his head throbbing from 50 feet away.

"Where's a kudu," he whispered, not quite sure we weren't playing the sort of cruel, demented joke he knew we were all quite capable of. Dave pointed downstream and the next moment the two of them were hunchbacking behind the sparse bank vegetation in an effort to shrink the range. Soon they were out of sight beyond a nearby hill. Meanwhile, the bull just stood there under the thorn acacia in charcteristic fashion—horns up among the overhead branches which apparently gives them some sense of security—like an ostrich with its head in the sand.

At the crash of Orv's 375 a minute or so later, we saw the bull lurch, then turn and disappear in a downhill rush.

As it turned out, we found Orv's kudu within 100 yards of where it had been hit, stone dead with a well placed shot in the chest. Its beautifully-spiraled horns went just shy of 57 inches, easily making it the best bull in camp.

Is my friend proud of his kudu? In a way, sure. It was a good shot . . . especially under the head-pounding circumstances. And it's certainly a trophy-class animal. But *is* it a trophy? Only Orv can answer that, but I can tell you he takes more pride in a number of lesser-quality heads that adorn his den because he worked harder for them. With his kudu he feels a little cheated.

Ideally, no extraordinary specimen of game animal should ever be killed through sheer luck or happenstance, or under conditions other than a long, back-breaking stalk culminating with one perfectly-placed shot. Hell, it's only right if one's going to shoot a record head! But alas, such is not often the case. Indeed, I'd wager that

the vast majority of animals listed in the record book—especially the Boone & Crockett—were simply stumbled onto by hunters who otherwise would have gladly shot a lesser quality head had it crossed their sights first. I single out the B&C here because their minimum entry scores are so high that only the most extraordinary specimens will qualify. A head that even approaches the minimum would prompt 999 out of 1000 hunters to pull the trigger. More easily achieved is a listing in the Safari Club record book which sets its minimum scores at much more attainable levels. SCI takes the position that their scoring standards for record book entry are high enough so as to ensure that only above-average specimens will qualify, but on the other hand, not so high as to discourage would-be trophy hunters. There's something to be said for

(Right) Actual "hunting circumstances" can determine trophy status, in a subjective way. This average-size black bear becomes a genuine trophy when you've taken it with a flintlock like this hunter did.

(Above) Two average mule deer, but real trophies for the two young men from the East who had to save for 2 years to make this Wyoming hunt. Unless and until they hunt mule deer again, and successfully, these hunters can be justifiably proud of these heads.

A record-book head like this western red stag taken in Spain by Basil Bradbury, is something to behold. Imagine the discipline needed, says Sundra, to pass up a bull two-thirds this good.

each position since both encourage selective hunting; they only differ in the degree of excellence required for record book admission.

The Trophy Hunter

Just as there are different levels of trophy excellence, so too are there different levels of trophy hunters. Entry level status is achieved the first time we consciously choose to not pull the trigger when we have a legal critter in our sights. Now, obviously, there's a real chasm between the guy who passes on a button buck the first morning of the first day of the local hunting season, and the chap who turns down a 75-pounder on the last day of a 3-week elephant safari 'cause he's got 80-pound tusks straddling his fireplace back home. The aforementioned examples are extremes but illustrate just how broadly selective hunting can be interpreted.

Unfortunately, there's a lot of misunderstanding and ill-will among those in our own ranks toward the trophy hunter . . . or what they perceive him to be. For the average guy who loves to hunt but knows he'll probably never have the chance to do it outside his own state, let alone in a foreign country, the image of a globe-trotting sportsman isn't always a flattering one. Indeed, some see the trophy hunter as a disgustingly rich dilettante who hunts 6 months a year, while spending the other six planning where he'll hunt the next six. He's a dude who refuses to shoot any animal unless his guide assures him it will "make the book." He's not really a hunter but a head collector who's ob-

Trophy whitetail hunting—to Boone & Crockett standards,—is often as near an exercise in futility as one can come, says author. This magnificent buck, taken in Pennsylvania by Mike Sullivan, was the best taken in the state . . . and was a full six points short of the minimum 170 needed for B&C admission!

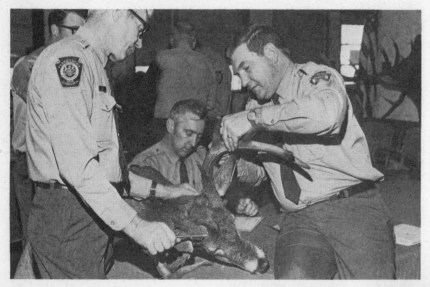

trophy room wall. And when asked how his last hunt went, he answers not by telling you what a great experience it was, but rather how many heads he put in the book and what each one scored.

Not a very flattering perception to be sure.

Are there really people like that? You bet, but they're mercifully few and no more representative of the hunting fraternity as a whole than poachers and slob hunters are.

The way I see it, a trophy hunter, in the best sense of the term, is simply a guy who is more selective about what sort of animal he'll shoot. Trophy hunting represents a natural progression: The more experienced one is at hunting, the more selective one be-

sessed with accumulating trophies in more quantity and/or at a faster pace than whomever it is he's chosen to be in competition with. Somewhere along the way those motives which separate hunting from killing have been mislaid by that hunter. His respect for animals as being noble, worthy adversaries is gone, as are the sensibilities that make us want to leap for joy at the fair and hard won taking of a beautiful trophy . . . yet weep over its lost majesty. He's not above buying a set of horns or antlers then lying about how they got on his

Scoring systems differ as to the degree of excellence required, but all are stringent enough to ensure that only *well-above-average* specimens will qualify.

Author Sundra and Professional Hunter Bryan Smith measure a reedbuck. Trophy quality is important to Sundra, but though he's taken many "book" heads, he's never entered a single one. "So long as I know," he says.

comes. After all, as long as we're out there by choice rather than necessity (assuming we're not relying on game for our very sustenance), the prospect of coming home empty-handed shouldn't bother us that much. This is especially true when we're hunting locally or in our home state where we know there'll be other chances. Perhaps on our next hunt we'll get that big 10-point we've been dreaming about. But if not, and a spike buck shows itself on the last day and we plug it for the freezer, fine. If not, that's fine too.

Occupying the next rung on the trophy hunting ladder is the nimrod who shells out hard-earned and long-saved money to go on an out-of-state hunt—a hunt he knows he may never be able to do again—and still musters up enough self-restraint to pass up a

tion he deserves. After all, the gent who has the time and wherewithall to come back as often as necessary is one thing; to know it's your first and probably last hunt and still be selective, is something else again. It is the kind of conduct we should *all* aspire to.

Adding to the difficulty of maintaining high (let alone record-book) standards, is the prospect of passing up a good head early on, then not seeing anything close to it for the remainder of the hunt. Conversely, when you fill out early in the hunt with a critter you had doubts about at the time, it usually turns out those doubts were warranted. Sure as hell you wind up seeing something better afterward. I went through both the aforementioned scenarios just last year.

In January I was in Sonora Mexico

hunting mule deer. On the first morning of the first day I had two bucks in two different basins visible from the same vantage point. We had plenty of time to evaluate them through the spotting scope, and I was sure both of them were *as* good, and probably better, then the 28½-inch head I had back home. But, hey, here I was with two good bucks on the first morning of a 5-day hunt . . . So I passed, figuring I'd surely see something better. Sure I would.

In August I was hunting Asiatic buffalo in Australia. On the first day we saw a bull my guide assured me was a good one—probably as good as I was going to see. Of course I'd heard that line plenty of times before . . . and usually don't pay attention to it—not that early in the hunt. But this time I did. Okay, so it was the *second*

Here, again, it's easy being a trophy hunter, even though judging horn length among these black lechwe is as difficult as setting up the shot.

(Right) It's much easier to hold out for a "book" head under conditions where you're sure to see game every day. Here Sundra checks out his Namibian gemsbok.

good buck or two on the first half of the hunt. Make no mistake: everyone's a trophy hunter the first morning, but that level of selectivity usually drops with each day's passing. No one wants to go home empty-handed, so it is especially difficult to not pull the trigger on a decent buck late in the hunt on the diminishing chance that you'll see something better. But those who *do* manage to do that are to be admired, in my opinion. And the less likely it is that this fellow will return sometime in the future to hunt that specie again, the more admira-

Trophy hunting is 99.9 percent "looking." These two hunters are glassing for Montana pronghorn. Finding one is easy. Finding a *trophy* pronghorn is another story. It takes stamina, dedication and discipline.

(Below) To shoot or not to shoot, that's the question that plagues the would-be trophy hunter. Pressure usually favors the former rather than the latter.

I'm a journalist puts even more pressure on a guide to culminate the hunt. After all, no game, no story.

The point I hope I've made by now is that trophy hunting is kinda' neat, but it is not the easiest thing in the world to do with consistency. When done in the proper spirit though, it is hunting on its highest plane. Do I consider myself a trophy hunter? Sure I do, because like I said, I believe that *selective hunting* is something everyone should aspire to. Seems to me that if it truly does take experience, more than anything else, to become a trophy hunter, more experience is the one thing every hunter wants. So in the final analysis, I think most of us are trophy hunters of one type or another—to the degree we can afford to be and to the extent that our experience allows. •

smallest bull out of seven taken that week.

The would-be trophy hunter, then, has all kinds of mind games working against him, making it difficult to be selective. And let's not forget the subtle pressure applied by the guide to shoot something less than what you may have had in mind. When you've got the crosshairs on the sort of animal you know most hunters would be glad to hang on their wall, and you've got this guide whispering non-committal BS in your ear like: "It's not a bad head," or "We'll have to work to find a better one than that," etc., it's tough not to shoot.

In my particular case, the fact that

IN 14 STATES, they are considered songbirds. In the remaining 36, they are game birds and are hunted harder, longer and by more shooters than any other feathered game in this country. Although tiny, the mourning dove, Carolina turtledove or *Zenaidura macroura* is the game most sought after by this nation's shotgunners.

Several factors contribute to the amazing popularity of dove shooting. First, dove season is generally the first hunting season after a long, hot summer. Next, the birds are more widely distributed than other game birds. Finally, they are *difficult* targets; enough so to attract the attention of any shotgunner.

Dove aren't particularly difficult to drop. That is, they aren't difficult to drop if you can hit 'em! I've seen expert shotgunners blast away through a box or more of shells without ruffling a feather although those same shooters were holy terrors in the duck or goose blinds. After they get their mental gears shifted to potting a 2-ounce target, they do very well. But there are few funnier sights than a first-time dove hunter.

Whoever decided to adopt the dove as a symbol of peace had obviously never known one personally. They cruise along lazily until a hunter shoulders his shotgun, then kick in the afterburners and throw rapidly alternating punches at left and right rudder. The resulting erratic flight pattern is almost enough to make the average shotgunner take up bowling! Application of a few time-tested techniques can help even the odds between dove and hunter, however.

Almost any shotshell and choke can be used effectively. Some experienced

by DICK EADES

dove hunters opt for high velocity shells stuffed with No.6 shot. At the other extreme, some elect an open bored gun with loads of No.8 or No.9 shot. Selection of shells and choke is a matter of personal taste coupled with a smattering of common sense applied to choice of hunting sites and shooting conditions.

Probably 99 percent of the dove taken each year are shot within a range of 40 yards with possibly 75 percent being taken within 25 yards. For this reason, there's simply no call for a Full choked shotgun. Many shooters prefer a Modified choke, and I won't dispute that choice, although much of my shooting is done with a Skeet gun. My ammo? Since most of my shooting is over small water holes, I also usually select No.8 or No.9 shot.

Tips and Tactics

Before hunting season, or at least before you tackle dove shooting the

"... When you hunt doves be sure to bring a spare bucket of ammo and a buddy with a sense of humor—you'll need 'em both!"

DOVE

Walking up birds is only for the hardy hunter and is usually less productive than water hole or grain field shooting. In this case, camouflage is of no value since the birds will be on the ground feeding and will flush when approached.

(Left) Doves sitting on the ground will explode in whichever direction they are facing rather than gathering into a formation for takeoff like most ground nesting birds. Hunters who walk the fields will often find the shooting to be quite fast. One advantage to field hunting is the fact that a "flushed" group of doves will often settle down in the same field (in pairs and singles) after they have been shot at. This gives the persistent hunter a chance to follow up, and continue to fill his bag. Cut wheat fields of 50 acres or larger is where this sort of shooting will be found.

(Right) Some states have split dove seasons with the second season in late December or January.

first time, spend some time watching flight patterns and try to learn the daily habits of the dove in your selected hunting area. This will not be foolproof since the birds may suddenly, for no apparent reason, change their habits overnight. Knowing where the birds are will usually, however, give you a better chance for good shooting than just trusting to luck or searching for them when you could be hunting.

After hunting season begins, continue to observe flight patterns and feeding places. A field that is loaded with fallen grain and covered with birds on Monday may be completely ignored on Tuesday. If you are hunting a "hot spot" that seems to cool suddenly, start watching for a change in the birds' routine. One field may be best for morning hunts but be vacant in the evening.

There are almost as many methods for hunting doves as there are hunters. Some may elect to "walk them up" by marching through grain fields during the heat of the day flushing the birds while they are feeding. This method is probably very popular with doves but should be used only by the hardiest hunters. Unlike ground-nesting birds such as quail, dove will flush wildly in whatever direction they are facing, rather than gathering for a take-off in formation. It's quite common to have several birds rise at one time, each on a different departure course.

Many hunters prefer to station themselves on an established flight pattern and intercept birds as they travel in and out of their feeding grounds. This works well with a large group of hunters who can ring a field without leaving much uncovered territory. Once a few shots have been fired, the birds seem to know which lanes to avoid unless there are enough hunters to cover all avenues of entrance and exit.

Many hunters ignore the fact that doves, like most birds, have exceptional eyesight. Each season, I see hunters clad in very light, almost white shirts and glaring yellow golf caps. I know it's hot during dove sea-

Full camouflage, including face net and gloves, can help the hunter fully blend in with brushy background. Both the face net and gloves are made of an open mesh which provides excellent ventilation and does not interfere with vision.

son but, c'mon fellas, the birds can still see!

My personal choice of clothing for dove hunting is usually camouflage, but I will also simply wear dark, non-reflective clothing much of the time. A hat, in my opinion, is a necessity since it shades the face and prevents the sun from spotlighting it. If you think that's not the case, have a friend stand against some trees in the sun, with and without a hat. Notice how much easier it is to see his face when the hat is removed.

Some hunters will go for full camouflage, including either a face net or camo paint on their faces. While not always convenient, this method of dress is certainly better than any other and will assure a hunter of very low visibility from the doves' point of view. I have also seen a few hunters with camouflage covers or camouflage tape on their shotguns. Though I have never tried this approach, it must be said that a shiny shotgun can be easily seen on a bright day. Camouflaging your gun should add to a dove hunter's desire to blend into the landscape.

In arid parts of the country, the favorite hunting method is to stake out a water hole and simply wait for the doves to come in for a drink. With rare exceptions, every dove in a given area will seek water twice per day. Don't simply stand out in the open. Get in among the trees or brush on the shaded side of the waterhole and conceal yourself.

Dove will ignore a large body of water or a running stream in favor of a muddy stock pond or a small spring. The best water hole for an ambush will have gently sloping banks that permit the doves a walking approach to the water which they seem to prefer. A few trees nearby provide convenient watchtowers and gathering places for the birds so they can get together at the end of the day and exchange tales about how many hunters they frustrated that afternoon.

Quantity of water seems less of a consideration than the other factors mentioned. Small water holes are advantageous for the hunter since, over a large body of water, every dove (so it will seem) will sail in on the other side, just out of range of your shotgun. I am equally convinced that dove can read choke markings on shotguns from a range of about ½-mile! They also know exactly how far the shot will carry and always manage to add *exactly* 5 yards to that range for their flight path! A flock of birds boring

through the sky enroute to water can suddenly change course and split for the next county if they see a hunter. Oddly enough, they will sometimes proceed directly in, even if the hunter stands up. That's just one more "inconsistency" that makes dove hunting a fascinating sport. *Never* count on dove to do anything normal or to repeat any action.

Within the past few years, dove decoys have gained considerable popularity. Hunters who use these decoys report best results by placing a "spread" in trees surrounding a water source. They simply conceal themselves within shooting range of their decoys and wait for the birds to come in. Dove decoys are available in both flat silhouette and fully formed, painted models. Both types seem to work although it seems the fully-formed variety should be better. Both types are usually equipped with spring clips similar to those found on clothespins. As a result, those decoys are easily attached to tree branches. Remember, doves favor barren limbs for resting and observation so pick a similar spot for your decoys.

Guns and Ammo

Earlier, I mentioned shotguns and shells very briefly. I almost hate to make a recommendation since I know successful hunters who use almost every imaginable kind of gun and every make and style of shotshell. The easiest way to start a fierce argument with a group of dove hunters is to state that a slide-action 20-gauge or an autoloading 12-bore (or anything else) is the "best" shotgun for dove hunting. The "best" shotgun for dove is the one you are the most comfortable with and the one *you* shoot best. (It should also, of course, be one which you can fire enormous numbers of shotshells through without developing a flinch.)

Although any shotgun may be used effectively on doves, there are a num-

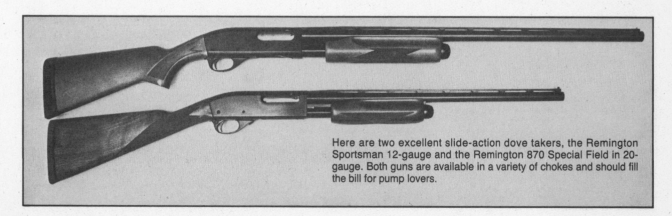

Here are two excellent slide-action dove takers, the Remington Sportsman 12-gauge and the Remington 870 Special Field in 20-gauge. Both guns are available in a variety of chokes and should fill the bill for pump lovers.

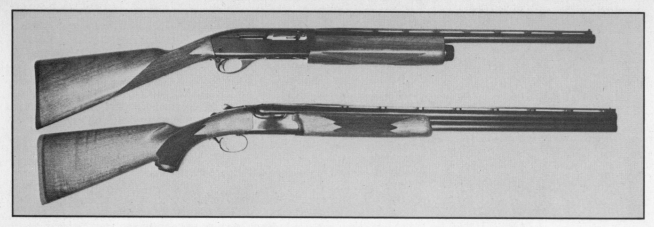

This Remington 1100 Special Field (top) and the Ruger Red Label over/under are 20-gauge guns. And both have relatively open chokes which are ideal for dove potting near water.

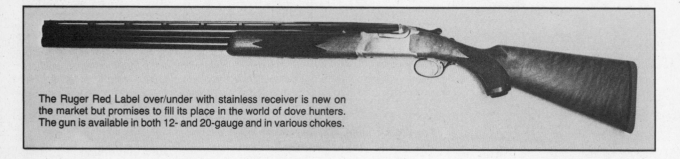

The Ruger Red Label over/under with stainless receiver is new on the market but promises to fill its place in the world of dove hunters. The gun is available in both 12- and 20-gauge and in various chokes.

ber of points to look for when selecting *your* dove gun. The shotgun should be relatively light since some walking will be required, even if you are pond shooting. It must also be fitted with a recoil pad, even if you don't normally use a pad. Recoil can become a major factor when dozens of shots are fired from strange positions in a few hours.

I have always favored double-barreled guns, either stacked or side-by-side, but any fixed-breech gun can quickly tire the hunter by its punishing recoil. If you do select a double, choose your ammunition carefully to minimize recoil. A sore shoulder and a bad case of "flinchitis" can easily dim the beauty of a featherlight double gun rather quickly.

Another factor in choice of shotguns is a bit more difficult to describe. The gun must "feel" and "swing" right. Doves fly faster than most other game birds and the gun must respond quickly to the hunter's demands. An overly long or heavy gun will be difficult to swing fast enough to keep it on target. If shouldering the gun requires conscious effort to get it properly positioned, the gun doesn't fit well enough for dove hunting.

A slow, deliberate mounting style which pays off in a duck blind would be useless for dove hunting. The rapid, erratic flight of doves makes rapid gun mounting and fast pointing essential.

Before the dove hunting season ar-

rives, a few rounds of Skeet from the "low-gun" position should pay excellent dividends. If your local Skeet range will permit it, try shooting from off-station positions. In other words, try standing to the side or in front or behind the marked stations. Such changes in position will offer different shooting angles as well as slightly different ranges than are normally encountered on a Skeet range. It also helps to have the person triggering the targets let them fly when *he* wants to instead of when *you* call for them. (I have yet to get a dove to respond to a call of "pull" and show up exactly when and where I expect him!)

Unless you are a handloader,

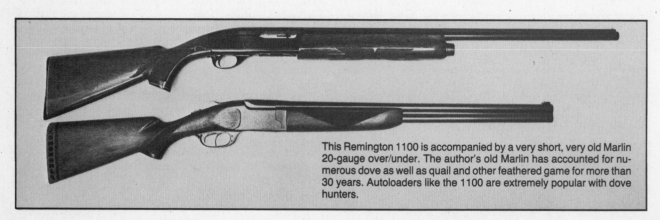

This Remington 1100 is accompanied by a very short, very old Marlin 20-gauge over/under. The author's old Marlin has accounted for numerous dove as well as quail and other feathered game for more than 30 years. Autoloaders like the 1100 are extremely popular with dove hunters.

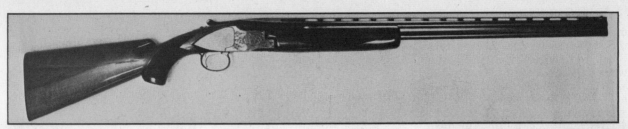

(Above) Only the big boys attempt to tackle dove with .410s. This little Winchester 101 has accounted for a sizable number when short-range pothole shooting was the order of the day.

(Left) If you have the opportunity to use an unusual clay bird range like this one, by all means take advantage of it. This range uses a trap placed high above the shooter and birds are released through trees and brush. Misses are more common than hits. It serves as a perfect dove-shooting training ground.

(Below) Twelve-gauge loads of 3¼, 1⅛ are very popular with dove hunters, the choice of shot size ranging from No. 6 to No. 9. The ACTIV shotshells seen here are all plastic, easily reloadable and are beginning to appear more frequently on dealer shelves. They're a solid bet for doves.

Use of camouflage clothing, and the ability to shoot from a sitting or kneeling position, can add birds to your bag. Be certain you are sufficiently clear of brush to maneuver your shotgun—dove are notorious for coming in from the direction *least* expected.

choose your shotshells by price as much as anything else. I can't imagine a shotshell that won't bring down a dove. Hunters who insist on premium quality shotshells with especially hardened shot for dove are, in my opinion, wasting money. There is no valid reason for choosing high-velocity shotshells for dove hunting unless you make a habit of blazing away at birds that are out of the range of ordinary shotshells.

Most successful dove hunters consider a bird more than 30/35 yards away "out of range." A few hunters will habitually shoot at birds much farther away, but they don't connect very frequently.

Users of 12-gauge guns will probably find a standard field load of 3¼/

1⅛ suitable for doves. For years, that was my standard dove load but more recently I have been successful with the newer, lighter loads. This year, I am using the new Winchester Xpert light field load of 3¼/1 in 12-gauge and the 20-gauge load of 2½/⅞.

Shot size is largely a matter of personal taste. Many shooters wouldn't be caught dead with shot smaller than No.6 but I prefer, as I said earlier, No.8s or even No.9s. At the short range at which dove are taken, I prefer to put a greater number of shot in the air. If you are more comfortable with No.6s or No.7½s, I won't criticize your choice.

A few hardy souls hunt dove with 28-gauge guns or even with the tiny .410. If you are good enough with any

shotgun, the 28 or .410 should prove to be the ultimate challenge. I often use a lightweight 28-gauge Skeet gun for dove hunting when I know I will be shooting only close birds.

Generous bag limits are the rule in most states and only the good shotgunners are able to limit-out on every hunt. Fortunately, dove hunting is usually readily available and enjoyment isn't limited to only the best shooters. Even on bad days, there's a lot to be said for being outdoors and for the smell of burning gun powder. Maybe that's the real reason for the popularity of this early season game bird. Whatever the reason, when you hunt doves be sure to bring a bucket of ammo and a buddy with a sense of humor—you'll need 'em both! ●

"ALABAMA HAS as many if not more deer per acre than any state in the nation," Gary Moody, Assistant Chief of the Wildlife Section for Alabama's Department of Conservation, says. "Although over 200,000 deer are harvested each season, the state has approximately 1,000,000 deer.

"Bowhunters can hunt 109 days each season and harvest 124 deer per man during their season. Gun hunters can hunt 77 days and legally harvest 92 deer per season. During the state's either-sex season sportsmen can bag two deer a day for 15 days. And there are over 2.5 million acres of land available to the public to hunt either for a fee or at no charge."

Therefore Alabama is the promised land for the deer hunter. All of the land in Alabama is considered *posted,* and the sportsman *must have* the written permission of the landowner to hunt. However, the state of Alabama has 21 wildlife management areas (WMA's), a total of 624,000 acres, where deer hunts are conducted on a regular basis. There are also five national forests in Alabama with over 400,000 huntable acres which are not

by JOHN E. PHILLIPS

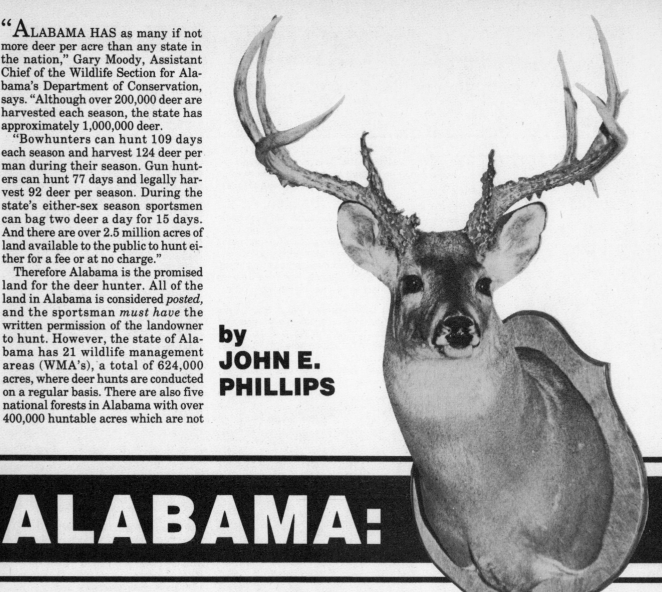

ALABAMA:

included in the WMAs. Additional land is available to hunt from the Tennessee Valley Authority, the Corps of Engineers, U.S. Military Bases and the Fish and Wildlife Service on the National Wildlife Refuges found in the state. And there are numerous hunting lodges that have private lands where outdoorsmen can pay a day-rate to hunt. Alabama truly has plenty of deer and plenty of land for the deer hunter.

How It All Began

Alabama has not always been the deer-rich state that it is today. Actually deer were nearly erased from the state in the '30s. But, in 1940, Alabama began an aggressive restocking program. At that time the state had an estimated deer population of only 12,000 animals, concentrated primarily in the west central and southern regions in the big river bottom

swamps—far removed from large population centers.

According to Moody, "In 1940 when Alabama's Department of Conservation began its restocking program, the people of Alabama wanted to see the deer return to a huntable population. Therefore when the state began its restocking program, landowners and sportsmen alike protected the deer. The season was closed to hunting.

"Then from 1940 until 1965, 3,100 deer were trapped and redistributed throughout the state. The deer for these restocking efforts primarily came from Alabama's Sumter and Clarke counties, which had always homed a remnant deer population. Located in west central and south Alabama, these two regions today boast the highest population of deer to be found in the state. And because of the diversity of habitat, terrain, soil

type and the years that the animals were stocked in, Alabama's deer herd is in different stages of development throughout the state."

Alabamians have a right to be proud of their herd, their Department of Conservation and themselves for bringing the whitetail deer back from near obscurity to one of the strongest deer herds to be found anywhere in the nation.

The Many Faces of Deer Hunting in Alabama

Habitat, terrain, tradition and food availability all dictate the hunting methods used in the state of Alabama. In the early years, Alabama was primarily a dog/deer hunting state. Farmers and townfolks would get together with a pack of hounds on any

If you're a traveling hunter, take heed! These seven bucks were taken at the Westervelt Lodge located near Aliceville, Alabama.

Number One for Deer?

given Saturday during hunting season and go into the forest to drive the deer out to the waiting shotgunners. The "hunt"—not the bagging of the deer—was the most important reason for going into the woods.

But in recent years, the state has become more of a stalk-and-steal hunting state than a dog/deer hunting area. Thousands of deer are taken over green fields and in clear-cuts. Many more thousands are bagged by silent stalkers as they slip quietly down woods roads and firebreaks.

And if the Alabama hunter has changed, so has the land he hunts. Once primarily an agricultural state, Alabama has become in recent years

Yes, Alabama has hardwood deer hunting country. With a generous 77-day deer hunting season available, the average hunter can easily expect to see deer like this.

(Right) Too many traveling hunters overlook "Dixie" as a prime whitetail source. This big 'Bama buck is just a taste of what southern deer hunting hospitality has to offer.

more industrialized and mechanized. Small patch farming has given away to large field farming. Big urban centers have sprung up where once were only small villages. The virgin timber that used to be seen throughout the state has been replaced with pine plantations and second growth forests.

The Blue Ridge Mountains are part of the northern section of Alabama and provide some hills and hollows for the deer hunter. The central part of the state is flatter and richer than north Alabama, the many river systems providing excellent habitat—plenty of river-bottom swamps along with fields of soybeans, wheat, corn and other grain crops. In the more southern part of the state, where Alabama meets the Gulf of Mexico, the land is even flatter, wetter and more

(Right) Like deer hunting across the U.S., the Alabama experience is a family affair, often involving the use of dogs.

As mentioned, dog-driving techniques can be tops when it comes to a successful hunt. Dogs, hunters, and the better part of a dozen bucks down—that's hunter success any way you care to cut it.

(Right) Driving deer is a standard practice in Alabama. This, of course, breaks up the hunting party into two factions—*standers* and *drivers*. As a result, most 'Bama deer hunters have their preference when it comes to this type of hunting. It's quite common for bucks like this to remain motionless when driven. A sharp-eyed driver can connect as easy as a stander can.

fertile. As the habitat changes, so do the hunting tactics of sportsmen in each region.

The "Dog" Hunter

The hunting methods in Alabama are as varied as the men who hunt the whitetail. There are many hunting clubs in the state where sportsmen ban together and use dogs to drive deer. Usually, a large area is surrounded by hunters sporting shotguns. One of the favorite shotguns of the southern hunter is the Remington Special Purpose 3-inch magnum which sports a short barrel and a sling and has the power to throw buckshot or slugs into heavy cover. On a dog drive, deer will more than likely be running through heavy cover, so a rifle with a scope is impractical. Shotgun hunters take many deer each season in the heavy cover of clear-cuts and river bottom swamps in Alabama.

One such shotgun hunter is Danny Fields of Oak Grove, Alabama, who is a "driver." The drivers are the men who go into the woods with the dogs to try and jump the deer out of cover and move the animals toward the "standers." The drivers have as good an opportunity to bag a deer as the standers do. And to Fields' way of thinking, ". . . the drivers have a better chance than the standers for taking a deer. As a matter of fact, I think that I can bag more deer driving than I can standing.

"Drivers don't *always* stomp through the woods screaming and hollering. Yes, drivers do make noise, but they move carefully and cautiously through the woods in an attempt to flush the deer. However, when we hear the dogs coming in our direction, we can be quiet and wait, just like the standers do to see if they bring a deer by us.

"Another advantage to being a driver is that oftentimes you can take

driver looks carefully as he is walking and hollering through the woods he will, on many occasions have the opportunity to bag a big buck in its bed. I have walked within 10 or 12 yards of a buck in a bed and been able to shoot him without his ever jumping up.

"The trick to walking up on a buck, when you are driving deer, is to keep

like jump-shooting quail. Generally your first shot is your best shot. I aim quickly for the center of the deer's back between the two front shoulder blades. In that way I can lay a pattern of 000 buckshot from the deer's neck down to the center of his back—usually breaking the spinal column, the neck and the shoulders—often pene-

(Above) It takes a sharp-eyed hunter to spot a trophy whitetail in Alabama's brush country. Binoculars? You bet.

(Left) Tree stands work well, regardless of the area of the U.S. they're used in, and Alabama is no exception. The use of the stand gets the hunter above the game and out of the way of traffic. It also increases the amount of territory a hunter can see into, and over. The benefits are obvious.

(Right) Acorn flats often prove to be highly productive areas when hunting Alabama. This black powder hunter connected on this nice eight-pointer by following that advice.

the bigger, smarter bucks that won't flee from the dogs and drivers. I believe that big bucks, on land that is regularly dog-hunted, know that if they are bedded down when the hunt begins, they won't leave a trail for the hounds to follow as do deer that are up and moving—especially if the bucks bed down 2 or 3 hours before the hunt begins. These deer have also learned that as long as they can hear the drivers and the dogs (and oftentimes see them) they can stay motionless and avoid danger. For this reason, if a

hollering. As long as a buck can hear you, he knows where you are and believes that he is hidden well enough so that you can't see him. For that reason, you should walk in close before you shoot. But if you stop hollering, the deer doesn't know where you are. Therefore he will become *really* nervous and usually jump up and then run.

"Although I prefer to shoot a deer in the bed before he sees me, I have taken many deer when they have jumped. Jump-shooting deer is much

Though Alabama's terrain can vary, expect to encounter thick brush like this. When the going gets tough, shotguns are the best bet.

(Right) Using the stalk-hunting techniques discussed by the author, this magnificent whitetail was taken by Don Taylor. Don't overlook stalk-hunting—it works!

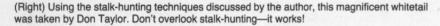

If you're headed South and looking for a rack with width, try Alabama's clear-cut areas. You'll find trophies like this.

trating the heart. If for some reason I miss the first shot, the deer will most often veer to the left or the right offering one or two shots before he is out of range.

"Before I started shooting a 12-gauge, 3-inch magnum, I was using a 2¾-inch, 12-gauge automatic. Since we can hunt with our guns unplugged in Alabama, I usually would have two, 00 buckshot shells to be fired first. Then I had three, No. 1 buckshot following the two, 00. My reasoning was that since I should have the closest and best shots first, I wanted the heaviest lead and the fewest number of pellets going after the deer at close range. The further the buck got away from me, the more pellets I needed so I would sacrifice the size of the shot."

As a driver, Fields is extremely effective in harvesting bucks on a dog drive. But there are many standers who are equally successful at taking whitetails. Although, on the surface, any stander appears to have equal opportunity to get a shot off on a deer that is being driven or pursued by dogs, this is not the case. What a stander does on his stand often determines his success as a hunter.

The successful standers assume there is a deer looking at them as soon as they arrive at their stands. I have known several hunters who have bagged their buck with 10 minutes of going on the stand. Why? The buck

was lying in its bed, within gun range, and was *not* frightened off by the approaching hunters.

Most good standers sit motionless on their stands until they see deer. They use binoculars and look for ear twitches and tail swishes because bucks will many times try to slip past the stander rather than run past him—especially if the dogs are a good distance away. Good standers *never* smoke or eat on their stands and are *always* searching for deer. And they are also looking for places to shoot the deer. Many times the stander misses his buck because he is shooting at the animal through cover. The trees and bushes absorb most—if not all—of his shot. An effective stander will pick a clearing in which to shoot at a running deer. When the deer breaks into that clearing, the hunter will fire.

Although dog hunting for deer may seem dangerous (because the drivers walk straight to the standers), the drivers and the standers are easy to see in the woods since all the hunters wear fluorescent orange. Accidents are rare.

The Silent Stalker

Many of the deer harvested in Alabama are taken by stalking hunters. These men slip quietly and silently through river bottom swamps, along mountaintops and creek bottoms and through acorn flats. Don Taylor of

In some of the flooded areas of Alabama, the use of a canoe will provide the best access to whitetails. The author recommends using the lightest boat possible for this chore.

Birmingham, Alabama, is a stalker.

Taylor says, "I have been fortunate enough to take some big bucks since I have been stalk-hunting. And one of the reasons for my success is because I hunt extremely thick cover. I look for areas where hunters either can't or won't go. Maybe these are large briar and cane thickets, galberry thickets or other dense ground cover where visibility may be limited to only a few feet.

"I hunt these thickets by finding a small creek, stream or drainage ditch that runs through the cover. I have learned that oftentimes these thickets will open up once you get past the outer perimeter—then you can find a spot where you may be able to see as far as 20 or 30 yards. Many times I have spotted a big buck in these kinds of thick places. I believe that the reason the bigger deer are there is that they know the hunters won't penetrate these regions."

But thick cover is not the only place Taylor hunts. "I also slip down firebreaks and woodsroads."

One of the reasons Taylor's stalk-hunting pays off in his taking 10 to 20 deer per season is because he begins his stalk long before other hunters start theirs. He also moves slower than many hunters and studies carefully all he sees.

"I take about 30 percent of the deer that I harvest each season within the first 50 yards of my vehicle," Taylor explains. "When I pull up into the woods and stop my truck, I wait for 10 or 15 minutes for the woods to settle down before I get out of my vehicle. Then when I do get out of my truck, I am careful that the door doesn't squeak. I get out as quietly as possible, and I don't slam the door.

"Once outside my four-wheel-drive, I use my binoculars and begin to look for deer. You must remember that deer become accustomed to vehicles during hunting season—especially around rural farm lands. And if the animals are bedded down close to a road you plan to hunt near, you can oftentimes get out of your truck, see the deer and take him before he moves.

"To be an effective stalk-hunter, I have to train myself to move slowly. I believe that walking *slowly* through the woods is the most unnatural thing a hunter can do. So I began to notice my wristwatch. It helped me slow my gait. I would look up the road and see a tree that I determined was 50 yards away. I would mentally decide that I wouldn't arrive at that tree for 45 minutes. To move that slowly, I would continue to check my watch to make sure that I didn't get to the tree *before* the appointed time.

"I realized that by moving slowly, not only did I *not* spook deer, but I didn't spook the birds and the other animals that would, in turn, spook deer. I also learned that every time I took one step forward, I could see 50 percent more of the woods. Therefore I use my binoculars to carefully study everything I see. From daylight until 11 AM I will usually only walk ¼- to ½-mile. By slowly walking I have been able to take deer that never saw me—although some were as close as 25 yards and others as far away as 150 yards.

"When I am stalking, I use a 6.5 Remington Magnum with a 140-grain Hornady bullet, which puts out a little under 2700 fpe at the muzzle, when traveling at around 2900 fps. I like this bullet because it leaves a good exit hole and makes blood trailing easy if you have to follow up your shot. Another rifle that I use is a 270 Winchester Featherweight. A 130-grain bullet in this gun also does a good job of downing the animal, although I don't believe it is as effective as my 6.5 Remington Magnum. For a scope, I prefer the 2x7x Leupold variable. And when I am stalking in thick cover, I usually leave the scope set on 2x to get maximum field of view. However if I see a deer in the distance, I can quickly zoom the scope out to 7x.

"I also rely heavily on the small, shirt-pocket size binoculars made by Simmons. With these little binoculars less motion is involved in taking them

(Left) Don't overlook Alabama's green-field hunting opportunities. There are plenty of bucks in 'Bama's farm country. (Below) Here is a nice, corn-fed whitetail taken in farm country.

from your shirt pocket to your eyes and then returning them to your pocket than when using a bigger pair that hang down around your stomach. You also have a lot less motion for the deer to see using these smaller binoculars than if you use your rifle scope to look for deer.

"I believe that moving slowly, looking close, and starting to hunt when you get out of the car are important keys to taking more bucks—not only in Alabama—but anywhere else too."

The Green-Field Shooter

Some of Alabama's Wildlife Management Areas have open fields planted by Alabama's Department of Conservation to aid the hunter in harvesting deer. Some landowners and private hunting clubs also plant green fields, and many commercial hunting operations like Westervelt Lodge near Aliceville, Alabama, and Burnt Corn Lodge near Burnt Corn, Alabama, offer hunting over green fields.

Green-field hunters simply take a stand on the edge of a planted field and wait for the deer to come into the field to feed. However, knowing where to place that stand, and when to move it, is critical to successful green-field hunting.

"There is usually one spot on a field where most of the deer will funnel into it," David Smith, a noted green-field hunter says. "I usually try and place my stand so that I am about 50 yards from the spot where I assume the deer will come into the field.

"During the first of the season before the deer have been shot at too much, this type of stand will generally produce deer. However, once the season has been in for a few weeks and the bucks learn that there is danger on the field, they will often hold 50 to 100 yards away and wait on nightfall before entering. When this begins to happen, I follow the trail 50 to 100 yards back into the woods and try and set up a stand downwind and about 30 to 50 yards off that trail. In that way, when the hunting pressure is on and the bucks are waiting in the woods before they come into the field just after dark, I can still take my buck during the daylight hours.

"Another critical thing to remember about green-field hunting is that the more you hunt a field, the less likely you are to see deer on it. I try not to hunt over any one field more than once a week. I always make sure that I am downwind when I am hunting. If the wind changes and carries your human odor into the field, you may as well leave and go to another field."

The size of the green-field often dictates the rifle to be used. On big, open fields most hunters prefer guns like Remington's 22-250 or a Mannlicher 30-06. In short, a 243 is more than adequate on smaller fields of 100 yards or less.

The Clear-Cut Hunter

Because Alabama supports a large timber industry, there are many clear cuts on both public and private lands. Hunting in and over these clear cuts can be extremely difficult. There are two hunting techniques I use that have proven to be effective for me. The first is what I call my "high-tower" technique.

Carrying a portable tree stand, I search for a tall tree near the center of the clear cut that will permit me to look down into the cover. If I can't locate a suitable tree, my next option is to find a tall tree on the edge of the clear cut. When using my high-tower technique, a good pair of binoculars is essential. For armament I prefer my Mannlicher 30-06 or the Remington 22-250. Although I have seen deer moving through the thick growth of a 3- to 5-year-old clear cut, more often than not you will see the deer bedded down. A variation of the high-tower tactic is to take a stand on a hill that overlooks a clear cut. From that van-

(Left and right) Yes, you can find some beautiful trophies in Alabama. However, the author recommends that the traveling hunter look for trophies like these on private, pay-as-you-go hunting grounds. (If you're planning to travel to Alabama for whitetails, drop the author a line in care of GDHA '87. We'll pass it on for possible assistance.)

tage point you can spot a deer moving down in the cover.

The second method for hunting this dense underbrush is to use the stalking technique that Don Taylor utilizes when he hunts thick cover. Move into a clear cut along drainage ditches, small creeks or any other type of break in that cover. Since the shooting will be close, a shotgun loaded with buckshot might prove to be more effective than a rifle. If I do use a rifle, under these conditions, I prefer a Remington 700 in 243 with open sights.

Some of Alabama's Best Public Deer Hunting

Alabama's 21 Wildlife Management Areas may be the best public hunting for out-of-state hunters. If you are looking for a trophy whitetail, "Then Lamarion WMA on the Lamar/

Marion county border may be your best bet," Gary Moody suggests. "The deer on this WMA have never reached the carrying capacity of the land, and there only has been light hunting pressure at Lamarion. Therefore the bucks have acquired enough age to become trophies. The sportsman will see fewer deer on this WMA than he will on many others. But I believe that his chances of seeing a really big deer are the greatest here.

"If a hunter just wants to take a buck deer, Skyline, Barbour, Butler and T. R. Miller WMA's may offer the hunter his best chances. There are a greater number of deer on these WMA's than on Lamarion, and the hunter success ratio is also higher. If out-of-state hunters want more information about hunting dates or public hunting lands, they can write Alabama's Game & Fish Division of the

Department of Conservation at 64 North Union St., Montgomery, AL 36130."

Alabama's deer herd has grown rapidly over the last 46 years and there are plenty of hunting lands available to the sportsmen—both private and public. But the hunter cannot merely drive to Alabama, get out of his car and begin to hunt.

"Even on state Wildlife Management Areas the hunter must have written permission before he hunts," Charles Kelley, Chief of the Game & Fish Division for the state, mentions. "All land except the national forests are posted. So the hunter should make sure that he has the permission of the landowner before he begins to hunt."

A long season, a liberal bag limit and an abundance of hunting areas make Alabama one of the nation's leading deer hunting states. •

GUIDE or CLIENT

Who Calls the Shots?

by DWAIN BLAND

Your first experience on a professionally-guided hunt shouldn't be your last. Here's how to avoid problems, before they start.

DREAM HUNT, or nightmare . . . Which will it be?

If you're the average hunter, you've lain awake countless nights, eyes wide open, your mind conjuring up all sorts of hunts for that trophy-of-a-lifetime. Perhaps you see yourself settled into a sitting position, the scope's crosshairs zeroing on a full-curl, bighorn ram just coming into view through the lifting mountain haze. Or, maybe you're a longtime waterfowler, and you have always dreamed of hunting Maryland's famed "eastern shore," where *all* the honkers are big; no small geese there. Whatever, we all have yearnings for that "hunt-of-a-lifetime."

Such a hunt will become a reality for many of us, but only after diligently studying maps, game regulations, the habits of the quarry we hope to bag, and gleaning what we can from other hunters' experiences. Telephone calls and letter writing will help fill in

the information blanks we'll need.

Perhaps you can pull it off on your own. Some people are good at it, some ain't. Many will need "outside" help. For them, such a hunt will only come about through the enlistment of a hunting guide or an outfitter. Often it boils down to just being able to "buy" a place to hunt for several days.

The average bighorn sheep hunter

Through letter writing, chance conversations, magazine ads, and newspaper articles, hunters can locate good places to hunt. This particular hunting camp, in south Florida is a good example of a "good commercial" hunting camp. They offer wild hogs, whitetails, wild turkeys, good food, lodging and guides.

In the early planning stages of a hunt, the client should inquire as to what types of lands the hunt will take place on as many guided hunts are on public lands.

Only a few weeks ago I was sent a list of wild turkey guides from across the United States, many of whom I knew had not killed a handful of turkeys. On the list was a man I've known for many years, and with whom a friend of mine once hunted. My buddy was instructed to: "Shoot any turkey you can, we'll look later to see if it's a hen or a bird we can keep." This was during the spring gobbler season. Ethics? The so-called "guide" probably couldn't spell the word.

Reputation is the only quality to search for when trying to locate a good hunting guide. Such guides live in a "man's world," where the guide's reputation follows him like a shadow and is built on his word to *produce.* When you hear the name of a guide, try to find someone who has hunted with him, then call that person and ask him a few questions about the guide or outfitter you have in mind. Ask how long it's been since he's hunted with the guide. You'll get a truer picture if they hunted together

(Right) Clients should be informed if the hunt will be "one-on-one," or if the hunter will be sharing the guide's time with one or more hunters.

just last season, versus 10 or 15 years ago. Inquire as to how much game was seen, how long it took to find game, and if the game was located where the guide thought it would be. Did they hunt from dawn to dark? How long was the noon hour? Did the guide offer to shoot the client's game? Did the guide take care of bagged

doesn't own a string of pack animals or the small mountain of paraphenalia required for a big-game hunt back into high country. That hunter will need an outfitter who has all this, plus the know-how.

Which will it be? Dream hunt, or nightmare?

You are calling the shots. How it all ends is determined by what you do before the hunt.

Locating a Reputable Guide

Locating a reputable hunting guide is a job that should be done "in depth." Hunting guides are just like places to hunt—there are good ones and bad ones. And, I wouldn't stake too much on asking a guide for a list of references I could write to verify the guide's qualifications. Even the worst guide is going to send a list of folks he knows will give him a good recommendation. Nor can a person rely on other organizations to cull out the good from the bad. Lists of hunting guides and outfitters can be found in the classified sections of all the popular hunting magazines, but the magazine staff cannot afford to check out these people. So, while the bulk of them are reputable, there can always be a rotten egg in the bunch.

Many big-game hunts require the use of horses. And for some of those hunts, a great amount of time will be spent on horseback. The client should be warned so he can then take whatever action he deems necessary, beforehand, in preparing for this exercise.

game—field dressing, skinning, etc? Did the guide appear to have the desire to follow game regulations and to hunt "by the rules?" Did the guide remain near the hunter?

Thorough, but careful, questioning of a former client can give the prospective client a good insight into the guide's personality and what that guide can offer him. Any telephone conversation with the guide himself should delve into game populations *now,* and what the guide thinks the chances for success are. Inquire as to how much walking is anticipated. Will you hunt from horseback? Does the hunt end with the killing of game? What about lunch, transportation, and the land you'll be hunting on? Does the guide care if you have a shot of "hooch" in the middle of the afternoon? I wouldn't hunt with one who did. Guns and whiskey *don't* mix.

When speaking with the former client find out if there are any little extras the guide provided but for which the hunter had not paid, such as photography. Maybe just the offer of a candybar at mid-morning, or a cup of coffee. Little things which make a hunt enjoyable. Did the client hear from the guide in the weeks after the hunt, or did the guide just "take the

perhaps he wants a trophy animal, or wants to hunt terrain he has always wanted to see, or requires special accommodations in camp. Many guides and outfitters are like me and would prefer to *work* with a client, to learn what the client wants most from the hunt, and then talk prices once this is known. All of this communication back and forth also brings the two parties into closer contact and helps them to get to know each other. If there are any personality conflicts, they will hopefully surface at this time.

In taking hunters back into Mexico's Sierra Madre mountains for a Gould's wild turkey, I won't take anyone I have not known for some time, or with whom I have not hunted. Camp conditions are *tough* back in those dry, cold regions, which means it's no place to find out that you hate the guts of the guy you're hunting with and guiding.

money and run?" Then ask the prospective guide if there will be other hunters, or will the hunt be one-on-one? What about the terrain, is it rough, and does the hunter need to "get in shape" in the months prior to the hunt?

Throughout this culling process cost will surface numerous times, and the hunter should make absolutely certain what he is getting for his money. Few guides or outfitters use written contracts, nor do clients ask for them. Again, it's the "man's world." It's one man's word against another. Of course, the reputable outfitter, or hunting guide, realizes that he'll give the client the best hunt possible, work his tail off, and really not realize much profit in the end. You'll never find anyone in today's blue-collar world who works as hard for a day's wages as does a hunting guide. It's strictly a "labor of love."

Most guiding outfits will ask for a down-payment on the hunt. It's something that's known among older guides as "serious" money. In other words, "put your money where your mouth is." Every guide has been burned by the client who swore verbally that he would be there at a set time for a hunt, and then failed to show up. Very often the guide loses a few days hunting time, and some income.

This down-payment is often "not refundable," and yes, the client should find this out before he plunks down his cash. The amount? It varies with

(Above) The guide should inquire, before the hunt, as to his hunter's desires to rest during a noonday lunch break. Unfortunately, many people are not accustomed to hard hunting. Likewise, the hunter should do his best to get in shape well before the hunt starts. Also, it's the hunter's responsibility to inform his guide of any medical problems that might limit his participation.

The hunter should strive to make certain the guide knows what grade of trophy is being sought, during the early planning stages of the hunt. The client should ask the guide, outright, if the chances are reasonable that such a trophy can be found within the guide's hunting territory.

outfitters, some asking one-fourth the total cost, and others asking for as much as one-half down. After a 10-year layoff, I've returned to active guiding and now ask for one-half down, at least 60 days prior to the hunt. It's best to make your "serious" payment far in advance, particularly if you want to retain the services of a highly reputable guide. The best hunts are invariably those planned far in advance, and since each hunt is built around a hunter's particular desires, it becomes a custom-made hunt. Therefore, prices vary depending upon the preferences of the hunter—

How Can you Get the Most Out of a Guided Hunt?

Number one, ask the guide or outfitter what kind of conditions can be expected in terms of both the terrain and weather. Is it going to be tough on the person who smokes? What about the old ticker? Should a person with even mild heart problems make the hunt? Are there other hazards? Some hunters are petrified of snakes. I've hunted in areas where ticks were so bad that hunters have refused to hunt with me if I intended on taking them there.

Knowing the combination of weather, terrain, hazards, and "how hard the guide hunts," will tell the hunter what to expect, enable him to get into the best physical condition possible and help him choose the proper personal equipment to make the hunt enjoyable. All reputable outfitters will instruct the client as to what specialized equipment is needed.

Guides and outfitters often keep a few extra clothes for those "just in case" incidents which arise—an extra raincoat, camp cap, heavy jacket, etc. But, extra boots? There isn't any way the guide can keep extra pairs of boots, in all sizes, for all hunters. And footwear is the *one* thing which causes hunters the greatest amount of discomfort, and it invariably happens in some back country haunt where the hunter is simply stuck with what he's got. Much hunting involves *considerable* walking, often on bad, rough, uneven terrain. The best hunting guides

but as the hunt draws near, extend your hikes. If you know there is going to be uphill climbing, find a hill near home you can practice on, or get permission to use a local sports stadium. Once you have your feet toughened, begin wearing a light daypack to develop your breathing capacity, and add weight to the pack as your stamina increases—you'll learn how to handle weight going both uphill and down. If nothing else, this will prepare you for carrying a rifle.

Eyeglasses are another item that

Tucson bed, it's no more'n lying on your belly, and covering it with your back.) Today's veteran outfitters and hunting guides sleep in the best sleeping bags they can afford. Not many of them use the "mummy" bags. Guides know that a bone-tired hunter will rest far easier in a large bag, where he can stretch, out. If you bring your own sleeping bag, be sure to purchase an insert "liner" for it. That liner will add to the bag's warmth and versatility. It can also be easily removed for washing. Here's another tip: roll up

The guide or outfitter should tell the prospective client what can be expected insofar as camping, game and hunting conditions are concerned.

(Left) Many hunters like to help throughout a hunt, such as taking up a decoy spread on a goose hunt. Most hunters expect the guide to clean the game, though that responsibility should be discussed well prior to a hunt.

The big-game outfitter, and any hunting guide, should make it a point to keep the hunter informed about the country being hunted, along with its various forms of wildlife, habitat, and other facts of nature. The hunt should be interesting.

like to walk, realize they will get nearer game by doing a considerable amount of it, and know deep in their hearts that true hunting, in the deepest sense of the word, involves the hunter going to the game *on foot*. You may ride a horse to the area, but in the end, you'll make the shot on your own two feet.

The hunter owes it to himself to put on the footwear he intends to use, and not only break it in, but break his feet in as well.

Break in your feet, and boots, at home, in the weeks *before* the hunt. Make short jaunts in the beginning,

no outfitter can have in an emergency. Carefully pack an extra set where they won't be lost or damaged. This goes double for any special medicines. Inquire as to whether the outfitter will have a well equipped first-aid kit in possession.

A hunter who has booked with an outfitter and is going after big game should ask about bedding. Will a ground sheet be needed, as well as a tarp to protect the bed roll? The days of sleeping on a Tuscon bed, like the rawhide tough old-time cow waddie did in the last century is a thing of the past. (If you ain't acquainted with a

sliced from the carcass hanging over my sleeping bag, and slipped into a frying pan of sliced potatoes, onions, and some beans, simmering on a oil-drum-turned-to-wood cookstove. Oh, don't forget to break a few eggs into this slum gullion before it's done.

When you are hunting in the Sierras in the dead of winter, it's difficult to put on enough clothes, but on a late spring afternoon, it's just as hard to find a place in the shade with a cool breeze. There are American hunters who turn up their noses at such a camp, though it is fairly comfortable compared to others with less comforts. American's have become spoiled and soft from the good life. A guide or out-

your pillow from home, in the liner, just before you leave for the hunt; you won't regret it.

Booze?

Many guides and outfitters do not furnish liquor, leaving this to the discretion of the hunter. Recently I read a newspaper account of a big game hunt into Colorado's Rockies. The article was nothing but a long sad tale of how a hunt went sour. First off, the hunter bemoaned the fact that the wrangler's horses were too wide, which indicates that they'd at least been looked after, maybe too well. But, this hunter had known there would be horses used, yet he was griping about riding one. As soon as this hunter and his companions hit camp, it began snowing. These hunters apparently did not like hunting in the snow. The hunter next lamented that they "soon ran out of whiskey."

I really didn't need to read any further to understand why their "dream hunt" had bellied up. But I did. It got worse. The man's next complaint was that it was too far to get water for camp (200 steps) and that the return trip was an uphill trek. Nor could they catch fish from the stream, nor was there any shootable game walking through the camp. Then they ran out of food. This man was irate because the outfitter had not brought more food to camp and had left them there with insufficient foodstuffs. Obviously, there had not been enough communication between hunter and outfitter prior to the hunt, or these things would have been ironed out. But, too much whiskey does not mix any better with high-elevation hunting than do too many cigarettes, moreso to flatlanders not acclimated to hunting in high mountain country.

(Above) Newspaper headlines tell the story of one hunter's "dream hunt" which turned sour. This would not have happened had there been more thorough communication between hunter and outfitter.

The guide should keep the client-hunter informed as to the hunting plans. That information will enable the client to better handle his portion of the hunt. The client who listens intently to instructions, and who can follow orders, will have the greatest chance for success.

Go easy on the booze, and the smokes.

Supplies and Game Licenses

It's up to both parties to learn what the other expects in the way of supplies if, for example, the hunter is to be dropped off by airplane or horse at a fly-camp. The guide can't over-emphasize the primitiveness of such outings. The log cabin I hunt from back in Mexico's Sierra Madres is what I term as a "purty nice place." Water's scarce—there's barely enough to brush your teeth with. Meals are usually a tortilla washed down with home canned pears eaten from a quart jar. Or, *venado* (venison to you and me)

fitter should give any prospective client a *vivid, true picture of what conditions will be throughout the hunt,* because once they hit camp, it's too late to back out. It'll perhaps save some hard feelings, later on.

Licenses, big game permits (all of these things) should be discussed by both guide and client well before the hunt. A few guides will furnish licenses and permits, but most do not. In many instances, special permits must be applied for through a drawing many months before the season. For instance, if a hunter wants to hunt spring bears in Arizona, he can get in contact with Neal Reidhead, who lives in the small town of Nutrioso, and learn first if he was booked up. He's a hard hunting bear man, and he'd also tell you what your chances were for taking an animal. Once that was settled, the hunter would then obtain a set of current regulations, and after studying them, realize that to hunt spring bears in that state, an application would have to be sent in prior to January 7. This would involve a $3 permit application fee, $53.50 for a non-resident hunting license, and $50.50 for a non-resident spring bear tag. Of course, if the hunter would be so unlucky as to not draw a permit, these fees are refunded.

First-class guides and outfitters try to see that non-resident hunters are aware of game regulations concerning the game being sought, though it is definitely the hunter's responsibility to know "the letter of the law." Yes, you may encounter local hunting prejudices. The shooting of doe deer comes to mind in this regard. There are many places (where does are legal game) where you'll hear a local native remark, "We don't shoot does around here." If you are an "outsider" hunting there, you'd be smart to pass up does too, as you're going to be frowned on if you down one, even though it would be perfectly legal. The savvy hunter will draw out, through conversation, what's okay, and what's not, and take a clue from what he's heard. Even today, if you get back in country where living is tough, where times ain't so good, and where there are lots of hardwoods, with tiny spring branches trickling from the head of a hollow, you could stumble onto a "still." You know, the down-home device that churns out moonshine whiskey. *Mountain run, coffin varnish,*

Kansas sheep dip—call it what you want, it's illegal stuff.

If you want to come back to hunt that neighborhood again some day, you'll walk on; *you didn't see nothing.* Oh, don't kid yourself, you just *think* nobody knew you was thereabouts. Before nightfall, the folks in that hollow'll know more about you than your mother does. Or, maybe it's a tiny cultivated patch of ground you stumble onto, neck deep in some weeds. You best look again, those "weeds" bring fancy prices. Back in the High Sierras they pronounce it "marry wanna." Responsible outfitters and guides try to keep hunters steered clear of such shenanigans.

Making the Shot

What it all boils down to, what we today call "the bottom line," is the shot itself. The guide owes it to the hunter to have a solid, thorough knowledge of the game being hunted, then having the savvy to put the hunter within easy killing distance. When the guide whispers "shoot," he's done his part, at least up to this point. The hunter now owes both himself and the guide the benefit of making the shot count, with *no* cripples, *no* follow-ups, and *no* misses.

One November morning, while guiding on a hunting block assigned me out of Fisheating Creek Hunting Camp, a few miles west of Lake Okeechobee, Florida, I scattered a small band of old gobblers from where they'd been roosting in a few pines scattered among big cabbage palms. Following the direction they'd fanned out towards, I positioned my hunter some 15 yards to the front of me, waited a spell to let things calm down, then began the long waiting game of making a *cluck* now and then. It wasn't long before I got a *cluck* back. Me and the turkey talked back a few times, the bird being off to our south, more or less straight ahead of my hunter, out probably 200 yards distant.

Suddenly, without so much as a "I-beg-your-pardon," here comes a Feathered Lord thundering through

(Above) Many guides insist on being very near the hunter when shots are fired. This enables the guide to "call the shot," as he will better know the range, will have a thorough knowledge of angles and bullet placement, and by being within talking distance, can easily relay shooting advice. This often has a "steadying" effect on any nervous hunter.

Many early-day guided hunts offered generous shooting opportunities. This is a photo of an 1880s era hunt into the Cherokee Strip, now northern Oklahoma. This well equipped camp lacked nothing, particularly turkeys. Note that the guns are all side-by-side shotguns. (Photo courtesy of the Kansas State Historical Society, Topeka.)

The hunter owes it to himself, and the outfitter, to sight in his rifle, or pattern his shotgun prior to a hunting trip. He should also do this while keeping in mind what game is being sought, what type of ammo will be utilized, and the ranges at which the bulk of the shooting can be expected. Additionally, topographical charts should be studied, and throughout the planning stages, they should be discussed with the outfitter or guide.

the fan-topped palms, but from behind us. Winging in from my back left, the gobbler all but flies across the shoulder of my hunter, wings tumbling the oak leaves as the old bird trots to a halt 20 yards from the hunter's barrel. Straight down the gun barrel.

The gobbler sized up things right quick and with head high, eyes alert, took a couple of pausing steps, then clucked the danger *pert*. My heart stopped. That bird would be gone in a twinkling.

Not seated right beside my hunter, I had no way of knowing if he was ready for such action. Gobblers flying to the gun have a way of upsetting folks. *Booomm.*

That answered my hopes. Yep, the man was well up to the situation. We both ran over to where the old longbeard was thrashing the leaves. Slapping him on the back, I shook his hand. He'd done his part.

Too often I've seen hunters travel hundreds of miles, only to miss. It doesn't do much good to buy all the equipment, arrange to hire an outfitter, pay good money to travel far and

wide, when you *cannot* shoot, accurately. What's worse, this is almost like a slap in the face of the guide who has worked his guts out to see that the client gets a killing shot.

Can you handle a gun safely, keeping it pointed away from people at all times, loaded or not? Have you shot the gun hundreds of times, or, just a time or two? Have you shot the gun with the load you intend to use when hunting? Have you shot it at simulated targets of game, or, just at circles on a firing range? Can you kill moving game? I do mean *kill it,* not just put a shot into the bird or animal anywhere?

These are just starters. The list of things a hunter should know about using a gun are almost endless. In hunting wild turkeys, as is the case with many big game animals, very often there will be a chance for one shot, oft times a quick shot, but if the hunter has done his homework, a second shot will not be needed. Hunting "partridge," (ruffed grouse) in Vermont, or prairie chickens in east Kansas, is much the same. You walk all day, perhaps late in the afternoon you get a

chance, *one chance,* and if you miss, you'll hope somebody applies his foot to the seat of your pants. One for every time you missed.

I invariably ask my turkey hunting clients if they've ever shot at a turkey. If they have, I can then hope they realize what marvelous eyesight these birds possess. It is extremely difficult to get across this point to someone who has not hunted them. When a bird is called into easy gunshot (25-yards), and once the hunter makes a move to shoot, that time is running out, *fast.*

In some instances, the guide will need to leave the hunter. When that happens, it's the hunter who must make the decision about shooting. In most instances, however, the guide will be with his hunter when the shooting starts. In goose hunting, for instance, the guide furnishes a pit, sets out a decoy spread, and does she calling. He'll "call the shot" when the flock of honkers appears to be where he thinks his hunters can cull out a few. A turkey hunting guide will often sit against the same tree his client is next to, rubbing the hunter's back, whispering, "don't move," or "bring your gun up smooth, when he walks back of that big tree," so the client won't spook off a whiskery old turkey that's coming to see the hen that's clucking in the guide's wingbone caller. Out in quail country, the guide might be talking to the dogs, as they've locked down on a bevy of birds, his two hunters standing pat as he goes in to flush. And, up in the high country, whether it's Yellowstone country in Montana, or down in the Tonto Basin under Arizona's Mogollon Rim, thousands of times next fall a guide will whisper to his client, motioning the next move, praying the quarry will stay put just a little longer.

Nobody—outfitter, hunter, nor guide—wants a hunt to turn into a nightmare. Nor should it. The hunter should make plans well in advance, and then *maintain solid contact* with the guide or outfitter of his choice. The outfitter and guide should see that the client *fully* understands what he is buying. All parties should work as a team, striving for a well defined goal.

Only dream hunts have happy endings. And a happy ending means you all did your respective jobs, the way they had to be done. Only then can you sit back, kick up your feet, think about what just took place, smile, and know you "called the shot correctly." ●

WHETHER THE javelina is a small- or big-game animal is open to argument. Truly, if it were just a matter of size we could reduce the disagreement to, simply, a discussion of dimensions.

The little javelina is a pig-like animal, with grizzled hair of grayish black and a pale collar (hence the formal name of collared peccary) that stands from 17 to 20 inches at the shoulder and averages between 28 and 36 inches in length and from 30 to 60 pounds in weight.

From these numbers, the little critter comes in smaller than a Texas Hill Country whitetail (one of the smallest deer on the continent) and a tad bigger than a coyote. If you want to call it a small-game animal, then so be it. I'll stick with my favorite moniker: America's small big-game animal.

For many years these animals were considered vermin throughout most of their range. Because they were believed to destroy crops and kill livestock, they were normally killed on

by
FRANK PETRINI

sight. It's only been in the last two decades that the javelina has achieved game status with protection from indiscriminate killing.

Dangerous?

A lot of fiction has been written and related about the little peccary. Early American writers described the animal as aggressive and ferocious, exaggerating its danger to man and beast. There have been hundreds of published accounts of men being treed and even gored by the little animals. Most of such writings are rubbish.

The javelina generally flees from

JAVELINA
America's
Small
Big
Game

"The little collared peccary may not be a wild boar, but it's plenty fun to hunt."

For U.S. hunters, the little collared peccary, or javelina, is located only in Arizona, New Mexico and Texas. Generally, a good-sized mature javelina boar will reach an over all length of about 3 feet and tip the scales at about 60 pounds.

man, although it will fight viciously when cornered and has been known to severely cut or gore hunting dogs using its sharp, fang-like lower canine teeth. As small as the animal is, it has few natural enemies excepting, of course, the armed hunter.

Some of the misconceptions about the javelina arise because of its poor eyesight. If, under changing wind conditions, it gets wind of a man, it will (normally) quickly flee the area, but because of its poor eyesight may appear to be charging. On the other hand, while the little critter doesn't charge unless cornered, I think a bit of healthy respect for his fighting capabilities is recommended to avoid foolhardy hunting situations.

On one recent hunt in the brush country of south Texas a companion shot at, and appeared to have wounded, a small boar in a thick tangle of thornbrush. The animal squealed and plowed deeper into the entanglement, out of sight. Without thinking, both of us dropped to our knees and began scrambling into the brush, squeezing between the trunks of the bushes on our hands and knees.

We had our revolvers in our hands—his a 357 Magnum and mine a 41 Magnum—both stoked with full-house loads. After getting about 20 feet into the brush, and seeing dark shapes weaving through the cover, I quickly realized the stupidity of what we were doing. If we cornered one of

those tusked creatures in that confined space, we could have a real blood-letting on our hands—our blood. So, in spite of the artillery, we backed out. Once we were in the open we circled to the other side of the brush and, luckily, collected the boar on its exit.

It hadn't been wounded, by the way, and shivers ran up my spine when I thought about what could have happened. A 200-grain 41 Speer jacketed hollow point slug at 20 yards did the deed, but I wouldn't have wanted to rely on it to stop a crazy fighting brush pig while tangled up inside the flora.

Habits and Habitat

The range of the javelina, or collared peccary, is pretty limited in this country. While it and many related cousins range greatly over Mexico and most of Central America, the javelina is only found (in abundance) in three states of the lower 48. First, there are plenty in Arizona, primarily in the southeast quarter, inhabiting the brushy draws and frequenting scattered water holes in that arid part of the country.

Arizona has done much to elevate the little pig from the unofficial status of kill-on-sight varmint to a recognized game animal. Back in the late '60s that state instituted regulated seasons for the pursuit of the peccary, usually 1 or 2 months long, in late

winter or early spring. Of course, the little critter was then protected the rest of the year.

That single conservation act did much to halt the wanton slaughter, although no doubt, in Arizona and the rest of the animal's range, there are those who still believe the javelina is responsible for wholesale losses of crops and livestock and should be eliminated for economic reasons. Apparently this kind of thinking is on the wane, for the peccary population remains healthy, if not increasing, throughout its limited range.

In *New Mexico* hunting is somewhat restricted since the peccary population was just about annihilated there some years back and reintroduced in the 1970s. When seasons are held they are usually offered for residents only.

The little animal inhabits the southeast and southwest corners of the state with the largest population in the Animas and Peloncillo mountain ranges of Hidalgo County.

Texas probably has the largest number of javelina. They roam the south Texas brush country, from San Antonio, south all the way to the Mexican border, and west across that corner of the state. However, it's more difficult to hunt javelina in Texas than anywhere else in its range because, while the Arizona and New Mexico range covers much public

The javelina's eyesight is, at best, poor. If a hunter *is* spotted, however, the peccary's usual response will be to head for the hills — *fast*. However, if you are unfortunate enough to wound and corner one of these devils, look out. Those teeth can inflict serious damage.

land, the areas of concentration in Texas cover primarily private property—ranches, oil leases, or private hunting operations.

Hunting in Texas, therefore, is a proposition of either getting an invitation or paying a hunting fee. And since these lands are also prime whitetail areas, the javelina is normally pursued as an adjunct to deer hunting. Some ranchers offer package hunts for deer and javelina, with room, board and guide services combined. For the nonresident to get in on these kinds of deals it's best to contact the Chambers of Commerce in the areas being considered. As you may have guessed, fee-hunting in this part of the country is *big* business.

Javelina are gregarious; they live and travel in bands of five to 10 or more. They are also creatures of habit. Both of these traits help the hunter. First, a band or drove of pigs is easier to spot or track than a lone animal. And second, by knowing where a particular band hangs out, the hunter can pretty well find it again, usually in the same general area. They use the same water holes day after day and frequent the same feeding and bedding areas.

Because of their habitual nature, a guide who has done his homework—preseason scouting of the local peccary haunts—can be worth his weight in gold to the traveling hunter. In Arizona, guides operate out of Phoenix and are usually worth their fees. But even without a guide you can do a creditable job hunting these little animals by knowing a bit about their daily habits and diet.

Like deer, peccary feed early in the morning and late in the afternoon. So to spot them while feeding, or on their way to and from their feeding areas, you must be out hunting at dawn and at dusk. Their favorite foods are prickly pear cactus and the roots of several different desert plants, so hunters normally keep their eyes open for any cactus that's torn or shredded or any other signs of recent eating activity such as torn up soil where the pigs may have been digging at plant roots.

Javelina have a keen sense of smell and a decent set of ears. But, as mentioned earlier, their eyesight is poor. If the wind is right you can walk up to them if you're cautious and move slowly.* On the other hand, the little animals are so low to the gound that a single pig is not easy to spot among all the low brush and cactus cover. A band of them, however, is more difficult to overlook.

When they feed, undisturbed, they don't seem ever to be in a hurry—they just poke along. Their slow move-

---

*Ed. Note: We *don't* recommend it.

In the deer country of south Texas, javelina hunters often use deer stands in an effort to glass more countryside when looking for a band of pigs.

ments may not catch the hunter's eye, so binoculars are required equipment for scanning the brush for their presence.

Finding Your Javelina

Probably the most productive way to locate a band's area is to inspect water holes for tracks or other signs of javelina activity such as shallow rootings and wallowing spots. Non-experts complain that javelina tracks can be easily confused with those of small fawn deer, but there *is* a difference if you take the time to examine the tracks closely.

The javelina have blunter toes than small deer. An active watering area is usually crisscrossed with these small-footed tracks. Why? When *one* goes to water *the entire band* follows. It usually doesn't take long for a hunter to easily identify their signs.

When watering holes are found and the hunter knows a band is in the area, he can proceed to stillhunt (into the wind) and glass for movements in low brush, draws, dry watercourses and cactus-studded clearings.

Surprisingly, javelina don't care for the heat. Once temperatures approach 80 degrees Fahrenheit they hold up and bed down, usually in the shaded areas under a rimrock or thick-canopied brush. Generally,

The "desert pig" is not difficult to kill. Usually, a single solid hit in the heart or lung area will put a javelina down for the count.

Many hunters cruise the dirt roads, glassing as much acreage as possible, looking for signs of javelina "band" travel.

out territorial markers with urine.

Whatever the purpose, the musk gland and its smell is helpful to hunters. If the wind is right as you approach a band, you can often smell 'em before you actually see 'em.

Incidentally, when field dressing one of these desert pigs be careful you don't get this musk oil on your hands. It has a disagreeable odor which takes a number of soap scrubbings to eliminate. The first thing you do upon dropping a pig is to use your knife to cut the skin around the gland and peel it off like a postage stamp before proceeding any futher. In that way you'll avoid getting any musk on yourself or on the meat.

It's difficult to tell the difference between a boar or a big sow, and it really doesn't make much difference; either is desirable as a trophy, although a young sow makes better eating. However, be sure you *don't* fire at any adult javelina that has small ones following it. The reasons should be obvious.

Javelina may be born at any time of the year and litters contain one or two. So, whenever you hunt there's a possibility of coming across a sow with her very young.

The Tools

Most any caliber of firearm can safely dispatch a javelina. Most experts, however, avoid the 22 rimfire and recommend anything from 22 WMR on up. The main consideration here is the possibility of wounding an

they'll bed throughout the heat of the day and reappear during the later afternoon hours. Many hunters therefore take a siesta during midday. For those who prefer to hunt at this time, the best bets are those areas nearest to water where there may be some cool shade.

On cooler, overcast days the little pigs may feed all day long. Only then does it truly pay to hunt from dawn to dusk.

On south Texas ranches and oil exploration properties the thick, brush-infested terrain is crisscrossed (almost endlessly) with jeep trails and roads. Many hunters cruise these trails in 4WD trucks while glassing to locate javelina bands feeding or on the move. Others stop frequently and get up on trucktops in order to see above the thick and high brush, to glass a wider territory.

Indeed, finding a band is the hardest part of the hunt as that band often inhabits an area of 1,000 acres or more. Once spotted, those javelina can be easily stalked to within shooting range by the hunter who makes the most of the available cover, pays attention to wind direction and moves quietly.

A side note: The little critter's *smell*. They have a musk gland just above the hump on their backs that gives off a smelly, oily substance that has a fairly unpleasant odor. Biolo-

gists aren't too sure of all the functions of this musk gland, but there's agreement that the animals use the smell to locate one another and to stay together as a band. There's also reason to believe that the oily substance is rubbed on brush and tree trunks to identify the animal's, and the band's, territory, much like a wolf pack sets

Once the javelina's musk gland is removed (as discussed by the author) the gutting-out starts. These little pigs make *great* eating, tasting more like beef than pork. (Be sure to get the animal cooled down as soon as possible.)

animal and having it take off into the thick brush. In places where I've hunted in south Texas there are brush patches that'll take up ½-acre and more. Let a wounded pig get into that maze of entanglement, and there's no way to get it out short of crawling in after it—which I *don't* recommend. So while they're not particularly difficult to kill, you want to use good marksmanship and a cartridge with enough zip to anchor one with the first shot, if at all possible.

Because of this I never recommend even the 22 Magnum unless you're hunting in relatively open country where tracking a wounded pig is possible. Among rifles, probably the best caliber choice is one of the 6mms, either the 243 Winchester or 6mm Remington. A soft point bullet in the 80- to 100-grain range should prove more than adequate. Just about any deer rifle will also do the job. Be sure to mount a telescopic sight on that rifle if you feel the shooting distance will be over 50 yards.

The peccary is a top target for the handgunner. With a little luck you can often stalk to within 50 yards of the animals. With an automatic pistol there's little doubt that the best caliber is the 45 ACP with one of the 185- to 200-grain jacketed hollow point loads. The 9mm Luger or Parabellum is, in my opinion, the lightest autoloading cartridge that should be used, and then only with a fast-expanding, jacketed hollow point slug weighing no less than 115 grains.

My favorite javelina hunting handgun is the revolver. Why? It's available in more potent calibers than the automatics and provides additional firepower over a single-shot. Yes, I've hunted with handgunners who used 22 Magnum revolvers, but I personally recommend nothing smaller than the new 32 H&R Magnum with a load that safely pushes an 85- to 100-grain

bullet to about 1400 fps.

In my experience, most any fullhouse 357 Magnum load will anchor a javelina in its tracks with a hit in the vitals. And I usually recommend a jacketed hollow point in the 140- to 158-grain range at a velocity of at least 1300 fps.

One favorite 357 target load of mine has also proven to be a top pig getter. This one takes the 168- to 172-grain (depending on the bullet alloy used) Keith-style semi-wadcutter cast bullet (Lyman's mould #358429) designed originally for the 38 Special. I seat this one over 13.5 grains of Hercules 2400 in regular 357 Magnum casings with Federal Small Pistol primers. Velocities run around 1350 fps from my 6-inch barreled revolvers—it's plenty for the javelina; the few I've shot with the load didn't go far.

I've shot more javelina with 44 Magnum revolvers than any other and consider this cartridge a top pigshooter. When I don't feel like handloading, I've found I don't lose anything if I go with the Federal 180-grain JHP factory load. This light slug exits the 7½-inch barrels on my Ruger Redhawks and Super Blackhawks at better than 1500 fps and is a reliable hunting slug on game the size of javelina out to at least 50 yards.

Probably my favorite javelina cartridge is the 41 Magnum. I like this chambering particularly in the Ruger Blackhawks but also shoot two Ruger Redhawks, a Smith & Wesson Model 57 along with a Dan Wesson stainless revolver with 6- and 8-inch interchangeable barrels. All are superbly accurate, the first requirement in any hunting handgun, no matter what the game. The 41 load I always use on these small animals utilizes the 200-grain Speer ¾-jacket hollow point bullet and maximum load of 22 grains of Olin's 296 along with CCI-550 mag-

num primers. Velocities from my 6½-inch barreled Blackhawks run between 1350 and 1400 fps.

When hunting with revolvers I usually restrict my javelina shooting to within 50 yards. This is not too difficult to do since there's usually plenty of brush and other range-limiting cover when stalking in pig country. Once in a while, however, I'll miss out on one because I simply can't get close enough. Yes, by mounting a long-eyerelief telescopic sight on your handgun you can increase your effective range to, at least, 100 yards. Again, however, it would be wise to stick with a scoped centerfire rifle (to guard against crippling shots) if the anticipated shooting will be *over* 100 yards.

The little collared peccary may not be a wild boar, as far as dangerous game goes, but it's plenty fun to hunt. And if you get a relatively young one, it's also good eating.　　　　●

Petrini prefers to hunt the little desert pigs with open-sighted handguns like this Ruger 44 Magnum Redhawk. If at all possible, try to drop your javelina with one shot — trying to find a wounded javelina in his native thick cover can be frustrating at the least, and dangerous at the worst.

(Left) If the shooting is going to be done at a distance of over 100 yards, the author strongly recommends the hunter use a rifle. When it comes to desert pigs, the author's rifle choice is a scoped bolt-action chambered for either the 243 Winchester or 6mm Remington.

THE 30-06

by HOWARD FRENCH

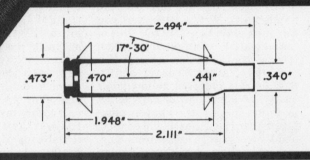

The '06 has everything. It's got history, versatility and reputation for hunting excellence that's 80 years young.

IT SEEMS AS IF just about every American hunter has owned a rifle chambered for the 30-06 cartridge. And why not! Most first-class military cartridges have always been used as sporting rounds! The 30-caliber 1906 cartridge certainly proves that. Used in two World Wars, plus the Korean conflict, its military prowess cannot be mistaken, and as a sporting cartridge, it has been used all over the world on a variety of game animals.

As a hunting round it has always had that unique sobriquet that many other rounds are often compared to it, to better or lesser degrees. Often another cartridge is "just so much better," at certain ranges, than the '06. Of course, nobody ever talked to the animal being taken. The chances are the animal didn't know the difference. With proper bullets, and good shoot-

ing, *any* North American animal can be taken with the '06 cartridge. Now, if any of you want to raise up on your hind legs and state that you wouldn't use the 30-06 on grizzly bear, don't expect me to stop you. The '06 certainly *has* taken grizzly, but then only on special hunts. (If you have checked the prices of hunting those hump-backed bears, you'll understand why they're "special." I would certainly not argue if you picked a 338 or 375 as your personal arm for grizzly hunting.)

History

The point is that, after some 80 years of usefulness, the '06 is still one fine cartridge. Even more amazing is that the 30-06 and several other cartridges all came out when smokeless powder was first being used in mili-

The 30-06 has been, and still is, chambered in a number of action types. **(Opposite page):** the Remington 700 Classic; (from left to right) Ruger's Model 77RL "Ultra Light," the Remington Model 6 pump, a Remington Model 4 auto and Ruger's No. 1 International.

tary arms. The military inventors at the close of the 19th and the opening of the 20th centuries came up with cartridges that are still being used all over the world. Need proof? Just consider that Mauser gave us the 6.5, 7x57, 7.65 and 8mm; that Mannlicher introduced its own 6.5; that England gave us the 303; and that Krag-Jorgensen provided still another 6.5, not to mention our own 30-40 Krag. They're all military cartridges that are *still* being used as sporting rounds! When you also consider the fact that many other sporting rounds were formed from some of these same cases, it is amazing that so many are still on the sporting goods dealers' shelves. (When you get down to it, even the venerable 45-70 cartridge is still being used, although much of its use is due to modern, smoke-

less loadings and the presence of modern firearms chambered for that round.)

The rifle that seems to epitomize the '06 cartridge is the Model 1903 Springfield. I am sure many people wonder why a 1903 rifle uses a 1906 cartridge case. The first 1903 rifle did indeed use a 1903 cartridge case which had a slightly different (read that "longer") neck than the eventual '06 case. The origin of the Model 1903 rifle goes back to the Spanish American war. At that time, the "militia" was armed, if you can call it that, with trapdoor Springfields chambered for the 45-70 black powder round; the Navy had their 6mm Lee straight-pull rifles, while the Regular Army plied its trade with 30-40 Krags. (Yes, there were some rumors that Roosevelt's Rough Riders purchased some

1895 Winchester rifles chambered for the Krag round.) In battle our series of arms proved to be sadly beneath those of the Spanish forces who were armed with the 1893 7mm Mauser. The Mauser was easily loaded with a stripper-clip that held five cartridges—it was a *fine* battle rifle. Although the 1893 Mauser is now looked down upon (compared to the Model 1898 Mauser), it was used as a battle arm up to WWII.

The rapid-firing Mausers were deadly when pitted against our militia and their black powder 45-70 cartridges. Once the black powder arms were fired, the cloud of smoke revealed the militia's position and invited a steady stream of 7mm fire from the Spanish soldiers. Against our regular forces, armed with the Krag rifles, the Mauser was also superior—

Just a single shot from the author's 30-06 Sako carbine took this black bear. The Sako carbine with its 20¼-inch barrel, dropped the animal without a fuss.

the Krag had to have each round *singly* loaded into its box magazine. This left our troops scrambling to return fire against the clip-charged fire of the Mausers. Of course our Krag-armed soldiers did get their crack at some Spanish troops armed with black powder 11mm Remington single shots, but when push came to shove, the Mauser was a *much better* bet than the Krag. So, the Army started looking for a new rifle.

I suppose our Army looked at many rifles—Britain's 303, the French Lebel, the Mannlichers, the Russian Moisin-Nagant—but those troops who faced the Mauser 1893s seemed to have the final say as to which rifle we picked for our forces. Consequently, our new rifle, the '03 Springfield, was really just a refined version of Germany's latest rifle, the '98 Mauser.

Ammo? The original 1902 cartridge was rimless and was loaded with a 220-grain bullet that was similar to the Krag projectile. Historians would say (and have said) that the rimless design was a wise move in light of the dawning of automatic arms. Velocities were said to have been about 2300 fps with the new 1903 cartridge, but some authorities said that barrel life was only about 800 rounds with those loads. Load data was reduced, and we ended up with a new rifle, firing a new cartridge, about like the old Krag round, but clip-loaded.

Meanwhile the Germans had come up with a new round for the 1898 rifle; it used a lighter bullet (than what had been used in the older 1888 cartridge) with a spitzer (sharp-point) shape. Our Army liked that idea and, in 1906, redesigned the Model 1903 case, changing the neck and using a pointed 150-grain bullet. The new round was a success.

It was also a success with sportsmen. Teddy Roosevelt took an '03 Springfield, chambered for the '06 cartridge, to Africa. T.R. also took along a good supply of full-jacketed 150-grain military loads. (Stewart Edward White, who was credited with being the best American shooter to hunt Africa, thought nothing of dusting off African lion with one round each from his Springfield loaded with 220-grain bullets.)

WWI taught a lot of men to like the bolt-actioned rifle. Men who served in the trenches with M1903 or M1917 rifles came back wanting bolt-action *sporting* rifles. There were not many available except for surplus WWI arms. There were some Krags, a few Lee straight pulls, a smattering of Hotchkiss and old Remington-Keene arms, but nothing that matched the velocities of the 1906 cartridge. The 30-06 was *the* cartridge that brought Americans into the sporting bolt-rifle scene.

My first 30-06 rifle was a Spring-

field that seemed to have been used to hold up one corner of the sea bag of a recently returned WWII Naval veteran. My high school cash surplus wasn't much, but I was able to turn up $20 which made me the proud new owner of that Springfield '03 rifle in A3 persuasion.

From the fit, fine bore and lack of usual combat weapon's fatigue marks, it occurred to me that this Springfield saw little use in our Navy's war on the enemy.

Now, owning that rifle and being able to shoot it were two different things in those post-war times. Ammo, like then-new 1946 cars, was difficult to come by. Fortunately I discovered a clever dealer who had stocked up on a rare supply of surplus '06 ammo. Unfortunately it was not from WWII. The headmarks sported date stamps reading *17, 18* and *19*— fresh from the *War To End All Wars.* Unfortunately, that "mixed" lot of '06 fodder had not been decently stored in 20-round boxes. Tracers here, ball there—I'm sure you get the picture.

That's when I first learned about the yellow phosphorus tracers from "Over There." Shooting that mismatched ammo could be rather exciting when one round suddenly blossomed into flame! Fortunately, the few rounds I did fire were in dry, desert areas and caused no problems. It also taught a young shooter to be

(Left) During the author's testing of various '06 bullet weights the author used a number of different rifles, with different barrel lengths. The shortest barrel length tested was 20¼ inches (on the Sako carbine to the far left). The longest barrel tested was a 26-incher on the 1917 Enfield, seen here to the right of the Sako.

(Below) On a "special-purpose" level, Weatherby's new Fibermark, complete with fiberglass stock, fills the bill nicely. Available in 30-06, the Fibermark is designed for "go" not show.

(Bottom) When it comes to researching the 30-06 cartridge, it's not difficult to literally come up with dozens of books relating to the history, use and reloading of the 30-06. Some of the author's 30-06 load data stretched back some 35 years.

wary of surplus ammunition—you might get something you didn't count on when you pulled the trigger!

Since those early days of firing WWI ammo out of a WWII Springfield, I've managed to burn up more '06 ammo than I had, perhaps, planned on. Over the years I have used the '06 on both American and African game. It always did the job. The '06 cartridge not only has an enviable record for accuracy, it also has a reputation for moderate recoil. In writing this article, for example, I fired in excess of 70 rounds over my Oehler chronograph in just a few hours time—and walked away with a shoulder that felt just fine, thank you. I won't say that the '06 doesn't kick, but its recoil is mild enough so that most people can enjoy shooting it.

Handloading

One great thing about the '06 is that reloading data *is* plentiful. Like most reloaders, my bookshelves are filled with data books. In no time I had material in front of me, from Ackley, Herter, Hodgdon, Lyman, Nosler, the NRA, Pacific, Sierra and Speer. In some cases I had multiple copies of data books that stretched back some 35 years. (In addition there were other books that also proffered up a wealth of more general information on the '06 cartridge.)

One of the first things you notice in these books is that they all do not, necessarily, have the same loading data. Which is not surprising. After all, each source used their own test arms and, often, their own bullets. As a result, velocities will differ, from load source to load source. (That's one reason why I have so many books on cartridge reloading.)

I decided to try out a series of reloads using one bullet, the 165-grain Sierra, loaded into once-fired Federal cases primed with Winchester caps. Additionally, eight different types of powder were used in the construction of those loads. Each load reached an estimated velocity of 2600 fps (feet per second), according to recipes taken from several data manuals. The powders were from Winchester, Norma, Hodgdon and DuPont. The rifle used in the testing had a 24-inch barrel.

How did all this loading data, using various powders and data from different sources work out? Rather well I thought, as the average for all of these loads was an instrumental velocity of 2541 fps, which is pretty close to the allowable 2600 fps I was trying for. Frankly, I take my hat off to the pub-

Using an Oehler chronograph, the author determined the extreme spread of velocities, the average velocity and the standard deviation of a great number of '06 loads using five different bullet weights. The results were interesting.

many people are hunting with snub-barreled rifles. The reasoning is simple: Short-barreled rifles are handier in the woods, and you don't suffer any appreciable velocity loss at normal ranges.

Most people feel that a game rifle is adequate to kill a deer if it will put its bullets into about 8 inches at 100 yards. I am sure you can nail a deer with such bullet placement but, when push comes to trigger squeeze, and maybe just a bit of buck fever thrown in, I would like a bit more accuracy from my own rifles. But let's look at the worst possible situation. Suppose you had driven to your favorite hunting camp, just outside of Fort Fungus, and discovered you had brought along every conceivable thing for your hunt . . . except ammunition. You immediately go to the local gas/gun/fishing-lure emporium and ask for a load that approaches your own, handloaded dream.

Reluctantly you accept whatever weight bullets the emporium has to offer in '06 cartridges—at least you knew they *would* have 30-06 ammo in stock. (Obviously, the best bet is to remember to bring your own ammunition and avoid this problem; however, I *have* been on one hunt where the shooter *did* lose his ammunition.)

But where do all the various bullet weights available for big-game shoot-

lishers who compiled that reloading data!

There are so many different rifles chambered for the '06 round, some newly made, with others assembled from military arms, that barrel lengths vary widely. Just to get an idea of what you can expect from the performance of your loads I took three rifles, each sporting a different barrel length, and fired 150-, 165-, 180-, 200- and 220-grain bullets from them all.

My longest-barreled gun was a Model 1917 U.S. Enfield with a 26-inch tube. Next in line was a Mauser M77 with a 24-inch barrel followed by a short-barreled (20¼-inch) Sako. The M1917 Enfield turned in velocities higher than the other two rifles regardless of bullet weight. But who really cares? Let's face it, few hunters are going to tote around a 26-inch barreled '06 rifle.

When you compared the 20¼- and 24-inch barreled guns, the velocity loss really shrank. The most velocity difference was between the 150- and 165-grain bullet, the 24-inch barrel beating the 20¼ by only 79 fps. The least amount of loss was the 180-grain bullet, the Mauser beating the little Sako by only 42 fps! It sort of makes you think that if I had only pulled the trigger just a might harder velocity would have . . .! So, for practical hunting purposes I would not feel worried about using either gun.

Actually the 180- and 200-grain bullets were quite close, just 58 fps difference between the two loads. And finally, the big 220-grain slug from

the 24-inch barreled Mauser beat the 20¼-inch barreled Sako by just 63 fps.

Actually, comparing the highest velocities (from the 26-inch barrel) to the lowest velocities (from the 20¼-inch barrel) showed that the short barrel was never below 95 percent of the velocities of the longest barreled gun. That, my friends, shows why so

In developing your own 30-06 loads, be sure to carefully inspect the brass for splits and signs of high pressure. Stay within the limits indicated in your own loading manual and *never* exceed listed powder charges.

(Left and below) There is an old adage to the effect that all the bullet placement you need to kill a deer at 100 yards is to have your bullets hit inside an 8-inch circle at that distance. In firing five different bullet weights (150, 165, 180, 200 and 220 grains) at 100 yards, all five rounds could have gotten you a deer. The maximum spread was under 4 inches! (Note inset for a closer look at this rather remarkable target.)

(Left) Most hunters who are familiar with the 30-06 feel that the 150-grain bullet (far left) is the minimum bullet weight for big game hunting. The others, second from the left to far right, are: 165-grain, 180-grain, 200- and 220-grain weights, all suitable for hunting on the North American continent.

ing strike a target at 100 yards from the muzzle? Well, I am not going to tell you what they will do in your rifle, but from my 24-inch barreled Mauser, five rounds, using five different bullet weights (150-, 165-, 180-, 200- and 220-grains) provided a *single group* well under the magical 8-inch mark at 100 yards!

All five bullets hit into an area of just 3⅞ by 3¼ inches. In short, you could take a deer with any of those loads at 100 yards, regardless of original sighting data for a specific weight of projectile. Also from that particular rifle, the 165-, 180-, 200- and 220-grain bullets nestled into just 2¼ by 2⅝ inches, rather deadly at 100 yards. The real surprises were the 180-, 200-, and 220-grain bullets—

they pinpricked a 1½- by 1½-inch area at 100 yards. If they will do that in your rifle, it's obvious you have a series of loads that has tremendous 100-yard versatility; i.e., sight-in, say, with the 180-grainer and you're prepared to take on any animal you want to by simply selecting any bullet weight ranging from 180 to 220 grains. That's versatility!

Selecting the Proper Bullet Weight

Looking at bullets for the '06 cartridge, it soon becomes obvious that you can pick almost any weight you want. Usually you can have your choice of bullets ranging from 100 to 220 grains in weight. Bullet style? That's easy. Take your pick: flat base, boat-tailed, round nose, soft point, full

metal jacket, spitzer, hollow point, flat nose, Grand Slam, Spire, Solid Base, Partition, Mag-Tip . . . well, you can just about name it—and you can find it.

Not enough you say? OK, let's turn to the folks at Barnes Bullets. They make a monstrous 250-grainer. They also provide enough loading data to turn the '06 into a modern counterpart of the old Westley Richards 318 Rimless Nitro Express. (That was a caliber that never got too much space in the magazines, but it was well known in Africa as a fine cartridge.)

With all of the choices just mentioned, I'm sure that you want to know which bullet you should use for *your* type of big-game hunting. Well, I'm not going to tell you! I don't know whether you are sitting in a haystack shooting a broadside whitetail at 50 yards or if you are looking at the wrong end of a mulie crashing through a thick growth of aspens.

While the 150-grain bullet is usually quoted as "ideal" for deer, there is nothing wrong with going with a bit heavier slug, say the 165- or 180-grain weight, if your shots may be dif-

ficult. If you are going after game larger than deer, and some that might bite back, the heavier bullets are the best bet. As to which brand or type you should purchase, well, that's the fun of reloading. The cost of a box of bullets is minor stuff when compared to the success of a hunt. Try out several brands and see what works best in your rifle.

What should you expect from a soft point bullet, as far as expansion is concerned? I cannot answer that. A few years ago I shot two wild boar with cartridges from the same box of ammo. The first shot was known, outside of the state of Texas, as a "Texas Heart Shot." I didn't lead the animal enough and the bullet struck the rear hams. The pig went down instantly and never moved, although he was given a finishing shot. The bullet broke both rear leg bones and was discovered as a mere shadow of its unfired state. Smashing through the rear leg bones, that slug lost more than half of its original weight.

The second pig took an identical round, just aft of the shoulder, ran off and dropped dead. The neatly mushroomed bullet was dug out with my knife blade in the gristle hide of the far shoulder. The bullet had lost only a few grains of its original weight. I guess if you asked the bullet maker what was wrong with the bullet that lost weight, and what was good about the bullet that mushroomed perfectly, he might rightfully ask, "At what point were you dissatisfied with either bullet when both killed the animal you were after?"

When you start going through your game-bag of recovered bullets, and we will assume that each came from an animal you killed, what happened immediately upon bullet impact? Did you make a note of how the animal reacted to the shot? What bones were hit? How deeply the bullet penetrated? What the bullet actually looked like, in terms of expansion, upon recovery? It might make an interesting study. And you should keep that information in mind when you purchase new bullets.

Whatever bullet weight(s) you choose for your hunting chores, be sure to consider the tremendous versatility the 30-06 offers the hunting handloader. From woodchucks to whitetails (and beyond) there is, I can assure you, a bullet weight (or weights) that'll do the job—in spades.

That's the way it is with the 30-06. It's a workhorse that refuses to die. And if you don't reload for your "hunting '06," you just ain't hunting! ●

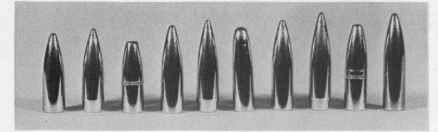

Speer makes a line of bullets that cover weights ranging from 150 on up to 200 grains for big game hunting as well as lesser weights. Speer also has its 165- and 180-grain Grand Slam specialty hunting bullets, not shown.

Hornadys' 150- to 220-grain bullets include the following (left to right): 150-grain Spire point, 150-grain boat-tail soft point (BTSP), 165-grain Spire point, 165-grain BTSP, 180-grain Spire, 190-grain BTSP and 220-grain round nose.

If the handloader looks hard enough he can even find foreign .308-inch diameter bullets for the 30-06. On the left is a 150-grain Dynamit Nobel offering. To the right are some 185-grain Finnish Lapua bullets.

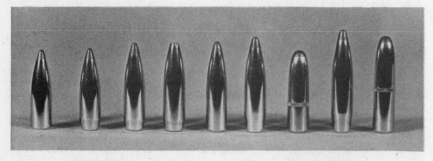

Sierra makes a series of 150- to 220-grain bullets that cover most big game shooting needs. (Like other makers, Sierra also has lighter bullet weights for other shooting/hunting needs.)

THE TEACHER was trying to present a word to the class. "Ubiquitous," she said. "Anybody know what it means?" Everyone's eyes got real interested in something on their desks lest the teacher call on someone for an answer. "Sam, how about you?" Was she surprised. I knew the word. I'd just read it a few days ago in a hunting article.

"It means everywhere at once," I said, and my classmates' heads snapped up and their eyes left their desktops for the first time in minutes.

"Use it in a sentence," the teacher commanded.

"The cottontail rabbit is ubiquitous," I said. "It appears to be everywhere at the same time." The teacher looked at me as if to say, "I might have guessed hunting was involved here somehow." But I was right, not only about the word, but about the rabbit. Cottontails do inhabit most of our land. The rabbit is often our first game hunted, and I wonder if he's not sometimes our last as well, for even in our twilight years we could, certainly,

negotiate the usually-gentle terrain of the rabbit.

I got my hunting start on rabbits. Probably you did, too. And we never will outgrow hunting the cottontail. Fathers and grandfathers start new shooters on the rabbit because the rabbit is there, close to home and fairly easy to come by. The rabbit, in turn, gives the newcomer some field responsibility, experience in gunhandling, enhanced and increased hunting skills and familiarity with hunting equipment—all of which transfer

COTTONTAILS *West!*

Shotguns, rifles or handguns—take your pick. The "ubiquitous" cottontail is ideal for the beginner— or the old-timer.

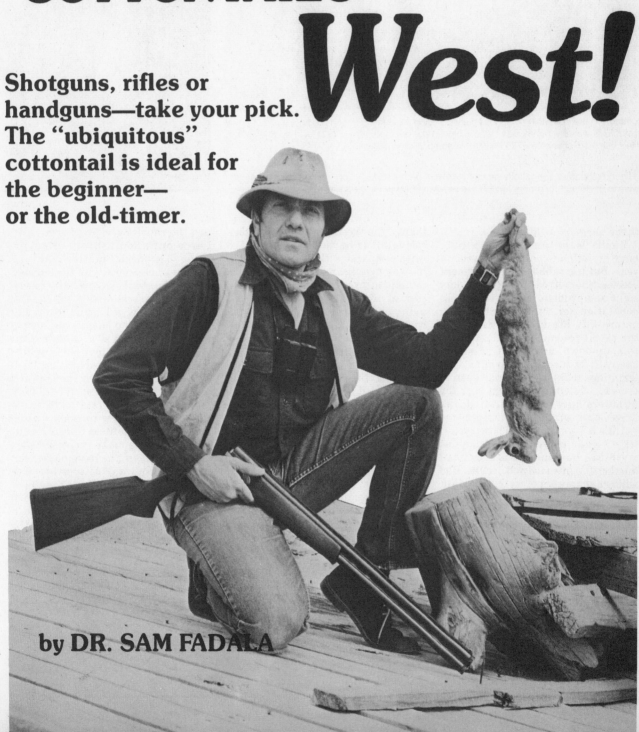

by DR. SAM FADALA

Cottontails are something you don't outgrow—and the hunting doesn't require a pile of fancy gear. This western hunter has taken a lunch-hour break to pursue rabbits in good weather. He's using a Remington 572 Fieldmaster pump. Nice cottontail.

(Right) Repeaters and rabbits go together well. Be it a lever-action, pump or semi-auto, it's wise to make sure of proper feed, fire, ejection and accuracy *before* you head for the field.

to the big game field later.

Prolific is the cottontail. Litters are large and often come more than once a year. But the rabbit is a replacement species. Short-lived anyway, it is only right and prudent to crop the excess population, for if the hunter doesn't, nature will. Population dynamics for the rabbit resembles a roller coaster ride, up-down, up-down. One season the rabbits may be swarming like lemmings making their mad dash to the sea, while the very next year the numbers may have dwindled like leaves on a winter aspen tree. Some say it's a 7-year cycle. Those cycles, like 7-year itches, are somewhat mythical, but the fact is cottontail numbers *do* increase and decline. Bad winters simply wipe 'em out, too. But, somehow, they always bounce back.

The rabbit is the beginner's delight, and he is the most popular small game animal in the world. But these reflections shine truer in the East

than in the West. In fact, the western cottontail is quite unsophisticated when compared with his eastern cousin, who has figured out that he who cometh on two legs wants to make a stew of him. Hunting with dogs and using shotguns is a wise approach when it comes to eastern cottontails. In the West, the firearm is more likely to be a 22 rimfire rifle, and the dog usually stays home. Where I live, in Wyoming, the season is ½-year long, and the limit is 10 rabbits per day, 20 in possession. Where I grew up in Arizona, the limit was the same—but the season never closed!

The Guns

I said western rabbits were easy. That's right. But they do get the message if hunted enough. And where I bag bunnies, there is some hunting pressure, so I use my 22 rimfire early in the season, but switch to my shotgun when the "scare factor" increases

and the rabbits are jumping from 30 yards out and dashing for cover. Gauge? It doesn't matter much, as long as you are good with the gun and fast on the swing. I know hunters who regularly harvest rabbits with a .410. I prefer a 20 or a 12, but I've found that in either one an ounce of shot is plenty. I like No. 5 shot. In my experience, only three or four No. 5 pellets are needed to drop a rabbit cleanly.

I've also hunted with the bow and arrow with success. I love a black powder rifle, too, and have filled many a game bag with rabbits using my 36-caliber Hatfield flintlock rifle. Handguns also make sense. If he's a good marksman, the handgunner can use just about any caliber to head-shoot his rabbit meat. I use the Ruger Mark II Standard Auto pistol with bull barrel, or a Super Single-Six in 32 H&R caliber—head shots are the byword. Quite frankly, the handgun can be perfect rabbit medicine, espe-

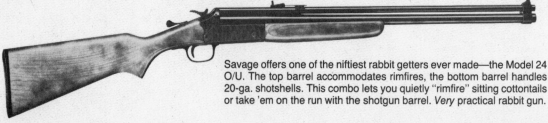

Savage offers one of the niftiest rabbit getters ever made—the Model 24 O/U. The top barrel accommodates rimfires, the bottom barrel handles 20-ga. shotshells. This combo lets you quietly "rimfire" sitting cottontails or take 'em on the run with the shotgun barrel. *Very* practical rabbit gun.

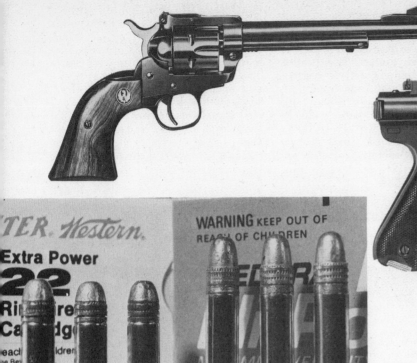

If you're a handgunner, and you're out to sharpen your eye on rabbits, here's a pair of rimfires that should do the trick. Below is the old version of Ruger's Mark II, complete with bull barrel and fully-adjustable sights. At left is Ruger's New Model Super Single-Six.

On the left are three 22 Short H.P. rimfires—a trio of similar fodder on the right, only in L.R. persuasion. The author prefers the somewhat more economical Shorts, finding them ideal at ranges up to 50 yards.

One of the author's all-time favorite bunny busters is this old Remington Model 121—it accounted for the pair of cottontails in the background. Slide actions are ideal for rabbits as second and third shots are only a "pump" away.

Scopes have their place on rimfires. Head shots are easier, and you won't waste an ounce of meat. For rabbits, the author prefers a 13-yard sight-in—be the sights iron or glass. The 13-yard sight-in will handle any shot right up to the 75-yard mark.

cially when the outdoorsman is on the big game trail and looking for some choice camp or trail food.

One season I was hunting antelope and deer above the Platte River in plateau country. From my lofty viewpoint I could see a shallow, beautiful river, and since I was backpacking, my supplies were with me. I descended the steep slope and built a temporary camp right along the river. Using a compact fishing rod, I quickly nailed some breakfast trout and then proceeded to take my sidearm and bag a few cottontails for supper. These particular rabbits had pure white meat from end to end—they were delicious in the fry pan!

But, all in all, I prefer and recommend the 22 rimfire rifle for western cottontail rabbit hunting. I'm a fan of some of the older 22 rimfires, and I have several, including a couple of Remington Model 12s and a 121, rifles which often account for limits of rabbit. When using these rifles, my favorite ammo, believe it or not, is the 22 Short hollow-point. I've never lost a rabbit after that little 27-grain bullet thumped home through either the rib cage or the head. Of course, the head shot is the ideal shot for fine eating.

Knowing that head-shot rabbits mean less meat waste, my two sons turned to scope sights for their own 22 rimfire rifles, mostly because the scope makes that head shot easier courtesy of its clearly defined aiming point and magnification of the target. But I still don't overlook the use of iron sights in my rabbit hunting. Cottontails represent a wonderful practice medium. And since I shoot various iron-sighted rifles, muzzleloaders and 30-30s mostly, the transfer value from small game to big game is a solid benefit. When it comes to sighting-in, be it for scopes or irons, I choose the

13-yard mark. Why? It's perfect. The 13-yard sight-in allows for a rabbit-taking hold-on from anywhere right under your nose on out to about 75 yards. While a practiced shot can take cottontails up to 100 yards with the 22 rimfire, I find no reason to shoot so far. Most of my shots come at 50 yards and even less. If I were to make a habit of trying shots over 75 yards, I believe I'd trade my 22 Short hollowpoints for Long Rifle fodder.

Hunting Methods

There are a lot of ways to hunt cottontails, as hinted at earlier. Stillhunting is my preference. Stillhunting means moving quietly. It does not mean "staying still." Moving quietly is what I try to do, and to move quietly you certainly have to move slowly. Take a few steps. Stop. Look. Take a few steps. Stop. Look. That's the way to stillhunt for rabbits. I sometimes do

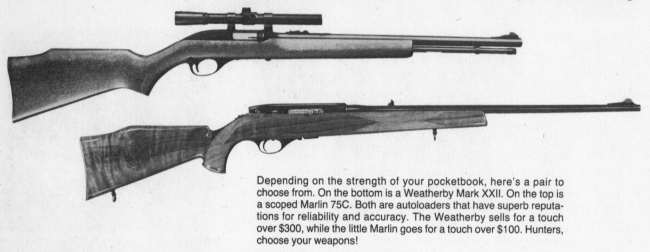

Depending on the strength of your pocketbook, here's a pair to choose from. On the bottom is a Weatherby Mark XXII. On the top is a scoped Marlin 75C. Both are autoloaders that have superb reputations for reliability and accuracy. The Weatherby sells for a touch over $300, while the little Marlin goes for a touch over $100. Hunters, choose your weapons!

my looking with both the unaided eye and the binocular, too. The glass can show you what your naked eye would have missed. I search around woodpiles and right on into brushpockets. Wherever man has left behind the things he has no further use for, a rabbit may have made a home, so keep a sharp eye out for junk—anything from building materials to dilapidated farm structures.

While stillhunting is my favorite western method of hunting cottontails, sitting can pay off, too. I don't mean stump-sitting, waiting on trails or hoping to have the rabbits come and pay a social call to your camp. I mean sitting in between walking. I've taken short-time stands which have often produced a bag of rabbits. Stalking, while thought of as a big game maneuver only, can be, and often is, a part of western rabbit hunting. While these rabbits may not be as alert as the eastern variety, it's never a surprise to me when one darts into a hole at my approach. So I have learned to stalk instead of boldly walking up to a "found" rabbit.

And you can successfully pair up on bunnies, too. An example would be one hunter moving around a likely bush or woodpile while the other circles the opposite side. Of course, safety is the big word here. Each hunter must know *exactly* where the other is

at *all times*. No shot should ever be fired if the location of the other guy is in question. My little 5-year-old daughter and I have safely bagged more than a few rabbits with the above methods. Of course, her rifle is a lever-action cork gun, but all the same she stalks around and gets a well-aimed shot or two. "Hey, Dad," she says, "I see one," and she usually does.

It is a safe sport, rabbit hunting, and it can also be a topnotch family sport. Since it requires less effort and risk to harvest a rabbit as opposed to a lion or bighorn sheep, even the younger members of the clan can participate in a bunny hunt. I especially like the fact that the kids get to see hunting for what it is—a harvest. They not only get a chance to watch the shooting, they also get to see the dressing, the field care, and later on the processing and the cooking of that game. In short, they learn to appreciate the complete hunting cycle, and they come to understand that the rabbit—all game, in fact—is a renewable resource that must be harvested, for it cannot be stockpiled like cordwood.

Field Dressing, Meat Preparation and Cooking

Knowing what to do with a cottontail after you have it is just as important as knowing how to bag it. I like to have my rabbit field-dressed either immediately after shooting, or certainly within a ½-hour of the event.

The skin of a rabbit comes off easily. I tug in the middle and separate the hide away in both directions. A slit all the way through the aitch bone (and also through the sternum) will reveal all internal organs which can be removed from the carcass with a quick downward motion, hanging tightly onto the feet, of course. If you

Rabbits are easy to field dress. The hunter simply pulls the hide from the rabbit as soon after the harvest as possible. The entrails are removed and the body cavity washed and cooled. It can then be carried out of the field in a plastic sack. (An easy way to skin a rabbit is to start in the middle and tug the fur off over both the head and feet.)

After cutting the rabbit into sections, the meat should be soaked for an hour or two in cold water, to which has been added a handful of salt and a little vinegar. The amounts of the last two may vary without harm. The author used 5 tablespoons salt and ½-cup of vinegar on this batch.

All white meat, that's a Wyoming cottontail. The cleaned and soaked pieces await the fry pan, where they will be cooked slowly to a golden brown.

have water handy, rinse the carcass. Let it cool. And when cool, slip the meat into a plastic bag. (The small white plastic sacks used to line wastepaper baskets work fine for this.)

Once you've butchered your rabbit drop the pieces of meat into cold water to which has been added some salt and some vinegar. The amounts of salt and vinegar are not critical. If the container is a couple gallons in capacity, then ½-cup of vinegar is plenty. Salt can vary from 3 tablespoons to 4 or 5. Soak the meat for an hour and then rinse it in cold water. Dry the meat and freeze it after it has been double wrapped. This means a good plastic freezer wrap followed by regular freezer paper. This double-wrap saves the meat from freezer burn, but even so, I find rabbit meat somewhat delicate and try to eat it within 6 months' time. If you have only a few on hand, don't freeze 'em. Eat 'em. Fresh is best.

Table Fare Tips

Stewed rabbit is good food. There are many ways to stew a cottontail, of course, and I have no secret to share. I like a simple approach, which includes an initial half-done frying of the meat. The meat is then transferred into a pressure cooker and well covered with water. Splash a little Worcestershire sauce in the pot and a tablespoon of soy sauce. Add one can of chicken or beef broth, too. Sprinkle in some garlic powder (just a sprinkle), and pepper to taste. You may wish to add ½-teaspoon of sweet basil leaf. If you have dried onion, drop a handful into the pot. Attach the lid of the pressure cooker and then cook for 30 minutes.

After 30 minutes have passed, pour cold water on the lid of the pressure cooker to let the steam off and carefully open it to see what you have created. The rabbit meat should be very savory at this point. Drop in ½-cup of Sherry wine, boil for 5 minutes and then transfer the meat and its sauce to another container. (You can thicken the sauce into gravy, if you like, with either flour or corn starch and water.) Cook the family's favorite vegies—we like potatoes and carrots—and add them to the meat/gravy. You now have a stew the lazy and fast way. It's good, too!

Fried rabbit? It's my favorite! Coat the rabbit with a flour, salt, pepper mixture. Melt a little pure lard mixed with some margarine in a skillet and toss in the flour-coated rabbit pieces. Cook on low to medium heat until tender. For a tasty fried rabbit, use some spices such as a sprinkle of garlic powder, or maybe some parsley chopped fine. You can add a little onion, too. Toward the end of the cooking, splash a little wine into the skillet and pop the cover back in place.

Steam the rabbit for a while and then have a feast. There are many alternate ways of frying rabbits, and I seldom cook mine exactly the same each time. (By the way, good game cookbooks usually have plenty of cottontail recipes. Buy one!)

This game animal, small as he is, furnishes not only fine hunting, but also fine eating for a great many people. Hunting the rabbit can hone those shooting abilities, too. And in some areas, rabbit hunting is very good exercise, not very difficult walking, but walking all the same. The cottontail also gives the new hunter easy access to hunting success. If we all had to wait until we were able to mount a full-scale big game hunt in order to experience the outdoors with rifle in hand, many hunters would never get started. But the rabbit is close at hand, not difficult to come by and not expensive to chase.

Hunt him alone. Hunt him with a friend. Take your family along. Start your boy or girl on rabbits. Hunt him with a bow and arrow, an air rifle, a shotgun, a black powder rifle. Use a handgun if you wish. Hunt him for his own sake or as a part of your big game trek. I'll do all of these, but most of the time it will be a hunt for the rabbit himself that will bring me out, and I'm most likely to be going with rifle in hand. That's generally the style "out West."

Finding Wounded Big Game

Losing a wounded trophy animal is one of the worst hunting experiences a hunter will ever encounter. Here's how to avoid trophy game loss.

by CHUCK ADAMS

I LEARNED MY first important lesson about finding wounded big game when I was only 12 years old. After six tough weekends of busting the brush for blacktail deer in my native California, my dad finally flushed a nice little 3x3 buck across the canyon below me. I opened up with a barrage that sounded like a minor war, spewing 130-grain 270 slugs all around the deer as he bounced in my scope 150 yards away. As the buck tore up the far hillside in fifth or sixth gear, my old pre-'64 Winchester finally ran dry. As I watched helplessly, the animal charged over the far lip of the canyon and bounded out of sight.

To say I was disappointed would have been the understatement of the year. I was crestfallen, heartsick, depressed. The chance had not been especially easy, but California bucks never stand around and gawk like barnyard cows. If one tears past you in high gear, you open up and hope for the best. If you're a good enough shot, you sometimes manage to connect.

Ten minutes after the dust cleared, Dad came huffing and puffing up to my vantage point and asked for details. He immediately said we should go take a look in the area the buck had disappeared. I told him I had missed, but he insisted we check the situation out. I was glad he did.

We found the deer's big, splayed tracks beside a tree just at the top of the canyon rim. Dad fell in on the trail like a terrier after a rabbit, walking along with nose dropped toward the ground. There was no blood, no hair, no *nothing* aside from tracks. After 100 yards, I lagged dejectedly. Dad continued out of sight into the next little draw.

An unexpected whoop snapped my head up with a jerk. I dogtrotted over the hill and found Dad admiring a beautiful buck barely 50 yards from where I had stopped! My deer was drilled neatly between the shoulder blades from above, and there was no exit hole in the brisket. The animal had left no blood on the ground, but the well-mushroomed Sierra boat-tail had literally exploded the deer's lungs and heart. The buck had been dead on its feet when it disappeared over the hill.

The foregoing story is one that most serious riflemen can identify with. Almost every seasoned hunter has seen (or experienced) a similar occurrence during his days in the field, because big game animals *quite often* run away after being hit without the slightest clue that they are hurt. As a result, it is every hunter's sacred responsibility to search for each animal he shoots at, no matter how pessimistic he is about the outcome.

Always following up your shots at deer and other animals is the first cardinal rule of hunting big game. This single procedure puts thousands of animals on the meat pole each year that would otherwise be lost. Every hunter owes such diligence to the game he hunts and, more selfishly, to himself. Hard, skillful hunting and straight shooting are necessary for taking any big-game trophy, but every bit as important is knowing what to do after you finish pulling the trigger. Here's a thumbnail course on precisely how to proceed once the shooting stops.

One important (and obvious) hunters' tool is a quality pair of binoculars. Spotting wounded game with the naked eye can oftentimes be, at best, a hit or miss proposition. Our advice would be to buy the best binoculars you can afford.

Note Game Reactions

Hard-hit animals sometimes fail to show any sign of actually *being* hit. However, more often than not such critters will in some way indicate their plight. They may stumble, hump up in the mid-section, or tear blindly away with bodies held low to the ground. In some dramatic situations, a hit is clearly indicated as the animal cartwheels tail over teakettle or drops like a wet sack of oats. More often, a hunter must note subtle reactions that tell him if he scored a hit and where that hit might be.

A few classic reactions are fairly easy to analyze. An animal that humps up in the middle and ambles

away is probably hit in the paunch. An animal that sags in the rear end might be hit in a ham or the area between the hams and paunch. A critter that charges away pell-mell with body held low and with little regard for where it is going has probably been hit through lungs or heart. Other reactions, like slight flinches, falls, or rearing up are impossible to interpret for sure but generally mean some sort of hit.

Reactions, like a deer dropping its tail or veering sharply up or down a hill, mean far less than some hunters believe. Such big game behavior is often caused by fear, not actual projectile impact. Similarly, the solid "whump" you think might be bullet impacting flesh often turns out to be bullet impacting dirt, a rotten stump, or a tree trunk. By all means note such clues if you can during the shooting action, but don't rely too heavily on iffy information.

Look, Listen, and Wait

All too many hunters charge after an animal the instant the shooting stops. This is a terrible mistake. There is no way a person can overtake a healthy animal, and pushing a crippled one only spurs the poor creature along. If your trophy is dead already—like my very first buck—you'll find it just as easily 15 minutes after it disappeared as you will at once. In game pursuit, haste definitely makes waste on most occasions.

What you should do is remain where you shot from once your target has disappeared. Watch for the animal to run over an even farther ridge, sneak out of the brushpile it dove into,

The clear majority of big game takes off running when shot at— even after solid hits are made.

One of the keys to finding any wounded game animal is hunter persistence. Without it, this hunter would have lost this nice buck.

or double back toward you in confusion. Keep your ears wide open for sounds the animal might make after it melts out of sight. Quite often, a hunter can track a deer, elk, bear, or similar animal by *sound alone* as it crashes through trees or brush, or scrambles over rocky terrain. At times, the random thrashing of a downed animal or even its death gurgles will tell you your game tag is filled, even if you cannot actually see your trophy.

After shots are taken, you should wait at least 10 minutes before following big game. If you stay alert during this period of time, you might determine whether or not you hit the mark from animal reactions. If so, you should definitely be able to pinpoint where you last saw or heard the animal you were shooting at.

Clearly Mark Your Shooting Locale

All too many hunters storm after an animal without marking the place they shot from. This is well and good if you shot at an elk from a prominent rocky outcropping or a deer from a stand in a tree. Such locales are easy to find a second time. However, in

(Left) Tree-stand hunters are fortunate in that they can easily relocate their shooting locale. Ground-bound hunters should *clearly* mark where they shot from to avoid confusion later on.

A hunter should carefully inspect likely escape trails for signs of blood, hair, bone, etc. Note the position of the hunter. He has wisely positioned himself to the *side* of the trail. Why? He's trying to prevent the accidental obliteration of any tell-tale sign.

many situations hunters leave their shooting locale, become disoriented in densely wooded hillsides or monotonous brushy flats, and permanently lose track of where they were when they took their shots. In many instances, not knowing where you shot from means you haven't the foggiest notion where your animal was last seen or heard, either. Too many stone-dead deer and other trophies are left

to rot because the bozos who shot them have rushed into the woods becoming instantly confused about where the action took place. If you know precisely where you shot from, you can always return to this site and become oriented once more as to where your target animal was when you pulled the trigger.

It is riduculously easy to mark where you shot from. If you're proper-

ly prepared, you'll have a roll of fluorescent orange, blue, or yellow surveyor's tape to drape on nearby trees or bushes. In a pinch, toilet paper or any bright article of clothing will neatly serve the purpose. A last-ditch effort that works is laboriously blazing a few nearby trees with a hunting knife or belt-carried hatchet. If you don't have a hunting knife, you shouldn't be in the woods at all!

Proceed to the Hit Site

Once you've marked your shooting locale, it's time to proceed directly to the place you last heard or saw your animal. If you are alone, move forward carefully with gun ready and eyes and ears alert for hints of a still-living animal. If a hunting friend is along, it's best for one of you to hang back if this offers a superior vantage point and a decent chance for a finishing shot if the animal is still alive and

A *running*, cloven-hoofed animal, like a deer, leaves a track like this one. Note the fully splayed toes and dew claw impressions in this track.

(Left) Knowing that a "wounded" buck runs can be helpful when it comes to sorting out the tracks of *your* deer from others that may be present.

comes squirting into the clear. The buddy-system of animal recovery works especially well in canyon country, where one hunter can drop into the brush or trees to rummage for trailing clues while the other watches from on high.

Search for Signs of a Hit

Many beginning hunters expect every "hit" animal to leave blood on the ground in easily-seen quantities. If such nimrods do not discover blood sign after a minute or two of casual looking, they assume they've missed their shot. In reality, I think it's safe to say that over 50 percent of hard-hit deer, elk, and bear leave no blood at all initially and bleed sparingly between hit-site and where they finally keel over. A hunter should certainly look for blood, but he should look for less obvious signs of a hit as well.

The easiest signs to find in areas with mud or soft dirt are the running tracks of the target animal. Freshly scuffed dirt is always darker in color than older tracks because subsurface moisture has been recently uncovered. Running tracks are generally deeper than those of walking animals, and in split-hooved game like deer and elk, the running tracks tend to be splayed at the toes with dewclaw impressions clearly imprinted behind the main hoofprints. Such knowledge should make tracking *your* animal fairly easy, even if hundreds of other tracks litter the immediate area.

If you can find the tracks of your animal, follow them as best you can while looking ahead for the animal itself and looking for other forms of sign. Bullet impact often cuts a little hair and scatters it on the ground—a sure sign of a hit. *Lots* of hair usually means a non-fatal "creasing hit." At times, a solid hit also leaves a little fat or bone scattered near the hit-site.

Blood and other body fluids are primary things to search for when following up a potentially hard-hit trophy. A paunch hit often leaks clear or yellow-green fluid—fluid which can sometimes be seen on dirt, rocks, or logs. Blood is not as easy to see as some hunters might suspect, especially if it's being dropped in small quantities. I've often blood-trailed mortally hit animals on hands and knees, finding as little as one match-head-sized drop every 10 or 15 feet. Go slow, eyeballing every leaf, rock, log and blade of grass for blood. Crisscross the hit area for sign if tracks are not visible, making wider and wider loops in search of blood, hair, etc. And be sure to look for blood *above* the ground,

too—blood often squirts or gets smeared on tree trunks, limbs, or high-growing grass and waist-level brush.

If you saw or heard something that indicated a hit before you actually went to the hit site, you'll be especially fired up to search hard for signs of a hit and the animal itself. However, you should search diligently even if chances are good that you missed entirely. Persistence often pays off with blood found dozens of yards from the hit-site or the animal itself found sprawled dead on the ground. Never give up looking without a *diligent* effort!

Trailing Without Blood Sign

In a surprising number of cases, animals will take a solid hit, run 50 to 300 yards, and drop without leaving one speck of blood on the ground. This is especially true with *high* chest hits, which promote internal bleeding. Even more often, animals like deer and elk will make a frantic *death-run* that carries them several yards before blood wells up and begins spurting to the ground. In such cases, a hunter must trail a bit without blood to recover his animal.

If tracks are visible, following a bloodless trail might be easy. If no sign can be found, a hunter must use his noggin and try to second-guess his target's escape route. Hard-hit animals almost always head for some sort of "safety zone"—a thick clump of brush, a deep, rugged canyon, or a distant basin with a good view of danger.

If running uphill is necessary to reach such a place, a hurt creature will often take the tougher route. However, most animals hit solidly in the body take the easiest escape path they can—*downhill*, if possible, and usually along a well-traveled game trail. Only when almost dead and thoroughly panicked will an animal rush blindly without regard for specific paths through the woods.

If you cannot find blood right off the bat, circle the area carefully, widening your search as time goes by. Pay special attention to more likely escape routes, snooping along trails, through openings, and around the

(Left) The hunter should remember that a big game animal, once hit (with arrow or bullet), will often hole-up in heavy cover.

(Below) Unless a wounded animal is "dead on its feet," it will generally seek out, and stick to, easy escape paths like this well-defined trail through the heavy brush.

edges of especially dense cover. Such efforts often produce blood sign or a glimpse of the animal itself.

Blood-Trailing Tips

If you do find blood, follow it slowly to one side of the trail to avoid missing sign or destroying it with your feet. If blood is skimpy, it's a good idea to leap-frog your "markers" (like two white handkerchiefs), placing one alongside the last blood seen and carrying the other forward to mark any new blood found. This technique helps you stay on the track as you cast ahead for fresh sign.

Blood is most easily seen on leaves, rocks, logs, snow and other uniformly-colored surfaces. If leaves are abundant on the ground, your animal has probably flipped some over with its feet as it ran or walked along. If blood is especially tough to find, inspecting leaves on both sides sometimes turns up valuable splashes or flecks of this precious trailing commodity.

Additionally, the *color* of the blood you find on a trail can indicate a lot about where you scored your hit. Dark red blood, in short supply, often indicates a superficial flesh wound from a surface vein, especially if blood appears in *big, round* droplets. Bright red blood which seems to be squirted out in streams usually means a deep artery hit and the good chance of animal recovery. Dark red blood in good quantity sometimes means a hit in the liver area—a fairly slow-killing but deadly shot. Pink, frothy blood indicates a hit in the lungs—in this case, proceed with confidence even if blood is sparse. *Lots* and *lots* of bright red blood probably means a hit in or near the heart.

When blood-trailing deer or other big game, always keep an eye out for sudden directional changes that might throw you off. Wounded animals sometimes veer sideways unexpectedly, and occasionally backtrack a full 180 degrees before peeling off in a brand-new direction. Such moves can puzzle a hunter who is not trailing slowly and paying attention to both sides of the animal's escape route.

Typical Trailing Scenarios

If you find some sort of hit sign after a search, several scenarios might follow. Here is what you can expect.

• *Big, dark-red droplets of blood in good quantity often peter out to nothing after 50 to 300 yards of trailing.* This usually indicates a surface hit in the brisket, ham, neck, etc. The animal will probably survive nicely with the wound healing quickly.

• *A skimpy or nonexistent blood trail that turns to heavy blood trail* generally indicates a solid chest hit and a dead trophy at the end of the line. Why? The animal's chest has filled up with blood, increasing exterior flow through entrance and/or exit holes.

• *Uniformly skimpy blood can mean several different things.* The animal may be surface hit in an area where body movement keeps the wound open and produces a light but constant flow of blood. Such blood sign might mean a broken leg that is

(Left) Another point to be aware of is the fact that crippled game sometimes heads for vantage points that provide clear views of any approaching danger.

Once you have nailed your deer, and it's on the move, you should "leap-frog" blood markers. Doing so helps the hunter systematically follow his trophy. This hunter is using strips of old sheeting as his blood markers.

bleeding slowly but steadily. On the other hand, the animal might be dead on its feet and merely bleeding inside. By all means follow as long as you can find trailing blood—the end result might very well be cause for celebration! Even if your hit is not a fatal one, you always have the chance of overtaking the animal and shooting a second time.

● *The best trailing scenario of all is, of course, the classic buckets-of-blood trail you can follow at a lope.* Many animals hit solidly in chest or ham leave such a highway to follow, and the result is always a short trail to a buck or bull on the ground.

Never Forget Safety!

Any crippled big game animal is potentially dangerous. When following a blood trail or crisscrossing an area for sign, always look about *regularly* for the animal itself. A wounded buck deer surprised in dense brush at close range can lacerate a hunter with antlers and hooves. And a bull elk can do even *more* damage. Also remember that bears of any sort can be *potential killers* when riled. There's no need to be paranoid when following up shots at game, because the danger is certainly minimal unless your quarry is a grizzly bear, rhino, Cape buffalo, or similar death-dealing machine. However, always watch your step when a hurt animal might be lurking nearby.

A savvy woodsman follows up his shots with the same enthusiasm he exhibits when stalking the hills and leveling his sights to shoot. By persistently dogging every trophy that might be mortally hit, such a hunter never wastes precious wildlife and always makes the most of chances to fill his big game hunting tag! ●

Never presume you "missed" your buck. The author once made that presumption when he was starting out, years ago. His father, seen here, urged him to reconsider. They tracked, trailed and found a nice buck. *That's* hunting.

Big game animals always "head for the hills" when shot at, or hit (even vitally). It's wise to remember that not every vitally hit big game animal drops in its tracks.

by DON ZUTZ

THE APPLE TREES were gnarled and dying. The farmer had long ago quit tending the orchard that swung around the base of a small-but-steep hill. Tall grasses blended into the trees from the edge of the uncut corn field, offering easy "sneaking cover" for any pheasants that slipped ahead of hunters who, like me, worked the tall stalks without a dog. Most often the birds would run and skulk, leaving the impression that there was no game around; and I assumed that, with the pheasant season having been open for several weeks, the remaining roosters knew all the tricks. Not only would they sit tight, but it would take a lot of walking to get a bird up, thanks to the absence of canine assistance.

Readers need not be steeped in Sherlock Holmes mysteries to sense the thickening plot or to anticipate the climax. For whatever reason, a long-spurred cock bird didn't keep running into the orchard ahead of me.

PHEASANTS

Used within its range capabilities, the 28 can be a practical pheasant gun — especially if the hunter can center the bird with the 28's small, 20-/24-inch diameter pattern!

It flattened in the fringe grasses and, as sheer luck would have it, my booted foot came down threateningly close to him. He registered a brassy protest, vaulted skyward, then banked and turned back over the corn. But it was still close range, and I was mentally prepared for the moment. So was the 28-gauge Remington Model 11-48 Skeet gun which folded him cleanly. The retrieve was easy; he lay where he had fallen, solidly anchored. Then I went back to look for my empty hull for future reloading.

There is probably nothing overwhelmingly unique about that opening narrative. More than a few pheasants are taken annually by sportsmen using 28-gauge shotguns. In fact, each year the little gauge seems to attract a few more followers. But if one considers the relatively light shot charges thrown by the 28, he must sooner or later ask an important question: Is the 28-gauge a *legitimate* pheasant gun? For although the 28

has a tremendous reputation for breaking 100x100 in Skeet, and although it can sparkle on close-range woodcock and bobwhite, the ringneck pheasant is another ball game. Roosters *can* carry lead! Even the larger 12, 16, and 20 gauges have feathered and lost their share of tough ol' cocks, and one must be intelligent enough to realize that the 28's lesser shot charges invariably contain less energy than those of the larger bores simply by virtue of fewer pellets.

The 28-gauge was developed in Europe before the turn of the century. Unfortunately, some misconceptions attribute this creation to the famous Parker Gun Co. of Meriden, CT, which isn't true. European publications had already mentioned the 28 long before Parker made its first gun in that gauge. (For that matter, the Europeans also had 32- and 24-gauge shotshells *prior* to the 20th century.)

Initially, the 28 was given ½- and ⅝-ounce shot charges, and its bore di-

ameter was standardized at 0.550-inch. Since then, the advent of slow-burning powders has brought the basic 28-gauge load to ¾-ounce, and some commercial and reloaded rounds have been taken to ⅞- and even to 1 ounce.

There can be no doubt that the 28-gauge performs better with a ¾-ounce load than does the .410 bore with practically the same payload weight. People who do poorly with the .410 on Skeet often come off their first round with the 28 beaming proudly and saying, "It breaks 'em like a 12!" And hunters who happen to center game with the 28 on one of their first outings with it tend to come away equally impressed with its prowess as compared to the crippling done with a 3-inch .410. Essentially, there are three reasons why the 28-gauge does so much better with a light shot charge than the .410 bore.

First, the 28's wider bore produces a shorter shot string. Secondly, the

& THE 28?

There are pros and cons on this one, but there's an intelligent way to approach "the problem." Read on!

The Remington 870 pump chambered for the 28.

(Far left) One reason why the .410 is less efficient than the 28 (despite similar shot charge weights) is its long, narrow, pressure-laden shot string which causes pellet deformation, relatively low velocities in the 3-inch length, and terribly long in-flight shot "tailing." The .410 wad doesn't have any cushioning section, either.

(Left) The 28's patterning prowess comes from a short shot string fired at a snappy velocity from a plastic wad that has a proper cushioning section.

(Right) The 28-gauge hull (right) isn't all that much bigger than the .410s to the left, but the wider 28-gauge bore certainly improves the ballistics and the patterning potential.

volumetric capacity of a 28-gauge hull permits some cushioning via a longer wad. Finally, the 28's bore diameter gives a more efficient pressure/velocity ratio than that of the pencil-barreled .410. Thus, the short shot string puts more pellets on the plane of the target at the point of interception, and the larger 28-gauge bore gives powder gases greater expansion room and a broader wad base upon which to push. In general, the 3-inch .410 has a starting velocity of roughly 1,135 fps, while the ¾-ounce 28-gauge commercial field load takes off at 1,295 fps. On the basis of patterning and velocity, then, the 28 outdoes the 3-inch .410—in spades!

Realistic Pattern Tests

All that ballistics stuff sounds good, of course, but it's mainly academic unless we can develop an answer for our primary question: What does it mean when applied to pheasants?

Much of the answer pivots on pattern and pellet power, meaning choke and shot size selection. The 28 does *not* automatically throw rifle-like patterns that casual hunters mistakenly believe come from a smallbore shotgun. The firearm's industry tests 28-gauge chokes and loads on the same basis as the 10, 12, 16, and 20—namely, into a 30-inch-diameter circle at 40 yards. Only the .410 bore is tested dif-

ferently, being checked with a 20-inch-diameter circle at just 25 yards. Thus, an Improved Cylinder 28-gauge barrel spreads its shot charge over as large an area as an IC 12-gauge, while a modified 28 barrel is supposed to deliver the same percentage and pattern width as a modified 12, 16, or 20. And the full-choked 28 is regulated to put at least 70 percent of its shot charge into a 30-inch circle at 40 yards, just as is a full-choked 12 or 3-inch 20. Indeed, if you're one of those people who thinks all smallbore shotguns punch out fist-sized clusters, forget it!

The 28's obvious weakness is that its light shot charges don't pack enough pellets to fill out the 30-inch circle for guaranteed multiple hits into the vital areas of a game bird. In other words, the 28 doesn't throw a smaller pattern than the larger gauges—it throws a *thinner* pattern due to the comparatively fewer pellets in the original payload.

Just how does this thin patterning affect the 28's field performance? To illustrate, I ran some patterns with a Remington Model 1100 28-gauge field gun choked Modified. I used both 6s and 7½s at *30 yards*, which I deemed a justifiable working range for the rig. After patterns had been fired and outlined, I worked a life-sized pheasant profile (obtained by tracing a mature

rooster) into the 30-inch circle to evaluate both shot sizes for consistency in putting multiple hits into vital areas. Remember, now, that the overall size of a game bird means nothing relative to target-pattern relationship, for a hit just "anywhere" in a bird's anatomy won't bring it down. Unless a pattern can place multiple hits into the *vital* areas of a game bird, and do so with adequate energy for penetration and bone breaking, there is more potential for crippling than for clean killing. On a pheasant, the vital areas include the head, neck, wing butt segment and chest cavity ahead of the diaphragm. Nipping the outer wing does nothing but leave a runner; hit the leg, and the bird'll keep flying; glance pellets off the back or put them into the rear end, and ol' rooster will also sail away into heavy cover. Thus, once the patterns were shot and outlined with a felt-tipped pen, I analyzed them according to: **A.)** basic percentages; **B.)** pellet distribution within the 30-inch circle; and **C.)** coverage on a pheasant profile traced at random on the target sheet. My feeling was that the results would be indicative of the 28's ability to place multiple hits into a ringneck because of the *relatively short range,* the 28's *short shot string,* and the field load's *snappy velocity.*

With both 6s and 7½s, my Reming-

Next to the "gigantic" 3½-inch 10-gauge Magnum, the 28-gauge doesn't seem like much of a shotshell. But it can fill out a 20-/24-inch-diameter pattern quite well for those who have the skill to employ it.

This pattern was shot with ¾-ounce of 6s over 30 yards. This Modified-choked 1100 has a target-saturating pattern for the inner 20-24 inches, but as the pheasant profiles show, a fringe hit won't automatically place multiple pellet hits in the vital areas of the bird. And ringnecks can carry a lot of misplaced lead.

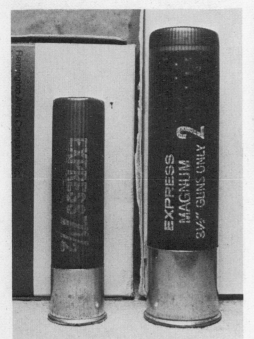

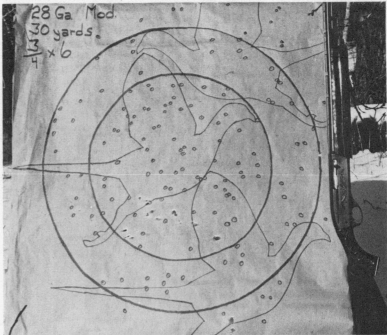

28 Ga. Mod.
30 yards.
¾ × 6

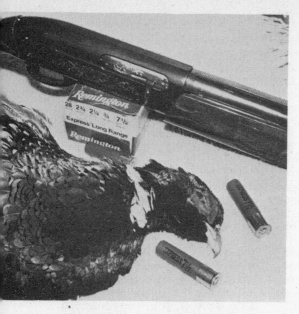

Number 7½ shot will help fill the core of a 28-gauge pattern when ¾-ounce loads are used, but the writer prefers 6s for their greater energy, especially if the range begins to exceed 20 yards.

When you consider a full-grown rooster's overall size, the bird does take up a considerable portion of the pattern's 20-inch core. But rather than look at the whole bird, consider just the vital areas — head, neck, wing butts, and forward chest cavity — and you'll see that it's difficult to insure multiple pellet hits into that reduced vital area.

ton 1100 28-gauge Modified barrel gave honest Modified percentages at 40 yards. However, since I didn't regard the Modified 28 a true 40-yard gun, I did the serious analytical work over 30 yards, at which point the Modified barrel was still holding about 70-percent patterns. Those tighter percentages should have given the little shotshell an advantage, but, alas, there was a glaring fault. . . .

As the accompanying photos show,

the 30-yard patterns gave adequate density only in the 20-inch-diameter core. A pheasant profile placed anywhere in that 20-inch core would have picked up multiple hits in the vital areas with either 6s or 7½s. But once outside the 20-inch core, the pheasant profile rarely showed multiple hits in the vitals unless one laid the profile precisely to match the distribution, which isn't how it happens afield. With the element of chance that's always involved in wingshooting, the

outer 5-inch ring of a 30-inch-diameter pattern from a 28 doesn't seem able to insure positive coverage so that clean kills are registered no matter where the bird fits in.

With the 6s, patterns at 30 yards averaged 120 pellets overall, but only 46-52 ever found their way into the outer ring; all the rest were concentrated in the 20-inch core. The nearby photo of a typical pattern with 6s illustrates the distribution. The pheasant profiles traced on that pattern of 6s show how a bird can be nipped by the pattern's outer ring without absorbing strikes to the vitals. And we do not need to draw pheasant profiles on the pattern of 7½s, also shown nearby, as just eyeballing that spread will indicate a weak outer ring. Interestingly enough, this is basically the same pattern distribution thrown by Full-choked 28s at 40 yards and Improved Cylinder 28s at 20 strides: The core is dense, while the outer ring is patchy at best. Thus, although other guns may pattern differently than those I've shot, the session indicated that the 28's *effective* pattern isn't really a 30-incher! While it actually puts some pellets outside the 30-inch circle, the main mass tends to be concentrated within 20-24 inches. If a hunter can slap that 20-24-inch core on a pheasant, he has enough density to be highly effective. Nip John Ringneck with the edge of a 28's pattern at most distances, however, and you're likely to hang a handful of feathers in the air rather than folding him like a wet dish rag.

Why not sweeten those pattern ring/fringe areas with heavier shot charges? That may happen with some guns, but in my own patterning with

As this pattern of 7½s fired over 30 yards shows, the 28 doesn't pack enough pellets to fill out the entire 30-inch-diameter patterning circle. Pellet-free patches inside the outer ring indicate crippling hits. An eyeballing of the area between the 20-inch-diameter core of the pattern and the outer 30-inch ring will show obvious weakness.

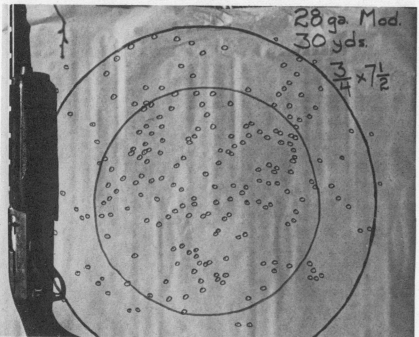

28 ga. Mod.
30 yds.
¾ × 7½

⅞- and 1-ounce charges, the distribution characteristic remains intact: The added pellets tend to show up inside the 20-24-inch-diameter core, *not* in the outer rim. Moreover, there are a trio of complications in "magnumizing" the 28: **1.**) There are no deep shotcups for these charge weights, which leaves the pellets (at least in part) exposed to bore scrubbing; **2.**) velocities drop and chamber pressures rise with the heavier loads; and **3.**) the shot string lengthens *á la* the 3-inch .410 for less effective in-flight "tailing." From this writer's vantage point, the ⅞-ounce 28-gauge Magnum may well be the best, as it can still move briskly (Federal's commercial offering did about 1,250 fps) at sane chamber pressures. But, alas, handloaders have not been able to accomplish much with the one-piece plastic wads currently available, as they take up too much room. One of the best handloads for the ⅞-ouncer is this one worked up by Tom Browne in Hodgdon's lab:

Case:	Federal plastic 28-ga.
Primer:	Winchester 209
Powder:	18.0/Hodgdon HS-6
Wad:	Remington SP-28
Shot:	⅞-ounce of shot
Pressure:	10,500 lup
Velocity:	1,178 fps

One-ounce reloads in the 28 have never excited me, but for those who think more is better, here's another from Hodgdon:

Case:	Win. AA-type 28-ga.
Primer:	Winchester 209
Powder:	20.0/Hodgdon HS-7
Wad:	Overpowder cup cut from WAA28 wad + ¼-inch filler wad
Shot:	1 ounce of shot
Pressure:	11,100 lup
Velocity:	1,144 fps

Frankly, though, anyone who wants a 1-ounce shot charge should simply go to a 20-gauge gun where the larger bore will do a better job. But if somebody were to produce a suitable shotcup wad, the 28 could, indeed, handle a ⅞-ounce shot charge *efficiently*.

Which choke for the 28-gauge pheasant gun? The answer seems twofold, depending on whether the hunter uses a double or a single barrel. In a side-by-side or an over/under the combination of Improved Cylinder and Full seems closer to the ideal than the standard Modified and Full

duo. The IC can handle close-flushing birds out to 20 yards or so, while the Full choke follow-up barrel puts maximum density into the air for longer shots. I really don't view the Full choke as a handicap beyond 27-30 yards, as by that time it has opened up and the shooter's technique is more important than a few more inches of overall spread that a Modified choke can give. This combination of IC&F isn't generally available, but it can be had by buying a double bored M&F and having a quality gunsmith open the Modified barrel to IC (about 50-55 percent at 40 yards). If the double 28 has 28-inch barrels, so much the better, in this scribe's opinion. A 28 with 25-26-inch barrels can be somewhat whippy; the longer 28-inch tubes help steady the already-trim gun for smoother swinging and a more positive follow-through.

Clip a tough old ringneck with the 28's outer ring or fringe, and you'll need a good dog to run it down and make the retrieve.

Currently Available 28s

Twenty-eight-gauge doubles are getting easier to find these days. Stateside, Browning is the main man in over/unders. The Citori line comes in both hunting and Superlight models with 26- and 28-inch barrels. Because these guns are already so small, there is little difference between the standard hunting grade's weight and the Superlight's heft. The main difference is in the stock/fore-end design, which has a racy straight-hand grip and slight schnabel on the Superlight while the standard Citori wears a full pistol grip and a thicker fore-end. If you're into the 28-gauge for pure aesthetic appeal, the Browning Grade III and IV Citoris are eyecatching.

In the side-by-sides, there's mainly the Spanish and Italian imports such as the AyA, Grulla, and Churchill

This 28-gauge boxlock is made by Vouzelaud of France. Note the English-style, fine scroll engraving.

(Windsor). However, Winchester has made a limited run of Model 23s in 28-gauge for '86 and '87.

Also new this year is the 28-gauge side-by-side from Parker Reproductions. There's some good news here. You can, on special order, get that gun in the IC/Full choke combo mentioned above. The price for that D-Grade Parker runs around $2800. Not exactly cheap. However, the wood is gorgeous, the engraving is top quality and the whole outfit comes wrapped in a superb hard (leather) case.

There are also some ultra-fine 28s being custom made in Europe and the U.K. by the likes of Holland & Holland, Westley Richards, Powell, Piotti, and the smaller houses of Belgium, like Forgeron, Dumoulin, and Lebeau-Courally. In fact, the current American importers of doubles like the Darne (now Bruchett), Vouzelaud,

and Forgeron tell me that the 28 is one of the most popular gauges because of its overall trimness. Friend Tony Falise (Midwest Gun Sport—Belgian Headquarters, 1942 Oakwood View Dr., Verona, WI 53593) has had some classic 28s handmade in Belgium for his clients; they are superbly high quality, but not as expensive as the prestigious British houses.

When it comes to single-barreled repeaters, the Modified choke seems to be the best compromise in a 28-gauge pheasant gun. (An Improved Cylinder or Skeet-bored 28 gives up the ghost too quickly. I carried the Skeet-bored Model 11-48 mentioned earlier in this piece only in anticipation of close-range shots; I was mentally prepared to pass up anything that wasn't inside 20-25 yards.)

As in the case of doubles, there aren't many 28-gauge repeaters

made, albeit in small numbers, and their collector's value is going out of sight. But Model 12s were always well made, and a 28 is sure to attract the attention of any knowledgeable shot slinger. Others with a collector's bent may find it fun to dig up one of the old 28-gauge single shots formerly made by Savage, Stevens, Winchester, and H&R. These guns are invariably Full chokes, but what the heck.

From the gist of these proceedings, one can surmise that the 28-gauge can be a legitimate pheasant gun with its ¾-ounce load. If the hunter realizes range limitations, if he or she can work with the 20-24-inch core of the pattern, and if he or she can overcome the temptation to believe that the 28 is indeed a 12-gauge—then it can legitimately be employed for ringnecks. It can be made even more legitimate if the hunter does some patterning to

(Top) Remington 1100 semi-auto and (bottom) Browning Citori. Both are chambered for the 28, and are readily available across the U.S.

Trim European-style smallbores usually can get the 28-gauge's pattern on target sooner than many heavier 12 gauges.

around. However, the all-around excellence of Remington's Models 1100 and 870 in said gauge makes up for the shortage. Both are readily available streamlined guns that tote easily, move as responsively as most doubles, and point naturally. Recoil is nonexistent on an 1100 28, which makes it perfect for sensitive beginners or milady—as well as making it possible to throw in very fast second and third shots. With an extra IC or Skeet barrel for close-in woodcock, quail, or off-season clay-target busting, the 1100 or 870 can cover a lot of ground for the 28's admirers who can't exactly put down $10,000 for a custom-made double. The Remington 1100 I used for hunting and patterning this past fall functioned perfectly in every respect, as did an 870 I had earlier when that gauge first became available in the Wingmaster line.

Hunters who happen to be gun nuts on the side might hunt up a Winchester Model 12 in 28-gauge. These were

find the best load for his individual 28, and if some time and money are spent on off-season Skeet shooting. Skeet can teach a lot about the 28. For although there are a lot of thoroughly shattered Skeet clays in 28-gauge events, there are also weak fringe hits that chip or merely dust the targets; and these light hits, so often forgotten in favor of the smokeball impacts, are the ones which tell us that the 28 is still "only a 28"—complete with its thin outer rim and fringe areas that are prone to crippling. Thus, the 28 gauge's light loads have definite parameters, as does the typical hunter have his or her level of skill as a wingshot, and these factors must be intelligently assessed before the 28 can be considered a viable pheasant gun. Centered hits by the 28's pattern core tend to make it look a little better than it really is overall. But use those center 20 inches of pattern *expertly*, and the 28 *can* deliver clean kills at modest ranges. •

by **BOB BELL**

BOLT-ACTION

I HAVEN'T ALWAYS been a bolt-action fan. There was a time when I thought the Model 94 Winchester carbine was the greatest gun in the world—light, fast, and just so nifty looking. I worked all summer to get one, and few thrills in my life have surpassed what I felt when I pulled that shiny, blue-black 32 Special—serial number 1,260,210—from its tan box. I was 12 years old.

But in a short time I was pondering something bigger, and my thoughts focused on the Model 71 Winchester 348. It was big enough for elk—even Elmer Keith agreed to that, though he'd have preferred the same case opened up to at least 375, and preferably bigger. I'm not sure why I was already thinking about elk. I was born and grew up in Pennsylvania, and when I got the 348 at age 17, I'd never been more than 100 miles from home and the nearest wild wapiti was thousands of miles away. Still, I got it, as a high school graduation present, and it was everything I wanted—a beautiful hunk of machinery, smooth as grease, chambered for a powerful cartridge, and accurate enough for the only kind of hunting I was familiar with then. And it, like the little 94, was a lever

gun. Who would want anything else?

It was the spring of 1943 when I got the 348, but it would be the fall of 1947 before I shot anything larger than woodchucks with it. World War II intervened. At least my share of it. I enlisted in the Army shortly after high school graduation, was sent to basic training at Camp Sibert, Alabama, and was issued a spanking new M1903-A3 Springfield, SN 4, 831,662. In case anyone doesn't know, that was a bolt-action rifle. It was a sort of illegitimate offspring of the legendary '03 Springfield, in the view of many card-holding competitive riflemen of earlier years, but I didn't know that then. What it was to me was a revelation. It changed my life.

Admittedly, the A3 lacked much when compared with the earlier M1903. Not only was the A3 crudely finished and fitted with assorted stamped parts, but half the grooves in the barrel were missing. I didn't care. That just made it easier to clean, a necessary chore in those days of corrosive primers. And it shot. My first round at 200 yards was a pinwheel, and at that range it tended to keep most of its bullets in the 5-inch spotter, even with the Class C ammo we

had in training. That's 2½ minutes of angle, which was better than I ever got from the famous M1 Garand in subsequent years—and I won't even mention the 30-caliber Carbine's patterns. Fact is, I doubt that the old-timers' lamented '03 did significantly better than the A3.

However, I hadn't given up on the lever guns. During the early post WWII years, the 348 downed a truckload of deer and elk for me, and I even tried varmint shooting with a Model 65 Winchester 218 Bee. But memories of the way that new/old Springfield had shot in basic and the way a Weaver-scoped '03-A4 performed on later occasions lurked in my mind. It was obvious that when it came time to hit a small target at long range, the bolt-action was the logical answer. But I couldn't find one.

It might be difficult for most of today's shooters to understand, but not many centerfire big game bolt-action rifles were commercially available in this country in the years immediately following World War II. Truth is, not many were even in theoretical existence. Those that come quickly to mind are Remington's Model 30, a civilianized version of the WWI M1917

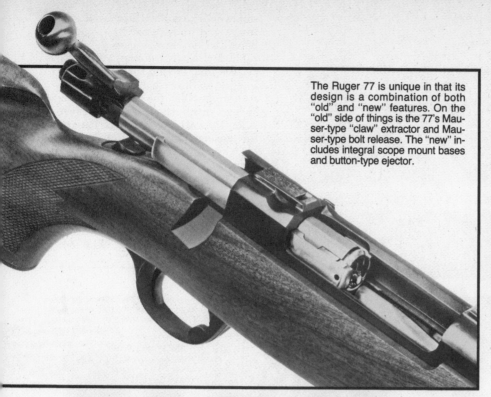

The Ruger 77 is unique in that its design is a combination of both "old" and "new" features. On the "old" side of things is the 77's Mauser-type "claw" extractor and Mauser-type bolt release. The "new" includes integral scope mount bases and button-type ejector.

action; and for those who needed more *oomph* for moose, elk and the like, the 35 and 405 Winchester loads could be found in the Model 95 and the 45-70 Government in the Model 86 lever guns. Most hunters who had some sort of yen for a bolt gun settled for the 30-40 Krag, an effective outfit that could be had in the inexpensive (like a buck and a half!) military surplus Krag.

Yet, the bolt-action caught on, as simple observation in any of the world's big game fields proves. Why? (We should point out that we are referring to the Mauser-type turnbolt here, not the straight-pull bolt, of which there were a number, nor the Mannlicher, a sophisticated but less influential design.) To begin with, riflemen were becoming interested in long-range cartridge efficiency. Hunting and competitive shooting conditions demanded it in some cases, and

BASICS

To many seasoned hunters the bolt-action is king of the hill. Here's why.

Enfield, and their Model 720, an "improved" Model 30 introduced in 1941 but rarely seen; the Model 54 Winchester, dating from 1925, of which only 50,000 or so were produced, replaced in 1936 by the Model 70; Savage's Model 1920, a neat hunting outfit that weighed under 6 pounds, and their Model 40. Doubtless there were others, but not many.

There are two important things to note here. First, the paucity of numbers, not only in models but also in simple availability. Few, if any, had been made during the war. Postwar production had not started, and when it did, none of these models except the Model 70 reappeared. Second, the fact that many bolt-action names which American shooters take for granted today—Weatherby, Ruger, Browning, Colt, Alpha, Champlin, DuBiel, Kleinguenther, Shilen, Wichita and others—simply did not exist.

The lever-action had dominated American gamefields prior to World War II. Only riflemen with guncrank instincts opted for the bolt during the 1920s and '30s, despite its use by millions in the trenches in 1914-18. Hunters such as Teddy Roosevelt, Steward Edward White, Col. Town-

send Whelen, Col. Jim Crossman, Capt. Paul Curtis and others used and wrote about bolt guns, especially a customized version of the military '03 which became known as the "Springfield Sporter." But such rifles were the stuff of dreams for the average shooter. In the 1930s, this country was deep in the Depression; the $25 or so a Model 94 Winchester cost was more than a week's wages for many workers (a big percentage had no job at all), so three to 10 times that for a fancy bolt-action just wasn't in the cards. Furthermore, most hunters were not excited by the bolt. They saw it as slow and clumsy, when compared to their lever- and slide-actions, and they had little need for high-velocity loads such as the 270 and 30-06, to say nothing of such esoteric imports as the 300 H&H Magnum, which long-range competitive riflemen were experimenting with.

Truth is, for the routine shooting most hunters did, the high-intensity loads weren't necessary. The 30-30 and 35 Remington class handled deer and black bear in the woods; the 300 Savage was available for those who wanted moderate bolt gun ballistics in the overwhelmingly popular lever-

the innate drive and curiosity that afflicts humans was doubtless operative in countless others. And of course there was the military situation which, in the early part of this century, had led the U.S. government to abandon the slow 200-gr. round nose bullets of the 30-40 and the 30-03 and go to the high-velocity 150-grain spitzer bullet in the 30-06. Official military cartridges always become popular hunting loads, and it's doubtful if any other cartridge ever attained the worldwide popularity of the 30-06. When, two decades after the '06's introduction, Winchester necked down this case to form the 270, whose lighter bullets were given even higher velocities, the possibilities for significant change existed. Not that everyone jumped on the bandwagon—just as some humans are driven onward, others inevitably hold back. But now it was possible to buy commerical rifles chambered for cartridges that at least doubled, and in some cases tripled, a hunter's effective range on big game. This was a quantum leap forward. And slowly, shooters' interest grew.

The basic change was a result of one thing: safe use of high-pressure car-

sights necessary for efficiency at long range and under poor light conditions; and, of course, *accuracy*.

Much of the bolt-action's strength derives from having the locking lugs integral with the bolt so there is direct support for the rearward pressures against the head of the case when the cartridge is fired. Having the lugs near the front of the bolt, as they are in most bolt-actions, and turned tightly into matching solid steel recesses, locks everything into what is essentially an enclosed one-piece unit at the moment of firing. The diameter of the receiver ring into which the barrel is threaded can be anything within reason, thus it is

(Above) Perhaps the most famous commercial bolt-action rifle ever made in the U.S.A. is the pre-'64 Model 70 Winchester. Seen here in typical prewar dress, this Model 70 sports a Zeiss scope on period Stith mounts. Note the generous (and fine) checkering as well as the early safety. In short, this is the rifle by which others have been measured for the past five decades.

(Top left) The now-discontinued Remington 788, in all the calibers it was chambered for, found favor with a large group of shooters and hunters. Beyond its *reasonable* price, the 788 was noted for two things: multi-rear-lug lock up and *superb* accuracy.

(Left) Seasoned hunters have long known of the bolt-action's finer qualities: accuracy and reliability.

tridges. The older ones—the big bore, heavy bullet designs intended primarily for lever guns—were loaded to 30,000-35,000 psi or so. Many of the guns couldn't be trusted at higher levels. But the 30-06 cartridge was loaded to upwards of 50,000 psi, and some 270 loads reportedly went as high as 55,000. No lever gun then available could handle such pressure. (A few Model 95 Winchesters were chambered for the 30-03 and 30-06 cartridges, but to me it always seemed an iffy thing to shoot one.) So the only repeating action available in the early days that could routinely handle such loads was the bolt. Thus the rifleman who was intrigued by high-performance, long-range loads had no

choice but to face up to that fact.

Bolt-Action Advantages and Features

What were the advantages of the bolt-action that set it apart? Strength, obviously. Also simplicity; durability; the ability to function under adverse situations; compactness while still having the size to handle long, reasonably large diameter, powerful cartridges; escape vents to allow gas venting if a primer should blow or a case break; an enclosed vertical magazine; a long threaded section of the action to hold the barrel; a one-piece stock that supports and protects the barrel; easy acceptance of the scope

easy to make it large enough to handle the internal pressures which are highest at this point.

The bolt-action is operated simply by rotating a handle which extends conveniently from the rear end of the bolt itself. This turns the locking lugs out of their seats and permits moving the whole unit back, extracting and ejecting the fired empty; shoving the bolt forward picks up and chambers a new cartridge, and then everything is locked securely on the downturn. With practice, this becomes a wiping, back-ramming, forward movement with the palm of the hand. The leverage created by turning the bolt approximately 90 degrees with the 2¼-inch handle is vastly multiplied by simple cams to apply great power for seating a slightly oversize cartridge or extracting a case that wants to stick after being subjected to perhaps 55,000 psi of internal pressure. A typical Mauser-type bolt is said to apply about six times the extracting power of a lever-action, so the advantages under rough conditions are obvious.

The bolt and receiver are massive enough, and the bolt is supported so well under stress, that the action normally lasts indefinitely—through numerous rebarrelings and restockings, if necessary. In addition to the unit's solidity when closed, its design permits easy cleaning (even if dropped in a mudhole), and the bolt itself can be quickly disassembled for cleaning and

ways had tubular magazines, and early repeating bolt guns had magazines that projected below the stock. The latter functioned acceptably but made for a clumsy rifle as they were located at the normal carrying point. Stacking the cartridges into a pair of staggered rows lessened the required depth enough that five rounds would fit within the normal stock line. Having them arranged in this way made it possible to safely use spitzer bullets, which gave superior downrange ballistics. Such bullets weren't usable in tubular magazines beneath the barrel or in the stock, for under the shock of recoil, a sharp-pointed bullet could detonate the primer of the cartridge ahead of it, causing a serious or even deadly accident. The box magazine also eliminated a shift in the rifle's bal-

mate military bolt-action, perhaps the ultimate bolt-action, *period*. It was made in incredible numbers—over 100 million, according to one estimate. The 98 was Germany's basic infantry rifle in both world wars, has been a standard in all the gamefields of the world, and is the progenitor for most of today's popular bolt-actions. Not only were the military '03 Springfield and the 1917 Enfield its direct descendants, but also most of the Remington bolt guns from the Model 30 on, the Winchester 54 and 70, the Ruger 77, the Savage 110, the Weatherby Mark V, whatever. . . This is not to say that significant changes from the Model 98 weren't made in these and other bolt-actions, but the ancestry is obvious.

And so the bolt-action has become the premier big game hunting firearm. It can be had in any power level commensurate with the intended quarry, from the 243 class for deer and pronghorns to the '06 level for most North American game, on up to the 338 Winchester, 340 Weatherby, and 375 H&H Magnums for this continent's largest game, and the 458 Winchester and 378 and 460 Weatherbys for the world's biggest and

In recent years the arms makers have gone to light, short-barreled bolts. Why? The hunters want 'em. Seen here is an Ultralight Ruger 77. Even when fully loaded and scoped, guns like the Ultralight Ruger weigh in at a manageable 7 pounds—a clear 2+ pound weight savings when compared to "standard-weight" rifles.

Since its introduction in the late '60s, the Ruger 77 bolt-action has become a real favorite. Accuracy reports from shooters seem to range from "very good" (at the least) to "superb" (at the best).

lubrication. The fact that it's hollow permits a straightline firing pin inside, activated by a powerful spring for fast lock time and positive ignition. Changing the bolt-action's overall length does not alter its basic design, so it is comparatively simple to make in sizes to match different cartridge groupings: a *short* for the 222 class, *medium* length for 30-06, etc., and *long* for the full-length magnums. It is also easy to attach a trigger, either a simple, sturdy, two-stage military type or a complex fully adjustable one.

The enclosed box magazine of the bolt-action has received little comment in popular publications, but it is highly important. Most lever guns have al-

ance as cartridges were expended, and made it easier to clear a jam if something got hung up.

Bolt-action rifles gained military importance before they were adopted by hunters. Many of the world's national powers were armed with bolt guns before the arrival of the 20th century, but it was not until post-WWII years that they were chosen by significant numbers of American hunters. Even before that, of course, the military had moved on to autoloading and automatic weapons. Nevertheless, the qualities which had made bolt-actions the favorite of the military for over a half-century were beneficial to hunters also.

The Model 98 Mauser was the ulti-

Bell was hunting moose when this nice whitetail popped into view, which explains the 338 Magnum. When cartridges like this are necessary, no other action is as good as a bolt.

toughest. It can be had chambered for cartridges such as Remington's 25-06 and 7mm Magnum, Winchester's 264 and 300 Magnums, and Weatherby's big 300 if long-range effectiveness on large game is required. If one's needs are centered closer to home, in the woodlots or cedar swamps where whitetails lurk, perhaps, Savage's plain-Jane 340 chambered for the equally plain-Jane 30-30 cartridge could be the perfect choice. Truth is, one bolt-action or another, from one end of the price spectrum to the other, can handle the cartridge you need. No other action type can do so except, perhaps, the single shot which has an overly obvious built-in problem which only aficionados are willing to put up with.

On a personal level, I might mention that after getting my first custom varmint rifle in 1946, a 257 Roberts put together by P.O. Ackley on a 98 Mauser action, my first big game bolt-action, a wildcat 7mm Magnum on an FN Mauser a few years later, I never went back to the lever guns. The bolt-actions just had too many advantages to be ignored.

Scoping the Bolt-Action

To take advantage of the power and long-range accuracy of many of today's cartridges, a scope sight is necessary. These are mounted so routinely that many bolt guns have no manufacturer-installed iron sights. I'm not sure that's the best idea if a rifle is to be used on a tough trip that takes you far from a gunsmith's services—backup irons could save the

day in case of a destructive fall or whatever—but that's how it often is nowadays. In such cases, a spare scope and the necessities for mounting it could be good insurance and won't take up much space in your duffle.

The proper scope permits precise aiming at any range where any cartridge that can be fired from the shoulder is effective. The important thing is to choose the best one for your needs, mount it properly, and zero it in to take best advantage of your load's trajectory.

Most scopemakers say the 3-9x variable is the best seller today. Buyers obviously feel it is the best compromise, giving enough field of view at 3x for woods shooting and enough magnification at 9x for extremely long shots. My personal choice for all-round use on a magnum for big game would be the 2-7x. I've found more need for an extremely wide field of view at the bottom end than for the extra power at top. If the scope were on a 6mm Remington, say, and used primarily for deer in the fall and woodchucks in the summer, the 3-9x would be first choice, as the 9x would be useful on these small targets at long range. But the times one might need 9x on big game come up about once in a lifetime. Meanwhile, a lot of deer, bear, elk and moose hunting is done in the thickest cover, where a mostly obscured target might be in view for only microseconds as it races for safety. Here, magnification is unimportant. Iron sights would work fine if they gave a clear, bright picture in the dimness and could be precisely zeroed in beforehand. Irons don't have these qualities, so the best choice is a low power scope with a conspicuous reticle.

The 2-7x is the best choice. As proof, compare the fields of view of representative examples from a top scopemaker, Leupold. In their Vari-X II line, the 2-7x has a 44-foot field of view at 2x, while the 3-9x has only a 32-foot field of view at 3x. In my opinion, 12 feet is a tremendous loss to suf-

Don Lewis' bolt-action was plenty fast working for whitetail in pines, as was his choice of a 2-7x variable.

From top to bottom: A Ruger 77V, Winchester Model 70 Featherweight, Browning A-Bolt, Remington Model 700 "Custom," Savage 110-C and a classic SAKO Mannlicher from Stoeger. All of these rifles will handle just about any cartridge a shooter/hunter could want. Prices? Depending on where you buy 'em, cost can run from *around* $400 and *up*.

The rings which come with most Ruger Model 77s are higher than ideal—note clearance between objective lens and barrel. (The Ruger's locking system does not permit a lower position.) Careful bench testing and zeroing gives the rifleman a good sense of his points of impact, making for deadly long-range shooting when the opportunity arises in the field.

fer in return for only 1x increase in power, particularly since the extra power isn't needed at close range. And keep in mind that most big game critters are shot at much less than 100 yards. One-third to one-half that distance is not uncommon, which means that field of view is *vitally* important. You need all you can get. Truth is, I have 1½-4½x's on both my 338s, a Leupold and a Kahles, in order to get the tremendous field-of-view advantage at 1½x. I've never had an occasion where I needed more than 4½x on a 338, but for the rare shot that might come up, I'll concede the utility of a 2-7x. But not a 3-9x. Besides its smaller field of view, it is a much larger and heavier scope. It has to be because of the larger objective lens

Remember, the gun should be chosen to fit the hunting conditions. Short, handy 788 Remington with Redfield 1½-4½x scope fits Bell's needs near home.

The ocular lens of this Lyman Alaskan just clears the bolt of this 284 Mauser, while the comb of the custom stock is sometimes scraped by cocking piece of bolt. There's no practical way to change anything further, yet the scope line is still higher, in relation to the aiming eye, than iron sights.

Bill Nichols stocked his Mauser 257 to suit himself—which meant an unusually high comb to get good alignment with the scope.

needed to give adequate light at top magnification. And so you have to put up with that extra weight and bulk every second you lug your rifle, all on the possibility that someday, somewhere, you'll get a shot which 7x won't handle. Meanwhile, you're handicapped in the brush.

As if that weren't enough, the 3-9x usually requires a higher mounting system than a lower power scope. This is not a major problem, but it's something worth considering. The higher the scope is, the higher the face must be on the stock to look into it. This means less facial support and therefore a less steady aiming position. Younger hunters have put up with this so long—all their shooting lives, probably—that they fully accept it. They don't know that it's a lot better to have the bottom of the cheekbone pressed tightly against the comb, rather than the jawbone, with most of the cheek then supported, and thus the head and the aiming eye.

This was the norm with a properly stocked iron-sighted bolt gun. But when scopes became readily available, it was obvious there was no way to install them as close to the action. Some of the early ¾-inch tube models of the 1930s came close, but the enlarged-eyepiece 1-inch tubes that came along after World War II were a whole new ball game. Even if installed right down on the receiver bridge, which a few mounts made possible, they were still significantly higher than iron sights. To help solve the problem, the comb of the stock was raised as high as possible. But that couldn't be high enough, as the bolt had to be operated and the cocking piece had to clear the comb nose. The stockmakers' last gasp effort was to give a reverse slope to the comb, making a Monte Carlo that's a first cousin to a canoe paddle—and there it ends. The comb still isn't high enough to properly support the face when using a big high-mounted scope, but there's no practical way to go further.

And so I prefer small scopes mounted as close to the action as possible—at least for big game. On chucks, crows, prairie dogs and such, there's plenty of time to get organized, and even if you don't get a shot off there's no big loss. But on big game. . . Well, you see what I mean.

Zeroing In

Once the scope choice is made and everything is assembled (and an effective load is developed or purchased), the outfit still has to be zeroed in. The usual goal is to adjust the scope so that the bullet's path is as close as possible to the line of sight out to 300 yards or so, and to learn where the bullet impacts in relation to the aiming point to the maximum effective range of the rifle/cartridge/scope/shooter combination.

With most of today's high-velocity loads, zeroing 3 inches high at 100 yards is said to put you 3 or 4 inches high at 200 yards, on zero at 275 yards or so, and a bit low at 300. This means a dead-on hold will give a solid hit at any distance up to that range, as the target's size will absorb the plus or minus inches. However, it isn't safe to assume that your *actual* trajectory will match the *theoretical* one, even if sighted in precisely 3 inches high at 100. Actual shooting from the bench on measured ranges will often give different points of impact than theorized, so the only way you can be sure of where you'll hit with your own gun and ammo is to test it properly.

Once past the zero point at 275 yards or so, the bullet will always be beneath the aiming point, of course.

However, with today's most popular reticle, the Duplex, a second aiming point is available, the top of the 6 o'clock post. The exact distance at which the down-arcing bullet will intersect the top of this post must be determined by actual test-firing. (If we have the actual chronographed velocity of the load, know the ballistic coefficient of the bullet, and have bench tested it to 300 yards, drops to 500 or 600 yards can be calculated reasonably well, but even these should be checked by actual firing.) At any rate, it's possible to find the distance at which the bullet and post top will coincide (usually about 450-500 yards with a spitzer bullet out of a magnum case). With this information we know that the bullet's impact will always be essentially between the crosswire intersection and the top of that post at any range where any of us have a reasonable expectation of placing a killing shot.

With such preparations, a good bolt-action of appropriate caliber, mounted with the proper scope, is the best answer to almost all of today's hunting situations. ●

There are times when it's possible for the hunter to overlook a vast expanse of land for big game. In such cases, a shot may come at any range, so the rifle/cartridge/scope combination must be capable of handling the roughest chance. Logic dictates that a bolt-action be chosen.

BOBWHITE QUAIL

by
JOHN E. PHILLIPS

LIKE CARVED granite, Bell stood on point, her nose telling me there was a covey of bobwhites hiding beneath the briar thicket just in front of us. Her bony pointer's tail curled over her back so rigidly that I thought if I thumped it, it would shatter like broken crystal. Right paw up, Bell was so intent on her point that she appeared not to know we were right behind her.

Where to find 'em, how to hit 'em and how to keep the population of bobwhites healthy!

Bell, a beautiful lemon and white pointer, had all the qualities of an outstanding bird dog, except one—the small brass bell that hung from her neck told the story. Bell was deaf and could not hear us when we called. The small brass bell around her neck signaled her movements to us. When I could no longer hear the bell tinkling, I knew Bell was on point and the search was on.

SOUTHERN STYLE

Although some hunters would cull a dog like Bell (and find a bird dog that wasn't defective), she had a good nose, a great personality and was a joy to hunt. Also, I knew I wasn't the world's greatest shot as I often let birds get away that should have been downed. But since Bell couldn't hear, she didn't know when I missed or when I connected. Therefore, I didn't feel too badly about her not being able to hear. And my not being the world's greatest wing shooter did not matter to her. However, when Bell went on point, all of the beauty showed in the staunchness of her point.

As Jamie and I moved in to flush the birds, I could hear movement under the briars. Then the quail exploded. But flying out of thick cover retarded their speed of flight somewhat and the first cock bird had not gotten up a full head of steam when my Remington 1100 with a 26-inch

the heavy cover we were hunting. I patted old Bell on the top of her head, and she began to search. Because she couldn't hear, she would search, then look back at me for directions. Once Bell had recovered and retrieved all four quail, I took her by the collar, led her out of the briar patch, petted her real good and sent her on her way once more.

Bell had learned to continue the search for quail until I had her by the collar and led her out of the search area. Having our own communication system, the dog and I hunted well together for many years. But that was when quail were more plentiful in the South than they are today—before. . .

. . . small patch farming was replaced with large field, intensive farming agriculture.

. . . urban sprawl engulfed much of my hunting territory

. . . big timber companies discov-

Where to find 'em: Winter wheat fields are usually highly productive when it comes to finding bobwhites. Work the wheat—that's where you'll find success.

(Left) Look at the face. Look at the eyes. He's the partner of a lifetime. In short, use a dog and you'll bring to bag every bobwhite you tumble. Enough said.

barrel spit out the No. 8 Winchester birdshot. The quail tumbled. The second bird veered to my left as I turned quickly, fired and debarked a pine tree. The third passed in front of me. I fired just as the range was becoming questionable. Another speckled bobwhite tumbled from the air. Jamie had also downed two birds.

The keenness of the dog's nose was critical to the recovery of the birds in

ered the fast-growing southern pine and began to clear-cut vast tracts of land and turn them into tailored pine forests.

As the land changed, so did our methods of quail hunting.

Hunting the Middle Grounds

Since much of the South has moved to soybean and wheat farming in large fields, there is often an abun-

dance of food for the bobwhite even though the cover is sometimes very sparse. After the crops are harvested, the birds have to covey up in the narrow strips of thick cover and hedgerows between the fields. These are commonly called the "middle grounds"—the land between the fields. I had just begun to hunt the middle grounds a few years ago when a friend of mine, Alex Thomas, invited me on a dogless quail hunt.

"We'll take quail and rabbits by simply walking through the middle grounds," Alex said. "I would suggest you use your bird gun, but No. 6 shot would probably be better suited than No. 8 shot for the type of hunting we are going to do. I like No. 6 shot because it's heavy enough to tumble a bunny yet small enough to give you a fairly dense pattern for quail—and it doesn't tear up too much meat."

(Above) *Where to find 'em:* Abandoned dove fields are often a prime quail haven. The wise bobwhite buster won't overlook acreage like this. The action speaks for itself.

(Left) When quail "jump," the shooting must be fast and accurate. These regal buzz-bombs not only make for fast shooting—they're also some of the finest wild game tablefare available.

As we began to walk through the middle grounds, the experience was much like going through a haunted house at an amusement park. You knew something was going to happen, but you didn't know where or when it was going to occur. After we had walked about 30 or 40 yards down the center of this particular patch of middle ground, we had taken a rabbit apiece. Just as I stepped into a thigh-high briar thicket, a covey exploded. I fired twice and dropped one bird.

"Mark your bird down," Alex hollered. "You'll have to find him since we don't have a dog."

As we moved forward to retrieve my quail, another single bird got up and headed out across the cut field. I tumbled the quail and was relieved that it fell on clean ground. After a few minutes of searching, I picked up the first bird, then went to the edge of the field and found my second bobwhite.

"Come on, John, we'll jump some more singles and maybe a covey or two before we get to the end of this middle ground," Alex encouraged me. And as we continued to walk through the drainage ditch and brush, I bagged five quail and four rabbits, while Alex took eight rabbits and four quail. I won't begin to tell you how many we missed. The hunt had lasted only 1½ hours, and we had only walked through one patch of middle ground before lunchtime, but limited out on both quail and rabbits.

The best time to hunt the middle grounds is right after harvest when the birds are concentrated in the hedgerows, still have plenty to eat and haven't been harassed by hunters.

Hunting Clear-Cuts

When an area has been clear-cut and replanted in pine seedlings, it provides excellent habitat for the bob-

white quail for about the first 3 or 4 years. Sedge, briar, honeysuckle, Johnson grass and many other shrubs or grasses will soon sprout up, providing the birds with plenty of food, cover and a place to dust.

However, hunting these clear-cuts can be tough walking for the out-of-condition quail hunter and dog because the usually-rolling ground is covered with tangled briars. Many sportsmen will completely overlook these briar patches because the habitat does not look like traditional quail-hunting territory. Oftentimes, especially in the late season, the quail experience little if any hunting pressure and don't get up nearly as "wild" as coveys that have been hunted all season long. The older the clearcut is, however, the less likely you are to find quail in it. When the cover gets chest-high, the quail will be gone. But for a few years, hunting over a clearcut can be an excellent way to find a mess of birds for the skillet.

Hunting Dove Fields

The biggest event in the hunting season in the South is the opening day of dove season. That's when all of the camouflage comes out of the closet, the fried chicken gets loaded into the coolers and southern sportsmen go out to test their wing-shooting ability on the gray ghosts of the southern skies. In many areas farmers plant fields of seed crops like milo, sunflower and wheat to attract the doves. (That's when hunters pay from $5 to $25 each to shoot at the doves.)

However, after 3 or 4 weeks of dove

The quail hunter's best friend is the man who owns (or controls) prime quail-hunting acreage. In this instance, the landowner is serving as a guide. Locating, and securing prime bobwhite hunting turf is a must in many areas of the South. Note the fast-rising bobwhite on the left. (Also note the attentive reaction of the hunters!)

hunting (when other seasons like squirrel, rabbit, quail and, most importantly, deer come in), the dove fields are abandoned. However, many times these same fields will serve as home for two or three coveys of quail. I have learned that by hunting these fields late in the season I can find many unharassed coveys which provide outstanding shooting. Often only a portion of the fields will be cut during the dove season with the final cutting taking place as winter approaches. Therefore, there is usually enough food in the fields for the quail and enough cover along their edges to hide the birds.

Hunting Feed Lots

Many times cattle ranchers feed quail unknowingly. When ranchers put grain out to feed their livestock, excess grain spills on the ground inviting the quail to come in for a free meal. Check with ranchers in the area and they will be able to tell you if they have seen any quail around their feed lots. This can often save hours of hunting time and allow the sportsman to lead his dog right to the area where the birds should be feeding and roosting.

Hunting Woodlots

When all the grain is out of the fields, the quail will often move into the woodlots. Ed Childers, one of the South's most dedicated quail hunters once said, "To effectively hunt woods birds you must keep your dog in close to you so that you can direct him. I have also learned that the best place to search for woods birds is along logging roads and firebreaks. The quail like the firebreaks and logging roads because they provide certain elements that quail have to have.

"First of all the quail must have open spaces where he can move freely. Secondly, he needs a place to dust and a spot to drink. The woods road provides each of these necessities. There will often be mud holes where the birds can water and dry spots where they can dust. Along the edges of the roads the birds can generally find grass seeds. So to successfully hunt the woods birds, I take my dogs down the old logging roads. We usually find them coveyed up not far from the road.

"An advantage to hunting woods birds is that you rarely ever see another hunter. And most of the time when you find a covey, they haven't been hunted and will hold much better than field birds will. Woods birds are also less likely than field birds to leave a hunting area when you hunt them regularly. When hunting is tough and I can't find any coveys in the fields, I can almost always locate woods birds. But the disadvantage of hunting woods birds is that they are much harder to hit when they fly through cover."

Hunting the Middle of Fields

Although the quail's brain is not very big, and it relies more on instinct than it does on reason, even a dumb bird will figure out before long that if it stays on the fencerows every weekend it will wind up in somebody's skil-

let. Many hunters believe that when they can't find quail on the edges of fields that the birds have gone to the woods.

"But that assumption is not necessarily true," Ed Childers observed. "I discovered a little piece of information last year that drastically changed my quail techniques during the end of the season. After making a circle around the edge of the field, my dog, Jack, failed to pick up the scent of the bobwhite. So more out of curiosity than anything else, I decided to go to the middle of the field—which is where we found the quail.

"From looking at the ground where the birds had been coveyed up, they had apparently been roosting and feeding in the center of the field—never leaving it or going to the woods. I think those birds figured out that the pressure from the hunters and the dogs was on the field edges and that there was no hunting pressure in the center. Therefore the birds stayed in the center of the fields, wouldn't feed too far from their roost site and remained virtually unharassed by hunters until the season was over.

"Now I can't prove my reasoning, but I do know that many times when I can't find birds along the edges, I will find them holding in the center of fields. Towards the end of the season, I quit hunting the edges, begin to hunt the middles and continue to take plenty of quail all season long."

Whistling and Calling

Knowing and locating better places to quail hunt is not all that is required to be an efficient bird hunter. The sportsman must also determine the best ways to cover the most ground and find the most coveys.

A new discovery I made that I am sure is a familiar technique for many seasoned bird hunters is the quail whistle. The Knight and Hale Company in Cadiz, Kentucky, manufactures a small brass whistle that's designed to produce the bobwhite call as air is sucked *through* the whistle. By using the whistle, a hunter can go to the edge of a field, begin to call and locate the quail when they respond to the hunter's overtures. After the covey is flushed, the quail call can also be used to locate single birds, thereby eliminating much of the useless walking and searching that normally takes place.

Another advantage of the quail call is that it allows me to hunt the same covey twice in one day. Oftentimes the birds that I flush in the morning, I can go back to in the afternoon, relo-

indeed, to share with your friends.

Another important call that no quail hunter should be without is a *hawk* call. "I use a hawk call late in the season when I am hunting coveys that usually get up wild," Ed Childers explained. "When my dog begins to act 'birdy' and I feel that we are getting close to a covey, I start blowing

When it comes to actually locating quail, the quail "whistle" can't be beat. The use of the whistle will help save you valuable time in the field.

How to hit 'em: One of the most important things a quail hunter should do is to cover his bird with the muzzle of his gun as soon as the bird starts to rise. *Pick it up. Cover. Pull.* It should be done that quickly.

successful quail hunter.

Major "Bubber" Cameron of Panola, Alabama, is a man who trains bird dogs and quail hunters for a living. He once commented, "The first mistake most hunters make is that they are timid when they walk into the quail. There is something about birds exploding in front of you that

How to hit 'em: The moment a covey flushes, the hunter should bring the comb of his stock to his cheek. Unfortunately, too many quail hunters shoot with their heads "off the stock." Follow this advice and you'll bag more birds.

cate them using the quail call and hunt them again in the evening.

Also the quail call is an excellent tool for training young hunters. An example is my 11-year-old son, John-John, who accompanies me on bird hunting trips with his single shot .410. Even though he doesn't get in as much shooting as I do (and doesn't down nearly as many birds), he becomes an *important* member of the hunt by using the quail call to locate the coveys and the singles. It is *his* responsibility to find the birds and help direct the dog to them. When you are 11 years old, being *that* important to the success of any hunt is something,

on my hawk call to make the birds hold tight to the ground until we can get close enough for the dog to point them and for me to get off a shot. Since the hawk is the natural predator of the quail, rarely will the quail fly when it sees or hears a hawk. So by using the hawk call when birds have been getting up wild, I can usually get much closer to the quail and wind up having much better shooting than I would if I didn't use the call."

Bagging the Birds You Find

No matter how good your dog is or how many coveys you find, if you can't hit the birds that fly, you won't be a

causes hunters to be hesitant. I have actually seen hunters take one foot and poke at some bushes to try to make the quail flush rather than walk boldly into the birds and flush them. If you are going to shoot accurately, you must walk boldly into the birds first.

"The second mistake many hunters make is that they don't keep their cheeks down on the stocks when they shoot. If that cheek is not on the stock, then you can't aim and shoot properly. So keeping your head down and making certain you are looking right down the gun barrel when you squeeze the trigger is very important.

"I have seen some hunters go ahead and shoulder their guns and walk into the birds with their guns in that position! It's a mistake. If a sportsman trips or falls while carrying his gun shouldered, he could shoot himself, his dog or one of his partners. I also don't believe that hunters who have shouldered their guns prior to the flush aim as accurately. Hunters who hold their guns in their hands and shoulder them when birds flush, cover the birds with the muzzles of their shotguns." (When Cameron refers to *covering a bird*, he literally means placing the gun's barrel muzzle visually over the bird.)

"You will shoot properly and move more quickly when all you have to think about is covering the bird with the muzzle rather than trying to figure out what lead you should use and when you should shoot. Shot pellets move very quickly. If you have covered the bird with your barrel, and then pull the trigger, the shot pattern will cover the bird before it can fly away. I suggest that hunters use No. 8 shot because the denser shot pattern, even though shot size is small, will kill more birds and result in fewer cripples."

Utilizing Coop Management

To keep plenty of quail on the property you hunt, there are several necessary ingredients—food, cover and water being of primary concern. Once a covey's population has been dramatically reduced, replenishing it (after or during the season) is hard. Why? Because the mortality rate on pen-raised birds is usually about 85 percent. However Major Cameron has devised a method of introducing flight-conditioned, pen-raised quail into the wild with only a 20 percent mortality rate!

Cameron explained, "The reason that pen-raised birds don't survive well *in the field* is because they don't know *how* to feed, *how* to water or *how* to escape their natural predators. By using a coop in the field however, according to Cameron's specifications:

1.) Take four cedar posts, 6 feet long and put them 3 feet in the ground encompassing an area approximately 5 ft. x 5 ft.

2.) Stretch to these poles 2- x 4-inch, spot-welded wire as close to the ground as you can get it.

3.) Make a roof of plywood and tin to fit over the enclosure. The roof should be heavy enough so that predators can't knock it over but light enough so that one man can raise or lower it.

4.) Inside the enclosure place a feeder and waterer.

5.) Within the enclosure, also put a small cage that will hold a "call-bird," his food and water *off* the ground. (The call-bird is left in the coop so that he can call the covey together at night, into the pen, away from the predators.)

6.) Release your quail into this pen.

"Using this coop management system, a hunter can keep plenty of quail

As per the author's comments, the "call-bird" is an important element of pen-raised, field-situated, bobwhite quail. Note the lone call-bird cage at the top-center of the photo.

Pen-raised birds moved to coops located in the wild are the ticket when it comes to insuring a higher-than-normal survival rate. In short, bag 'em in the field—not the pen.

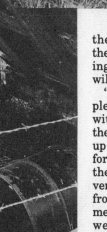

the birds still have food, water and the sanctuary of the pen while learning how to handle themselves in the wild.

"Generally the wild birds will supplement their "wild" food and water with the food and water provided in the coop and will use the coop to covey up in at night. The 2″ x 4″ wire mesh forming the sides of the coop allows the birds to pass in and out but prevents predators (like bobcats and fox) from getting into the coop for a free meal. I have discovered that within 2 weeks after restocking quail, the flight-conditioned, pen-raised birds will adopt all the instincts and habits of a wild bird."

To build a coop for restocking quail on the land he hunts," Cameron commented. "He can restock quail at any time and can replenish his coveys after the season to ensure that he gets maximum reproduction for the coming year. If a sportsman really enjoys hunting quail, he needs to try and ensure that he always has quail to hunt. Coop management is the best way I know to make sure the birds will be there when you are hunting them."

Quail hunting is great fun. Of course having a good dog and knowing where to hunt the birds is extremely important. But I also know that ensuring the future of your sport by restocking quail when the coveys get low can mean good quail hunting in the years to come. ●

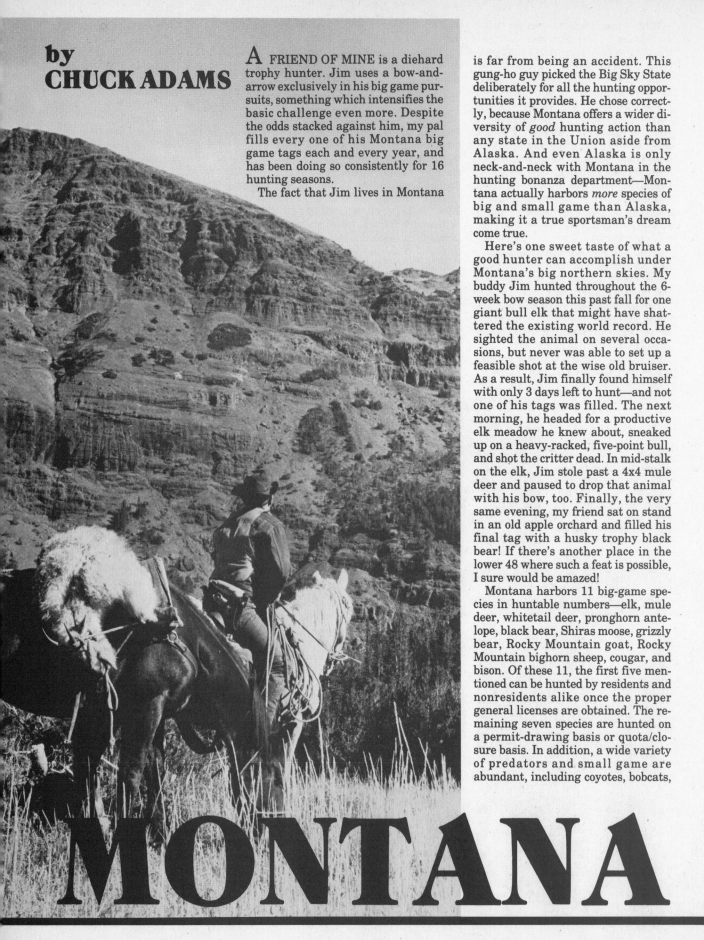

by CHUCK ADAMS

A FRIEND OF MINE is a diehard trophy hunter. Jim uses a bow-and-arrow exclusively in his big game pursuits, something which intensifies the basic challenge even more. Despite the odds stacked against him, my pal fills every one of his Montana big game tags each and every year, and has been doing so consistently for 16 hunting seasons.

The fact that Jim lives in Montana is far from being an accident. This gung-ho guy picked the Big Sky State deliberately for all the hunting opportunities it provides. He chose correctly, because Montana offers a wider diversity of *good* hunting action than any state in the Union aside from Alaska. And even Alaska is only neck-and-neck with Montana in the hunting bonanza department—Montana actually harbors *more* species of big and small game than Alaska, making it a true sportsman's dream come true.

Here's one sweet taste of what a good hunter can accomplish under Montana's big northern skies. My buddy Jim hunted throughout the 6-week bow season this past fall for one giant bull elk that might have shattered the existing world record. He sighted the animal on several occasions, but never was able to set up a feasible shot at the wise old bruiser. As a result, Jim finally found himself with only 3 days left to hunt—and not one of his tags was filled. The next morning, he headed for a productive elk meadow he knew about, sneaked up on a heavy-racked, five-point bull, and shot the critter dead. In mid-stalk on the elk, Jim stole past a 4x4 mule deer and paused to drop that animal with his bow, too. Finally, the very same evening, my friend sat on stand in an old apple orchard and filled his final tag with a husky trophy black bear! If there's another place in the lower 48 where such a feat is possible, I sure would be amazed!

Montana harbors 11 big-game species in huntable numbers—elk, mule deer, whitetail deer, pronghorn antelope, black bear, Shiras moose, grizzly bear, Rocky Mountain goat, Rocky Mountain bighorn sheep, cougar, and bison. Of these 11, the first five mentioned can be hunted by residents and nonresidents alike once the proper general licenses are obtained. The remaining seven species are hunted on a permit-drawing basis or quota/closure basis. In addition, a wide variety of predators and small game are abundant, including coyotes, bobcats,

MONTANA

(Left) Bighorn sheep are one of this country's historic big game trophies. They are also one of Montana's most exciting big-game resources.

Some of the finest trophy elk taken in the U.S., during the last 10 years, have come from Montana. During the 1985 bow season, the author took this excellent bull.

red fox, rockchucks, prairie dogs, ground squirrels, cottontail rabbits, snowshoe hares, jackrabbits and fox squirrels. Montana is also a bird-hunter's dream, with ten varieties of upland species prevalent and ducks and geese galore. This is one of the few states where even whistling swans can be *legally* hunted. The gunning and bowhunting opportunities are far too numerous for anyone to annually enjoy them all.

Here's a brief, fact-filled rundown on the major species offered to resident and nonresident Montana hunters. It is designed to help you decide what to hunt and where to go in this serious hunter's mecca.

Elk

Montana is one of the very best western states for hunting elk. A few states like Colorado and Oregon enjoy annual elk harvests higher than Montana's, but the Big Sky State generally yields 12,000 to 15,000 elk per year. Montana blows away all competition when it comes to trophy-bull production. A survey of bull elk entered in the Boone and Crockett record book since 1970 shows Montana with 15 heads, Arizona with a distant eight, and Colorado with only six. All other western states have produced five or fewer record-size heads for the book during the past 1½ decades. Montana's superb trophy-producing capability is probably a combination of three primary factors—good genetics, excellent elk habitat, and many remote areas where bulls are able to grow old.

Elk hunting in Montana is generally a deep-woods endeavor, with animals seldom straying far from heavy timber laced with deadfall logs and brush. Elk abound in virtually every mountainous part of this state—which means roughly the western half. In addition, a few isolated herds inhabit less typical country—herds like those along eastern Montana's Missouri River willow bottom. In the majority of top elk areas, country is torturously rough and steep and covered with dense foliage.

Montana's elk season opens with archery hunting in early September. A few parts of the state are also open to gunners during the mid-September rut. One such area is the Absoroka Wilderness just north of Yellowstone Park. General gun season for elk opens concurrent with most other gun seasons—usually during the last week of October. It runs through late

Room to Hunt!

Hunters seeking a nice whitetail in Big Sky country won't have to do a lot of regional hunting—they're abundant across the state.

Mulies are found at all elevations in Montana. Although this state doesn't produce many record-sized bucks, nice 4x4 trophies are plentiful.

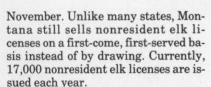

The record books don't lie. And when it comes to trophy whitetails in the West, Montana is tops.

November. Unlike many states, Montana still sells nonresident elk licenses on a first-come, first-served basis instead of by drawing. Currently, 17,000 nonresident elk licenses are issued each year.

For trophy bulls, an elk hunter should concentrate in the south near Yellowstone Park. Especially productive are the Madison and Gallatin ranges. For numbers of elk, the western Bitterroot Range is tough to beat.

Whitetail Deer

Next to elk, Montana is most famous for its big and abundant whitetail deer. This is the *only* western state with significant record-book whitetail potential. Since 1970, Montana has put 19 big whitetail bucks in the Boone and Crockett book, whereas the only other Rocky Mountain states to book a whitetail have been Idaho with *one* and Colorado with *one*!

Montana also harbors incredibly large whitetail populations. Hunters here annually bag about 30,000 bucks and does. In the eastern half of the state, bottomland deer are so abundant a hunter can take up to seven per year in some management districts! One archery-only area in western Montana allowed *unlimited* whitetail harvest in 1985—you could literally shoot as many deer as you wanted, provided you bought tags ahead of time. Seeing 200 whitetails per day is easy in many agricultural areas.

Every bottomland farming region in the entire Big Sky State holds huntable whitetail herds. However, major eastern river-bottoms like the Yellowstone and Milk Rivers are clearly most productive. For the largest antlers, the uppermost half of the state across its entire breadth has yielded consistently well. Good bucks are everywhere, but true giants live up north.

Whitetail seasons in Montana run, in one form or another, from early September till late December. However, the very best time to hunt is during the late-November rutting period because bigger bucks and smaller alike are easiest to locate and shoot.

Mule Deer

Montana harbors a very large mule deer population. Mulies are popular with both resident and nonresident hunters, with an estimated 70,000 mule deer taken by archers and gunners each year. Montana is one of the nation's best bets for a hunter to drop a decent-sized 4x4 or better buck, and mulies inhabit virtually every portion of this state from the high western mountains to the eastern sagebrush flats.

Montana is a relative dud when it comes to record-book mule deer racks. Compared to Colorado, which has produced 36 Boone and Crockett mule deer since 1970, Montana has produced only two. Only Oregon and California are more devoid of record-class mule deer than Montana, and that isn't saying much. Oregon has one record-book giant to its credit, and California has none! If you want a trophy mule deer book of *record* proportions, hunting Montana would be a solid mistake for the traveling hunter.

Pronghorn Antelope

Pronghorns thrive by the thousands on Montana's eastern sagebrush flats. These animals also live nicely near eastern grainfields, alfalfa fields, and cattle-grazing grasslands. Annual harvest estimates are not available for this species, but thousands of hunters bag Montana pronghorns each year. Success ratios approach 100 percent, with lots of animals for all.

Montana pronghorns are hunted on a permit-drawing basis. Some antelope units in the central part of the state offer a 50/50 or poorer chance when it comes to drawing a resident or nonresident permit, but better pronghorn ground to the east often goes begging for hunters. A few pronghorn management districts near Miles City have excess permits each year, letting true antelope buffs shoot two or three of these "prairie goats" instead of one. If you're a bowhunter, you can purchase a one-antelope, archery-only license valid anywhere in the state. This may be used during the regular September and early-October bowhunting season. Most general gun seasons for pronghorn run from mid-October through mid-November, with exact dates varying from year to year and unit to unit.

Montana holds its own quite nicely in the record-class antelope department. Wyoming is clearly the trophy-pronghorn king, with 81 giant bucks in the current B&C book. Arizona is second with 25, and Montana is third with 17. In Montana, however, Garfield and Rosebud counties in the east-central area of the state have produced the majority of truly giant heads.

Black Bear

For black bear hunting sport, Montana is second to none. This state offers both spring and fall general season on bruins, and a few areas are open for black bear from April 15 all the way through December 31! Limit is one bear per year.

It is illegal in Montana to run bears

In the expansive prairies of central and eastern Montana, nice bucks are par for the course. In short, the "mobile" hunter shouldn't overlook this state when it comes to nice antelope heads.

Interested in black bear? There's plenty to go around in Montana. And the season can be generous.

For those hunters who are lucky enough to draw a permit, Montana has trophy moose galore. The eating? From the standpoint of many hunters, moose is some of the finest table fare available.

with hounds or use bait of any sort. However, black bears are so abundant in most mountain areas that walking hunters can sometimes see several per day. Some of the very best bear hunting is enjoyed in northwestern Montana along the fringe of Glacier National Park.

Montana has never produced a black bear with a skull large enough to make the Boone and Crockett record book. However, bears with bodies in the 350- to 450-pound class are not at all uncommon.

Other Big-Game Species

Montana is blessed with several other big-game species which can be hunted on a limited basis by residents and nonresidents alike.

Moose: The entire western third of Montana is segmented by moose districts where permits are available through public drawing. Nonresidents are allowed to apply in approximately one-half of these districts. The rest are reserved for residents only. Montana yields moose to most hunters who draw, including quite a few record-class bulls.

Grizzlies: Montana is the *only* state of the lower 48 to allow hunting for grizzly bears. This hunting occurs largely in northwestern Montana, where grizzlies are quite abundant.

When a predetermined quota of grizzlies die in the fall, the season is automatically closed. Hunting is difficult, but serious gunners do take grizzlies in places like the Bob Marshal Wilderness and areas near Glacier National Park. Anyone can purchase a grizzly tag in Montana.

Mountain Goats: Mountain goats are abundant throughout Montana's western and southern ranges. Several hundred permits are issued on a

drawing-basis each year to residents and nonresidents. The chances of drawing vary from district to district, but odds of 50 to 1 are probably average. If you do draw a goat permit in Montana, your chances of taking a trophy are excellent. Record-book billies abound!

Bighorn Sheep: The Big Sky State is probably North America's very best place to bag a giant Rocky Mountain bighorn sheep. This state

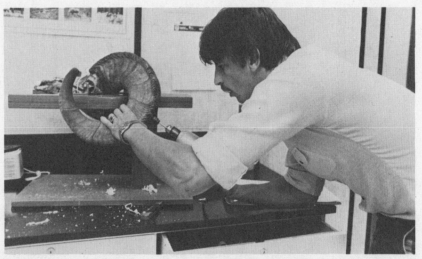

Montana game officials keep close tabs on the annual sheep harvest by "aging" and permanently plugging the horns of superb trophies with identifying seals.

(Left) In the annals of varmint shooting no animal has, perhaps, provided a greater challenge than the prairie dog. Montana abounds with these critters.

Jackrabbits? You bet. Montana's got its share. In fact Montana's lowlands provide great sport, on jacks, regardless of the shooting tool you opt for.

manages its sheep with trophy size foremost in mind. As a result, near-world-record rams are taken every year. The bad news is, most sheep districts offer permit-only hunting and drawing a permit can be tough. How tough? Odds range from 70 to 1 to over 100 to 1, making application a true toss of the dice. Montana is the only place in the United States with non-drawing, quota/closure areas for sheep, but such areas are typically steep, heavily timbered, and devoid of true trophy rams. A gunner in a Montana unlimited sheep area can easily spend a month without seeing hide nor hair of sheep. And when the quota for such an area is reached, the season is *immediately* closed.

Mountain Lion: Montana's western mountains offer superb mountain lion hunting late in the fall. Hounds are legal here, and record-sized cats are fairly abundant. However, heavy hunting pressure on cougars has generated talk of quotas in certain districts—something to look for in 1986 or 1987.

Bison: One last big game trophy deserves mention here. Montana recently opened a season on bison which wander outside the borders of Yellowstone National Park. These big brutes are overpopulated in parts of southern Montana, and some truly huge trophy bulls are available. However,

drawing a bison tag is not a high-odds proposition.

Varmints and Small Game

Coyotes, bobcats, and red foxes are incredibly plentiful in Montana. These are often bonus animals for hunters after other game. They also provide top-notch calling sport plus valuable winter fur. The best predator-hunting sport is found along the eastern-Montana riverbottoms.

Other sporting critters of off-season hunting value include rockchucks, prairie dogs, jackrabbits, and ground squirrels. Rockchucks are found here and there near high-country rockslides at timberline. There are also huge colonies of prairie dogs on the flats of eastern Montana. Jackrabbits are virtually everywhere in bottomland terrain. And little yellow-brown ground squirrels, locally called "gophers," are found by the *millions* from one edge of this state to the other at elevations below 6,000 feet.

Edible small game is surprisingly abundant and largely overlooked in Montana. Good populations of snowshoe hares inhabit higher timbered slopes, and cottontail rabbits abound at lower elevations. One interesting game animal along the river bottoms of eastern Montana is the fox squirrel—the same fat, tasty tree-dweller hunted so widely across the eastern

Varmint hunting, on a nationwide basis, is one of the most popular pastimes available to the dedicated shooter/hunter. Coyotes abound in Montana and provide some of the best varmint-shooting sport available in the North American continent.

(Below) For those who love both the art and science of waterfowling, Montana is an often "overlooked" haven. Even for the boys from the major flyways, Montana can provide waterfowl gunning that's oftentimes "stunning."

(Above) Nationwide, the turkey population is providing some of the finest "big-bird" hunting ever made available to serious hunters. Montana provides a good crop of Merriam turkeys in the southeastern quadrant of that state.

Surprising to many hunters will be the fact that the ringneck pheasant is the most popular upland gamebird in the state of Montana.

U.S. Few hunters in Montana concentrate on edible small game, but it's certainly there for all who enjoy stalking and eating critters under 5 pounds.

Upland Birds

An avid shotgunner from Montana might mistakenly think he'd died and gone to heaven. Blue, ruffed and Franklin's grouse all abound throughout the state. The season for these birds runs 3 full months, with a daily limit of four. Hungarian partridge are quite abundant in eastern Montana, with a 3-month season and a daily limit of six. Sage grouse and sharptailed grouse are also prevalent in eastern Montana. The fall season runs 6 weeks with a daily limit of three on each of these species. Chukar partridge inhabit western Montana, but the season is currently closed to allow populations to build.

Of all the Big Sky's upland species, ringnecked pheasants are most popular with residents and nonresidents. Cold weather and periodic dry spells cause pheasant numbers to fluctuate dramatically, but good hatch years mean positively superb gunning action. The grainfields of eastern Montana are especially good for rooster hunting, with a limit of four per day and 16 in possession! The pheasant season in Montana generally begins in late October and runs 6 or 7 weeks.

Wild turkey hunting has become quite popular with Montanans in recent years. The southeastern quadrant of this state is literally overrun with Merriam's turkeys—big, beautiful birds scaling up to 22 pounds and sporting beards up to 11 inches in length. There are both fall and springtime seasons in most hunting districts. The limit is one per year.

Migratory Birds

Mourning doves are abundant in Montana, but seldom hunted. The season here runs from early September through early November, with a limit of 15 birds per day. This is an excellent, untapped resource well worth checking out!

The "biggies" in migratory Montana birds are ducks and geese. Spe-cifically, big Canada geese and fat mallard ducks swarm this state in late fall and early winter. These birds are found along waterways everywhere, and provide excellent late-fall shooting sport. In addition, a variety of other ducks including teal, shovelers, pintails, wood ducks, mergansers, redheads and canvasbacks are also seen in fair numbers. In western Montana, snow geese are commonly seen. Special permits for whistling swans are available from Montana's Fish, Wildlife, and Parks office upon request. Limit is one swan per year. A final migratory bird of interest to shotgunners in Montana is the sandhill crane—a smart, sporting challenge that's available in many eastern-Montana areas.

Montana is truly a hunting state of plenty. Whether you enjoy big game, small game, upland birds, waterfowl, or all of the above, Big Sky country has something for you. For details on hunting this fine state, contact the Montana Department of Fish, Wildlife and Parks, 1420 E. 6th Ave., Helena, MT 59620. You won't be sorry! ●

BUILDING A HUNTER'S
Wildcat

by JON R. SUNDRA

Well-known hunter and gunwriter Jon Sundra wanted something special. Here's what he did—and how he did it!

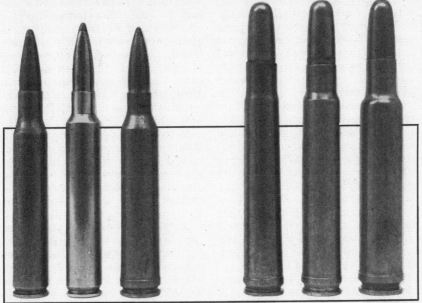

Relative case capacities of author's wildcats can be appreciated here. At left are the 280 Remington, 7mm JRS and 7mm Remington Magnum. At right are the 375 H&H, 375 JRS and 378 Weatherby.

MY GUIDE, Roger Morrel, eyed the cartridge he held in his hand with a quizzical look. "You say this wildcat of yours duplicates the performance of the Seven Rem. Mag.?" he asked, his nose wrinkled in skepticism.

"Yep," I replied matter-of-factly. "It'll do whatever the Remington will do, no more, no less."

"Then why go through all this?" he asked, raising the example of my 7mm JRS to eye level, then handing it back to me. "I mean, what's the point?"

A good question. And I'll never really know for sure whether I answered it to Roger's satisfaction during those few days we spent together hunting Dall sheep in Alaska's Wrangell Mountains. But then I didn't try very hard, either. I've found that such questions are generally asked by practical people expecting practical answers.

Indeed, why *would* someone go through the hassles and expense of building a custom rifle around a non-commercial cartridge that merely duplicates the ballistics of an existing one? After all, common sense tells us that if there's legitimate reason for a wildcat, it must be that it either fills some conspicuous gap in the caliber line-up or improves upon the ballistics of existing cartridges. Otherwise, as Roger Morrel said: "What's the point?"

Truth is that if there were any "caliber gaps" that *needed* filling, they have been. And within any given bore size there already exists a cartridge which provides the maximum velocity attainable within the practical parameters dictated by available propellents, case size, recoil levels and barrel life. Good examples of the latter category would be the 220 Swift, 257 Weatherby Magnum, the 7mm Remington Magnum, the 378 Weatherby, etc.

So then, if a handloader is looking to rationalize going the wildcat route these days, he's going to have to come up with reasons other than "gap filling" or sheer velocity.

Take my two feral felines—the 7mm JRS and 375 JRS, as examples; neither can claim to fill a genuine *need* even when viewed through the biased eyes of the proud parent. Yet both cartridges offer some unique advantages which to me at least, seem eminently worthwhile. Let me now recount the whole gestation and birth of my two "Cats", for I suspect that all other wildcats are rationalized into existence through similar processes. And a lot of it may sound very familiar.

It goes without saying that before one can seriously contemplate owning a wildcat one must first know his way around a reloading bench. Only through familiarity with various cartridges, loading data and ballistics can one begin to relate case volume to velocity. And only through extensive shooting at the bench and in the field can one appreciate other aspects of cartridge design such as neck length and shoulder angle; bullet seating depth as dictated by magazine length; case shape as it relates to smoothness and reliability of feeding, and other considerations.

The 375 JRS

Anyway, my first brush with feral fever was back in the early '60s when the 22-250 was still a wildcat. It was tame enough though that any gunsmith doing barrel work had a 22-250 reamer and virtually any gunshop carried dies in stock. Case-forming consisted of nothing more than running a 250 Savage case through the 22-250 sizing die to squeeze the neck down to .224".

A few years later when Remington announced it was legitimizing the 22-250, my status as a wildcatter suddenly went out the window. I saw no reason to contemplate another until a decade later when I was in the early planning stages of my first African safari.

By then I had, in the course of my writings, tested and done load development work for several 375 H&H Magnums and was familiar enough

Author with Asiatic buffalo taken with his 375 JRS in Australia's Northern Territory. Rifle is a rechambered Brno Magnum Mauser.

with the ballistics of the cartridge to know that I liked it. I especially liked its versatility—the fact it was the largest caliber for which you could get flat-shooting spitzer bullets, as well as round-nosed solids and soft points. With Hornady's 270-grain spire point loaded to 2600 fps, for example, you had a load that shot about as flat over 250 yards as a 180-grain spitzer from a 30-06 . . . and hit with 750 more foot-pounds of energy!

In addition to its capability of taking the largest of African plains game like kudu, eland, roan, gemsbok and wildebeest out at extreme range if necessary, the 375 with either soft or solid round-nose bullets was equally capable of delivering the power and penetration needed to stop buffalo, elephant . . . or Mack trucks for that matter.

As much as I liked what the 375 bore had to offer, and as much as I respected the opinions of the many experienced experts who flat-out venerated this 1912-vintage cartridge, I couldn't look at it without thinking how much better it would perform with a more "modern" case shape. Despite the 375's impressive ballistics, its excessively-tapered case and overly-long neck did not make the most efficient use of available powder space, given its length and diameter. By minimizing the body taper, shortening the neck, and increasing the shoulder angle, the volume of the case could be increased appreciably. Indeed, because of its sloping body and droopy shoulder, the belted Holland & Holland case benefited the most from this "improving" operation, as it's

known, and had been a favorite with wildcatters since the 1920s.

My thoughts, then, were hardly original. Wildcatters had been doing what I had in mind for over half a century. In P.O. Ackley's *Handbook for Shooters and Reloaders*, copyright 1962, there were four 375 wildcats listed, all based on "improved" versions of the H&H belted magnum case. There was the Barnes, the Mashburn, the Kodiak and the Ackley, plus the discontinued 375 Weatherby which differed from the others only in its venturified or rounded shoulder—a characteristic unique of all Roy Weatherby's cartridges.

Any of the five would have satisfied me since they were so similar to one another that the loading data was virtually interchangeable. All claimed velocities between 150 to 200 fps greater than the H&H version pushing comparable-weight bullets. Nominal ballistics specs of both Remington and Winchester 300-grain loads for the H&H were listed at 2530 fps; the 270-grain loading clocked in at 2690 fps. Muzzle energies were listed at 4265 and 4340 fpe, respectively. I figured if I got an honest 150 fps over the H&H I'd be more than satisfied. Though 150 fps may not sound like much, a 300-grain bullet exiting the muzzle at 2700 fps churns up nearly 600 fpe more, for a total of almost 2½ tons worth of bone-smashing energy!

It wasn't ultimate velocity in the 375 I was after; were that the goal I would have considered the 378 Weatherby whose huge case can push a 300-grain bullet out at 2900 fps. However, I figured that extra 200 fps came at too high a cost, for me anyway. The one 378 I had played with kicked brutally at the bench, even with the mandatory "sissy bag" between the Mark V's buttplate and my shoulder. And back then I was already "efficiency conscious" with regard to cartridges. To me, any case that required 20 more grains of powder to get 200 fps was too damn big. No sir. I knew what I wanted performance-wise: 2700 fps with a 300-grain bullet from a case based on H&H brass.

Another consideration which weighed heavily in my decision to go with some sort of improved 375 was that in a pinch, standard 375 H&H ammo could be used. Indeed, one of the ways to get brass for whatever wildcat I decided on would be to fire-form either factory or handloaded H&H rounds in the new chamber and,

On returning home I sent a letter to Max Clymer, the reamer maker (14241 West 11-Mile Road, Oak Park, MI 48237), along with a couple each of fired and unfired 8 Mag. cases. In effect, I had Max make me an 8mm Remington Magnum reamer . . . but with a 375 neck.

Once I had the reamer, I promptly turned it over, along with the Ruger, to the students at the Pennsylvania School of Gunsmithing for the relatively simple rechambering operation.

"What are ya' going to call it?" one of the students asked when I picked up the finished gun. When I told them I hadn't thought about it, one of 'em suggested my initials. Thus the 375 JRS was christened.

Because there's no magazine to dictate cartridge length on the single shot Ruger, I asked that the throat be

progressive neck expanders of .338", .358" then .375" (I also did it in a single operation using a tapered expander that opened the neck from .323" to .375" in one pass); and 3.) fire-forming the neck only.

Fire-forming 375 H&H loads worked perfectly, but I didn't like stretching the brass that much when it wasn't really necessary. As for necking up 8 Mag. cases, sometimes the expanders would buckle the shoulder a tad or distort the case mouth slightly. Of the three methods, I still prefer opening the necks by fire-forming 8 Mag. brass. I take a once-fired or virgin case, load it with 35 grains of SR-4756, tamp in a small piece of tissue as an over-powder wad, then fill the case to the base of the neck with cornmeal. I then jam the case neck into a bar of soap and withdraw it at an angle which breaks off a

(Left) The 8mm Remington Magnum case is, in effect, one which has been "improved" at the factory. At far left is the parent H&H case which, thanks to the presence of the 8 Mag. case, no longer has to be used, and subsequently "stretched," in improved chambers. Just necking up of the 8mm Rem. Mag. case was all that was required for Sundra's 375 JRS wildcat case at right.

viola, I'd have my brass.

When decision-time came, I decided to go with the old 375 Weatherby Magnum. It did no more than the Ackley, Kodiak, Barnes or Masburn versions, but it had the advantage of being an ex-production round of sorts for which reloading dies and factory brass were still floating around. And most barrel makers and custom gunsmiths had chambering reamers.

Just as I was about to send off my spankin' new Ruger No. 1 in 375 H&H for a rechambering job, the 1976 Remington Seminar for gun writers/editors came up. Lo and behold, they sprung the 8mm Remington Magnum on us, a new cartridge based on the full-length 375 H&H case . . . already "improved" with a minimum neck length and body taper, and a conventional, 25-degree shoulder. The moment I laid eyes on the 8 Mag. I knew I was looking at my new wildcat. All I'd have to do is neck it up from 8mm (.323") to .375".

With tapered expanders like this available from quality die manufacturers, it's possible to neck up from 8mm (.323") to .375" in one step. Sundra prefers to fire-form the neck as explained in the text.

cut so I could seat bullets out farther than normal which, in effect, gave me a yet larger case. The net result was that the working loads I eventually came up with gave velocities with Hornady's 300-grain bullets as high as 2745 fps in the 24-inch barrel of the Ruger. That's over 5000 foot pounds of muzzle energy.

I tried all three ways of brass forming: 1.) firing 375 H&H ammo; 2.) necking up 8mm Mag. brass using

sealing plug. Because all but the neck of the 8 Mag. perfectly fits the 375 JRS chamber, only the neck is expanded in the fire-forming process. It works like a charm.

Depending on the specific gun, my working loads range from 84.5 to 86.5 grains of IMR-4350 with a 300-grain bullet. Velocities vary between 2670 to 2750 fps, depending on barrel length. With Hornady's 270-grain bullet seated out to a point where the cannelure is about ⅛-inch from the mouth, 86 to 88 grains of 4350 is all I can get into any of my cases, and then it's slightly compressed. Again, depending on the individual gun and barrel length, velocities range from 2820 to 2890.

I went on to take my very first Cape buffalo with that Ruger, and my first elephant the following year. I've since built four more 375 JRS's: one on a Sako action; one on a Brno 602; another on a Remington 700; and a fourth on a lengthened '98 Mauser. All but the last one have been to Africa or Australia and have taken all sorts of larger plains game and buffalo. I'm as happy with the performance of this cartridge today as I was nearly 10 years ago when I first started working with it. Objectively speak-

Another of author's several 375 wildcats is this Sako which sports a Shaw barrel and Fajen, all-walnut, laminated stock. This buff fell in Zambia.

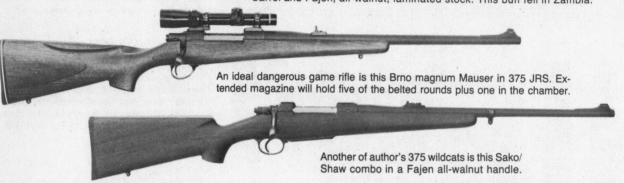

An ideal dangerous game rifle is this Brno magnum Mauser in 375 JRS. Extended magazine will hold five of the belted rounds plus one in the chamber.

Another of author's 375 wildcats is this Sako/Shaw combo in a Fajen all-walnut handle.

ing, it is a worthwhile wildcat in that it significantly improves on the justly-famous 375 H&H—*and does it without requiring an outsized action and case.* It also has the versatility of being able to digest H&H ammo, which it will shoot quite accurately and with little loss in velocity. Recoil with an average, 9-pound rifle comes in at just under an easily manageable 50 foot pounds. In all fairness though, it's no better than the old 375 Weatherby or the other feral kittens mentioned earlier; it's just *easier* to come by. To my mind that's what makes it a "usable" wildcat.

The 7mm JRS

As much as I like my 375 however, it is obviously a specialized cartridge of limited use. Since 95 percent of the world's game doesn't require such power, one can get a lot more use out of something smaller! Which brings us back to the 7mm JRS I mentioned at the outset.

My introduction to .28-caliber cartridges came in 1964 when I built up my first 7mm Remington Magnum from a Herter's barreled action and Fajen stock. I've owned at least six of them since and have done load devel-

This magnificent sable fell to Sundra's first 375 JRS—a rechambered Ruger No. 1.

opment work with at least a dozen more in the course of my writings. And when afield, if I wasn't totin' a 7 Mag., I'd have a 7x57, a 280 Remington or 284 Winchester in my hands. Offhand, I can count three 7x57s, four 280s and four 284s among my collection and all of them have been loaded for (and hunted with) pretty extensively. Yep, I'm a real fan of anything with a .284″ hole in the barrel. With

various versions thereof I've taken critters ranging from 7-ounce prairie dogs to 1,700-pound eland; from Dall sheep in Alaska to lions in Zambia.

Anyway, as much as I liked the performance of the 7 Mag., it seemed to me that its belted case was a little too large for the optimum balance between case size and attained velocity. I based that on the fact that with the several 280s I had worked with, I was

This 38½-inch Dall sheep was taken in the Wrangells with author's 7mm wildcat. These horns miraculously survived a 1,600 foot fall that destroyed the cape.

always able to achieve 3000 fps with a 150-grain bullet from a 24-inch barrel. The same can be said for my long-throated 284 Winchesters in which I could seat bullets out where they belonged. And believe me, I'm no hot-rodder when it comes to handloading. None of those loads were even slightly hot in my rifles. Yet with several of the 7 Mags. I worked with, I couldn't come up with any 150-grain load that would give me more than 3100-3130 fps without signs telling me I had "arrived," as it were, and should stop there.

As efficiency-oriented as I am, the 10 percent or so of unused powder space in the big 7 Mag. case bothered me . . . especially in light of the fact I was only able to get about 100 to 125 fps more for the extra 10 grains of powder I was using over that required for the 280 or 284. I had also gotten to the point where I really didn't like the belted case; it didn't feed as smoothly as a standard one; the belt itself would sometimes burr and cause sticky chambering at times; and the magazine capacity for the fatter case

was reduced by two rounds.

And so it was that I began to think about another wildcat. It seemed to me that with existing powders, the optimum case capacity for the .28-caliber was somewhere between that of the 280 Remington and the 7mm Remington Mag. As with my 375, I first looked for an existing wildcat—one that was already standardized and being chambered for by barrel makers/fitters like Douglas, Shilen, Shaw, etc., and for which dies could be ordered from stock. I mean, why make things unnecessarily difficult for myself?

I settled on the 280 RCBS Improved, a round which could be formed by simply fire-forming the standard 280/7 Express Remington ammo in the Improved chamber. I had Ed Shilen barrel a 700 Remington action for me and ordered the dies from RCBS.

The moment I started to fire-form my initial lot of brass I realized just how much additional boiler room was not being taken advantage of in the RCBS wildcat. By that I mean, the

In order to fire-form his 7mm JRS cases, the author did the following: First, he took a 280 Remington case **(A)** and necked it up to 308 **(B)**, then back down to 284 **(C)** in the 7 JRS die. . .but only to the point where the bulge on the 30-caliber portion of the completed cartridge's neck **(D)** allows the case to enter the JRS chamber with some effort on the downturn of the bolt handle. (This is strictly a trial-and-error process when it comes to die adjustment.) Thus properly head-spaced, these bulged-neck cases are loaded with any maximum load listed for the 280 Remington. A couple of hours is all that's necessary to prepare 100 cases which will, after fire-forming **(E)**, provide many years of shooting and prove to be no more difficult to load than any conventional cartridge.

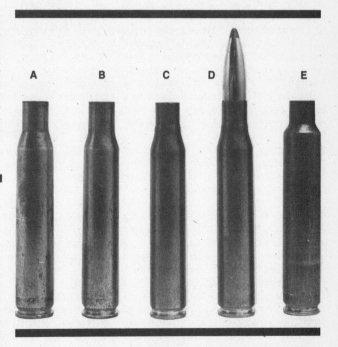

A   B   C   D   E

Sundra's first exposure to 7mm wildcat fever was in the form of the 280 RCBS Improved (center). When he found it increased case capacity less than 3 grains over the stock 280 (left), he went with his own version (right).

neck was longer than necessary, the shoulder was only 30 degrees, and there was still .020″ taper to the body. The net result was that where the stock 280 Remington case held 60.5 grains of a fine-grained ball powder when filled to the base of the neck, my new 280 Improved held 63.0 grains—a mere 2.5 grains more. Hardly worth it, I thought. It was time for another wildcat of my own.

Author's newest 7mm JRS is the Sako "Fiberclass" with an H-S Precision, blued, stainless barrel.

(Right) With various 7mm's author has taken some 60 species of game, from small antelope like this 45-pound "tommy" to 1,700-pound eland.

Figuring that a neck length of one caliber (.284″) was sufficiently long, I settled on .300″ just to be safe (the 7 Mag. and .284 both have shorter necks than that). I had heard of occasional feeding problems with wildcats having 40- and 45-degree shoulders so I settled on a 35-degree shoulder—the same as found on the 284 Winchester. And I decided to go with a body taper of only .015″; that meant .470″ at the head, .455″ at the shoulder.

I related those few dimensions to Max Clymer who, working from the specs for the 280 Remington case, was able to get all the necessary dimensions to make a chambering reamer. I then had E.R. Shaw chamber and fit a barrel to my Remington 700 action which I cradled in a Fajen, all-walnut, laminated stock.

Naturally I was anxious to see what kind of increase in case volume I had achieved with my "7mm JRS" over the 280 Improved, so after fire-forming the first few cases I repaired to the reloading room. Using the previously mentioned fine-grained ball powder as a volume-measuring medium, I found I could dribble in 70.5 grains before reaching the base of the neck. I then grabbed a 7 Mag. case and filled it to the same level; it held 80.5 grains. Though I never planned it to work out so precisely, my wildcat was exactly midway between the 60.5-grain capacity of the 280 Remington and the 80.5-grain capacity of the 7mm Mag.

I sent a couple of cases off to Steve Hornady and in a couple of weeks had a set of Pacific dies. Ultimately, after trying H-870, H-4831, W-785 and Norma MRP, I found the Norma propellant to be the best performer. Using 63.5 grains of it in R-P brass behind a 150-grain Nosler I got 3100-plus fps, *consistently*. The bolt

literally flops open with this load, and I also get at least six reloadings to a case before primers start seating on the "easy side." (I toss 'em out at that point.) The chamber is throated to take full advantage of the available case capacity, i.e., the 150-grain Noslers are seated just about flush with the base of the neck. As such, overall cartridge length is 3.425-inch—too long for a Mauser or a Ruger 77, but fits a Sako, Remington or a Model 70 with room to spare. Seating bullets a little deeper, of course, would allow any standard action to be used.

So what have I got? Well, as I see it, I've got a more ballistically efficient, beltless 7mm Remington Mag. of which I can stuff five rounds in the magazine instead of three. Not that I make a habit of using a fourth and fifth shot, mind you . . . but it's nice to know they're there!

Over the last 6 years I have used my 7mm JRS almost exclusively on some 25 different hunts on three continents, including four African safaris. My good huntin' buddy, George Daniels, also built a 7mm JRS and his results have virtually paralleled mine with regard to specific loads, ac-

curacy and velocity, though he prefers Hornady's 154-grain slug ahead of 63.5 grains of MRP for 2990 fps in his 24-inch barrel. As I write this I'm in the midst of building a second rifle; this one on an H-S Precision barreled Sako action, all nestled into a Fiberclass stock. As I'm sure you can tell, I like *this* cartridge too!

Again, my 7 JRS won't do anything *ballistically* that can't be done by the 7 Remington (or Weatherby) Magnum. And the 378 Weatherby will blow the doors off my 375. However, I hope I've shown here that there *can* be other reasons to justify wildcatting . . . though in the final analysis, the fact that it's *fun* is justification enough. And when all is said and done, perhaps that one fact—that wildcatting is *fun*—is the most important consideration of all when it comes to building a hunter's wildcat. Sure, I can also make a case for wildcatting being enlightening, challenging, rewarding and a lot of other drivel, but hey, if it ain't fun, I wouldn't do it. A good analogy would be a Ferarri and a Ford station wagon. I know which one is best suited for going down to the grocery store . . . but I'll take the lil' red thing. ●

WHEN A SHOTGUNNER has his head on straight, the woodcock (a.k.a.: "timberdoodle") can be an easy mark. One autumn back in the early 1970s I knew I had been shooting well, and over a toddy one evening, my gunning partner congratulated me on my recent smoothbore success. We both got to thinking about it. I hadn't missed a bird that day, limiting out on five shots. Then we started going back through the previous 2 days, hour by hour, minute by minute, flush by flush, shot by shot. That's when we came up with my first miss, by going backwards, and my tally was 14 straight. The next day, hunting alone, I missed the first 'doodle out, and it was a peeper, a shot I'd normally make. As I said, times can be easy—if the shooter has his head on straight. (It's equally important for one not to

get too big a head, especially after dumping a string of 'doodles!)

In contrast, back in the mid-60s I got into a slump with ruffed grouse, missing 23 straight chances. When I did finally score on a ruff, it was an almost impossible shot that turned my luck around and got my shotgunning back on track. Ruffed grouse are seldom an easy mark.

When most woodcock seasons begin—from Pennsylvania north through New York, the New England states and the Maritime Provinces (New Brunswick and Nova Scotia), as well as throughout the upper Great Lakes states—almost every leaf is on almost every tree. This is when woodcock sport is at its sportiest. As the leaves begin to tumble, timberdoodles become easier and easier marks, for the brushy overstory of the bird's habitat

is falling to the ground. When the leaves are gone, many woodcock shots are a piece of cake for an experienced gunner with the right smoothbore.

The Guns

An ideal woodcock gun for tight cover, when plenty of leaves still cling tenaciously to their moorings, is what I call a "poker," as opposed, say, to a "swinger." Case in point: Last September, gunning in one of the upper Great Lakes states, I was carrying what I call a "swinger" early in the day. It was a Ruger Red Label 20-gauge normally weighing just a bit over 7 pounds. However, Jesse Briley (1035 Gessner Ave., Houston, TX 77055) had made up a set of his .410 and 28-gauge high tensile strength Skeet tubes for it. I had the .410 tubes in for that woodcock day, which added an-

WOODCOCK

AN EASY MARK?

by

NICK SISLEY

other 14 ounces to the Ruger. The first 'cock came up on my left and swung across in front at about 15 yards, driving to my right—a classic swinging shot. The Briley-tubed Ruger sent that bird spinning with a perfectly centered .410 hit. I smiled broadly. *Not bad for ½-ounce of shot,* I thought.

The next three birds, however, were darting, twisting chances, but more or less, straightaways. Each time I'd poke that slightly heavy and fairly tight-choked gun in the direction of one of those fast disappearing woodcock, I'd be a tad left, a tad right, a tad over. I'd hit the trigger anyway. Never drew a feather with the little .410 on that latter trio. With a wide open pattern and ⅞- to 1⅛-ounce of shot I know I would have killed every one of those tims.

So, the type of shotgun I like and recommend for early season woodcocking is what I call a "poker." This would be a fairly light, short-barreled, short-coupled smoothbore—and one that's capable of carrying the previously mentioned payload of ⅞- to 1⅛-ounce. The choke? It should be nothing—Skeet bore at the tightest. One specialized piece of woodcock ordnance I had made up some years back is a side-by-side that came from an outfit called Mario Beschi, in Italy, and was imported by what was then JK Imports in California. I don't think they're in business today. It is a 20-bore, and I got to name my own stock dimensions, opt for a pistol or straight grip (I chose the latter), bea-

vertail or splinter fore-end (again the latter), plus got to name my chokes and barrel lengths. That choice was Straight-cylinder and Improved-cylinder—in 24-inch barrels. To my mind it is the ultimate 20-gauge "poker." At 15 to, say, 22 yards, in extra thick cover, the man behind it merely "pokes" it in the general direction of flushes and birds fall. It only weighs about 6 pounds. Of course, birds fall mainly because you're scattering a lot of shot out over a wide area.

In the same mold is a 12-gauge Franchi 48/AL autoloader I have.

Sisley refers to the ideal early-season woodcock gun as a "poker!" It's any shotgun that's very short of barrel and extremely quick in the user's hands.

(Left) A brace of woodcock and one of the author's favorite "pokers," his short-barreled Mario Beschi 20-bore. Chokes? The author likes 'em open.

Sporting a 24-inch barrel, its overall length is still considerably longer than the Mario Beschi 20 due to the inches taken up by its comparatively elongated receiver. I had Darrell Reed (Clinton River Gun Co., 30016 S. River Rd., Mt. Clemens, MI 48045—phone: 313-468-1090) rig that barrel with his Reed Screw-In chokes. I have eight of those inserts—obviously, of every conceivable constriction. The "wide open" screw-in is always in place when woodcock are on the day's agenda.

But, as Paul Harvey says, "And now the rest of the [Franchi] story." I sent that gun to Darrell, and had him highly modify it (the details of which appear elsewhere in this book, in my article on grouse hunting). At any rate, the result was an 8-ounce weight reduction, lowering the overall weight of an already light 12-bore to 6 pounds even. Further, the reduction in weight was all "out-front" weight, thereby adding to what I've been calling the gun's "poking" qualities.

Another case in point: On the final

day of that aforementioned hunt in that upper Great Lakes state, after turning my nose up at the .410 "swinger" for any further use and running out of 20-gauge shells for the Mario Beschi, I carried the revamped, shortened Franchi with the new Reed Screw-In chokes. I promptly sent a limit of five woodcock tumbling into the bases of the young aspens from which they had flushed.

"Poking" rather than "swinging" a shotgun is not classic fashion. It won't get you into the winner's circle in any serious trap or Skeet competition. The method won't win you any bucks at a live pigeon shoot either. If it's ducks, doves, driven partridge and the like, leave your "poking" gun at home. You won't be able to hit with any degree of consistency. Poking isn't something you can practice much either. You pick up your "poking" baccalaureate by shooting a heck of a lot of shotgun shells in heavy cover every year. Some fellas are born with such gunning ability. Others come by it more honestly; they work for it.

Ammo

Though the right gun is an important aspect of successful woodcocking, the shells aren't nearly as critical. I like to chamber ⅞-ounce 20 loads, or a 12-bore 1-ouncer, a 1⅛-ounce factory if I can't get what I want in 1 ounce. Number 8s are my favorite for tims, but either 9s or 7½s are OK. One load that Federal has discontinued was a favorite—1⅛ ounces of No. 10s backed by a 3½-dram equivalent powder charge.

There's always a good chance of flushing a ruffed grouse as one negotiates good timberdoodle cover, and I never felt under gunned for either of

these heavy-cover birds when I had that big Federal 12-gauge load of 10s speaking in my behalf, particularly if most of the leaves hadn't fallen to the ground. I have two ancient boxes of those paper-cased 3½-dram 10s left. I'll judiciously fire up one of those this season, leaving only one more to savor the following fall.

I don't know when I bought the case of Smith & Wesson 20-gauge, ⅞-ounce 2½-dram loads. Probably when they were on special at the local discount store back in the early '70s. They're No. 8s, ideal for 'cock in my estimation. But it's the price per box that I've mused a great deal about in recent seasons—$1.99! This past autumn I used up my last of those also discontinued S&W's. I think I have something like six or seven individual shells left. Like good guns and good dogs, I'll miss 'em when they've gone.

Let's get back to business . . . Skeet reloads carrying ⅞-ounce of No. 9s are fine, but chilled No. 8s are better. More expensive and much better loads like the Federal Premiums and Remington Premiers are excellent, though probably not necessary for close-up woodcock shooting. Today's 12-gauge trap loads contain high-antimony, extra-hard shot in No. 7½, 8 and 8½. Most of these contain 6 to 7 percent antimony, while Skeet loads of No. 9s contain less, reportedly about 3 percent. Trap loads will thus deform less, producing slightly tighter patterns. The bargain-priced Federal loads that always find their way to discount sporting goods shelves each fall—12- and 16-gauge 1-ounce, and 20-gauge ⅞-ounce (always select No. 8s, if possible)—make super, inexpensive woodcock medicine. They contain chilled shot.

Nick Sisley cautions his pointer with a "Whoa" as he walks in with an over/under at port arms.

Habits and Habitat

Successful "woodcock finding" centers on knowing *where* to look and developing an eye for ideal 'doodle cover. How does one do that? Like most anything, you have to pay your dues, but here are some keys. Woodcock are mainly earthworm eaters, and they can devour a *tremendous* number of them every day (read that, *night*). In one 24-hour period, for example, a single woodcock can eat up to 100 percent of its body weight in earthworms—that's *eating*!

Worms only abound where it's wet. Consequently, lowlands, along stream bed edges and flood plains are the places which hold these birds. They don't like high trees around them, maturing or even semi-maturing woodlands. In the upper Great Lakes states look for 'cock in aspen, more specifically young aspen that's no more than 16 years in age. (Aspen of that maturity really aren't all that tall in the northern Great Lakes region.) In mid-September, when hunting seasons commence in much of this part of birdland, I've found woodcock concentrated in even younger cover—4- to 7-year-old aspen stands.

In the Maritime Provinces of New Brunswick and Nova Scotia the classic woodcock cover is alders. The same goes for much of Maine, much of the rest of New England and other prominent 'cock states. An intermixture of low tree and shrub species can be the best cover type to seek in many areas because this is where this bird

With his long bill, the woodcock probes under the ground's surface, mainly for earthworms, the staple of this bird's diet.

thrives. In most states where I hunt I keep an eye peeled for a mixture of aspen, crab apple, gray dogwood, silky dogwood and the like. You don't have to have a degree in botany, but it does pay to learn how to identify many of the tree and shrub species in covers where you find birds.

In acre-spanning stands of all aspen or all alders, I have found plenty of woodcock, but in many states there's little, if any, of this type of habitat. This is when one must seek the aforementioned intermixtures. Here also is where there should be little openings between the varying tree and shrub species. I'm not talking football field size clearings, but ones that might be a third that size right on down to a chunk of space no larger than a spare bathroom.

Another important facet of zeroing in on real woodcock habitat is that there should not be thick grass on the ground. A bit of grass is fine, but

The woodcock's ear openings are well forward on the bird's head — which makes it a bit easier for it to hear underground movements of its favorite food, earthworms.

The author is working aspens in the early part of the season. Note the leaves and high bracken fern understory — it's typical woodcock habitat at the beginning of the season.

woodcock like to walk around as they feed, and they can't do that if the grass is thick and wiry. The right feeling under your boots should be sought as well. Timberdoodles can't drill their long bills into ground that's excessively hard. Worms won't be in such terra either, or if they are, they'll be too deep for even a 'cock to reach. When I'm strolling through potential woodcock country and suddenly it feels like a thick, luxurious, expensive carpet under my boots, I'm suddenly more conscious of my gun, my mouth begins to feel a tad dry and salty and I urge my dogs in, cautioning them to be careful and hunt close.

Woodcock also leave calling cards— their droppings. Called "chalk" or "spattle," these droppings are often as big as a half dollar and as white as an egg fresh out of a skillet. When you

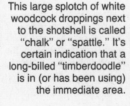
This large splotch of white woodcock droppings next to the shotshell is called "chalk" or "spattle." It's certain indication that a long-billed "timberdoodle" is in (or has been using) the immediate area.

spot one or more of these chalk marks on the covert's floor, there are, or have been, woodcock right where you're walking. A closer inspection will tell you how long ago. If the chalk is wet and slippery, maybe even warm, the flush could come before you stand back up. Dry and crusty spattle obviously means the droppings are old, not so much reason to be over anticipatory.

This bird is one of nature's most interesting avians. Its eyes sit well atop its head, thus enabling the bird to look upward for possible predators— even with its head down feeding. Its ears are well forward and much lower than the eye. Evolution has evidently resulted in this positioning to allow the birds to listen for underground movements of earthworms, thus better suggesting where they should

The woodcock's long and pointed wings make the bird well suited for migratory flights.

(Below) Sisley's pointer, Magic, sits mannerly with the morning's bag, a full limit of woodcock. As Magic is pointing out, early season timberdoodle hunts can get a dog, and hunter, pooped out in a hurry. Clothing? Go prepared to peel off a layer or two. Lightweight camo jackets, as seen here, are a good bet. Also remember that woodcock like the damp areas — choose your footwear accordingly.

probe the ground. These ear openings are particularly big, too.

With fairly long, pointed wings, 'cock are ideally suited for reasonably long flights. These are migratory critters, most of them wintering within 200 miles of the Gulf of Mexico, but a fair share winter along our southern Atlantic Coast as well. Their hearts are almost the size of that of the grouse, and so are their livers. The meat is a deep red, the cooked flavor of a woodcock often being described as "powerful." As table fare, the flavor of a woodcock is *so* pungent there's little room for middle grounders—you either love it or hate it. Consequently, the most robust Burgundy or Cabernet Sauvignon never overpowers the flavor of woodcock.

In some hunting areas brush bustin' duds of the highest order are required for hunting this bird. Otherwise, one's thighs, arms and wrists will be ripped to the bleeding point, regularly. However, in some sections, briars and the thickness of the vegetation aren't nearly on the same par. Blaze-orange clothing is highly recommended, in fact legally essential in a mushrooming number of states. Not only does the blaze orange help you keep track of your partner(s) in the thick brush, it also permits other sports who might be in the cover to see you as well.

Over the years woodcock have become known as tight, tight sitters, making them ideal for the pointing type of dog. It's true that today's woodcock have learned to run plenty,

but they are still great birds when it comes to a good pointer. Cocker spaniels were developed to hunt the much bigger European woodcock (thus the name "cocker"), so flushing spaniels or retrievers trained to hunt close and flush, are also used successfully by a large number of hunters.

Summary

On the Atlantic Seaboard woodcock have not been doing so well the last 5 or 6 years, mainly due to dwindling nesting habitat. Daily limits have justly been reduced to three birds, and the season length has been cut—by more than half! Further, there's cause for alarm in much of this bird's wintering habitat due to the clearing of land, the draining of wetlands, the quest for oil and other environmentally disruptive reasons.

The only bright picture in the woodcock's overall habitat exists throughout the upper Great Lakes region, where heavy demand for wood pulp is causing more and more land owners to consider cutting their trees. As these forests grow back, they tend to provide ideal woodcock nesting, resting and feeding habitat, par excellance!

Here's a bird that deserves every consideration by game managers. Large tracts of excellent habitat *can* be maintained for the foreseeable future. All hunters and game managers have to do is to make certain the loss of existing habitat is curbed. In my opinion, a federal woodcock stamp is a superb way to generate the funds needed to set aside, and manage, significant acreages of prime woodcock cover. If you are, like me, a dedicated woodcock hunter, you probably share similar feelings. The best way to ensure the future of woodcock hunting is to drop your congressman a note and express your feeling. For those of you who have just joined the ranks, be assured there *is* a future for the woodcock. It just takes time, energy, money and sound conservation practices. The woodcock is worth the effort. It's one of our greatest gamebirds. ●

Editor's Note—Grouse and Woodcock: An Upland Hunter's Book, *by Nick Sisley, the author of the foregoing article, covers two of the nation's most challenging game birds. There's hunting how-to, technique, dog training tips, how to shoot better and more. Those of you who know Sisley's work, and are dedicated grouse and woodcock hunters, can get the book from: Impact, Alder Acres, 509 1st St., Apollo, PA 15613 for $11.95 plus $1.50 for postage and handling. PA residents add 6 percent ($.72) sales tax.*

I WAS GRATEFUL for the full-size lenses of my binoculars. Compacts work fine when the light is good, but there's no way they can equal 35mm (or larger) objectives in the big timber gloom of late November when dawn is just a hint above the eastern ridges. Some people might wonder what anyone is doing out at such a time, alone, ½-mile from the Jeep, a scope-sighted rifle hanging from one shoulder, shivering. Squirrel snipers know. This can be the prime time of the day, for big bushytails often raid a cornfield before daylight, returning to the woods as the sun's first beams, colorless and cold as springwater, penetrate the black tree trunks.

That's where I was, and my 7x35 Bushnells were focused on a walnut-sized lump protruding above the crotch of an oak limb 40 yards away. I was braced against another tree, motionless as I could make myself, trying to be certain that what I was looking at was a squirrel's head instead of just a gray protuberance on the limb. Even as I studied it, the growing light gave me a better view. Now I could make out an ear, the glint of an eye. I lowered the binoculars, shrugged the rifle from my shoulder and found the small target in the 6x Leupold. The Lee Dot blacked out the gleam, settled motionless. Gentle pressure, imperceptible trigger movement, *Spaaat*. Half-cartwheeling, legs extended, wide but weightless tail floating, the squirrel thumped on the dry oak leaves. It was my first kill of the day.

Squirrels are one of the most popular game animals in the country, if numbers bagged are any indication. Admittedly, they don't have the glamor of big game, or perhaps even of grouse or turkey. But hunters of all ages and degrees of experience go for them when conditions permit—and sometimes when it means forgetting a hunt for a more glamorous species. In my home state of Pennsylvania, hunters take more squirrels than any other critter. Squirrels took over the number one position in 1978, edging out cottontails that year, and have held the top spot ever since. In the five more recent seasons for which reports are available, 1980 through 1984, Pennsylvania hunters have bagged over 13 million squirrels, compared to

SQUIRREL — THE

Go into the cold, the dark and the damp. Sit motionless. Wait. Know your game. Then you s-q-u-e-e-z-e- that trigger. That's squirrel hunting at its best.

The barrel on the author's old customized 52 is heavier than normal for a hunting rig, thus easier to hold steady when no rest is available.

Species

Two species of squirrels are normally hunted for food, the gray squirrel *(Sciurus carolinensis)* and the fox squirrel *(Sciurus niger)*. Interestingly, the first word in each Latin term derives from the Greek words *skia* (shadow) and *oura* (tail); thus a squirrel (from the French word *écureuil*) is a creature which sits in the shadow of his tail. Even a person who has never been closer to a forest than Central Park would recognize that the name is beautifully accurate.

Sciurus carolinensis ranges over the eastern half of the U.S. and edges into Canada, and thus this species is usually called the eastern gray squirrel. There is a western gray squirrel only a few inches longer but bulkier in the body. A weight of 2 pounds is common, however 3 pounds is not unknown. The fox often looks like a big gray squirrel with rust-colored marks, though in some regions most are a reddish color.

When you have animals the size of gray and fox squirrels—1 to 3 pounds, say—present in good numbers over approximately half the area of the 48 contiguous states, and their meat is tasty, there's little doubt that boys and men with guns are going to take notice. That has been so since pre-Revolutionary days, when budding frontiersmen whetted their flintlock skills on these branch runners—and almost bankrupted the colonial Pennsylvania government which had

RIFLEMAN'S GAME! by BOB BELL

less than 12 million rabbits. That makes for an awful lot of panfried good stuff, to say nothing about countless kettles of squirrel potpie. In my opinion, no other meat that comes out of the woods, except possibly the broiled chops of a yearling whitetail, equals fried squirrel. That alone would be enough to make me abandon the thick ringneck covers in late November and head for the big woods. But in addition, squirrels provide some of the most challenging shooting a rifleman can ask for.

Perhaps it should be pointed out right now that squirrels—tree squirrels, we're talking of here—are *rifle* game. I'm not suggesting a shotgunner should pass them up. That's up to the individual and the circumstances of the shot. There's no doubt that a startled gray squirrel racing through the deep oak leaf cover of a gloomy woods can be as tough a shot as any small game. In years past I shot quite a few that way—and missed more than a couple. Still, in my mind, a scoped smallbore rifle is the perfect tool for this kind of hunting. More on that later.

(Sciurus griseus) in the Pacific Coast states, and an Arizona gray *(Sciurus arizonensis)* in the southeastern part of that state. The fox squirrel's range overlaps most of the eastern gray's, except for the region above southwestern Pennsylvania.

An adult gray averages about 20 inches in length, including its 9-inch tail. It weighs 1 to 1¼ pounds. Its color, from a short distance, is silver-gray except for an off-white belly, but in the hand it can be seen that most individual hairs are gray near the body, turning to off-brown, then black, with white tips. A black color phase is common in northcentral Pennsylvania, and white grays are not unknown; in fact, I see one or two fairly often in my backyard. (No, I've never shot one, though I've been tempted at times.) The fox squirrel is noticeably bigger than the gray, not

Don Lewis, gunwriter for *Pennsylvania Game News* and a dedicated squirrel hunter, pockets a McKean County, PA, black squirrel taken with Walther KKJ. This color phase of the gray squirrel is common in northern Pennsylvania. White grays are rare, but not unknown.

placed a 3 pence bounty on them in the futile hope of reducing crop damage on the minuscule forest-enclosed farms.

There was no way that shooting was going to control squirrel numbers in the mid-1700s. Not until the vast forests were reduced, eliminating the necessary habitat, did the squirrel population dwindle. The trees supplied living quarters and food—acorns, hickory nuts, walnuts, hazel nuts, pecans, butternuts, beechnuts, wild cherries, buds, seeds, etc. They still do, but there aren't as many trees now. On the other hand, there are many large farms now, where corn is a staple crop, and as shown in the opening of this article, corn is a favorite food of squirrels in some regions. They usually eat only the germ end of the kernel, but this destroys the entire ear and wastes most of it, a practice that doesn't endear them to farmers in areas of high squirrel population. They also eat insects and grubs on occasion. When water is

available, squirrels readily drink, but they can go for months without it, subsisting on moisture in their food.

Habits and Habitat

Gray and fox squirrels differ in more than size. Wild grays, as op-

posed to the pathetic peanut-eating city park squirrels, are creatures of the woods. They can be found in small woodlots on most every farm, but are also common throughout vast forested areas, on mountainous ridges as well as in lowland swamps—anywhere

(Right) One of the nicest things about squirrel hunting is that youngsters, properly supervised, can do it too. And it teaches them the value of patience and precision shot placement—qualities that should be learned by *all* hunters.

A lot of gray squirrel hunting is done in gloomy woods, so Bell prefers full-size binoculars (7x35 Bushnells here) to compacts. The bigger objective lenses provide more light at a given magnification, and that's vitally important in early morning and late afternoon, when most shooting occurs.

they can find the mature trees whose occasional hollow trunks make weatherproof homes and whose canopies supply the highly nutritious nuts which are these animals' favorite food. Leaf nests, less protective than tree dens but perhaps more pleasant, also are built and utilized. Some of these are rather sophisticated, essentially weatherproof, and used even in winter—more often by fox squirrels than grays. That might grow out of the different kinds of territory these two species prefer. Rather than the big woods the gray likes, the fox squirrel lives in more open country, the edges between woods and farmland, even solitary fencerow trees some distance from heavy cover. He is less frenetic than the gray, less vocal.

It is often claimed that fox squirrels spend more time on the ground than grays. That could well be true, or it could be a deduction based on their comparative body sizes which would seem to make the fox less agile in the sub-stratosphere where the gray is so comfortable. However, the late C.S. Landis, a prolific gunwriter and dedicated squirrel shooter who had decades of experience on eastern grays, told me he believed they spent as much time on the ground as in trees. Maybe with the larger variety, an even greater percentage of time is spent searching among the fallen oak and hickory leaves. I don't know. I

With one big gray already bagged, Don Lewis prepares to squeeze off another shot from his KKJ Walther. This high-quality rifle is fitted with set triggers, which are a help in precise letoff. I doubt if there's a more dedicated squirrel hunter in the country than Don. He'd rather make six butt-of-ear shots on grays in a morning than take a 40-inch sheep,

live in gray squirrel country. Regardless, it isn't unusual to see tree squirrels on the ground.

The foregoing gives some indication of where to hunt squirrels. Mostly it boils down to finding an area where their preferred types of habitat and food exist together or nearly so. They prefer to have bed and board within reasonable distance of each other.

Grays are early risers. They're usually up and around before sunrise, before even the best scope permits aiming, so the first shooting hour is probably the best. It's not uncommon for a hunter easing onto a deer stand in the dark to see the fleeting shadows of scurrying grays. They're active again in late afternoon, but their midday hours are mostly spent snoozing or sunning in the den, along a limb, or in a high-protected tree crotch. I'm not sure if weather has much to do with their choice. Sometimes they're out on the most miserable days, motionless perhaps, but exposed to the determined hunter with a good pair of binoculars.

I remember accidentally spotting a gray huddled into a tree crotch one

cold wet December morning. He was hunkered into the classic squirrel pose, wide tail fanned close above his back, apparently sleeping. It was an awful day, freezing rain soaking my clothing, cold vapor coming off the snow-covered ground—the kind of day you wish you were back at the cabin, snuggled into your old down-filled mummy. For 10 seconds I nestled my Zeiss Zielsech's Lee Dot between his ear and his closed eye, shivering finger carefully held away from the set trigger of my 22-250, wondering what even the Hornet-level handload would do. Then I lowered the Mauser and eased away. I was after bigger game that day. By chance, several hours later, I returned past that same tree. The squirrel was still there. He hadn't moved a millimeter.

Hunting Tactics

Most squirrel hunting isn't done under such adverse weather conditions. October and November are more normal months, when at least two-thirds of the time the weather doesn't threaten the stand hunter with pneumonia. And that—sitting and looking—is the conventional way to hunt squirrels, if a non-active activity can be called hunting. Most riflemen find an area that harbors a reasonable number of bushytails, take up a position which they believe will offer

safe shooting opportunities, and wait. Most create a comfortable seat at the base of a tree, lean back. . . and wait. Others sit behind a smaller tree, to have the advantage of a rifle rest. . . and wait. I prefer to sit between two trees that are spaced sufficiently apart for both leaning against and rifle support. And then I wait. Waiting is a large part of the squirrel shooter's repertoire. Maybe that's why some of these guys make such good snipers when the shooting is serious. Neither pursuit calls for indiscriminate spraying with full-auto fire; rather, one shot, carefully placed after full and patient preparation, does the trick.

Picking the stand is important. Although squirrels live throughout large forested tracts, more are usually found along the edges than deep within. Food is important. If a cornfield adjoins the woods, it's not unusual to find ears of corn, most of them kernel-less, under den trees. A nearby stand will pay off. Squirrels also like to run old fences and stone rows that divide fields and connect woodlots, or tree-grown fencerows. Look for fresh-chewed nut and acorn shells, and cuttings that have drifted down. Look for an assortment of trees—the big old wolf trees that provide warm dens, the mast-producing species, maybe a wild cherry—the kinds that produce foods at different times of the year, the kinds that have an interlacing

Don Lewis watches carefully with binoculars as partner Bill Nichols prepares to drop a squirrel with his Redfield-scoped Model 9422 Winchester, an attractive and handy outfit for those who don't care for bolt guns. Lewis likes bolts, though, and his choice on this hunt was a Kimber M82 with Weaver T6. It would be hard to make a better choice.

(Top) Profile of Model 52 shows barrel has been chopped to 21 inches with Remington 700 ADL trigger guard substituting for original stamping. Maple stock has been glass bedded all the way, including a ½-inch wide and deep cut that runs most of the length of the Mannlicher-style fore-end. Why? To eliminate warpage. Also, Wardrop added a recoil shoulder on the bottom of the barrel, perfectly glassed, to solidify things even more. Though the barrel and action were built decades ago, it would be hard to find a better squirrel killer than this rig.

(Inset) When Bell cobbled up his Model 52 squirrel shooter, no mount could be found to install the 6x Leupold in the position he wanted (just ahead of bolt on uplift). So gunsmith Al Wardrop made a filler block to fit barrel taper ahead of receiver ring and to accept standard Conetrol base.

(Right) Anyone who is willing to spend a reasonable amount for his squirrel rifle can find some excellent choices. Here are three used by Bell's friends: Savage/Anschutz M54 with Bushell 3-9x scope; KKJ Walther and 10x Redfield; Remington M541-S with Weaver KW6x. These are precision outfits.

canopy which makes high-level travel easy for these four-footed, parachute-tailed aerialists. Sure, they can race wildly to the very tip end of a tiny branch and hurl themselves a dozen feet to the nearest extension of a neighboring tree, to scramble onward and out of sight, but most of the time they doubtless prefer to do things easier. Give some thought to what they do and why and how they like to do it.

Fox squirrels are generally lazier than grays. At least they tend to get a later start in the morning. They stay active longer, though, before slowing down in the afternoon and then stirring again a few hours later. Their routine is pleasant to some hunters who like to get up at a reasonable hour and eat breakfast before heading toward the back forty.

Squirrels have good eyesight, so it's not enough for a hunter to wait, he has to wait motionlessly. This is never easy. Few Americans have the ability. It conflicts with our national get-up-and-go makeup. But anyone who would become a squirrel sniper must learn to do his gittin' at the approximate speed of a glacier. Once you've made a comfortable spot for your seat, facing so the sun won't shine in your eyes, and have a no-stub tree trunk for leanin' against, boots in a no-slip position and rifle comfortable, it's time to be *quiet* (no coughing, no nose-blowing, no whatever). Any movement, even turning your head, should be slow. Keep your arms close to your body, so turning to study a new area won't radically change your silhouette.

Then wait. Study everything with binoculars. Listen. Gray squirrels are not the quietest critters in the woods. They chatter and bark and chew noisily on occasion, they clip leafy twigs

This Browning T-Bolt with a little Bushnell 4x is a slick-working and accurate rig that will handle most any hunting chore where a 22 rimfire is suitable, including elusive squirrels.

an individual rifle, as can be done with centerfires. Yet 22-caliber rifles are as finicky in their ammo likes and dislikes as any of the big bores. Maybe more so. So the only recourse is to bench test an assortment of ammo in your own gun. Chances are excellent that one or two makes will provide excellent groups, while the others will range from so-so to poor. I don't know why this is so—I doubt that anyone does, or they'd have done something about it—but that's the way it is. No big problem. In fact, it's sort of fun as it gives a good reason to do some shooting. One thing to keep in mind, though. Rimfire ammo—again as with centerfire stuff—varies from lot to lot, so when you find a batch that your gun likes, it's advisable to lay in a good supply, or you'll have to go through the testing procedure again. To start off, it's enough to buy one box of each of a half-dozen kinds. That's enough to fire four or five 5-shot groups to get a reasonable idea of accuracy and consistency. (Don't worry about the leftover stuff, even from the so-so boxes. Use it for offhand practice prior to the big game season. It'll be more precise than you are, so will serve a useful purpose.)

that drift to the ground, they rattle through the dry leaves on the forest floor, scrambling full speed for no apparent reason only to stop abruptly and intently look at something outside your ken, or maybe just scratch a flea. Sometimes they're more interesting to watch than to shoot at.

Guns and Ammo

But shooting is why most of us are out there. That requires a gun of some sort. I long ago quit shooting squirrels with a shotgun, even as incidental game on a pheasant hunt. I don't criticize anyone else for doing it, and I'd do it myself if I needed the meat at any given time. But that's rarely the case, so I do my squirrel hunting with a rifle. A good scope-sighted 22 seems the perfect tool for the job. It's accurate, quiet, portable, deadly at any range where the game can normally be seen if the hunter has done his homework and shoots well.

Proper preparation means finding the best ammo for his individual rifle, getting precisely zeroed at some specific range, and learning the bullet's path in relation to the scope reticle over the distance at which closer and longer shots will be taken. It helps to spend some time on range estimating procedures, too. This is not as critical on squirrels as with some kinds of big game—certainly a missed shot here is not as traumatic or expensive as it would be on a sheep hunt—but it makes sense to take care of all the details of a hunt. Knowledge adds to success, and all of us get more satisfaction out of a productive hunt than a nonproductive one, especially when the difference is our shooting ability. If we don't see anything to shoot at,

we tend to blame it on poor luck or lack of game, though it may actually be a result of poor hunting ability; but when we see game within range and miss it, there's nothing to blame but our own ineptitude. So it makes sense to be prepared.

Rimfire ammo cannot be handloaded, so it isn't possible to tailor a load to

Most any kind of 22 can be used for squirrels. Here are lightweight pump and bolt actions flanking a sophisticated target gun and an older Model 75 Winchester with 12x Litschert. The hunter who isn't bothered by the small field of view and unusual appearance of limbs and twigs in a target scope can get by with a 10x or 12x scope, but most hunters will be better served with a 4x or 6x. The "big game" models, because of their large lenses, are more suitable in dark woods than the small "22 scopes" because of their comparatively superb light-gathering qualities.

Testing is best done at 50 yards, with sandbags fore and aft. There's usually enough difference in group sizes to be noticeable at this distance, allowing you to make a deliberate choice, and any ammo that groups well here will handle squirrels in the woods. From a good scoped 22, 5-shot groups at 50 yards will usually go into 1 inch or so, occasionally in half that. That means every shot will drill a squirrel's head, if the hunter does his part. I'm talking about high-speed Long Rifle hollow points here, a type of ammo not known for such accuracy a few decades back. Anyone who hasn't tested today's high-speed production fodder might be pleasantly surprised. Target ammo usually does better from an accuracy standpoint, but doesn't kill as well unless the bullet hits the brain or the forward part of the spine. Since the high-speed HPs deliver plenty of accuracy, it only makes sense to go with the faster, more efficient bullets. This reasoning does not apply to the super-velocity rimfires, though. At least not in my

rifles. They do have extra speed, but I've never consistently got the accuracy out of them required for squirrels. Also, their extra power just isn't needed—and truth is, it isn't that much more at 50 yards and beyond. They start out faster but also slow down quicker, so the net gain is negligible.

Rimfires can be more cranky than centerfires on the bench, possibly because their velocity is so much lower that shooters subconsciously relax after the trigger breaks which can cause rifle movement before the bullet clears the muzzle. A competitive shooter tightly wrapped in a sling doesn't have this problem, but it often shows up on the bench. So make sure you're following through if results seem unusual or inconsistent.

The only rimfire rifles I own are bolt-actions, so I can't comment personally on the accuracy others will deliver. I can't help feeling they don't equal the bolt's, but know that the slide-action Winchester Model 61 was a deadly outfit in a friend's hands. As a general observation, lever-actions

don't seem as accurate as other repeating designs.

I still occasionally use my first 22 for squirrels. It's a Model 72 Winchester wearing my first scope, a 29-S Weaver in a Stith Streamline mount. I got it in 1937, which is awhile ago now, but it still can do the job among the hickories and white oaks. One nice feature is its tubular magazine. Stuffed to capacity, it'll handle all the chances anyone's likely to have even on a good day. Despite the sentimental reasons, though, the ¾-inch tube of that little Weaver just doesn't transmit as much light as I like on gloomy mornings.

Years ago I decided that a game animal as challenging as the gray squirrel deserved the best equipment, so I decided to get just the rig I wanted. When I was a kid, the ultimate 22 was the Winchester 52 sporter. Maybe it still is. Unfortunately, collectors have driven the price of this model beyond what any rational hunter will pay, but Model 52 target rifles are plentiful and comparatively reason-

(Right) Bell has found his 52 Winchester, sporterized from a standard-weight Model 52 Winchester target rifle, as efficient a squirrel killer as anyone could ask. The 6x Leupold has two Lee Dots, 2 MOA at intersection, 1 MOA 6 minutes beneath. The first subtends 1 inch at 50 yards, and thus fits neatly inside a gray's head. The smaller dot makes some unusually long shots possible, though such chances rarely arise in the woods.

Bob Wise tries out Bell's 541-S Remington with 3-9x Shepherd Dual Reticle scope. Bell recently replaced the 3-9x with smaller 2-7x Shepherd, as the sizes seemed more fitting for a lightweight rifle. (Editor's Note: The good news for fans of the 541-S is that Remington just announced the reintroduction of that rifle at the 1986 S.H.O.T. Show.)

able in cost. I got one on a trade, an early speedlock version with standard barrel. Al Wardrop cut the barrel to 21 inches, added a recoil shoulder and installed a 6x Leupold in a modified Conetrol mount. I restocked it with a nice piece of tigertail maple, glass bedded all the way, and took it to the range. It worked so well I spent many evenings just sitting at the bench and squeezing 'em off. I dunno how many rounds I fired at paper before squirrel season arrived, but it was thousands. Perhaps the most interesting part wasn't that it shot well—52s *always* shoot well—but that there were significant differences in the way different makes of ammo grouped. There's no use listing what the various makes did in my gun, as each one is a law unto itself. What was worst for me could be best for you, so try an assortment.

I also took the time to zero precisely at 50 yards, then with the same hold shot groups at 10-yard intervals from 10 yards to 60. This is the only way you can be certain of trajectory with your own gun, scope and ammo. I don't care what the ballistic charts or computer printouts or your hunting buddy says, the odds are great that *their* results and *your* results are going to be different. Maybe only ½-inch, which would be nothing on a deer, but it's highly significant on a critter with an aiming point smaller than a golf ball. So do your own testing. Chances are the differences come from variations in delivered velocity from different barrels, heights of different scopes above bore line, even differences in the way the rifles are held and rested. But for consistent kills you have to know these things, and the only way to learn them is by shooting.

You might be surprised to find how close the arc of the bullet's path comes to your aiming point over 50 yards. A lot of shooters believe they will have to hold several inches high or low over this range, but that's not necessary. The scope's height above the bore compensates for most of this, and once the line of sight and the bullet's path first coincide at 10 or 15 yards, even fractions of an inch separate bullet impact from aiming point.

I used the 52 for years with perfect satisfaction, and still use it, but somewhere along the way thought it would be nice to have a lighter outfit for some hunts. I had a chance to get a 581 Remington, which weighs only a bit over 5 pounds with 24-inch barrel. Even with a 4x Lyman All-American, it is a true lightweight compared to the 52—and the difference in accuracy is negligible. I'm not saying it equals the target-barreled 52 (it doesn't), but it will group in a squirrel's head all day at 50 yards, so who needs more?

Both the 6x Leupold and the 4x Lyman have Lee Dot reticles subtending 2 MOA. This means they cover 1 inch at 50 yards, which happens to be a size that snugs neatly between an adult gray's eye and ear or between the two eyes from the front. That makes for a good range estimating system, as well as a precise aiming unit. These scopes were designed for big game, so are built on 1-inch tubes with enlarged objective lenses. They transmit enough light for pinpoint aiming under any conditions where game can be seen.

Three rifles oughta be enough for anyone to hunt squirrels with, but somewhere along the way I got involved with another Remington, the dolled up 541-S. For several years I used one of Dan Shepherd's 3-9x Dual Reticle scopes on it, and results paralleled the others—which is to say, it was a very accurate rig. But the scope seemed larger than necessary for a 22, so when the 2-7x Shepherd came out, I substituted it. It still shoots as well as ever, and to my eyes, the somewhat smaller scope gives a neater appearance. Its multi-coated lenses also make it a honey in the woods.

I might as well admit to one more squirrel gun. It, too, is a bolt-action, the Ruger M77/22. The good Lord knows I didn't need it, but you know how things go. It's such an attractive thing, and with a 4x Leupold Compact it shoots so damn good.

Yeah, I know there are others out there. I keep hearing names like Kimber, Kleinguenther, Anschutz, Walther and. . . . But I've got will power. I don't need any more squirrel rifles. Not one. Still, it's nice to know they're there if I ever should need another one. . . •

Bell's latest squirrel rifle, here used by Brian Graybill, is a Ruger M77/22 wearing a 4x Leupold Compact. It's beautiful to look at, deadly efficient, and can be obtained simply by walking into a sporting goods store and plunking down some money. A great choice for those hunters who like to do things the easy way.

Here're a
few hints and tips
designed to help
the rimfire hunter..

GET THAT RIMFIRE READY!

by JIM WOODS

GETTING READY for the rimfire hunting season is only slightly more simplified than preparing for the big bore, big game season. Why? First, it's simpler because there are no new loads to work up, no new bullets to test out. (Of course, if you don't "roll your own" centerfires, and are dependent on factory rounds, then you are in pretty much the same situation as the rimfirer.) Secondly, and probably more importantly, getting ready for the hunting season is easier for the rimfire shooter because it's likely that your smallbore rifle was not used *just* for last fall's hunt, then put away for a full year. The 22 rimfire rifle may well have been used off and on all year, the shooter staying familiar with his gun's operation, and perhaps its quirks. Also, let's not forget that our shooter probably spent a fair amount of time with his rimfire just keeping his shooting eye in shape.

Assuming that a hunter does use his 22 year 'round, then with the coming of the fall, small game hunting season, that hunter will continue to use the same old reliable 22 rifle with which he dispatched pop cans and small varmints all year long. Also, assuming that no real functional problems have been noticed with the rifle, it should *almost* be ready for the meat-hunting season. This supposition is based on continued use of the rifle being accompanied by continual maintenance—periodic cleaning,

checking scope mount screws occasionally, and protecting the rifle from knocks and bumps during transport and storage. If any of these routine care items have been neglected, the results will probably start to show up in missed game shots—when that happens, the shooter had better head for a session at the target range.

Cleaning

Before any shooter heads for the shooting range to sight-in his rimfire, a little gun cleaning and general maintenance is in order. This should, in my opinion, apply to both *new* and used 22s. However, before *any* cleaning is attempted, be sure the chamber is empty and all ammunition is removed from the gun.

From the factory, a new rifle will come lightly oiled, both internally and externally, so the first chore is to run a couple of patches through the bore to wipe it clean. This helps ensure that no obstructions, such as remnants from manufacturing or packaging, have been left behind to create a hazard. Use a solvent-soaked

patch first, followed by a dry one, or several, to ensure that the barrel is free of any gunk that will attract and hold other fouling. Treat the dirty barrel on your old rifle the same way; however, if it's really grungy, you may have to use a bronze brush soaked with solvent for the first pass. (Suggestion: Try Shooter's Choice or

RIG 44—they're two of the best bore cleaning solvents to come along in the past several decades.)

Do these bore-cleaning operations from the breech end, if at all possible, to prevent any sludge in the barrel from being pushed into the action, and to prevent the possible deformation of the muzzle which can degrade accuracy. Fortunately, cleaning from the breech is easy to do with any bolt-action rimfire; you simply remove the bolt completely by (usually) holding the trigger back as the bolt is withdrawn. This gives you a clear tunnel through the receiver housing to the breech end of the barrel.

Bolt-action rifles with removable box magazines or clips will present no obstacle to the cleaning rod if the magazine is removed, as it should be, prior to cleaning. Tube-fed bolt-actions, however, like the Marlin Model 781, have a spring-loaded cartridge lifter that may interfere with free passage of the cleaning rod. For tube-fed rifles like the Marlin 781, that lifter should be carefully depressed to permit the cleaning rod tip to pass over it, on its way to the rear of the chamber. (Depress that lifter "gingerly" to avoid any damage to it.)

This shooter is cleaning out his new bolt-action *before* he shoots it for the first time. Doing so removes all factory packing grease or any remnants of manufacture.

When cleaning tube-fed rimfire repeaters from the breech, it's best to carefully depress the cartridge lifter *before* you run a cleaning rod through the rear of the action and on into the chamber. Depressing the lifter, and gently sliding the cleaning rod tip *over* it, will avoid damage to that usually thin, stamped-steel part. (It'll also help save your rod tip!) Bolt-action single shots, or box-magazine fed repeaters are simpler to clean from the breech: Simply open the bolt, move it to the rear, pull the trigger, and the bolt will slide right out the rear of the receiver. In the case of a box-magazine fed repeater, remove the magazine. As always, remove *all* ammo from the gun and make sure the chamber is empty *before* you start any cleaning procedure.

Rifles like the Winchester Model 9422 lever-action can be cleaned from the breech, without complete field stripping, by using a string-type cleaning set-up. Cleaning any rifle from the breech helps avoid damage to the lands and grooves (or the rifling) at the muzzle. Damage to that area can, literally, ruin the firearm's full accuracy potential.

Ruger's 10/22 can be cleaned from the rear of the breech via barrel removal—a procedure best left to an experienced gunsmith. Cleaning from the rear is better accomplished with a string-type cleaning system. Yes, the 10/22 can also be carefully cleaned, from the muzzle, with a conventional 22-caliber cleaning rod. To do so, remove the rotary magazine, make sure the chamber is empty and lock the bolt in the rearward position, as seen here.

Single shot 22 rifles that have a removable bolt, or those that break open, are also easy to clean from the breech end. However, the popular lever-actions, semi-autos and the few available pump-actions are a bit more difficult to swab out from the rear end. The lever guns, pumps and autos usually have enclosed or shrouded receivers, and even with the action open, access to the breech is very limited. As a result, your cleaning options are limited to: 1.) *carefully* cleaning the bore from the muzzle end with a conventional cleaning rod; or 2.) constructing a weighted, string-type cleaning device that will allow cleaning from the breech.

Sighting In

Rimfire ammo is *amazingly* consistent. In fact, the mechanized manufacture of 22 rimfire ammo has reached a level of quality and reliability unexcelled in any other manufacturing operation. All of the major ammo makers share in that tribute, and they produce millions of rounds each year. However, almost every 22 rifle will show a preference for a particular brand or type of ammo.

In fact, the variations in accuracy performance between *brands* of ammo, and even between manufacturing lots of the same brand can be quite surprising. The general cure for this sort of thing is to try out several brands and types of rimfire fodder. Usually, one of those brands, or types, will provide ragged-hole groups.

Sighting in a rifle need not take a lot of time or result in the expenditure of a lot of ammo. Why? Because of the relatively low intensity of recoil with the 22LR cartridge, and the slight reaction and counter-movement of the rifle. In my experience, it's possible to sight in a scoped rimfire by firing 5 rounds, or less!

There are some rifle scopes marketed as "22" scopes, and they often are inexpensive, and usually inadequate for serious rimfire shooting. These "22" scopes are usually of ¾-inch or ⅞-inch diameter, and they just don't transmit the generous amount of light that a full 1-inch diameter scope does. If you are going to use your 22 rifle for hunting and want to use telescopic sights, spend the money for a full-sized scope. It's true that 22 ammo is inexpensive, and that 22 rifles are low priced, but it just doesn't follow that the telescopic sight has to be budget priced and of low quality. The object is still to *hit* what you aim for, and to compromise on scope choice may keep you from doing that.

I prefer a good, 1-inch diameter, 4x scope for serious rimfire work. Additionally, I've had good success with 4x scopes that have been parallax corrected for 50 yards—not 100 yards as is the norm for 1-inch scopes. (Manufacturers will usually be happy to correct the parallax of one of their 1-inch tubed scopes for a nominal fee.) Why a 4x? Why parallax corrected to 50 yards? Simple. The 4x provides plenty of power out to 50 yards. And let's face it, 250-yard shots on bushytails, with a Ruger 10/22, are a bit ambitious. Finally, when adjusted to be parallax free at 50 yards, that 1-inch 4x scope will be *crystal clear* over the full range of normal (25-75 yards) shooting distances.

This shooter is wisely trying out a variety of different brands and types of 22 LR fodder in his Ruger semi-auto. He'll be looking for both functional reliability *and* top accuracy from one or more types/brands of ammo.

When selecting a scope for your own rimfire, consider the use of a full-sized, 1-inch tube model like the Burris 4x seen here. Most scope manufacturers will be happy to parallax-correct your scope to 50 yards—an optimum parallax correction for a scope that's to be used at practical rimfire ranges.

in this instance the shooter has found Remington Standard Velocity LR ammo to be the top accuracy performer in his scoped 9422 lever-action. The next step is to practice, practice, *practice.*

At what range to sight-in? Try 25 yards—dead on. With that sight-in, 25- to 50-yard head shots on rabbits or squirrels are pretty much a hold-on proposition. Yes, there will be some variation on this theme, from gun to gun—that's why you should head for the range with *your* gun, *your* scope and *your* ammo!

If your 22 rifle is to be used with iron sights, I would, again, recommend you set the target up at 25 yards. Support the fore-end on a solid rest, and put the butt solidly into the shoulder. Set the front bead just down into the rear notch, and forget what you've heard about "fine bead" and "coarse bead." Just be sure to use a "consistent bead" for every shot you make.

Open-sight shooters often like to hold at "6 o'clock," the bead just under the target. That's okay for some shooting games when bull's-eye targets are the only things to be shot, but that's no way to get ready for a hunt. In my opinion, you should put the bead "right on target" when a rabbit or squirrel is the object. If you sight in

and practice with the bead covering the part of the target you wish to hit, you'll be much more likely to put meat in the pot.

The main thing to remember is that you can become proficient with just about *any* sighting system, iron or glass, just as long as you are willing to *practice.*

Conclusion

Twenty-two Long Rifle ammo provides effective killing power well out beyond practical rimfire hunting ranges. However, if you can't see a rabbit or squirrel at 75 to 100 yards, why set your sights for that distance? Forty yards is plenty distant for a zero, and 25 is usually adequate and often preferred by experienced rimfire riflemen. At any rate, there's little to be gained by shooting at distances beyond the shooter's ability to put hits on target.

It was noted at the start that the 22 shooter had no reloading activity to clutter his hunt readiness process. Well, there is one more ammo decision to make—selecting solids or hol-

low points. If you're a meat or pelt hunter, the choice is clear—opt for the solids. Hollow points are fine for rimfire varminting, because tissue destruction is inconsequential. To preserve both meat and pelts, though, use the 40-grain solids instead of the 37-grain hollow points. In rifles of recent manufacture and in good condition, the hyper-velocity, lightweight solid bullet fodder from all the major ammo makers can be exceptionally good game getters.

Whatever ammo you select, make head shots if at all possible. Such hits waste no meat and kill quickly—two things that should be the aim of all hunters.

Hunting with the 22LR does not mean that such hunting is "minor" sport. The 22 is the *most used* hunting round here in the U.S. Hunting with it deserves all the pre-hunt preparation and care that is given to readying for the big bore hunting season. Like any other shooting/hunting activity, rimfire hunting is a matter of the right gun, the right sights, the right ammo and *practice, practice, practice.* ●

by MIKE VENTURINO

Hunting Big Game
from HORSEBACK

To MANY HUNTERS the actual taking of game is the sole reason they are involved in the sport of hunting. All their preparations, therefore, are intended to further this aim. That is why they choose the most powerful, and flattest shooting rifle topped with the best scope money can buy. That is why they buy the best binoculars available, the best hunting clothes and boots. That is why they hunt hard and long for the biggest trophies.

I am *not* one of those fellows.

As blasphemous as it may sound in some quarters, the actual killing of big game animals is not as important to me as the aesthetics of the hunt. That means that for the hunt to be ultimately satisfying, the type of firearm I use must be the type I am currently "in love with." That the shot I made was decent and required at least a modicum of skill. And lastly, that the hunting was done with horses.

This last requirement may sound strange to some. How do horses figure into the hunting experience except as beasts of burden to get you to places higher and farther than you would normally walk? Otherwise, are they not expensive complex, noisy, and often contrary brutes?

In this modern era it is often fashionable to denigrate horses as large, insensate animals given to wild fears, unpredictable fits of temper, and possessed of amazingly low IQs. They are often said to be no smarter than common pigs. As far as I am concerned that latter accusation may or may not be true because my experience with pigs goes no further than store-bought bacon. What is true is that one would look downright silly riding around the hills on the back of a boar hog!

Horses are majestic, graceful animals. No other animal, save for dogs, has captured the public's imagination more than has the horse. Horse novels, horse jokes, horse movies, and TV shows starring horses have been popular for decades in America. My wife and I are lifelong horse lovers and sacrifice many other of life's pleasantries in order to feed and keep a small assortment of the big beautiful critters. A busy work schedule keeps us from using them daily, and winters in Montana often preclude one from enjoying the out of doors on the back of a horse. Therefore, we feel that hunting season is a perfect time to use our horses

In those areas that are difficult to get to by foot or vehicle, the use of a horse makes good sense. Also, when it comes to retrieving big game, like the elk seen here, horses can be invaluable.

in the mountains. If we are successful in our hunting, the reward has an added greatness. If we are unsuccessful then we still have the reward of having spent the day in our beautiful Montana mountains in the company if our equine friends. It's a good feeling.

Horses may not place high on the scale of intelligence when rated against humans, but that's comparing apples and oranges. In my opinion, horses do pretty well when it comes to basic intelligence. Especially when it comes to common horse sense!

For instance horses never find themselves lost. It's the humans who ride them who get lost. The old adage about letting a horse have his head and he will take you home *is* true. I have experienced it more than once. In late November of 1980, I was elk hunting out of a completely strange camp. We left early that morning before light and were returning well after dark. And I mean *dark*! There was a dense cloud cover and I could literally not see the ground under my horse's hooves. As a bonus, the wind was howling creating a wind chill factor that pushed the temperature well under zero. Due to the young guide's ineptitude we became separated, and I was left to make my own way back to camp. As it happened, I was riding an old and very experienced friend named Duke. He, too, was a stranger to this new camp, but as soon as I owned up to being totally lost, I merely dropped my reins on Duke's neck and let him have his head. He lowered

his nose to near the ground, and in this slow and deliberate fashion carried me directly back to camp. Old Duke is permanently lame now and up there in years, but I still own him and will continue to do so until he dies a natural death.

Hunting from horseback is not practical in many parts of the country. I can't imagine a horse being of much benefit while hunting whitetails in the dense forests of New England, or in the swamps and bogs of the deep South.

Where horses do come into their own, however, is when it comes to hunting elk and mule deer in the mountainous West. In the high country of Wyoming, Montana, Idaho, Utah and Colorado, the horse is still considered indispensable by professional outfitters and many private hunters. A look at the hunting terrain of those states will give you an idea why. Sometimes a hunter must cover as much 12, 15 or even 20 miles a day searching for elusive elk. Most of that traveling will be in steep country where it seems the "ups" come much more often than the "downs." For much of the hunting season it is also likely that the high country will be covered with snow and ice. The only hunters fully able to cover such terrain on foot are those in superior physical condition, and those practiced in such outdoor endeavors. Also keep in mind that the elevation may range from 2,000 to 12,000 feet. Even hunters in *excellent* physical condition at sea level will experience *ex-*

When it comes to covering healthy chunks of steep, mountainous country, the horse can't be beat. A horse can, in a few minutes, cover the same amount of hilly terrain a hunter on foot would spend ½-hour or more trying to cover.

If your horse's ears and attention quickly settle on a nearby area, don't overlook it. Chances are good that your mount has spotted game. The author has taken a number of deer this way.

treme physical exertion at the higher elevations.

Incidentally, this same elevation exertion also applies to horses. A couple years back I knew a young 18-year-old fellow who brought his own expensive, papered horse from sea-level Seattle up to the mountains on a hunt. He then proceeded to use his horse hard in the Absoraka-Beartooth wilderness area of Montana during very cold weather. Though that horse was in excellent health, it wasn't conditioned to the extreme elevation.That horse dropped dead under his young rider.

The feeling that horses are insensate beasts is a hard one to understand by those of us who have been around horses for many years. Few animals are more sensitive to their surroundings than the horse. For thousands of years they have been preyed upon by carnivores. Only awareness of their surroundings and fleetness of foot have allowed them to survive. Their sensitivity can be a great boon to the hunter if only he will allow himself the sensitivity to "pick up" on his mount's reactions and behavior. For example, horses will of-

ten spot your game for you. When riding, or even when walking while leading the horse, the hunter should pay attention to the horse's ears. If the horse spots or hears anything unusual, his ears will point, and his attention will be focused, in that direction. This is of great help in forested areas where a game animal's natural camouflage often hides it from the untrained human eye.

In less experienced days, I did not understand my horse's reactions. Many times I would be riding down a trail and my horse would suddenly perk up and stare at something to the right or left. I would just pull his head around until pointed straight ahead and think, "I wish this dumb horse would just watch the trail and quit seeing spooks in the trees." Then, as time went by, and my experience grew, I realized that it was *I* who was dumb, not the horse. Quite often that "spook" would prove to be a deer. I now pay strict attention to wherever my horse focuses his attention. Sometimes it is nothing. More often than not, however, I'll get a glimpse at a deer or two.

A horse is also amazingly sensitive

to the emotions of his rider. How often have you heard that if you are afraid of a horse he will know it? As a former dude wrangler, I know this is true. We often took inexperienced people (whose fear was obvious) out on horseback rides. Their nervousness was immediately transmitted to their mount, and the horse would then begin to fidget and show signs of uneasiness.

If a horse can sense fear, it stands to reason that he can also sense other emotions such as anger, impatience, frustration, or even happiness. In very subtle ways a horse's behavior will reflect his rider's feelings. If the rider is ill at ease, the horse will be also, and if the rider feels all is right with the world, then often the horse will too. The trouble is that because the horse *is* a sensitive animal, and his reactions are very subtle, the human rider often misses them completely.

Another problem is that outfitter's horses are ridden by dozens of people in a single season. Those riders can range from seasoned horsemen to totally inept dudes. As a result, those horses tend to develop a callousness that "tunes out" the rider. They know their job and go about it with little regard to the person on their back, especially if that person is a novice. This has given rise to the legend of the "plug" horse: the type of horse that travels head-to-tail with the guide's horse and cannot be coerced into following a divergent course. That, my friends, is *bunk*. The truth is those horses are gentle souls that have resigned themselves to their fate. They want to "get along" with a minimum of fuss. I have often seen an inexperienced hunter/horseman dismount from a *good, solid* horse and complain about what a "plug" he is. That man will always eat crow when a more experienced rider mounts that same horse and proceeds to do whatever job is at hand.

Television and movies have done much to enhance the romanticism surrounding horses, but they have also done the horse a few grave injustices. One such injustice is showing riders traveling vast distances at a full gallop. *Horses get tired and short of breath just like people do.* For all their strength and stamina, they too need to stop once in a while and catch their breath. I have seen people push a horse without a breather, in the type of steep terrain that they themselves would not even consider navigating afoot.

When a horse is packing me plus

(Right) In these deep woods elk camps, the sight of horses and mules is an everyday affair. It can be said that some of this nation's best big game country is accessible *only* with the help of horses.

(Below) The author has a deal going with his hunting horses. He will walk downhill, if they will carry him up! The author's deal is indeed a good one. Too many once-a-year hunters work their animals excessively, and at unfamiliar altitudes. (Editor's Note: When I was living in Cedar City, Utah, I once heard a veterinarian state that too many horses died of heart attacks in mountainous country, because they were simply pushed too hard by their owners. That vet was specifically referring to hunters who brought their animals in from other western locations where the altitude was thousands of feet lower than the Cedar City area. Working their often out-of-condition horses at a 7,000-9,000-foot altitude was cruel at the least — a death sentence at worst. Treat your horse with respect, not cruelty.)

my saddle, rifle, camera, lunch and other hunting gear, he is packing quite a load. Since I would never be able to get myself, and my gear, as far up in the mountains as he can carry me, I make a unilateral treaty with any horse performing that chore. In return for packing me and my gear around the mountains, I give a horse *frequent* breathers. I dismount occasionally and loosen the cinch, or once we have crested a hill and begun the descent, I will often dismount and walk rather than ride down.

A few years back in a nationally known monthly hunting magazine, there was an article on how to get along with your outfitter's horses while hunting. The author was obviously a dude. He said that since your horse was going to be undergoing such physical hardship you should let him eat at every opportunity. I'll bet hundreds of guides shed tears on those magazine pages.

I made the point earlier that horses are sensitive animals. However, that does not mean they are above taking advantage of a good thing. If you teach a horse he can have his head down in the grass at every opportunity, you will soon have a horse that is more interested in grazing than in traveling. No outfitter or guide likes to look back and see his hunter 100 yards behind, with his horse fully stopped and eating. The horse gets spoiled and becomes a problem. If the hunter and guide are stopped, say, for a rest or lunch, then perhaps the guide might let the horses eat a bit. If you're on a guided hunt, and feel you want to feed the animal you're riding, *ask the guide first*. Other than that, keep the horse's head high and keep up with the guide.

Shooting from Horseback

Another fallacy promoted by Hollywood has been the horse's insensitivity to gun fire. You've seen the movies that show people shooting firearms near horses and/or while on horseback. I have been asked many times if I have ever fired a gun from a horse's back. In truth I have, just to see what would happen, but also in truth I must admit that such doings are merely stunts. There is no instance I can think of, short of a life-and-death emergency that justifies shooting from horseback. Like most animals, horses have extremely sensitive ears and discharging a firearm in close proximity to their heads will cause them much discomfort. It can also cause you to be left afoot! I know from experience.

In 1982 I was hunting from a horse named Ben in the mountains of south-central Montana. We spotted a mule deer buck watching us from about 100 yards. I dismounted, pulled my 50-caliber Sharps from the scabbard, and wrapped the reins around my wrist. At the shot, the deer dropped in his tracks, and the horse merely tossed his head slightly. That time I was lucky and didn't even realize it.

The very next year, almost in the same spot, I ran across another mule deer buck, dismounted and again wrapped the reins around my wrist. This time the horse was named Buck, and the rifle was a 40-caliber Sharps. At the sound of the shot the deer bounded away unhurt, and Buck pulled loose and took off at a dead run. I had a l-o-n-g walk home, mostly uphill, and a lot of time think about shooting around horses that are not firmly tied up.

Carrying Rifles on Horseback

At first thought, the actual carrying of a hunting rifle on horseback sounds like a simple proposition. You merely put it in a scabbard and let the horse tote it. With experience one learns that carrying guns on horses is not quite that simple. Every year, in my hunting area at least, a few rifles are lost in the woods because they slipped from improperly arranged or ill-fitting saddle scabbards.

Basically there are only four ways to affix a saddle scabbard to a saddle. Those are: **1)** butt forward/left side; **2)** butt rearward/left side; **3)** butt forward/right side; **4)** butt rearward/right side.

There are a few other minor factors to consider, however. One is the bolt knob on a bolt-action rifle. Keep it to the outside away from the horse. For instance, a right-handed shooter should put the rifle on the right side of the horse, the top of the receiver facing *away* from the rid-

(Above) The author feels that the best way to mount a saddle scabbard is butt forward and pointing upwards. Your chances of losing a valuable rifle in steep, mountainous country is minimized. (Left-handers would position the scabbard in the same fashion, but on the left side of the saddle.)

This is an ideal saddle scabbard for a scope-sighted, bolt-action rifle. Note the slot for the bolt handle, and the button flap to secure the rifle. Also note the upward angle of the butt. (Some people prefer to mount the rifle right side up so the rifle's weight will not be bearing on the scope.)

er. A left-handed shooter should simply reverse the procedure. This keeps the rifle's bolt knob from pressing into (and irritating) the horse's side.

Some hunters prefer to scabbard a scope-sighted rifle rightside up so that the entire weight of the rifle is not pressing on the scope. Though I have no argument with that arrangement, I've never had a properly installed quality scope/mount setup get knocked out of alignment as a result of the rifle being carried, if you will, in the "scope-down" position.

Personally, I feel the butt-to-the-rear-of-the-saddle position for scabbard carry is out if you're hunting in steep terrain. Why? That's the way most rifles are lost during hunting season. Try to imagine it this way: You are coming back to camp after a long, cold day of hunting. It's dark, or nearly so, and you are riding up and down the mountainous terrain. If you are the last man in line, and your saddle scabbard butt is to the rear, who'll notice if your rifle slips out while you're traversing a steep grade? On the other hand if the butt is forward and you are going down a grade, you will likely see the rifle slip-

ping forward. If it's dark and you can't see your rifle, you may at least hear it fall or perhaps even hear the horse step on it—a miserable situation, to be sure, but better than losing a valuable firearm. It's also a good idea to arrange the scabbard in such a manner that the butt is angled *upwards* instead of riding parrallel to the ground. This will help keep it from slipping out in steep country.

Additionally, be sure to purchase a scabbard that *snuggly* fits your rifle. Scabbards meant for scope- or iron-sighted rifles are *not* interchangeable. The iron-sighted rifle will be loose in a scope-sighted rifle scabbard and, as a result, be more likely to fall out. Many saddle scabbards have a snap button or latch that goes around the bolt of a bolt-action rifle which are even more secure.

I often hunt with an iron-sighted Sharps or antique Winchester. Both are relatively slender and fit more comfortably under the leg than the wider, box-magazine bolt guns. Scabbards made for iron-sighted lever-actions or single shots almost never have a securing latch to keep the rifle in; but if the scabbard *is tight* the gun *won't* slip.

Here's another piece of advice: Never carry a rifle (while hunting on horseback) with the sling over your shoulder or neck. Yes, I have done this many times and am completely familiar with the problems. One is that it is extremely uncomfortable. Another is that the scope will often take a severe beating.

does take a tumble, you'll still have your rifle.

Lastly I would like to caution anyone against carrying a rifle on horseback with a round in the chamber. That is extremely dangerous due to potential falls or other rough treatment your rifle is likely to get. Almost all outfitters and guides will allow a hunter to load his magazine—but they will be insistent about leaving the chamber empty.

Yes, carrying guns on horses will be a bit rough on the ordnance. They will scratch and show signs of wear more

(Left) The author feels that this is the worst possible way to carry a rifle on horseback. Why? The scope takes a beating, the hunter takes a beating and the muzzle, should it intercept an overhead tree limb, will serve to dismount the rider. Very dangerous.

(Below) Although you often see saddle scabbards mounted with the rifle butt to the rear of the saddle, the author feels this is a poor way to carry a rifle, especially in mountainous country. Note how the butt of the rifle is literally slipping from the scabbard. Also note the "parallel" position of the scabbard to the ground—that only enhances your chances of losing a valuable rifle.

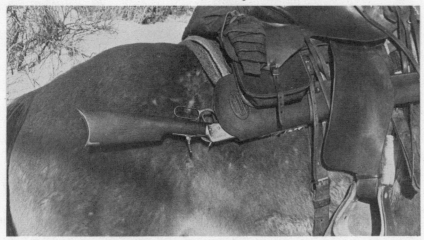

Thirdly, the rifle barrel will be projecting above the rider's head and will forever be snagging on tree limbs. In younger years I was once nearly pulled off a horse because a front sight hung up on a tree limb I tried to pass under.

One thing that hunters must keep in mind while hunting on horseback in snow country is that horses often do fall. Each year many rifles are damaged as a result of horses losing their footing and falling. If you use a rifle you value greatly, consider dismounting your steed and carrying that rifle over very steep or slippery terrain. If your horse

quickly than if the hunter only used them afoot. In an effort to minimize wear and scratches, some hunters buy "coverall" scabbards. However, as a rule, outfitters don't like using them as they are just too slow when it comes to getting the guns into action. Some wear and exposure is merely part of the game in carrying guns on horses. If minor firearms maintainance is performed regularly, no damage will result, and to my eye the honest wear a rifle accumulates is attractive. It's part of the horseback experience. An experience I'm not ready to part with!

Noisy?

Many people say that horses make so much noise traveling through wooded areas that the chances of seeing game are slim. There is some truth in that because horses can be awfully noisy. However, the remedy is in *how* one hunts from horseback. For instance, if you pick a hillside you think game is hidden on, and push up that hillside on horseback, you will probably push the game out ahead of you. On the other hand, if you know the country, you can circle around and come up the backside of the same hill and down on the game from above. That kind of maneuvering is possible with the added mobility of a horse. Since my wife hunts with me, we have worked out a system: Once we reach a ridgetop, I dismount and begin easing down the wooded slope on foot. She gives me a 10- or 15-minute head start and then begins bringing the horses down. This allows me to hunt the downslope quietly without having to walk back for the horse.

There Are Distinct Advantages. . .

Game animals are often *less spooked* by a hunter on horseback than a hunter on foot. Riders can often approach to within shooting distance of either elk or deer without disturbing them. I do not know why this is, but having done it *many* times I do know it is true. Just this past hunting season I was able to ride to within 20 feet of a small group of does without them running off.

On those occasions when you are horseback hunting, remember that your steed's quick mobility, as an asset, greatly outranks his noisiness as a liability. In 1982 I was hunting on horseback with outfitter Warren Johnson and C. Sharps Arms President, John Schoffstall. We spotted several six-point bull elk making their way up a ravine about 300 to 400 yards away. We only had a few moments to "cut 'em off at the pass" or they would be lost. Warren led us on as quick a horseback trip as I have ever experienced over broken, boulder strewn, sagebrush, and snow-covered ground. We made it to a vantage point, above the elk just in time for me to kill my first six-point bull. If we had not been mounted, getting a shot at one of those elk would not have been possible. As it happened, the horseback ride contributed to the excitement.

Once the shooting is done, the horse can again earn his keep. How many times have you heard, "After you

When using horses to hunt big game, the author and his wife have worked out a hunting system that has put whitetails and mulies in the freezer. The author dismounts on top of a hill, and proceeds to hunt the hill *down*, his wife waiting a predetermined amount of time before joining her husband.

shoot something, the real work starts!" That's true; but with the aid of horses the chore of retrieving dead game animals is much easier.

With the aid of a rope a horse can drag a deer over snow covered ground with very little effort. An elk is more difficult, but still easy for a horse in good shape. I once killed a mule deer well down the side of a mountain. To have dragged the deer uphill by hand to the nearest logging road would have taken many hours. With the horse doing the dragging, the mulie was in the pickup in 30 minutes.

There Are Dangers

As much as I enjoy hunting with horses, there are some dangers to beware of, especially if your hunting area is crowded. As sad as it may sound, every year horses are killed because they are mistaken for elk or deer. Believe it or not, that tragedy sometimes takes place with the rider on his horse's back. But more often than not it happens when the horse is tied to a tree in the woods and left alone while the hunter is off hunting on foot. For that reason my wife has made large panels for our horses out of blaze-orange fabric. When we ride, the panels are tied behind the saddle. If we dismount and tether our horses, we drape them over the saddles.

Without the aid of a horse, the author would have never bagged this nice bull elk. His mount got him back in among the bulls — something that would have been next to impossible had he been afoot.

The author's wife suggested the following "horse-safety" technique to the author some time ago. Resistant at first, Venturino now believes his wife's thinking to be rock-solid sound. Her idea was simple — tie swatches or panels of blaze-orange cloth to the pommel, letting the cloth hang down, draping the animal's shoulders. Why? Unfortunately, too many horses (some complete with rider) are shot by hunters who think they've stumbled onto an elk-trophy of a lifetime. It's not a laughing matter. Horse safety *means* hunter safety.

Standard stirrups almost caused a serious mishap when the author's wife couldn't get her heavy pack-type hunting boot dislodged from her stirrup. The solution was to have proper stirrups made up to accommodate winter footwear.

I was once walking and leading my favorite buckskin horse just before daylight in elk country. About 75 yards away two elk jumped from their beds and ran. Several other hunters began shooting at them before legal light. I looked at my buckskin and thought, "In this light he looks just like an elk!" Therefore, I took cover in some trees until full light. As a result of that experience I am now careful about getting out in the game fields during hours of darkness.

There is also another danger — the horses themselves. They *can* lose their footing. Hunters have often had their rifles badly damaged because a horse slipped and rolled over. Sometimes, under those circumstances, hunters themselves get hurt. It is a risk one takes when astride a 1,000-pound-plus animal.

While we were hunting, last year, a horse started to lay down with my wife on its back. Being an experienced horsewoman, my wife tried to quickly dismount, but her hunting boots were too large for the stirrups — her foot stuck. We were lucky. No damage to gear or rider took place. But, a lesson was learned. My wife had a saddle-maker build a set of covered stirrups similar to those used by the old-time cavalry. Now her foot can only be inserted so far, and is easy to remove.

Many years ago, when I was a youngster, a grown-up asked what my interests were. I can still remember replying, "Guns and horses!" As an adult I have not changed much; and I consider myself lucky to live in an area where I can pursue those interests in the out of doors. Hunting with horses, to my way of thinking, is the icing on the cake. •

the Dangerous Game HUNTING LION

by JACK LOTT

When it comes to hunting lions, you either do it right or they hunt you. It's a sport that has few second-place winners.

LION HUNTING, to some armchair enthusiasts, is highly symbolic. A result, no doubt, of the vicarious thrills experienced in the better-written hunting tales and the nerveless screen performances of dashing movie-star hunters. That's the fantasy. The reality is that lion hunting originated when some ancient primate first fought a cave lion over ownership of some game animal—the odds favoring the latter hunter. Lion hunting is a *deadly serious activity* which has cost the lives and limbs of more human hunters than the hunting of any other African species. It is an axiom that, sooner or later, those who seek the skin of the lion must eventually do so on the lion's terms—thereby not infrequently becoming a casualty.

According to D.G. Elliott, the American zoologist, the lion disappeared from Europe between 340 BC and 100 AD—a mere moment in the geological time scale. Today's paleontologists regard the lion as having been the most widely distributed of all large mammals, as recently as 10,000 years ago, with fossil specimens of the prehistoric American lion (*Panthera leo Atrox*) abounding as far south as Peru. The rich skeletal deposits of the La Brea Tar Pits of Los Angeles, California, include abundant lion fossils, thereby proving that today's would-be U.S. lion hunters were born some 10,000 years too late to save the high costs of air fares and overseas charges spent to hunt African lions!

In ancient times, the Greeks, Romans, Egyptians, Hebrews, Persians, Assyrians and others were familiar with the lion as a hunting trophy as well as a symbol of courage, strength and nobility. To Roman emperors and their subject spectators in Rome's Coliseum, the "contests" between the emperor's hungry lions and gladiators (or helpless Christians) were a national pastime. The Egyptian Pharaoh Amenhotep III, who lived from 1406 BC to 1370 BC, was a great lion hunter who killed 102 of the beasts, according to the hieroglyphics on a stone "scarabaeus" now in the British Museum. King Assurbanipal of As-

George Michael of South Africa has just fired his 10.75 x 68mm Mauser through this charging Botswana lioness that is in the act of charging the photographer. (Note the stones and dirt thrown up by the exiting bullet and the dropping head of the still-charging lioness.

syria had his scribes record the following in stone: *"I am Assurbanipal, the King of the World, the King of Assyria! For my regal amusement I have caught the Desert King by his tail, and on the instructions of my helpers, the Gods Ninib and Nergal, I have split his head with the two-handed sword."*

Historically, the lion has been used internationally as a symbol of royalty. In imperial Ethiopia the Emperor Haile Sellasie, was called the "Conquering Lion of Judah." In England, Richard the Lion-Hearted was another monarch whose courage and power were symbolized by the King of Beasts. Almost anyone understands what is meant by saying; "He fought like a lion;" or "He has the courage of a lion." "The lion's share" means the victor's share, and the names "Leo" or "Leon" mean exactly what they sound like—*lion.*

In Asia, with the exception of a limited number of Indian lions in a preserve in the state of Kathiawar, where they survive in the forests of the Gir Peninsula, the lion is extinct.

In the 19th century lions were widely distributed in the drier parts of India, and during the Indian Mutiny (1856-1858) English Col. Acland Smith killed some 300!

Today the lion survives in huntable numbers over widely spaced African territories wherever his preferred open and semi-open habitat and prey animals exist under the protection and management of enlightened game departments. Naturally, the lion's ancient status, as perhaps the most challenging and formidable hunting trophy, has been much enhanced in proportion to his reduced availability—the costs reflect this. The awareness that the lion can make a trophy out of *you* provides that extra piquance to the chase. This is not, I assure you, mere hype generated by the "heroes" of the typewriter. The records of game departments and the police of many African countries are replete with bloody accounts of man-killing by lions who settled scores with their human hunters.

"Man-eating" has always been en-

demic in certain parts of Africa, and during my almost-annual hunting trips to South Africa—the most developed African nation—not a year passes without several cases of man-eating, especially in the northeastern Transvaal along the borders of the vast Kruger National Park. Today, most victims are illegal aliens crossing through the park from Marxist Mozambique; but not long ago, two young girls were eaten by a lion near a village on the western borders of the park. Fantasy? It's *fact*. My friend, Dr. Roy Bengis, the park's chief biologist, performed an autopsy on the lion and retrieved bits of clothing and the undigested skin of the palms of the hands and soles of the feet of the two children. The fame (or infamy) of Kenya's turn-of-the-century man-eaters of Tsavo, remains the most sensational case of lion man-eating. A single pair of lions literally created a reign of terror, in 1898, lasting 9 months. The victims were 28 Indian "coolies"—laborers, dozens of blacks and an injured European—all working on

Leonard Eustace Vaughan with a Zambian buffalo-killing lion which weighed well-over 500 lbs. (Note the buffalo's partially-eaten carcass.)

the Uganda Railway's bridge over the Tsavo River between Nairobi and the Indian Ocean. The lions were finally killed after great difficulty, by Col. J.H. Patterson, the English engineer in charge.

Although the lion's original African range is considerably reduced from what it was in the 19th century, when it extended from the Mediterranean littoral (Morocco, Algeria and Tunisia) to the Cape province of South Africa, in recent years its South African range has increased slightly in areas of former habitat, long devoid of those animals. Now lions can be found in Zululand and parts of Natal in bushveld bordering game reserves and in Cape Province adjacent to the Botswana border and the Kalahari Gemsbok National Park. In South-West Africa lions survive in the huge Etosha National Park and occasionally on bordering areas outside the park, as well as in Kaokoland and parts of Damaraland. But in the cattle and sheep-raising areas of the South-West, an intruding lion is soon dispatched by farmer's bullets.

Kenya, once the classical lion-hunting land, is closed to hunting; but Tanzania offers some of the best lion hunting in Africa, as does Zambia and Botswana—the latter the home of the fierce and spectacular Kalahari black-maned lions. Tragically, Uganda is no longer a place to hunt. It's a result of decades of savage waves of mass-slaughter of both human and game species. Zaire has a large lion population, and despite conflicting re-

George Michael of South Africa with a Kalahari lion whose charge was stopped just in time with a 347-grain soft-nosed bullet from Michael's 10.75 x 68mm Mauser. (Note the one hole through the nose and the exit wound in left cheek.)

ports of available hunting, that country may be able to offer limited lion hunting in the eastern districts. Angola's once-fine lion hunting is closed due to civil war. Zimbabwe still has huntable lion populations in the Zambesi Valley, Matetsi and areas adjoining the Gona-re-Zho game reserve in the southeast. Mozambique, like Angola, once a great lion-hunting area, is off-limits for hunters because most of the bush is in the control of anti-Marxist guerrillas. In West Africa, lions are still hunted in the Central African Republic's savannah and that of the Cameroons. But the preferred lion-hunting areas for the overseas sportsman are Zambia and Botswana.

The lion is not a "jungle" species,

though it is sometimes found in pockets of grassland throughout the Congo Basin rain forests. It is essentially, a plains, desert and bushveld predator—a sight hunter, whose habitat is the same as that of his prey (the antelopes, zebra, pigs and buffalo). Mature lions weigh but one-fourth the weight of an adult bull buffalo, however, many become confirmed "buffalo-hunting lions" after a period of "studies" in perfecting the technique (during which many such "students" are killed by their intended victims). During my early hunting days in Mozambique, one located lions simply by finding a buffalo herd. There were always lions about which could then be baited with a buffalo carcass.

The Guns and the Danger

Lions have relatively light bone structures but massive shoulders, chests and leg muscles. Their paws, claws and jaws, as actuated by those powerful muscles (and added to a lion's considerable bulk), are terrible weapons designed for the taking of the largest prey animals. These weapons, combined with great attacking speed and agility, are basic reasons

mortal combat. A charge must be expected. Under these conditions a double's two quick shots are as much as one can give—and about as much as the lion can normally take. Remember: A lion can charge 50 yards in just over *2 seconds!* Because of this, and the lion's tremendous momentum and ability to do so much damage in a few seconds, most experienced British hunters of the early part of the century preferred a heavy "Paradox" 10-

armament has saved the lives of numerous lion hunters. Standing shots at a charging lion often result in the beast running "under the shot" as the angle changes the closer the lion gets to the hunter. This is why some professionals prefer to squat or sit, thereby delivering a parallel shot that fully rakes the charging lion. This technique, however, requires exceptional *sang froid* and precludes a quick last-minute sideways "jink" or

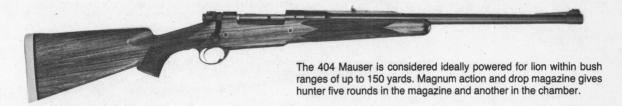

The 404 Mauser is considered ideally powered for lion within bush ranges of up to 150 yards. Magnum action and drop magazine gives hunter five rounds in the magazine and another in the chamber.

Royal Hammerless Ejector "Paradox" Ball & Shot Gun

Made in 12, 16 and 20 bore. With straight hand or half-pistol grip stock.

The "Paradox" has long been recognised as the most perfect form of Ball and Shot gun extant. To those sportsmen not already familiar with the weapon, we might mention that the results are achieved by rifling a short length of the muzzle, the rest of the barrel being smooth bored.

The weight of a 12-bore "Paradox" (chambered for the 2½ inch 65 m m cartridge) is about 7¼ lbs. and it handles and balances well.

We need hardly point out to practical sportsmen the great advantages of a weapon which shoots shot as well as a good cylinder gun, and conical ball with smokeless powder with the accuracy of an Express Rifle at short ranges.

SMOKELESS PARADOX

12 bore Cartridge with "Paradox" bullet, full size.

The famous Holland & Holland "Paradox" gun as widely favored for lion, tiger and leopard. It was available in 12-bore and 10-bore during the early part of the century. The conical 12-bore "Paradox" slug weighs 750 grains.

dodge. Lions have small brains, and like all cats they have no forehead. As a result, brain shots at a charging lion must be taken through the animal's mouth or nose, at the last few yards—say 5—of the charge. This shot is only taken as a last resort, since head shots invariably ruin the trophy. The trick is to hold one's fire for the last shot until the lion is within 10 paces. An ounce-and-a-quarter of buckshot from a 12-bore produces instantaneous stopping and is considered the professional's top choice for wounded lions, tigers and leopards. I recall an intrepid Englishman who hunted in Tanganyika, and whose specialty was to hunt the grasslands alone, locate a lion and "walk him up" until the provoked lion charged. That hunter would calmly let the charging lion close to within 10 paces before blasting it in the face with his 12-bore double.

There is but a small chance that an overseas sportsman will have to stop a lion charge, since that is the work of the guide. But guides can miss or be in the wrong place, and then the client must assume his own self-defense duties—perhaps to save the guide, a black tracker or himself. It seems obvious that if one is not prepared psychologically and armed appropriately to do the above should the need arise, then one should be hunting lesser game. Lion-hunting, with the danger excluded, is not "hunting"—it's mere-

for the lion hunter to use powerful rifles. For an adult lion or lioness—the former weighing up to more than 500 pounds, the latter up to 350 pounds—the absolute *minimum* caliber should be the 375 H&H Magnum, using a 300-grain expanding bullet. That is for an *unwounded* lion, but once wounded, a larger caliber, heavier bullet performs better, especially at the closer ranges where charges are launched in cover. This means that a better minimum would be a 404, a 416 or, in a double, a 450/400. Tops for a wounded lion or one in bushveld is a double rifle of 470, 450, 465 caliber, or better, a 500.

Once a lion is wounded, you are no longer "hunting"—you're engaged in

bore using a conical lead slug of 875-grains at 1,550 fps for a total 4,660 fp of energy. Some of the old hunters considered the "minimum" to be a 12-bore "Paradox" using a similar 750-grain conical slug. (Either of the above guns were considered superior to any double nitro-express.) Such projectiles always delivered their full energy to the beast, the lead bullets *never* breaking up.

In the event that one is seized by a charging lion, a fighting knife and a 4-inch 357 S&W Magnum loaded with metal-piercing bullets may provide one with a last-minute lifesaver when all else fails—providing one can reach the weapon and use it effectively. This may sound melodramatic, but lesser

The author's 350 Rigby Magnum Mauser is the same as those that were used by Southern Rhodesia's Department of Zoology (Game Department) in the '20s and '30s for lion and other thin-skinned game control.

The Winchester Model 95 in 405 W.C.F. caliber was "Teddy" Roosevelt's "lion medicine" rifle with which he killed a number of lions in East Africa on his 1909 expedition.

Author's 375 Holland & Holland Mauser Modele de Luxe. The 375 H&H Magnum round is author's absolute minimum choice for lion when unwounded and with scope mounted. The 375 is also the legal minimum caliber for lion and other dangerous game in many African nations.

Custom 458 Lott caliber pre-64 Winchester Model 70 by David Miller & Co. of Tucson, Arizona. Rifle takes 458 Win. Mag. and long 458 Lott Mag. in same chamber. Ideal for lion in bush country and for stopping charges.

ly shooting.

In addition to pointing out the need for powerful rifles of large caliber, I must also point out that lions have tremendous vitality. Like great bears, charging lions often drop to marginal shots, but then resume the attack, seemingly charged with extra energy, for a fight to the death. It is then that the "fun" begins! It is also then that the rifle and load with which one has begun the proceedings (our vaunted super-hot magnum) is suddenly very inadequate! This is not simply due to the lion's adrenalin, but the fact that instead of thin rib cage tissue and light rib bones, one now faces massive chest muscles, neck muscles, shoulder muscles, shoulder bones, facial bones, jaws and sloping frontal skull bones. Even the great 375 H&H Magnum, which I mentioned as an "absolute minimum" is, in my opinion, really *too light* for such work.

The fact that so many overseas lion-hunting clients avoid becoming casualties during charges is a tribute to the guide's skill, courage and armament, and also often to the prompt action of a brave African gun-bearer or tracker. This fact naturally diminishes the sportsman's share of credit for

the outcome, but then, nobody should be faulted for seeking a lion trophy minus death or mutilation at the jaws and claws of the "trophy!" The late Joe Shaw, a San Francisco civil engineer became such a "trophy" in 1963 when an Angola lion took exception to Shaw's too-close approach to his hiding place. Shaw ignored his guide's (Cornelis Prinsloo) warnings and tried to force the lion out so that he could shoot him with his ultra-high velocity 30-caliber magnum. Shaw's magnum meant nothing to the lion, who had not read the ads. That lion charged out, tore Shaw's arm off and inflicted fatal wounds in seconds before the guide and a gunbearer killed it with shots from a 375 and a 12-bore!

A dramatic illustration of a charging lion's appalling power when in full-charge occurred in Botswana to an American cinematographer on safari with a guide and two friends who were armed with two 375 Magnums and a 458. The idea was for the three armed men to find and provoke a lion to charge so that it could be filmed. Following the tracks of a big male for 3 or 4 hours, they found him under a tree watching their approach. The "irrationale" was that a phalanx of three

riflemen armed with such potent artillery would prevent any charging, wounded lion from reaching the unarmed photographer. One hunter fired at the lion to only slightly wound him. Being a good shot, he succeeded and the lion made off into thick bush. The "heroes" followed the blood-spoor for some 150 yards after being admonished by the guide that the lion was now very angry and very dangerous. The guide ordered the party to stop when he heard a growl of warning (the lion is a gentleman) from a patch of thick bush. At this the lion charged, the cameraman worked his cine-camera, and the three riflemen poured a volley of powerful bullets into the enraged animal, which came on relentlessly as if unscathed. The cameraman, noting that his viewfinder had filled up with lion's hair, looked up just as the lion shattered the "phalanx" of riflemen like so many nine pins. The lion grabbed the cameraman from behind as the man was attempting a fast retreat. Nobody could shoot while the lion was clawing and biting the man's back, but as the cameraman rotated his body and the lion turned his attention to the man's face, the cameraman grabbed the lion's

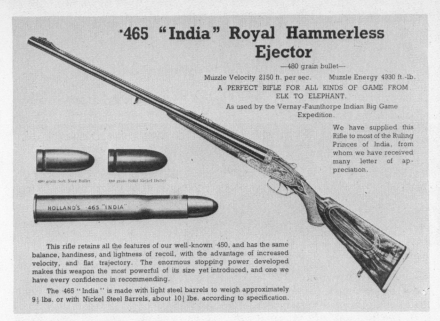

·465 "India" Royal Hammerless Ejector

—480 grain bullet—

Muzzle Velocity 2150 ft. per sec.   Muzzle Energy 4930 ft.-lb.

A PERFECT RIFLE FOR ALL KINDS OF GAME FROM ELK TO ELEPHANT.

As used by the Vernay-Faunthorpe Indian Big Game Expedition.

We have supplied this Rifle to most of the Ruling Princes of India, from whom we have received many letter of appreciation.

480 grain Soft Nose Bullet   480 grain, Solid Nickel Bullet

HOLLAND'S ·465 "INDIA"

This rifle retains all the features of our well-known ·450, and has the same balance, handiness, and lightness of recoil, with the advantage of increased velocity, and flat trajectory. The enormous stopping power developed makes this weapon the most powerful of its size yet introduced, and one we have every confidence in recommending.

The ·465 "India" is made with light steel barrels to weigh approximately 9¼ lbs. or with Nickel Steel Barrels, about 10¼ lbs. according to specification.

Selous was one of Africa's greatest lion hunters and the greatest of all the hunter-naturalists.

(Above) The Holland 465 double ejector is among the traditional favorites for hunting and stopping lions, especially in cover.

MODEL NO. 4
.350 Magnum

Price in London...£36/15/0
Price in U.S.A....$300.00

Weight of Bullet........225 Grs.
M. Velocity ......2600 Ft. Sec.
M. Energy ......3400 Ft. Lbs.

Bore—.350-inch.   Stock—Pistol Hand, Sporting.
Length of Barrel—24 inches.   Weight—8¼ pounds.
Sighting—Standard sight, 100 yards, and Folding Leaves, 200, 300 yards.
Foresight Ivory Tipped Bead.   Spare Foresight supplied.

The Improved Model of the already well-known .350-inch bore is the ideal all-around magazine sporting rifle. The cartridge is a powerful one with very flat trajectory and great striking energy and this action has been designed for it.

(Right) John Rigby's 350 Rigby Mag. was considered ideal for unwounded lions, and an early rival to Holland's 375 Mag. which finally swept all other medium-bore competition from the field.

tongue. The lion then grabbed the cameraman's leg and the cameraman (a powerful man) kicked the lion off his body. Undaunted, the lion turned his attention to, and attacked, one of the riflemen. He was biting the rifleman's hand when the guide blew the brave beast's brains out. A chartered plane took the cameraman to a hospital in Rhodesia, where a month's plastic surgery restored him to a semblance of normalcy.

Frank W. Lane wrote: "When a lion launches a short explosive charge, there takes place in his body a physical change, more akin to an explosion than a bodily function. The large adrenal glands pour their crisis-energy-producing secretion into the blood and cause a greater discharge of the vitalizing sugar from the liver to enrich the blood stream. The result of these chemical changes is that the lion's brain, heart, lungs and nerves are slammed into top gear, and its immense physical strength is concentrated into a violent outburst of energy which is expended in a few seconds . . . Once the charging mechanism has been activated and the vital organs have been energized, nothing short of the most violent action can stop a lion.

Even with its heart destroyed by a bullet, a lion may continue to charge!"

The Great Lion Hunters

Who were the greatest lion hunters among the whites of Africa? (I limit the context to them because I have no way of obtaining the records of the many native Africans and Asians who single-handedly killed lions throughout the centuries with swords, spears and bows and arrows.) According to the late Col. Stevenson-Hamilton, himself the victor of some 200 lion hunts during his long tenure as first warden of the vast Kruger National Park of South Africa, it was Californian Leslie Simson with a record of some 300. This is corroborated by Kenya's first game warden, A. Blayney Percival. Such bags were of course made in the "Golden Years" of African hunting—the first 3 decades of this century. The famed guide, Leslie J. Tarlton who, with his partner R.J. Cunninghame, guided Teddy Roosevelt's 1909 East African expedition, had a client in 1927 (a 70-year-old millionaire) who bagged 20 lions in 3 months! Those same guides had another client who bagged 26 in 3 weeks. "All quite honorably shot in

the open in broad daylight, but such a record would be impossible without the cars."

The Tactics of Lion Hunting

What methods are used in taking lions? Baiting lions with dead game is the most popular and generally effective method, but is banned today in some African countries. Zebra, wildebeest, hartebeest and other large antelope suffice for baiting purposes, but experienced hunters aver that lions cannot resist buffalo or elephant carcasses. Blinds constructed from branches and grass are utilized for such shooting, once the lion settles down for a feed. (Sometimes unethical methods are employed such as focusing a vehicle's headlamps on a carcass and turning them on when the sounds of feeding are heard; the shot is then taken from the car.)

A popular method used on the open plains is to drive around looking for vultures spiraling on thermals or sitting on trees—likely signs that lions are feeding nearby.

A dishonest variation of this method is for a guide to book a "block" and to regularly feed the lions so that they, being lazy creatures, will hang

A pride of lions engages in a tug-of-war over meat from a kill in Rhodesia's (Zimbabwe's) Wankie National Park. This is not a "lethal" fight, but sometimes it escalates into one.

around until the day the overseas client arrives. One morning the guide suggests to the unsuspecting client, "Since we've nothing on for this morning, let's drive out on the plain and look for vultures." After arriving near the feeding area, vultures are often sighted, and the guide, feigning surprise says, "How lucky can you get? Look at those vultures. I bet there's a lion nearby feeding on a kill!" Sure enough, there are lions on a zebra—surprise, surprise! Our client-hero readies his shiny wonder magnum and is driven to within a safe distance for the shot. Sometimes the client, being a sporting type, gets out of the car for the shot—few such dupes ever know of the deception. A friend of mine, to his dying day never knew that his fine trophy lion was the result of such a cynical charade.

Another, even more disgusting hunting method is not infrequently used, both on lions and leopards, whereby a steel trap is placed beneath the bait suspended from a tree branch. Sometimes the trap is tied to a log, a stake or the tree, but sometimes the trap is free so the lion is slowed down and becomes insane with the rage of pain. This slows down any charge, but the added "rage" makes the hunt more exciting for certain types who specialize in such atrocities. In South-West Africa, one can be guaranteed a maned lion and even pick out the trophy prior to the hunt. It's quite simple—the lions are all caged specimens selected for size and beauty of mane. After an enormous trophy fee and high daily rate (with a minimum) is contracted for, the "hunter" arrives and his choice is released, to be hunted down with certainty and with minimal effort or risk. The hunter usually, if not invariably, gets what he pays for. I'll also

state that one such "trophy" is listed near the top in one record book in the U.S. The "winner" of that great contest between the savage lion and the manly hunter is actually quite proud of his "trophy" and makes no effort to conceal the method used to take the beast. I dislike saying such things, but for the sake of clean hunting, such atrocities must be exposed to the ethical hunter who should be the first to condemn such things.

Let's go back to the "respected" methods . . .

Calling lions with homemade calls created from gasoline cans, as developed by South American jaguar-hunters, is a sport which met with some success as introduced in Mozambique by Jose Simoes, the Portuguese professional. This produces plenty of thrills when a male lion—anticipating a date with a lady lion—closes in

and suddenly realizes he has been duped!

Spooring-up (tracking) lions is one of the most sporting ways to hunt them, especially on sandy or damp soil, as practiced in the Kalahari Desert of Botswana. It is done by using bushmen trackers. After a lion's tracks are picked up in the morning, they are generally followed until the midday heat—a time when most lions lie up under a shade tree. When pushed under such conditions, the volatile Kalahari lions are apt to charge, thereby providing more thrills (*and risk*) than most hunters seek. Spooring-up lions in bushveld on foot is even more difficult and dangerous, especially when done by a lone hunter. However, there are benefits to hunting lions, alone, as those beasts are less liable to charge a *careful,* experienced lone hunter. Usually,

Here's a closeup of a black-maned buffalo-killing Zambie lion killed by the great professional hunter, Leonard Eustace Vaughan.

An understandably proud Craig Boddington, Editor of Petersen's *Hunting* magazine, beams beside the carcass of a fine Zambian lion taken with his left-handed converted pre-64 Model 70 in 375 H&H Magnum.

hunters of the type just mentioned can approach a lion closely without being detected. The more hunters and trackers following, the more risk of noise and sighting by the quarry. Sometimes a lucky hunter will encounter a lion while hunting other game, thereby providing him with an unexpected opportunity. But lionesses, especially those with cubs, should be absolutely left alone and given a *wide berth*. One cannot always spot the cubs as they may be bedded down in thick bush or in a cave. Again, never come between lion cubs and their mother. If you do, a charge can be expected. If you ever spot a lion cub, and not the mother, the best bet is to instantly freeze in your tracks and try to determine the whereabouts of the lioness, and then back slowly away with your rifle at the ready-fire position.

Undoubtedly the use of packs of hounds is a most effective way of hunting lions, as exemplified by the late Paul Rainey, an American who hunted in East Africa in the early part of this century. Today, this method is generally illegal (and considered unsporting) unless it's used to take a man-eater or cattle-killer. Quite different is the use of fox terriers, those small but brave and most intelligent dogs, especially when a wounded lion is waiting in an unknown ambush position in thick bush. This method of lion hunting can save lives and clean up a job badly begun. I advocate the above method only when, if you will, humanitarian reasons are involved.

The late John "Pondoro" Taylor, that great professional hunter and author put it sharply in his autobiographical book, *"Pondoro":*

I cannot warn you too strongly not to think of tackling any potentially dangerous game with a small-bore rifle. Remember it's by no means always the animal at which you're firing that constitutes the danger: There may be another one there of whose existence you're unaware. Just because these small weapons are used safely and satisfactorily on the open plains where men shoot at 200 and 300 yards range doesn't mean that they can be safely used in *bushveld, where the ranges are very much closer. It's one thing to shoot a lion on a short-grass plain with a scope-sighted high-speed small-bore at 150 or 250 yards, and it's quite another to shoot at a range of 20 or 25 yards in the bushveld. Even though you kill your lion stone-dead, as you ought to be able to, what if he has a mate concealed in the grass, with you unable to see her until suddenly she comes open-mouthed at you from 20 paces? You'll very likely regret not having a man-sized weapon for a man's work—that is, if you live long enough to regret anything!!!*

To me, the lion is the most coveted trophy of all—but I do not have to hunt him, successfully or not, to enjoy his proximity. The finest moments of my African hunting came when bedded down and looking up at the African night sky with its uncountable stars, listening to a lion's roar—sometimes answered by another. Such a moment is to be treasured in one's memory always. The roar of the lion is the voice of the African wilds—of a primeval freedom. It's the echo of prehistory!

AN EASY SHOT—a large fox squirrel moving slowly through the top of an old beech, clearly visible against a pale blue autumn sky through a screen of bronze leaves and small twigs. He stops to sample a few beechnuts, his outline clearly defined. I settle the crosshairs just back of the shoulder, gently increasing pressure on the trigger. The shot comes as a *surprise,* just as the books say it should. The squirrel spins around the limb and with a single flash of a bottle-brush tail vanishes unscathed, into one of the many holes dotting the top of the venerable beech, a good 70 feet above me.

With an angry sigh I wonder how I could miss a "sucker shot" like that. The scope is a good one, the rifle a 52 Winchester loaded with ammunition that had always delivered dime-sized groups at 50 yards. Having already alarmed the woods, I take aim at a small stub near the exposed tree top— a target less than 1-inch square, clear against the sky. I squeeze off a shot. The stub is clipped short as the bullet

strikes it dead center.

The day is getting late, and I leave with the conviction that it isn't the gun or the ammunition, it has to be the person behind it who's at fault and that's that. Yet, there is still that nagging image of crosshairs centered exactly where they should be, the shot squeezed off without a pull or jerk.

This experience was repeated in farmyard encounters with starlings and grackles who waited in tops of locust trees from which they swooped to the bird feeder to rob chickadees, cardinals and nuthatches of the meal I'd laid out for them. Could a few leaves, a twig scarcely larger than a pencil lead so deflect an accurately placed 22 Long Rifle bullet as to cause it to miss a better than 1-inch square target, at a range of less than 30 yards? It seemed implausible. I had seen those promotional pictures of sectioned, ⅞-inch pine planks drilled seven layers deep by a Long Rifle slug that made a

ruler-straight hole. And there, in General Hatcher's notebook, was a photograph of a 30-06 which had bored straight through nearly a yard of oak planks.

I began looking through my gun books for information on "brush busting" and deflection with negative results. The only exception was Franklin Mann's *The Bullet's Flight,* where I found the first confirmation of my suspicion that shooting through twigs or leaves could cause missed shots. Said Mann: "It has often been stated by hunters that the contact of a flying bullet with a small twig deflects it from the game, thus accounting for a miss. Others have questioned that small twigs exert any appreciable influence towards deflecting a bullet from the line of sight." I continued to read expecting one of Dr. Mann's finely constructed experiments that would not only resolve this question, but would tell me how much, and in which direction, a hypothetical bullet might be deflected. Unfortunately, the good doctor's ruminations on twig

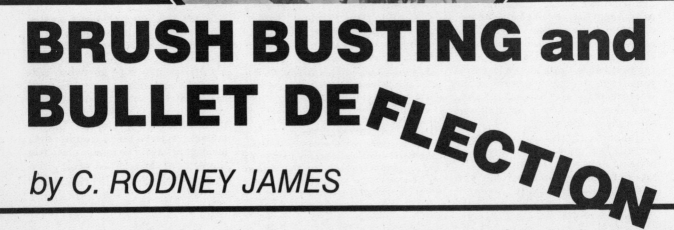

BRUSH BUSTING and BULLET DEFLECTION

by C. RODNEY JAMES

(Left) The tree branch deflection target was 20 yards from the firing point and 12 feet from the recording target.

Branches of standard dimensions were positioned so a straight portion of the branch was aligned with the vertical line on the record target. Horizontal lines were for secondary reference, since most deflection is lateral.

(Left) Milkweed and goldenrod stalks (right) and small twigs (left) readily deflected 22 Long Rifle bullets.

deflection came within the larger context of a study of "tack driving" accuracy and his experiment consisted of hitting tacks on their points and observing the behavior of these unbalanced, tack encumbered, bullets, with nary a twig in sight.

Rimfire Experiments

On a backyard range I made a recording target out of a 24x18-inch sheet of paper divided by a vertical line, crossed by horizontal lines to create a series of intersection points. In front of this I placed deflection targets of twigs and branches in a sand filled can that could be moved to align these with the vertical line on the recording target. Initial tests were carried out with a separation between the two of 6 feet. Deflections at this distance were less than 1 inch. On the assumption some of this might be the result of shooter error, the separation was doubled to 12 feet. The deflection targets were brought forward to be fired at from a distance of 20 yards with a Model 52 Winchester rifle on a sandbag rest.

Single leaves and leaf stems had no measurable effect on 22 Long Rifle match bullets, even when leaves were packed together six layers thick. Twigs, a nominal ⅛-inch thick, however, not only deflected these bullets, but caused them to "tumble" as well. Several types of wood were tested including locust, elm and mulberry. Both dead and live samples were tried. No significant difference in deflection was caused by this factor, nor did changes in variety of wood produce measurably different deflections. Green mulberry was used for all remaining tests since it was plentiful and seemed a good compromise between the fibrous elm and the brittle locust. A few weed stalks were tried from time to time yielding, to me, surprising results in tests with both rimfire and centerfire bullets. A dead ⅛-inch goldenrod stalk had a negligible effect, but a green stalk of that size caused a ³⁄₁₀-inch deflection on the record target 12 feet beyond the deflection point. A green milkweed deflected another match bullet ⁶⁄₁₀-inch, causing it to tumble.

Hitting ⅛-inch targets at 20 yards proved not too difficult with the aid of a scope, but placing shots at varying points within this space proved impossible. At length I lucked out, hitting a twig, but not cutting it. The bullet, after taking a notch out of the edge, printed a full inch out of line on the record target, the largest deflection so far. Such hits gave the first indications of the importance of bullet placement in the degree of its deflection.

In hopes of finding a particular style, weight or velocity of bullet that would prove more deflection resistant than others, I tried a variety of 22 rimfires ranging from 45-grain round and flat point 22 Winchester Automatic cartridges, at 1050 fps, which

A variety of 22 rimfires was tested to determine if bullet weight, style and velocity affected brush penetration ability. It didn't. (Left to right) Two styles of 45-grain Winchester Automatic bullets, a Stinger hyper-velocity, Yellow Jacket H.P., Viper truncated cone solid, Winchester match and high-velocity.

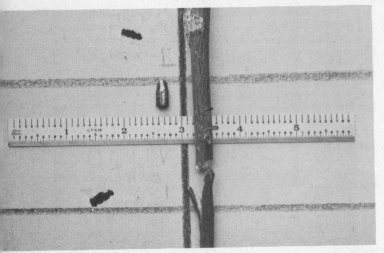

These two hits from a high-velocity 22 Long Rifle on a ¼-inch branch resulted in "tumbled" slugs.

Even the speedy C.C.I. Stinger 22 tumbled as a result of a left-of-center hit on a ¼-inch branch. (Note that the deflection is, clearly, to the left.)

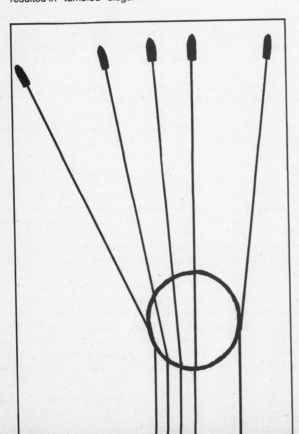

An idealized model of how bullets deflect from branches. No attempt is made here to compute actual angles of departure, but simply to illustrate the difference between center, center left, left and far left deflections. The far right strike represents a grazing shot. The degree of contact between bullet and branch on the extreme left and the extreme right, though perhaps differing a fiftieth of an inch, can produce markedly different deflections.

delivered excellent accuracy in my Model '03 Winchester; to mid-weight truncated cone solid and hollow point Long Rifles at around 1500 fps, to the CCI Stinger with its 30-grain bullets moving at close to 1700 fps. All were deflected by ⅛-inch twigs with no one bullet showing a marked superiority over any other. Minimum deflection was $^{3}/_{10}$-inch, the maximum was 1¼ inches. Most of the bullets lost stability and tumbled into the record target leaving typical keyhole entrance prints. Most of the twigs were cut by bullets striking them. Those not cut sustained hits on their edges. Such marginal hits caused a markedly greater degree of deflection—in some cases more than double that of centered hits.

A classic example of the result of an off-center hit by a 223 FMJ bullet.

Another "tipped" entry by a 223 FMJ projectile produced a large number of small holes in the target. In the author's opinion, those holes are the results of melted lead core spraying from the open base of the projectile(s).

Centerfire ammo tested for deflection include 12-gauge Brenneke and Foster slugs, four weights and styles of 45-70 bullets, two weights of 30-caliber bullets from a Krag and two styles of 223 Remington bullets (soft nose and FMJ).

High Velocity 22s

With the idea that a bullet having greater weight and higher velocity might make a significant difference, I plunged ahead with a plan to test cartridges that would bracket the main classes available in this country. This included high-velocity 22-, 30- and 45-calibers and shotgun slugs. These would be fired at what I considered brush-sized targets, which is to say branches up to about 1 inch in diameter. For the sake of consistency, I cut and selected straight branches of mulberry that were within $1/16$-inch of being $1/4$-, $1/2$- and $3/4$-inch in diameter. Twigs were trimmed and knots were avoided.

The $1/8$-inch twigs had little effect on 55-grain metal cased 223 bullets, from an AR-180 rifle, that clipped them off at speeds in excess of 3200 fps. Branches of the $1/4$-inch size, however, produced deflections of better than 1 inch at the 12-foot target. As I suspected, larger branches produced larger deflections, but here again placement of the bullet in the branch proved to have a far greater influence than mere branch size. A slightly right-of-center hit on a $3/4$-inch branch produced a $3/5$-inch lateral deflection, while a far right-of-center hit on a $1/4$-inch branch deflected the bullet $1^1/5$ inches. A far right-of-center hit on a $3/4$-inch branch deflected $3^3/5$ inches.

Soft point bullets proved no more stable than the spitzer-type FMJs. Nearly all tumbled into the record

target. One puzzling phenomenon was a peppering of sand-sized holes around the target entrance points of the metal-cased bullets. Mann noted that 30-caliber jacketed bullets which had been drilled or cut near their bases expelled particles of melted lead through these holes.[3] I can only assume that similar particles of melted lead were being centrifuged from the bases of the tumbling 223 bullets.

30 Caliber

A 30-40 Krag rifle was next tried, using two weights and styles of bullets—a 125-grain plain base at 1500 fps and a 220-grain metal case at 2000 fps. A precisely aimed (lucky) shot with the plain-based bullet struck a $1/4$-inch branch at or very close to its center and gave *no* deflection. There was only one such shot. Others averaged 1-inch deflections.

The 220-grain round-nosed jacketed bullet had a reputation for stability and there was only one instance of this bullet tipping as it struck the record target. Nevertheless, this bullet gave a maximum deflection of $1^7/_{10}$ inches on a right-of-center hit on a ½-inch branch and a $2^3/_5$-inch deflection on a left-of-center hit on a ¾-inch branch.

45 Caliber

A fair substitute for a handgun projectile is the 45-70 150-grain "collar-button" sized bullet at 1100 fps. Thus a small insight was gained in the area of handgun performance vis-a-vis deflection. Almost as wide as it is long, this bullet has most of its weight up front and for that reason looked to be a good candidate for a straight shooter. In a Sharps rifle these bullets delivered 10-shot groups of under 1 inch at 35 yards. I started with a shot at a tough weed (wild lettuce) with a ½-inch stem. A center hit drove straight through. A left-of-center hit, however, printed 1½ inches to the left of the sight line on the recording target. Quarter and half-inch branches struck slightly right of center resulted in bullet deflection of $3/_{10}$-inch and $7/_{10}$-inch respectively. A ¾-inch branch hit slightly right of center deflected $1^9/_{10}$ inches. The most significant aspect of this bullet's performance was its stability after deflecting. There was no evidence of bullet tipping or tumbling in the flight to the record target.

The 330-grain bevel-based hollow-

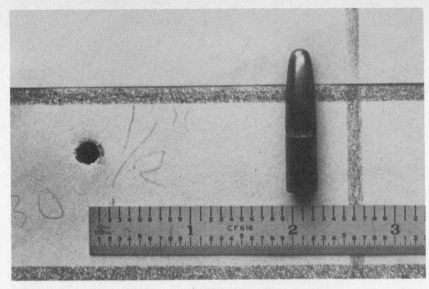

A 220 grain Krag FMJ bullet was no match for a ½-inch branch. The bullet did, however, remain stable after deflecting approximately 2.6 inches.

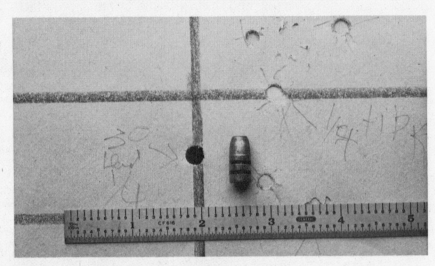

This 125-grain 30-caliber flat point bullet hit the exact center of a ¼-inch branch. Zero deflection.

A robust weed even deflected this 150-grain 45-caliber bullet traveling at 1100 fps. Again, note that the left-of-center hit on the weed stalk resulted in a "left-directed" deflection of about 2¼ inches.

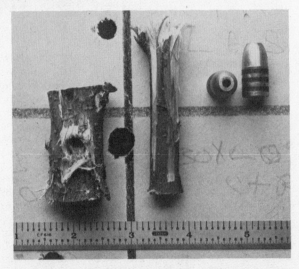

Centered hits were difficult to make, but evidenced little deflection at short ranges. (The bottom target strike was by a 330-grain 45.)

The big 405 and 500-grain 45-70 bullets fared little better than lighter ones. Centered hits by a 405 (top and bottom left) on a ½-inch branch remained relatively stable. A 500-grain 45-70 slug (right) was tumbled by an off-center hit on a ¾-inch branch. Note the deflection comparisons.

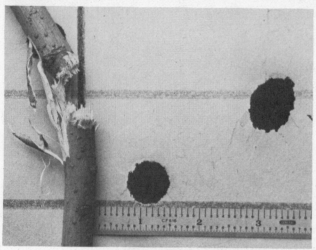

Less than ¼-inch difference in bullet placement made a big difference in where these bullets impacted after deflecting. Centered (bottom) and off-center hits (top) by Brenneke slugs tell the tale.

These nearly identical deflection impacts were made by Brenneke (top) and Foster (bottom) slugs after hitting a ¾-inch branch.

point at 1500 fps, though more than double the weight of the collar button type did prove to be better, but not an outstanding brush buster. Center hits on ½- and ¾-inch branches deflected $3/10$-inch and $1/5$-inch respectively with no tipping though the ¾-inch branch did produce some upset in the cast bullet. Grazing shots cutting the outside edges of ½-inch branches deflected $1\frac{1}{5}$ inches and $1\frac{2}{5}$ inches. A left-of-center hit on a ¾-inch branch deflected $1\frac{3}{10}$ inches. All three of these shots tumbled.

The original military and current commercial 45-70 bullets weigh 405 grains and are considered good brush busters, but performance in this weight class was no improvement over the 330. A left-of-center hit on a ½-inch branch by a cast 405-grain flat point bullet at 1400 fps produced a $3/5$-inch deflection; a second hit only slightly nearer the edge deflected $1\frac{3}{10}$ inches. Two hits on outer edges of ¾-inch branches both deflected; the first $1\frac{1}{2}$ inches after which the bullet tumbled, the second $2\frac{1}{5}$ inches, with the bullet entering the record target point first.

The 500-grain gas-checked bullets at 1350 fps proved less stable than the 405s. Nearly all tipped, with the greatest deflection from a ½-inch branch being $1\frac{1}{2}$ inches and from a ¾-inch branch $2\frac{1}{5}$ inches. Perhaps the only noteworthy feat performed by the big 500 was to cut ¼-inch branches without deflecting, which would at least qualify it as a "twig buster."

Shotgun Slugs

With hopes raised by the somewhat limited success—maintaining stability after hitting a branch—of the front-heavy collar button 45, I targeted 12-gauge Foster and Brenneke slugs. The 12-gauge Foster at 400 grains and the Brenneke at 485 both had muzzle velocities of about 1600 fps. Quarter-inch branches deflected the Foster $6/10$-inch and the Brenneke $1\frac{1}{5}$ inches. A right-of-center hit on a ½-inch branch deflected a Foster $2\frac{4}{5}$ inches while a right-side hit by a Brenneke deflected it $3\frac{3}{10}$ inches. Both tumbled. As I expected, ¾-inch branches gave larger deflections—$3\frac{1}{2}$ inches for the Foster and $3\frac{7}{10}$ inches for the Brenneke, tumbling both into the target.

Shot Patterns

The fact that weeds deflected rifle bullets set me to wondering what effect this kind of soft brush might have on shotgun patterns. The same 18x24-

A yard-thick bunch of weeds was used to test the spreading effect of soft brush on shot patterns. For actual testing the record target was 12 feet behind the weed clump.

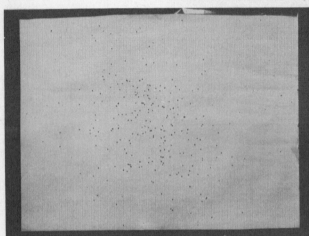 

The "unobstructed" shot pattern (above left) was delivered by a 12-gauge field load (3¼/1⅛/6) shot through a Full-choke barrel at 20 yards. Above right, you'll see the same field load after it hit the weed obstruction at 15 yards, printing on a 20-yard target. (Note the substantial dispersion.)

inch paper target was placed at a distance of 20 yards from the shooter. For the record a 12-gauge field load of 3¼/1⅛/6 shot was fired through a Full-choke barrel. Virtually all of the charge struck the paper. The test was repeated with the same load fired through a patch of dense weeds about 1 yard thick, 15 yards from the shooter. The pattern recorded on the paper at the 20-yard point—12 feet behind the weed patch—was about equivalent to that fired by a Cylinder-bored barrel. Had the weed patch been a solid mass stretching back to the record target, it is a fairly safe assumption that only a small percentage of the shot would have reached the paper.

Mathematical Models

As evidence mounted, the fact that bullet deflection was far more a result of bullet placement than any other factor became apparent. Although larger branches tended to give greater deflections than smaller ones, the ½- and ¾-inch sizes caused about the same degree of deflection, the major differences being the result of center hits versus outside hits.

In theory, hitting the exact center of a branch will cause no deflection, the bullets behaving in the manner of those penetrating flat planks. Such bullets in this test did continue in a straight line for at least 12 feet. In off-center hits, first contact between the cylindrical branch and the conical bullet, though it is initially on the point, is thereafter on the sloping ogive of the bullet after the point has passed through the branch. The net effect of this is for the branch to push the bullet to one side. Those striking to the right of center are deflected right, those striking to the left go left. As the angle of contact between bullet and branch becomes shallower—as the bullet strikes nearer the edge—deflection increases until a critical point is passed where only a small portion of the base of the ogive makes contact with the edge of the branch in a grazing hit which does little more than scrape the outer surface of the bark resulting in a very slight deflection. The logical reason for this pattern is that a bullet meeting a branch dead center is subjected to equal lateral and vertical displacement forces and will remain on course. As the point of impact deviates to one side, the displacement force exerted by the center (thick part) of the branch will be greater than that exerted by the outside (thin part) of the branch. Theoretically, the greatest deflection will occur where half the width of the bullet will contact a branch leaving the other half unsupported.

The flight path of a deflected bullet as it deviates from the line of sight can be viewed as a right triangle with the base representing the amount of deflection which increases in an equal proportion to the lengthening of the distance between the deflection point and the target—the long sides of the triangle. Using the 12-foot deflection model as a starting point; deflection at longer distances would be as follows:

Such a model assumes deflection occurs in one plane with the bullet moving away from the long (vertical) axis of the branch and that the path of the deflected bullet will be straight. It applies *only* to the initial hit. In point of fact, *unbalanced, tumbling bullets* may do all sorts of strange things, including taking an outward curving path that may both rise and fall as they deflect. Over any distance a bullet will have a trajectory, its motion influenced by its forward speed, air resistance and the force of gravity. In a deflected shot, to the above forces must be added those set in motion by the deflection which include *tumbling* and *increased unbalance* if the bullet has been damaged by the branch.

Short-axis (vertical) deflection, while less evident than long-axis deflection, *was* evident though to a far lesser degree. Where measurable, hits could be seen above or below the line of sight. These deflections followed no pattern, but seemed to occur perhaps slightly more often on edge-deflected shots. Vertical deflections were never more than about ½-inch.

A deflection profile of nine of the bullets tested gives a comparative look at the maximum deflections achieved by these bullets over a distance of 12 feet after hitting a ¾-inch branch. The differences, though mathematically significant, were hardly what I expected or hoped for. The 22 Long Rifle, for instance, had a deflection only 14 percent greater than the Brenneke slug—the second worst performer. While the 330-grain 45-70 was 230 percent better than the 22 Long Rifle, a slightly more than two times better performance by a bullet having more than eight times the Long Rifle's weight and muzzle energy hardly inspires cheering.

To bring this mass of data into a form useful to the hunter who would consider brush shots might be expressed in one word—*don't*. The deflection model presented here must be considered a mathematical ideal and not necessarily a practical one. Even within the ideal, a 4-inch deflection at 12 feet can mean a clear miss of a moose-sized target at 100 feet or 30 yards. The actual deflection values may well double or triple at longer distances as a deflected bullet curves, tumbles and drops. In a practical shooting situation, common sense would argue against taking any shot at a game animal through twigs and branches unless that shot can be made through a hole in the foliage screen. If a shot is taken that must pass through a branch, it should be limited to one, perferably small, and must pass through the exact center. Additionally, such a shot should be attempted *only* if the target is *very* close to the branch. A telescopic sight, while giving a shooter the advantage of seeing holes in foliage, has the disadvantage of blurring to near invisibility close branches that may lie in the bullet's path. A second disadvantage is the scope's foreshortening of perspective, making it exceedingly difficult to judge distances (depth) between objects in the field of view. Nevertheless, the advantage of seeing clearly and placing shots accurately far outweigh these negatives.

Though both large heavy bullets and light, high velocity ones will cut through brush, once having done so they are not capable of much else. Shooters planning on any form of hunting requiring shots through heavy weeds or foliage would be well advised to first run their own tests under conditions where they will be shooting and take their shots accordingly. I wish them luck. They'll need plenty. ●

NOTES.
[1]Julian Hatcher, *Hatcher's Notebook,* p. 406.
[2]Franklin W. Mann, *The Bullet's Flight From Powder to Target,* pp. 326,27.
[3]Ibid. p. 332.

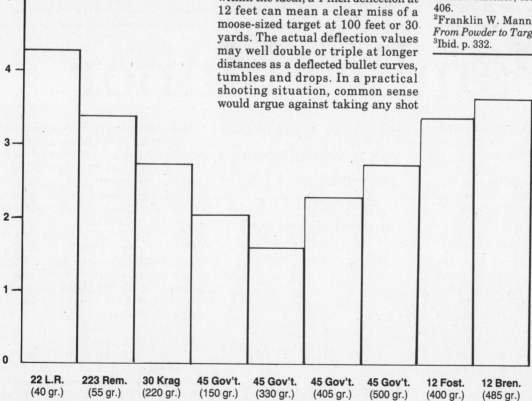

A scale illustration of maximum deflections at 12 feet from ¾-inch branches. There is no reason to assume these are the maximum possible. Such evidence would indicate there is no such thing as an accurate brush busting bullet.

| 22 L.R. (40 gr.) | 223 Rem. (55 gr.) | 30 Krag (220 gr.) | 45 Gov't. (150 gr.) | 45 Gov't. (330 gr.) | 45 Gov't. (405 gr.) | 45 Gov't. (500 gr.) | 12 Fost. (400 gr.) | 12 Bren. (485 gr.) |

A NEW EAST COAST HUNTING LODGE:

Pamlico Manor

PARKER WILLIAMS and I had been hunting all day. Hard. Parker *really* wanted to put me on a buck. We had "binoculed" several deer, although try as we might we couldn't make any grow horns. We bounced along in the Toyota four-by-four, dust leaking out from under its dash, my hand over the objective bell of my scope, trying to keep the lens clear.

The sun had long since dipped beneath the treeline, doing its best to thwart my first day's attempts at bagging a whitetail. And succeeding.

Abruptly my head slammed forward—narrowly missing a serious confrontation with the windshield—as Parker ground the brake pedal under his heel. "There's one! A buck! See 'im?"

I didn't. But I jumped out of the

Pamlico Manor — it's a 48,000-acre spot where, "The deer and the waterfowl play."

by

CLAY HARVEY

truck anyway, having earlier learned to rely on Mr. Williams' uncanny ability to spot game. I slipped off the dirt road, settled into a comfortable position, and peeped through my glass.

"See 'im?" Parker queried excitedly. "He's got a doe with 'im, yonder by that near brush pile."

The "near" brush pile was close to 200 yards away. I examined it carefully. By gosh, there *was* a deer standing there, shoulder-high in weeds, gazing intently at my handsome visage. No matter how hard I squinted, I could not make out his antlers.

"You sure he's a *he*?"

"Absolutely! Bust him."

I put the crosswires on the top edge of the buck's shoulder, where the leg nears the spine, and turned one loose. The big 300 H&H Magnum rocked me a bit. I barely noticed; I had called the shot good and was busy pulling the gun down out of its recoil arc so I could watch my deer fall.

He stood there, looking at me. I couldn't believe my eyes. So I made my second mistake. I held in the same spot, high on his shoulder, just above the tops of the vegetation, and sent another 180-grain Nosler along. I must have come pretty close to him that time, or perhaps he figured that giving me two shots was enough. He took off, quartering to my left.

My cerebellum communed with my cerebral cortex, then passed the findings on to my trigger finger. I remembered to hold *low*—finally—and touched off my third round. The fast-

My Remington 700 was zeroed about 2.8 inches high at 100 yards, which put its bullet around 4 inches up at 185-190 yards or so. Too high. That, plus my tendency to aim above any greenery that happens to be in my bullet's path, no matter how insubstantial said vegetation, caused me to overshoot that deer twice. But I'll never admit it.

Parker and the Squeaky Boots

Earlier that afternoon, I had spied a little band of deer down a side road. There were three of them, about ¼-mile away. We decided to run a stalk in hopes that one of them was a buck. Ditching the truck, we headed for the deer.

I was hunting. Equally natural was Parker's choice of footwear—hip boots. Rubber boots. *Squeaky* rubber boots. The objects under discussion were raising one helluva racket.

As my wife likes to point out, I am sometimes lacking in patience. When under the close scrutiny of a herd of skittish whitetails, I am pointedly lacking in patience. And tact.

"Parker, can you walk a little quieter? If those deer don't hear us coming, it'll be inhumane to shoot one. They'll be deaf."

I crept on. My concentration was so absorbed by the band of deer and my own stilted footfalls, several minutes transpired before I noticed that Parker's movements were completely muted. I glanced over my shoulder, mumbled, "That's much better. What'd you do?"

"Took off my boots," came the whispered reply. I turned around, glanced down the road. Fifty yards to our rear stood a pair of hip boots, looking a bit forlorn. Parker had been tiptoeing along in his stocking feet. It was near 40 degrees. Now *that's* a guide!

Alas, his sacrifice went to naught. The deer sashayed into the woods, unalarmed, several hundred yards to our front. We set an ambush, heard them walk by within 30 feet, but heavy brush screened them completely. Parker retrieved his boots and we hiked back to the truck. I with newfound respect imbued in my bosom. Parker, I suspect, with cold feet.

Parker Williams downed this fat five-point just after sunup. Note the flat country, not generally attributed to the South. Shots out to 600 yards are not unheard of, although such distances would be unsporting.

Author slew these two spike bucks within 30 minutes. Although there is marked disparity in size, both bucks were the same age — 1½ years old.

stepping Ballistic Tip struck home with a resounding *SWACK!* akin to striking a soggy blanket with a tennis racket. The buck humped up, zigzagged crazily, and departed for heath unknown. I'd hit him, but not quite right. (Remember that the next time someone tells you that power can make up for poor bullet placement. The little cowhorn buck had absorbed close to *3000* fpe, transmitted through a quick-expanding bullet, *and had run off.*)

Parker found him several hundred yards away, dead in a canal. His two single beams were nearly a foot long. (From whence the local term "cowhorn.") It's doubtful he exceeded 110 pounds on the hoof.

My mistakes, alluded to earlier, were not remembering to *hold low*.

The road wandered along between two thick stands of timber. At our end was the road we'd parked on and a large soybean field adjacent to that. At the deer's end was a clearcut; a pool of lambent sunlight backlit the deer. We advanced head-on as they ambled along the road.

Walking in single file, figuring to be less noticeable, we would take a dozen quiet steps, then stop to glass the deer. I use the term "quiet" advisedly. Actually, our anabasis wasn't quite as subdued as it might've been.

The problem was Parker's boots. The day prior to my hunt had seen a torrential rain along the entire Eastern seaboard; on my trip down, I had noted many homes completely surrounded by water. Naturally, much of that water was still in evidence where

Pamlico Lodge can accommodate just about any variety of deer hunting you like. Tree stands such as this one abound. Additionally, the black powder deer hunter hasn't been forgotten as Pamlico has thousands of acres of dense, heavily-wooded land to hunt on.

The Mid-Morning Buck and Br'er Bear

Traditional wisdom espouses that if you want your buck, you should be in the woods well before sunup. If you are freezing, starving, sleepy and generally uncomfortable, so much the better. Anson Byrd, ramrod of Pamlico Manor, upon whose board I had been wolfing my daily bread, believes otherwise. Mr. Byrd (I call him "mister" because he is about 6 feet 4 inches and 235 pounds) is the quiet, determined sort. Today—the second day of my first hunt—he had set himself the task of finding a mountable buck, pointing me at it, and hoping for the best. His lack of confidence in my shooting skill was perhaps justified by my performance on the aforementioned cowhorn. Still, it rankled. If Anson hadn't been so confounded *formidable,* I might have mentioned it. Being a petite, dainty sort, I kept my counsel.

We toured a good many of the 48,000 acres Pamlico Manor lays claim to, through deed or lease, and

beheld many a doe but nary an antler. Around 9 o'clock, we ran across Tommy Midgette, affectionately referred to as "Worm" by his peers, and Landa Gibbs, two of Mr. Byrd's inestimable employees.

Anson rolled down his window as Worm's truck veered to a halt, tilted his beard to the frosty air and canvassed his cohorts.

"Any deer movin'?"

"Ain't seen none."

"Been on fifth street?"

"Yep. Nothin' moving over there."

"Third avenue?"

(Above) Pamlico's guides take care of the skinning chores. The deer hunter can spend the rest of his day seeking quail, ducks, whatever is in season, for a small extra fee.

(Right) Big Anson Byrd is seen here bringing out the author's nice six-point whitetail. As you can see, much of the property is made up of open terrain. (This buck was taken at about 185 yards.)

"Naw. You might check it."

These fellows waste few words.

"We're gone," said Anson.

"Fellow hit a big bear out on the highway. Knocked his El Camino in the ditch," Worm informed us casually as he reeled in his window. "Y'oughta go look at it. Big one."

Anson said, "Wanna look at a bear?"

"Let's go." Didn't want to appear loquacious.

We sailed on over to Highway 264, arriving just in time to get a few photos of a big (B-I-G) black bear, thor-

oughly defunct, as it lay in the back of the battered El Camino. Even beside Anson the bruin looked big.

It was. The carcass was hauled to a local meat locker and weighed. It tipped in at *440* pounds! And Anson opined that it was just a bit over medium-sized for those parts. In fact, we had spotted four bear out in the open that morning as we looked for deer. At least one of those was larger than the recently deceased. Obviously, Hyde County, North Carolina is *loaded* with black bear. (There is a county-wide moratorium on bear hunting,

and has been for many years. Hence the burgeoning bruin population. If the county commissioners decide to allow an open season, even on a limited or permit basis, I'll stand in line to buy one.)

After ogling the big black for 15 minutes or so, we U-turned the truck and headed back for Pamlico property. We had no more than set tires on same when Anson glanced back over his left shoulder, growled, "There's one," and stuffed a size-12 boot to the floor. Once again, my proboscis came perilously close to denting a dashboard.

Anson performed a neat three-point turn, then eased the truck along to a wide spot on the shoulder. There was my buck, a fat six-pointer, doing his part in keeping the vegetation of manageable height in his neighborhood soybean field. Periodically, he would raise his head and peer unconcernedly in our direction. Perhaps he had heard of my gunning prowess.

I fooled him. He was quartering almost directly toward us. Anson suggested that I wait until he turned broadside, likely figuring that I needed as large a target as possible. Not me. I was in a steady position, had my crosswires astride the buck's left shoulder and about half the slack out of the trigger. The next time he upped his noggin to stare at me, I was going to stop his clock. I did, too.

His rack came up, I applied another few ounces of pressure, and the 284 pushed against my deltoid. As the muzzle whipped up in recoil, I got a quick view of a stone-dead buck. Never have I seen a big-game animal decked so abruptly. He just went DOWN!

Anson congratulated me on the shot, seeming genuinely pleased. (Perhaps he had simply been dreading a long tracking job.) We off-loaded a Honda three-wheeeler, and Mr. Byrd went to fetch my deer. I drove the truck to the far end of the bean field to pick him up. (The near end was bordered by a canal.)

While Anson was scooping up my prize, I sat in the truck and admired my little Alpha Grand Slam. We made quite a team, thought I.

When Anson returned with my buck slung over the back end of the Honda, I hollered, "Where'd I hit him?"

"In the cheek."

"Beg your pardon?"

The cheek. Look."

He was right. Obviously, the buck had lowered his head about the time I launched my bullet, taking the mis-sile in the right cheek. The bullet went on into the neck, just foward of the shoulder. Right where I'd aimed.

"Never saw a deer killed any quicker," said Mr. Byrd. "Legs were folded up underneath his body. Didn't even roll over on his side."

Praise from Caesar.

The next time Anson guided me on a whitetail hunt, several weeks later, he put me in touch with three deer within 30 minutes. I dropped one like it'd been poleaxed, with a shot to the neck, then reverted to my previous bad habit and shot over the next one. (I was again using the 300 Magnum.) A half-hour later, Anson stuck another buck in front of my nose. I shot this one in the spine at about 175 yards, and my morning's hunt was over. (North Carolina's limit on deer is five in some counties, but only two can be taken in a single day.) Two points to all of this: Pamlico Manor has a *lot* of whitetails; Anson Byrd can find them.

Bobby's Playground

When Bobby Rupert purchased Pamlico Manor Hunting Lodge a couple of years ago, it was more in a spirit of adventure than capital gain. Bobby *likes* to hunt, and the Lodge was a hunter's paradise. For years the area had been noted for its waterfowling, no surprise considering its proximity to North Carolina's famed Pamlico Sound and equally celebrated Lake Mattamuskeet. Of course, Bobby wanted the enterprise to pay its way, but he had other businesses with which to fill the Rupert family larder.

The Lodge was sort of his playground.

Anson Byrd, Bobby's longtime friend, business associate, mentor, and sometimes bodyguard, stepped in when Bobby was too busy to give the Lodge the attention it required. Things proceeded apace.

Finally, in 1985, Bobby geared up for some serious outfitting. He advertised in various regional journals, hired a PR man, enlisted the aid of Missourian Gerald Ryals in securing a herd of exotics, and engaged Gary Chapman as General Manager. Things began to happen.

From blinds like this, built along the edges of cornfields, Pamlico gunners keep busy when the geese are coming into the calls and decoys.

Gerald brought in a load of mouflan rams, sitka and fallow deer, some trophy-quality whitetails, and built a fence surrounding 600 acres of prime Pamlico turf. (I've seen a photo of one of the transplanted Missouri bucks. He would score 175 Boone & Crockett points!) In the offing are blackbuck, axis deer, elk and chukars.

Also in the planning stages is a trap and Skeet field, rifle and pistol range, a gun shop, a fine restaurant, and similar attractions. Bobby's playground sounds like a gunner's Disneyland. Currently, both wild and pen-raised quail can be hunted at Pamlico Manor, over your own dogs or the Lodge's. Pheasant may be available for the 1986 season. And I haven't mentioned waterfowl.

Getting Bobby's Goose

In early January, with deer season safely tucked away, my thoughts turned to icy mornings shivering in a duck blind. Bobby invited me down, once again.

Before dawn one blustery morning, taciturn Mr. Byrd and I were sliding along in the mud, trying to keep our footing as we made our way to one of the Manor's many impoundments. Actually, I was doing all the slipping and skidding; Anson just plodded along as if he were wearing magnetic boots on a cast-iron floor. I tossed him nasty looks whenever he faced away. That'd teach him.

A flight of some kind of duck or other whistled overhead just as we arrived at our blind. They settled on the opposite side of the pond, out of range but not out of mind. We waited. It was chilly and damp, not exactly cold. Clammy.

"Here comes a flight. Get down!" How could I see anything if I got *down*? "Now," hissed Mr. Byrd, just a second too late for me to hit anything. He dropped a pair. *Did that on pur-*

them a spell—straightening here, bending there—then trooped over to one of the blinds bordering the field. Anson and Bobby commenced to honking. Sounded like a barnyard.

Directly, a gaggle V-eed its way in our direction, skimming the treetops, honking queriously. Bobby and Anson tooted back at them, almost enticing them into range. But not quite. They veered off and planed away. Bobby said a bad word.

We spent a fruitless hour in the goose blind. Flocks continued to wing past, often just out of pellet reach. We let them pass; no sky-busters in this group. Eventually Anson gave me back my shotgun.

Swan Lake

Mr. Byrd had purchased a swan permit, legal in North Carolina. The huge birds were everywhere, their

"I've made better," he replied self-effacingly. "I was aiming at *the lead bird.*"

I Hate Snipe

After Anson decked his swan, I grew bored. He began to hoot on his goose call, giving me a headache and having no visible effect on any geese in the area; the skies remained empty of feathered life save for an occasional seagull and the omnipresent swans. When my snoring became too raucous to ignore, Anson suggested that I quit the blind and have sport with the snipe population.

I hefted my Citori 12-bore and excused myself. *Snipe*, I thought. *Just my speed.*

Wrong. I had no more than cleared my camouflaged rampart when a snipe flew past my nose and lit at the edge of the impoundment. *Aha*, I

Pamlico property is visited by thousands of swans. North Carolina offers a one-a-year permit to take a swan. They are superb eating, provided they are (like other waterfowl) *properly* prepared.

pose, I thought.

As the morning progressed, several more flights winged in, and I was offered several shots. Many shots. Once in a while I connected. In an hour or so, we had our limit of eight ducks. Anson's big Lab had spent a lot of time in the water.

Bobby Rupert rowed over, brandished his pile of ducks, suggested we go get him a goose. I climbed out of the blind without falling down, made it off the dam upright, then plopped in the mud as I reached the easement. Nobody laughed. Out loud.

We trucked a few miles to a cornfield in which stood rows of decoys somewhat resembling geese. Bobby and Anson were so bedecked with calls—both ducks and ganders—that they nearly walked stooped over. We hiked out to the decoys, fiddled with

plaintive cries a constant accompaniment. Ever generous, Anson asked me along to help him fill his tag; I was to provide moral buttressing in case he muffed his shot.

Another blind alongside another impoundment. You don't use a mechanical device to lure a swan. At least Anson didn't. He simply cupped his hand to his facial folliage and made a sound like a loon does when you squeeze it. Sort of. It worked. Swans zoomed in on us like pigeons to a freshly-unveiled statue. After a spell, Anson took a shot.

With cool assurance he rose, swung deftly ahead of one of the long-necked creatures, and adroitly pulled the trigger. The last bird in the formation tumbled out of the sky like a stricken 747, folded neatly in flight at 55 yards.

"Nice shot," I said.

thought, *what a foolish bird.* Not only foolish, but foolhardy; the little feller gave me a whistled notice when he decided to take off.

Did me no good. The bitsy needlebeak was not 20 yards distant when he took wing, but I missed him with both barrels. Little did it matter that I had my feet tangled up, my balance 10 degrees to port, and the sun (such as it was) in my eyes. I couldn't have hit that bird at 3 feet with a canoe paddle.

Ever see a snipe fly? Reminds me of *Woodstock*, Snoopy's avian companion. They seem to fly upside down, sideways, in every direction at once. "Erratic" is insufficient to describe the flight plan of a snipe. I walked up eight birds in a few minutes, fired both barrels at all but one, and cut not one feather. *Hate* snipe.

Author's hunting partner, Randy Smith (left), is discussing the fine points of bobwhite gunning with ace guide R.L. Vaughn.

side, a mother porcupine would have welcomed me as a prodigal. My jeans weren't completely ruined—there were several square inches relatively bereft of rips—but even my eldest West Highland terrier refuses to sleep on my coat any more.

The Tail Ends

If you enjoy hunting quail, if flights of ducks leave you in ecstasy, if honking formations of geese quicken your pulse, if snipe and rail and the chance at a swan perk up your ears, look no farther than Pamlico Manor Hunting Lodge. If whitetails are your meat, or mouflan sheep, or blackbuck or fallow or sitka, consider Pamlico Manor your hearth away from home. If you're an Easterner who yearns for the clucking of chukar, the quick rise of cock pheasant, the Lodge has plans for you. If a trophy-size whitetail or a monster black bear would look good on your wall, give Pamlico a buzz and see what the current situation is. You'll likely find me there.

Their particulars are: Pamlico Manor Hunting Lodge, P.O. Box 277, Englehard, NC, 27824-02277, (919) 925-6161. Ask for Anson Byrd or Gary Chatman. Tell 'em I sent you. They promised not to charge extra.   ●

The author's guide on ducks, geese, snipe and whitetails was Anson Byrd. Anson is the kind of man hunting myths are built around. He's big, quiet and minds his own business. And he's one of the best shots the author has ever seen in action.

Quail Are No Better

Randy Smith is the owner of Randy's Outdoorsmen's Shop in High Point, North Carolina. His store is without question the cleanest, niftiest, and best thought-out gun emporium I've ever visited. Not only does Randy run a tight ship, he's one of the best scattergunners it's been my chagrin to hunt with.

A few months ago, I was in High Point dickering with Randy over the price of goose-down suspenders, or something similar. Randy, being of obvious Scottish lineage, was clinging tenaciously to the exorbitant numbers affixed to the garment in question. Vexed, I changed tactics, switching from disputation to blandishment.

"I'm planning a quail hunt out on the coast after Christmas. Wanna come along?"

He eyed me suspiciously. "What'll it cost?"

I drew myself up, feigned an offended look, said, "I invited you. Of course it'll be my treat."

He dropped his gaze, shuffled his feet, cleared his throat. I had him now; his conscience, such as it is, was nibbling at him.

"Sure, I'd love to go. When and for how long?"

I spent the next few minutes adumbrating the hunt, craftily pushing the suspenders aside as if I'd lost interest. He was hooked; Randy loves to quail hunt. We settled on time and duration, method of transportation, and

ancillary business. I turned to go.

As if in afterthought, I queried, "Oh, how much for this little item?" I fingered the galluses in what I deemed a noncommittal fashion.

"Just how it's marked," returned Mr. Smith. I thought I detected a slight leer, but he turned away as I squinted up for closer scrutiny. I paid the tariff unhappily.

As I left the store, a sign just above the doorway read, "Gotcha."

When Randy and I arrived at Pamlico Manor some weeks later, we were immediately turned over to R.L. Vaughn and his trio of English setters and pointers. Despite the fact that the day was gusty and dry, R.L. and his canine pals did their part in finding bobwhite.

Randy did his part in hitting several of the birds R.L. flushed and I did my part in inflating Randy's ego by missing several of mine. In fact, my gunning was of such poor quality that I feared one of R.L.'s dogs was going to quit in disgust. Why should he work so diligently when I wasn't able to hold up my end, he seemed to be thinking. Likely, he was right.

But we had fun. Once, one of the pointers locked onto a single on the other side of a briar-choked windrow. A briar-*choked* windrow. R.L., like a true gentleman, did his best to open a swath through the thorns, beating and stumbling and using colorful language. Randy, being the gentleman he is, let me go first.

By the time R.L. and I made the far

MY BEST SHOT

We got a few of the gun writers on the phone and asked them to think about and write up what they felt were their "Best Shots." Read on. You'll find warmth, humor and marksmanship. It's the stuff memories are made of.

LEONARD LEE RUE III

R.S.L. ANDERSON

GENE HILL

CLAY HARVEY

BOB BELL

LAYNE SIMPSON

LEONARD LEE RUE III

IT WAS A DARK, overcast day. A day so still it seemed as though the earth was holding its breath. A gray day, a day to match my mood. It was the third day of our 6-day "bucks only" hunting season in New Jersey. I hadn't even seen an antler yet—except on the deer of other, successful hunters. I really didn't have that much time to hunt as my job as Chief Gamekeeper for the Coventry Hunt Club kept me busy patrolling.

I was on patrol with my good friend and deputy, Bud Disbrow. Bud had bagged a nice buck on the first day of the season. As it was now a mid-week day, things had quieted down after the hectic first 2 days.

We were patrolling on Ridge Road and I was driving my jeep. Just before we passed the vacant Hamilton House a fleck of brown up in the hilltop cedars caught my eye. I could see several does milling about on the hillside, waiting to come down and cross the road to go into the preserve area down along the river. I thought that perhaps a buck might also be with them. Pulling opposite the empty house, which was between us so the deer couldn't see me, I got out and had Bud drive on. Loading my gun, I sneaked out and got behind a huge hemlock tree and hunkered down, overlooking the trail the deer usually used in crossing this

Pigeons & Chucks

R.S.L. ANDERSON

I WAS ABOUT 15 years old, and it happened on a chuck hunt. My Dad was doing the driving and spotting. As the car came to a halt on the dusty road, I quickly found myself standing on top of a hill looking across a huge, Upstate New York alfalfa field. Smack dab in the middle of all that fresh-cut "green" was a large, lonesome chuck. Pop was pretty good at estimating distance. Together, we guessed around 450-500 yards.

Dad was watching, so I tried my best to please him. (I'm sure you've been there.) Neat guy, my Dad. The gun was a Savage 340B in 222 Remington. The load was 24 grains of Ball C (Lot 1) behind a 50-grain Sierra Blitz. No scope—couldn't afford one. The first shot was over, the second shot was under, the last shot clipped the chuck's spine. I was not unhappy. Pop smiled.

Then there was the time I was shooting barn pigeons in a stiff wind ... Pulled down on a fast moving single, hit the trigger and watched a 25 mph breeze take the south-bound dead bird right over the top of a barn at a total speed of about 50 mph. Quite a sight ... Especially when it landed in the bed of a north-bound pick-up truck also doing about 50 mph. The literal *explosion* of feathers off the butt-end of the truck was really something to see. We were about half bent-over in a combination of utter amusement/amazement! The guy driving the truck? We weren't sure. But our first clue was the fact that the pick-up's rapid stop left enough rubber on the highway to make a pair of waders. As the guy exited the pick-up the scene before us was not unlike a liquid-filled glass ball, complete with St. Nick, and vibrating snow. We really *tried* to be serious. A lot of difficult explaining followed. It didn't work. Somewhere around the town of Lyons, New York, I'm sure there's a guy who likes to tell about the time a 22-year-old wiseacre "threw a dead pigeon at a perfectly good pick-up truck."

Perhaps I Hung the Wrong "Deer" on the Meatpole

area.

There were just enough cars passing to make the deer wary about coming down, and they finally went back over the hill.

As it was just about ½-hour until the end of hunting time, and getting darker yet, I walked down the road to where Bud sat parked in the jeep. Climbing in on the passenger side I said, "Let's call it a day," and we started toward home.

We were on River Road, about ½-mile from my home when, in a patch of timber on the river side of the road, I saw a small herd of deer, but even more important, I saw antlers!

"Deer!" I shouted.

Bud started to put on the brakes and I said, "No, no, go on down the road, turn around, and I'll get out as we come back past them."

We went down the road for ¼-mile, turned, and started back up. I sat with my feet out the door, holding my shotgun and three shells in my hand so I could load the minute I stepped out of the vehicle.

"Slow down, but don't stop, and I'll jump out and the deer won't be the wiser," I said.

"I'll tap you on the shoulder when we get opposite the deer so you know when to step out," Bud exclaimed.

Bud seemed to be going awfully fast as I watched the snowy road flash by beneath my feet.

Suddenly Bud pounded me on the back, and I catapulted out the jeep, only to land in a heap on the road. As I lay there on my back I watched the jeep disappear up the road. I scrambled to my feet, loaded the magazine and fed a shell into the chamber.

I walked to the edge of the road and stepped over the guard rail. Out ran a doe. Then a second. Then a third. Where was the buck?

I knew I had seen a buck, but I wasn't seeing him now. Finally he stepped out from behind a big sycamore tree. My gun was up in a flash, and as the sights settled on his chest, I fired. At the blast I could see the buck drive backwards, but he didn't go down. As he whirled into the open on the other side of the tree I fired again. Instead of a roar, there was a feeble *PSSSSST* when I pulled the trigger and the buckshot literally fell out the end of the barrel. It's a good thing I was shooting downhill.

I pumped in my third shell and fired again, with the same results. (I was shooting some handloaded shells a friend had given me.)

I searched for a fourth shell, got it loaded and fired just before the buck made it up to the road.

I frantically searched my pockets for more shells but couldn't find any.

As the buck was running down the road, away from me, Bud was approaching from the other direction. As the jeep came by I jumped for the foot step and missed, only to end up flat on my back in the middle of the road again just as Bud ran over my foot. Only the snow kept my toes from being crushed.

Bud never stopped; he raced down the road after the buck which was trying to scramble up a steep roadside bank. As he got to the deer, it collapsed and fell backward down into the road. My first shot had been a good one.

I hobbled up the road, elated at the positive turn of events. Bud and I pounded each other on the back in congratulations. I eviscerated the buck, and we loaded him on the back of the jeep. It was only then that I noticed I had almost torn the sleeve off my new Woolrich jacket which I had caught on the truck's door frame when Bud had pushed me out.

My new jacket was torn, I was bruised from my fall, my foot was in *bad* shape but I was elated; I had my deer.

Back at my house Bud and I hung the buck on the meatpole and I hobbled in to tell my wife the incredible series of events and resulting "good fortune." Her reply was not the congratulations and sharing of joy I expected. Her only comment was, *"You're late; you knew we were going out tonight!"*

My Most Intelligent Shots

GENE HILL

AFTER GIVING this concept a lot of thought, I came to the conclusion that a great shot should be the routine shot: the stalk to minimize distance and error, the adequate rifle and load, the knowledge of animal anatomy and bullet trajectory—all ought to reduce the shooting of an animal to a total anticlimatic ending to a hunt; it should be like successful surgery—no surprises.

But the more I thought, about "My Best Shot," the more I realized that it wasn't the routine good shot, it wasn't a function of the trophy. It ought to be a shot that is memorable for more than the missing or hitting, and although I have done a few of both, my "best" shot

was anything but . . . that is, until I learned to look at it in the proper perspective.

It was late in the afternoon of my first day on safari in Kenya. We hadn't been hunting anything, just getting air, when our hunter stopped the car, asked the tracker for the 270 and said we needed some camp meat. At this point I found it impossible to say that I'd never shot an animal with a rifle larger than a 22; in fact, other than some Army business, I'd never shot a *big* rifle. I'd come to Africa as a shotgun shooter and realized, too late, that the hunter wouldn't believe I'd never used a hunting rifle.

I knew it was going to be bad; it was just a question of how bad. We

stalked to within easy range (about 125 yards), the professional set up his little shooting stick arrangement, I slid the rifle over it and tried to look at the wildebeeste through the scope. The crosshairs circled around the animal; I couldn't make them hold still. Finally, as they passed the chest area I shot. The animal stumbled, caught itself and began hobbling away. "You've shot him in the knee," the hunter said. I shot again, nothing happened. Again and nothing happened. The hunter thumbed in another cartridge, and by the purest of luck, this shot caught the spine and the animal fell. The hunter was angry, and I was humiliated. On the ride back to camp he said nothing, but I knew what was on his mind—and I had the same thing on mine; I vowed that I would shoot well or not at all.

The next morning I took my rifle and two boxes of shells and had the hunter fix up a range for me. What theory I had, I practised.

The rest of my safari went fairly well—not all one-shot kills, but the incident of the wildebeeste was *never* repeated or *ever* forgotten. So my "best shot" was a bungled horror. But what it created was a deep feeling about the responsibility of the hunter. Since then I have grown enough that I now take pride in saying "no" to the wrong shot.

In fact, my best shots may be my most intelligent shots—they're the ones I say *no* to.

Chucks, Deer & Elk

CLAY HARVEY

WHEN EDITOR BOB phoned to give me this assignment, I was somewhat dubious, to say the least. My best shot? On game? Layne Simpson insists that for me even to *hit* an animal *anywhere* at *any* range constitutes a miracle, not just a good shot! But Layne is prejudiced. He's seen me shoot.

Perhaps he's right. Wasn't it *I* who missed an easy shot at a running whitetail, just 20 yards distant, the season before last? Alas, it was. And didn't *I* blow an equally facile shot at a monster buck just 6 years past? Indeed; I confess. I miss

more groundhogs than I hit, which charges my hunting partners with glee but does naught good for my ego.

Ah, but just last year I made a first-shot hit on a crow not too far shy of 300 yards. That's a good shot in anyone's book, even rested over a truck's hood. And year before last, I pasted a woodchuck—first try—at 275 yards from the kneel with a lightweight 243 under a 4x scope. (Take that, Layne!)

But my best shot? My *very* best? Hmmmm. Perhaps my most *satisfying* attempt was on a fat doe, grazing, facing dead away, at 165 paced yards. No big deal, right? Maybe. But I had just chugged 50 or 60 yards imitating a deer, all hunched over, and I *knew* the little herd had me spotted, and my heart

Two Shots

BOB BELL

A FAIR AMOUNT of my time, for almost a half-century, has been spent peering into the rear end of rifle scopes and watching the effect of high-velocity bullets striking somewhere out yonder. I've no idea how many shots I've fired in these years, or even how many critters I've killed. Less than some shooters, I'm sure, and more than others. That in no way is meant as a brag; in fact, at times I've felt twinges of guilt about it. But I go on shooting. Sometimes the results have been impressive, even spectacular. Other times they've been pathetic, sad, funny. More than occasionally, the laugh has been on me. That's as it should be. If I never missed, I'd have given up shooting long ago.

Nobody can remember all the shots he's made. One of my problems is that I can't forget the bad ones. But this little piece is supposed to be about a good one, so that makes things easier. I remember that kind, too. Most guys do.

Several summers back, some friends and I loaded an assortment of rifles into a pickup and pointed it toward South Dakota's prairie dog country, a trip we make whenever time is available and the cases are loaded. We each had a pair of guns (to have something happen to your *only* rifle in the middle of a big dogtown would be legitimate cause for suicide), most of them 222s, 223s and 222 Magnums. These are the perfect choices for prairie dogs, which normally are taken between 150 and 300 yards. I had a Remington 40XB-BR 222 with Weaver T16 scope and a M788 223 with an 8x Lyman All-American boosted to 16x by Wally Siebert. Magnification was too high in both cases for midday use—mirage at times made them unusable—but early or late they worked beautifully. Regardless, I had a good week, so good that the guys started calling my 40XB "the Meatgrinder."

But it was the plain-Jane 788 that gave me the results I most remember from that trip. We were spaced out along the flat edge of a high butte overlooking a wide gray-green valley. Innumerable dog holes spotted the floor, with ranges out to infinity. It can be fun trying for the impossible ones, but with the wind that's always blowing in that country, any such hits are more the result of chance than ability, so don't mean much. We tend to try the more reasonable ones, preferring to be surprised by a miss rather than a hit. Anyway, it now was late afternoon of the last day, and I was snugged in solid, prone, looking at two dogs on a hole where I'd killed one sometime earlier. It was at least 350 yards out there, which is quite a piece for a 223, but from my previous hit I knew about how much hold-over I

(Continued on page 138)

was shuffling around and the adrenaline was gushing to and fro inside my plumbing, and she *wouldn't* turn broadside. *No way.*

I was toting a bitty 257 Roberts, stuffed with handloads featuring the 90-grain Sierra hollow point boat-tail. (I know. That's a varmint bullet. But the whitetails in the area I was hunting run to about 100 pounds, and so long as I avoided heavy bone, I figured I'd do okay.) So here I was with a varmint load up my chamber, the light failing fast, peering at a doe's caboose. I went to figurin'. If she would turn just a *little* bit quartering, I'd try to angle my slug in just behind the shortribs and on into the boiler room. She cooperated, shifting slightly, quartering to my left. I eased a bullet across 165 yards of turf; it zippered the front edge of her paunch, slammed into her heart, and disintegrated. She ran 15 yards and piled up. Perfect.

But, undoubtedly, my *best* shot came on a 1978 elk hunt. On the second day of a 10-day pack-in trip, I was offered a shot at a big old six-point bull. As I fell off my horse, he was busy hustling his 13-cow harem up the mountain. When I asked the guide how far, he suggested 400 yards. No hesitation on his part, you understand. *Four* hundred yards. I glanced around. No handy rocks, no deadfalls, no steadying tree trunks. The grass was waist high. To my horse. It was offhand or nothing. Four hundred yards. Uphill. At a running animal. My guide was shouting at me to shoot. I did.

I was so nervous, I rushed my first shot; I had *no* idea where it went. (We discovered later that I had poked a hole in his right hind foot!) Then I rallied. Tuning the guide out, I waited for the bull to reappear from behind a boulder, put the crosswires high and forward, and made a clean tug on the trigger. My 180-grain Nosler took him high in the lungs, and knocked his chin in the dirt. He got back up, traveled a ways. But it was fatal.

Everyone on that hunt—guides, wranglers, hunters alike—visited the kill site at one time or another. Range estimates varied from 350 to 450 yards. Let's settle on 375 or so. My best shot. Ever.

needed. Windage was another question. It was blowing harder now than it had been, and a 50-grain .224-inch bullet isn't the most efficient projectile under such circumstances. But that's what I had.

That pair of pups didn't look too big, even through the 16x scope. They just stood there, motionless as the number 2 and 3 pins on a bowling alley. I eased the crosswires onto the windward one. With the Remington's fore-end snugged tightly into its bipod, the reticle intersection seemed pasted into place, but I knew it was pointless to shoot. I'd miss by a mile. I started easing the aiming point out at 3 o'clock. The first foot was easy. But I knew that wasn't enough. Still, it took a definite mental effort to force it out farther. I got it to 18 inches, maybe 20, maybe a bit more. Light reflecting from a pebble made a reference point. I concentrated on it, shutting off all awareness of everything else, thinking of nothing but maintaining the quivering crosswires on that speck of light until somewhere in the distance the rifle cracked. The lefthand dog fragmented. The other one was still as solid as a fencepost. I fed another load into the chamber, found that shining speck once more, eased out enough to accommodate for the space that had existed between the two dogs, waited for the rifle to crack once more. Another explosion.

My breath went out in a long sigh. I watched through the scope for awhile, then shoved myself up. "That does it for me," I said. "Two clean kills at better than 350, holding 20 inches or more for wind, is as good as I can hope for. Another shot'll only spoil it. Those two hits will keep me happy till next summer."

They did. Nothing fantastic, I know. Not as glamorous as a long-range kill on a bighorn or as chilling as stopping a wounded brown bear in the alders, but nevertheless the kind of shots I like to remember. Good shots, the kind a rifleman can expect to make a reasonable percentage of the time if he's about on a par with his equipment. That's why I like to think about them occasionally.

"Mother Luck"
Layne Simpson

MY BEST SHOT? Gosh, Anderson, that's a tough one. Seems like good ol' Mother Luck manages to place her cool hand on my sweaty brow every few years or so. And I never know when she'll next come by and smile over my shoulder. Yep, the sweet gal has been awfully good to me.

I remember the time long, long ago when I snuggled down in a snow bank with my 25-06, held the crosshair several shoulder depths over a mule deer's spine and

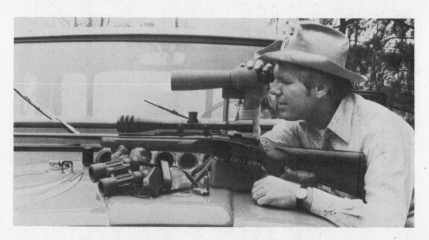

smacked him dead center of the lungs. He ran around in a circle four times and keeled over dead as a frozen mackerel. I really shouldn't have hit the buck, but I did.

Then there was the lucky shot I made on a pronghorn while afield with my Wyoming pal Dick Keenan.

"He's a very good buck," said Dick.

"He's too far away," said I.

"Try him anyhow, you don't see horns like that every day," argued Dick.

Mama Luck was there too. She said, "Now just be calm you handsome devil [honest]. Rest your .25-06 on this sagebrush, hold half a body length into the wind, over his back twice as much as you think you should, squeeze one off and drop by my place at seven." So I did. The buck dropped slightly quicker than "instantly." We paced off the shot—about 550 yards! The 115-grain Nosler Partition zipped through both shoulders.

Another "best" shot took place in a beautiful land once called Rhodesia. I killed a small monkey with my 375 H&H. Wait a minute, there's more to the story. Said monk and his chums were raiding pal Bob Swift's maze field. And, we were standing about three football fields from the unlucky one—the one with my crosshairs painted on his chest. After my shot I thought the Shona tracker's eyes would never stop getting bigger. (I haven't fired the rifle since for fear that someone might discover the truth.)

Another lucky shot happened more recently. Hal Swiggett and I were "wheezing" (not whizzing) down a rocky road on the Y.O. Ranch in his ancient Ford pickup. Suddenly a big flock of Rio Grande turkeys streamed across in front of us. Since I had a license, they were fair game. Hal hit the brakes and eventually shuddered to a halt in a boil of dust and flying gravel.

"You let them get away," screamed Hal.

"Just switch off the ignition [actually he was afraid to stop the engine] and turn me loose with this 257 Kimber," I replied.

"You'll never catch them!" countered Hal. But I did. After a stalk of about ½-mile through Texas thorn brush Mama Luck pushed a big airborn gobbler into an open pasture. And he hit the ground with both wheels spinning. Shooting offhand, I swung the little Kimber 84 through black feathers and squeezed the trigger as crosshair met beak. The gobbler tumbled wattles over tail feathers. The range was a bit over 200 paces. Hal was so excited he fell asleep!

But all my "best" shots haven't been made at breath-taking distances. A few years ago while attempting to dig a whitetail out of the thickets of South Carolina, I was suddenly afflicted by a splitting headache (the whitetails were winning). In my jeep, parked several miles away was a bottle of aspirin. So, with the little Model 600, 350 Magnum (great little whitetail digger-outer) cradled in my arm I was making good time down an old logging road. The thought of seeing a buck never crossed my mind. But I did. Actually, he knew about me first. And for an odd reason that only another deer might understand, the buck decided to sail across the road about 40 yards in front of me. Maybe he knew my guard was down. I really don't know. What he didn't know was that I was toting the fastest woods rifle ever built by mortal man. The little 600 leaped to my shoulder and barked its loudest. The 200-grain Core-Lokt actually caught him in midair and he landed like a baggie full of Jello. To this day I don't remember seeing the deer in the scope or pulling the 600's trigger. But that's the way of a deer rifle that fits you like a custom-made

quail gun or a hunting companion with the initials ML monogrammed on her Filson cruiser.

I could go on and on with many such tales. Like the time I killed not two, not three but four quail on the rise with a single ounce of number 8s. And the time I launched a broadhead at a big boar hog. The arrow dropped him, sliced on through and killed his chum on the far side. The chum, by the way was the bigger hog. But, since you're probably bored stiff by now (especially if you've already read Clay Harvey's tale) and since Anderson is paying such a pitiful amount of money for this piece, I'll close with my great squirrel deception:

Gerald Holden was 9, 2 years older than I at the time. It was Christmas day, 1948. Gerald dropped by and showed me what Santa had slipped down his chimney. It was the most beautiful shotgun I had ever seen. (Santa brought *me* a Gene Autry cowboy suit.) Of course, I had not seen many guns at the time, let alone a shiny new .410 single barrel. So, we headed for a patch of woods in back of my house.

I was just dying to try the little gun but that wretched Gerald wouldn't let me shoot it. On our way back to the house I suddenly screamed out, "There's a squirrel." (I really didn't see one.) "Where?"

"Up in the top of that white oak."

"I don't see no squirrel."

"Gimmie the gun before he gets away." *KA-BOOM!*

Would you believe it, the biggest, fattest grey squirrel in the land crashed down through the branches, ricocheted off a limb near the bottom and hit the ground with a thud, dead as a door nail. It did, honest.

To this day, ol' Gerald does not know the truth. Let him suffer. It serves him right. That's what you get when you mess with me and my pal Mama Luck ●

BY LEONARD LEE RUE III

THE WHITETAIL'S WORLD

IN AUGUST OF 1985 I was again lucky enough to be one of the featured speakers at the Georgia Wildlife Federation's Buckarama. This show gives recognition to the big bucks that have been taken in Georgia during the previous year. It's a must for anyone interested in deer.

Before I started my 2¼-hour slide presentation on the life history of the whitetailed deer, I made the following statement to the audience, the same statement I now make to you: "In about 2 years time biologists are going to discover that the whitetailed deer has scent in its saliva. I'm telling you now, that they have scent in their saliva; it's why they chew on twigs and lick sticks. And I have the photos to prove it." After my show was over, a well-known biologist said it was odd that I should mention this fact; he was about to embark on a 2-year study to see if there was scent in the deer's saliva.

Though I don't have the laboratory facilities available nor a knowledge of gas liquid chromatography and other scientific methods to prove my conclusions, I have spent countless thousands upon thousands of hours ob-

serving and photographing deer, and their activities, all over North America. I also have a large file of photographs, taken over many years, showing this peculiar deer behavior I talk about.

Glandular Scents

When I first started to hunt whitetails, about 45 years ago, there was little knowledge of scrapes, licking sticks, glandular secretions, scents, rattling antlers or calling deer. The old-timers looked for buck rubs in an effort to find out where the bucks had been working out. It was then commonly believed that a buck made just *one* rub, and that rub was made when he rubbed his velvet off. If there were 18 buck rubs in an area, it was believed that 18 different bucks made the rubs.

The only glandular scent then commonly noted was that of the tarsal gland. As a youngster I was advised to cut the tarsal gland off as soon as I shot my deer, before it tainted the meat. I quickly came to a differing conclusion. As a result, I have for years, lectured: "If that gland didn't taint the meat while the deer was

alive, it certainly is not going to taint the meat now that the deer is dead."

In the autumn of 1972 I photographed a buck in northwestern New Jersey rubbing his antlers on an elder sapling. This was in early October and his antlers had long been free of velvet so I knew that this was not the first rub he had made. My conclusion was that, like a boxer getting ready for a fight, the deer was getting in shape for the forthcoming rutting season. What was so interesting was that I also discovered that the buck was not rubbing the sapling with his antler tines, he was rubbing it with the antler beam and the burrs.

When a whitetail buck's antlers are growing, there are 24-26 major vessels supplying the blood that deposit the bone salts forming the antlers. If you will look carefully at any antler, you can see where the position of these blood vessels have been imprinted on the hardened antler beam bases; most are heavily corrugated, especially on the older, more mature bucks. These ridged corrugations are known as "pearlation." The roughness of these pearlations and the antler burr itself rasp the bark loose from

(Opposite page) This photo, taken by the author in 1972, shows a whitetail buck rubbing a sapling on the scent glands of his forehead.

This buck is chewing, or mouthing, the branch overhanging his primary scrape, covering it with the scent of his saliva.

OF SCENT MARKING

the sapling, literally shredding bark off like a vegetable grater. Usually the pearlation and the antler burrs are filled with impacted bark that has been loosened from the tree, the buck eating the shredded bark as he loosens it. But he also does something else.

Hours of observation have shown that, after the deer rubs off the bark with his antlers, he rubs that same bared spot on the sapling with his forehead and the area behind his antlers and in front of his ears. He's not rubbing to take off the bark, but rather to deposit his scent on the sapling.

I first became aware of the forehead scent glands when I watched the same buck rub a stiff, dead weed stalk on the center of his forehead between his antlers. He wasn't peeling any velvet off his antlers, nor was he strengthening his muscles—he was depositing scent.

When this same buck again worked out on some alders, the scent from his forehead glands so stimulated a nearby young spike buck that the young buck came over and began to rub his forehead scent glands on the same sapling. Amazingly—and contrary to

what others might care to believe—there was no animosity between the bucks. On numerous occasions I have even seen bucks take turns licking the scent from each other's forehead scent glands.

It is very important to remember that deer do not have a territory in the true sense of the word. A territory, by definition, is an area of ground from which one male animal will drive off all other rival males of the same species. Deer do have a home range which, in the case of the whitetail, is about 1-2 square miles, the bucks expanding that range to 10-12 square miles during the rutting season. They do not defend this area against all other males. They do, however, deposit scent in various forms, from various glands, that serves as an advertisement of their presence and of their availability. Additionally, it's my belief that the deposited scent may serve to portray a particular buck's place in the social hierarchy of a particular herd.

In Africa I photographed the little male *dik-dik* antelope creating an olfactory fence around his diminutive territory by rubbing his preorbital

gland (situated in front of the eye socket) on a weed stalk. On our western high plains, I have photographed the pronghorn buck doing the same thing by marking weed stalks with scent from his subauricular gland. In the Northeast I have photographed the whitetailed bucks rubbing their preorbital glands on branches and weeds to deposit scent. That this is commonly done is borne out by the pieces of vegetation that can be found in most bucks' preorbital glands. The preorbital gland of the mule deer is much larger than that of the whitetail and is flared when the buck is excited. The flaring undoubtedly allows the scent from this gland to escape directly into the air. I have not seen mule deer rub this gland on vegetation as I have the whitetail. Additionally, and unlike the mule deer, I have not seen a whitetail flare the preorbital.

Scrapes

The earliest record of scrapes, I can find, was written up in Volume 35, #1 of the *Journal of Mammalogy,* February 1954, by Dr. William Pruitt. Dr. Pruitt was at that time a professor of zoology at the University of Michigan and was studying the behavior of whitetailed bucks during the rut on the George Reserve.

Scrapes are the billboards of the whitetails' world. It is the buck's major means of advertising himself. Scrapes are found much more commonly in the South than they are in the North. The main reason is that in the South, especially in Texas, the ratio between bucks and does is closer to being 50/50. In the North, where the ratio may be three-to-five does per buck, the need to advertise is lessened. The competition is just not as keen.

There are several types of scrapes, only one of which, the primary scrape, should be of interest to the hunter because it is the only scrape that is of interest to the bucks and the does.

I have seen bucks walk along and suddenly stop for no apparent reason other than they just get the urge to stop and paw the ground. They make a few passes with either one or both front feet and then walk on. These should be called *pawings,* not scrapes, because they are not revisited and do not attract the other bucks or the does.

When a buck is following a pre-estrous doe, he does so with his head down and his tail erected straight up. As he follows her scent trail, with his nose, he often utters a grunting sound. When he comes to a spot where the doe urinated, he will smell deeply of the urine, checking for the pheromones that will tell him if she is about to come into heat. To better decode the odors he is taking in, the buck will breathe in the gaseous molecules of her scent and then trap them on the epithelial lining of his nostrils by curling his lip up, blocking the nasal passages. He will sometimes paw the ground at the spot where she urinated. This spot means relatively little unless the pheromones are present; if they are, every buck will stop and paw at this spot, which soon becomes a secondary scrape.

Most primary scrapes made and maintained by the bucks, and sometimes visited by the does, are located under a bush, tree, or sapling that has an overhanging branch the bucks can reach with their mouths. Most of these branches are 5 to 6 feet off the ground, although I have seen them so high (about 7 feet) that a buck had to stand on his hind legs to reach them. In many cases the branch was much lower to start with, but repeated chewing and antler hooking had broken off the lower growth. Because these branches are such an important

part of the scrape, you seldom find scrapes in a mature forest because no undergrowth or low branches are present. Deer are primarily creatures of second-growth woodlands.

When a buck approaches a scrape, he usually does so from the downwind side so that he can detect the presence of danger, or of a rival, before he actually steps out in view.

Yes, I have read that a small buck will *not* approach a scrape if it has been recently visited by the dominant buck in the area. However, I have not found this to be so. I have seen small bucks approach a dominant buck, on a primary scrape with extra caution; and I have seen smaller bucks stand to one side as the scrape was being used by the dominant buck. As a result, I do not believe that the lesser bucks live in constant fear of the dominant buck. Such a fear would be contrary to the entire hierarchy of dominance. So long as the lesser buck defers to him, there is no need for the dominant buck to do more than stare hard at the lesser buck to remind him of his lesser status. The lesser buck may not use the scrape while the dominant buck is standing there, but almost every buck uses almost every primary scrape he encounters, at some time or another.

When a big buck is on a primary scrape, he reaches up and chews on the previously mentioned overhang-

ing twig for several moments. This explains why such twigs are always broken and the bark usually stripped. I believe that the saliva of a deer is as individualistic as a human's fingerprints. The saliva, as a means of communication, is important only if it tells the rest of the deer precisely which buck deposited his saliva on the twig.

(I have not witnessed does chewing on the twig when visiting the scrapes, although they will smell them.)

After chewing on the twig, the buck then rakes the overhead branch with his antlers in an attempt to pull the branch down so it will make contact with his preorbital gland and his forehead scent glands.

The scent glands in the whitetail's forehead, both in front of and behind the antlers, become much larger and active during the rutting season and are quiescent during the spring and summer. The scent comes out from the hair follicles and follows the hair shaft through the skin. The presence of these scent secretions often darkens a buck's forehead to the point where it appears as if the animal is wearing a skullcap.

The bucks appear to be greatly stimulated as the branch rubs over their preorbital and forehead scent glands. It is stimulating; it is sexual; it is sensuous; it is very satisfying and enjoyable to them.

After licking the overhead branch, the buck then paws in the scrape itself. Here he is using his left forefoot.

After a few minutes of such rubbing, the buck begins to paw at the scrape with forefeet. (Believe it or not, most bucks begin to paw with their right front foot because most bucks, like most people, are right-handed!) The pawing removes any leaves that may have fallen on the scrape. When the pawing is vigorous, dirt may be thrown 2 to 3 feet into the surrounding area. A well used scrape may be 30 inches in diameter (or larger) and 2 to 3 inches deep.

After 4-8 pawings with the right foot, the buck will paw a like number of times with his left forefoot. Sometimes he will then paw again with his right foot but usually each forefoot is used just one time. Then the buck will bring his hind feet into the scrape, hunch his back upward, and rub his tarsal or hock glands together as he urinates on them. The urine combines with the scent from the tarsal glands and saturates the scrape with odor. This done, the buck usually walks out and away from the scrape without a backward glance.

The hock glands are the most conspicuous external glands of the whitetail. They have a strong odor of their own which is reinforced by the constant saturation of urine. The urine stains the tarsal hairs a very dark brown. The long hairs of this gland can be folded in tightly to reduce the amount of odor given off, or they can be flared widely when the animal is excited or alarmed. The more dominant the buck, the more frequently he urinates on his tarsal glands.

When strange dogs encounter one another, they smell each other's anal regions because of the identifying glands that are located there. When strange deer encounter one another, they check out each other's tarsal glands for the same reason. At times the deer will lick their own, as well as each other's, tarsal glands.

About 48-36 hours before a doe comes into estrous, she becomes exceedingly high strung and nervous, keeping on the go almost constantly. She is as anxious to be bred as the

(Above) One buck is licking scent from the other's forehead glands at the antler base.

buck is to breed her. If there is no buck in attendance, she will go to a buck's scrape and urinate. The telltale pheromones of her coming heat period are thus deposited where the buck can easily find them. As soon as a buck detects such pre-estrous urine the chase is on. A number of bucks may pick up on the same doe's odor, and they will all pursue her. The dominant buck then not only will chase after the doe till she stands for him, he will have to fend off the other bucks who are as interested in the does as he is.

Lesser bucks can usually be thwarted by the hard-look stare of the dominant buck. Any laggard is sent flying by a short charge. Large bucks, which may be almost equally ranked, may have to be fought. Each buck knows his rank on his home territory, when he is among bucks from the same area. When the breeding range is greatly increased, the dominant buck from one area may meet up with a dominant buck from another area, one which he has not tested before. That's when the competition gets tough.

It is because the scrapes may be the geographical center of the deer's breeding activities and may actually be the most pivotal point in the breeding range, that they are so important to both the deer and the hunters.

Licking Sticks

About 4 years ago I discovered what may be another focal point of the bucks' rutting activities. I call my discovery the *licking stick*. If other naturalists or biologists were aware of

When working a scrape, the final step is when the buck rubs his hock, or tarsal glands together and urinates on them, saturating the scrape itself with his individual odor.

Notice how this buck is rubbing the "licking stick" on the glands located behind his antlers and in front of his ears.

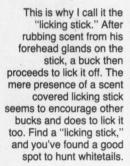

This is why I call it the "licking stick." After rubbing scent from his forehead glands on the stick, a buck then proceeds to lick it off. The mere presence of a scent covered licking stick seems to encourage other bucks and does to lick it too. Find a "licking stick," and you've found a good spot to hunt whitetails.

these sticks, they did not write about them, and I do know that I had the first photos published of a buck using such a stick.

The licking sticks that I have found are about the size of a man's center finger, about ¾-inch in diameter. The stick is a dead sapling that has been broken off about 30 to 36 inches above the ground. The sapling was probably broken off originally by the buck's sparring with it. Although broken off, the stick is not dry and brittle, but has considerable resiliency left in it. The top 6 to 8 inches will have no bark on it. There is no pawing or scraping done in the area. And it's odd that I

have not found the top section of the sapling lying in the immediate vicinity. The sticks can be anywhere in the woodland; they are not necessarily located near a trail.

The deer apparently start using the licking sticks while they are feeding on the fallen acorns just *prior* to the rutting season. In using the sticks, the bucks usually rub the glands that are located behind their antlers. After vigorously rubbing scent on the stick, they then proceed to lick it off. Other bucks visiting the stick will do the same thing. On the two occasions I saw does use the stick, they did not rub it, but did lick it. (And I have

seen no evidence of does having forehead scent glands.) Both does appeared to be stimulated by licking the sticks.

Although both does only "appeared" to be stimulated by licking, the bucks *definitely* were. They would rub the stick with their glands, then lick, rub, then lick for as long as 15 minutes at a time. The stick attracted bucks like iron filings to a magnet. I predict that if you can find such a licking stick in your area that you will find it *as productive* a spot to hunt as any scrape, and perhaps even *more so!* That's the licking stick. That's the whitetail's world of scent marking. ●

Western Hunting Rifles of Yesteryear

by
CONRAD SCHREIER, JR.

It's a perspective on what was available to, and used by, American hunters prior to 1900.

Hunting was a way of life in the West in the years after the Civil War. Breech-loading rifles were new, and game was far more abundant than people. Western hunters took to the big-bore breech-loading rifles as soon as these basically military arms first became available to civilians, about 1866 or 1867. The first of these guns were the U.S. Army's Allen "trapdoor" Springfield, the Remington rolling block, and the Sharps rifles that had been converted to fire the then-new metallic cartridges. These rifles, all single shots, could take any game on the plains or the mountains of the "wild West," and some of those animals were pretty nasty critters.

The most famous game animal of the early frontier was the buffalo. From just after the Civil War until about 1880, the buffalo was commercially hunted so intensely that its numbers declined to a point where there were literally very few left to harvest. Hunted primarily for their hides and a little of their meat, the

herds became so small and scattered they weren't worth chasing.

An awful lot has been said and written about how sad it was that the buffalo was hunted to extinction; it wasn't, of course, as the thousands of them on the prairie today prove, but little is ever mentioned about them as a wild animal. The buffalo is large (up to a couple thousand pounds for a big bull), stupid (he will stand still while being shot at) and a herd animal. Their charge can be extremely dangerous, and a stampeded herd was (is) practically unstoppable. Hide hunters took their shooting stands on high ground because the buffalo were unlikely to stampede uphill, and from a good stand, the hunters would keep killing their quarry until they finally got out of range. That was only 300 yards, or so, because that was about as far as their rifles could be counted on to shoot accurately, and fast.

The rifles those hide hunters used were mostly 50-caliber single shots—the trapdoor Army Springfield, the converted Sharps, and the Remington rolling block. These redoubtable big-bore rifles could take buffalo (or anything else) at ranges well past 300 yards, but only when the bore was wiped clean of the black powder fouling after each shot. It wasn't unusual for a hunter to kill an animal at 600 yards, but when shooting at a lot of animals from a stand, as fast as the hunter could reload, the range had to be short to accommodate a dirty bore.

As the buffalo numbers dwindled, so did another much more dangerous animal, the prairie grizzly bear. This savage predator disappeared around 1890. It was much like the mountain grizzly around today except that it lived out on the open flat lands. Like any bear, he would eat just about anything, but he had a more dangerous and unpredictable nature due, in no small part, to not having any place to hide much of the time. He'd attack almost anything, provoked or unprovoked. It took a good heavy rifle like a big-bore Sharps, Springfield or Remington to stop one, and even in the most powerful calibers, it could take more than one shot. The grizzly problem was one which led western hunters to want big-bore repeating rifles, and in the mid-1870s they began to come along.

It shouldn't come as any surprise that the most popular big-bore black powder repeaters in the West were the Winchester 1876s and 1886s. There were other lever-actions—the Burgess, Whitney, Marlin, a few Colt Lightning pumps, and even a few early bolt-actions. By the time these guns

came into general use, there were many big-bore black powder cartridges available, but only a limited number of them found any favor on the frontier.

Western hunting rifles had to be able to stop a dangerous *big* animal like the grizzly bear, and anything else from antelope to wolf, buffalo or bull elk. Pumas and plain brown bears were plentiful, and so were deer. Venison was as common as beef in the wild West. Rifles reckoned to be able to handle this type of game were pretty much those which used at least 70 grains of black powder to push no less than 250 to 300 grains of lead.

The 38- and 40-Caliber Cartridges

The smallest calibers used for old-time western hunting were the 38s—the 38-70 Winchester firing a 255-grain bullet in the '86 lever-action, the 38-72 Winchester which shot 275 grains of lead in the Browning-Winchester single shot, or the 38-90 Winchester single shot load. Any of these could be expected to shoot in a 10- to 12-inch circle at 200 yards which was fine, but their ability to stop large game was marginal; therefore, so was their popularity in the West.

Next in bore size were the 40s, a caliber seldom used any more but popular in the black powder days. The westerners favored the 40-70, 40-75 and 40-82, which were used in Winchester and Marlin lever-actions. A few used the 40-110, made for the Winchester-Browning single shot. The 40-70 was generally used in the

Springfield trapdoor rifles, the Sharps or the Remington rolling block. While the 40s were very powerful and effective on the game, they all pretty much had a reputation for poor accuracy past the 100-yard mark.

One old-time rifle caliber about which a lot has been written is the 44 Sharps. And a look at one period catalog shows a dozen or more 44s in this heavy class, running from the 44-70 up to the 44-110. Once again, they used powder charges from 70 up to 110 grains of black powder. They came with either straight or bottle-necked cases, but in the West they all sum up to two basic cases for many of the loads. One of these cases was the 2¼-inch bottlenecked-type that was loaded for anything from a 44-70 to a 44-90. Another was the 2⅝-inch case which took care of the 44-85 up through the 44-110. At one time the longer case was listed as the "Sharps necked 44-90 to 105 grs." Out of these 44s only a few were really popular in the West.

The 44-2⅝-inch case went back to buffalo hide hunting days, and it was very effective. Loaded well, it shot regularly to 300 yards, and as far out as 1000 when wind and weather conditions were perfect. The hide hunters fired the round in heavy, long-barreled rifles weighing 15 or more pounds, and in those guns it wasn't unpleasant to shoot because of the overall weight factor.

One of the problems western hunters had to face was the legendary "wide open spaces," and since most of them used horses to get around, they

The Marlin big bore repeater (which was a Burgess design) was used in the West, and was considered a good rifle. It was, however, nowhere near as popular as the Winchester.

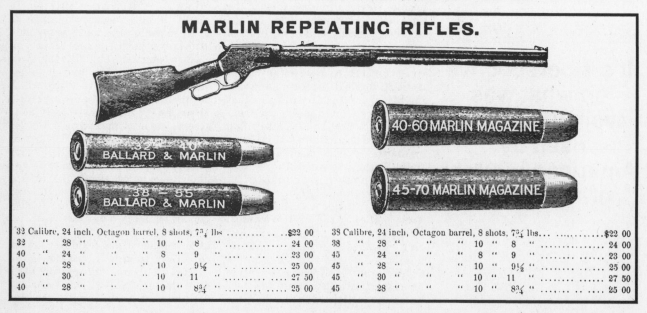

MARLIN REPEATING RIFLES.

32 Calibre, 24 inch, Octagon barrel, 8 shots, 7¾ lbs				..........$22 00	38 Calibre, 24 inch, Octagon barrel, 8 shots, 7¾ lbs				..........$22 00
32 " 28 "	"	"	10 " 8	"	..............24 00	38 " 28 "	"	"	10 " 8	"	..............24 00
40 " 24 "	"	"	8 " 9	"	..............23 00	45 " 24 "	"	"	8 " 9	"	..............23 00
40 " 28 "	"	"	10 " 9½	"	..............25 00	45 " 28 "	"	"	10 " 9½	"	..............25 00
40 " 30 "	"	"	10 " 11	"	..............27 50	45 " 30 "	"	"	10 " 11	"	..............27 50
40 " 28 "	"	"	10 " 8¾	"	..............25 00	45 " 28 "	"	"	10 " 8¾	"	..............25 00

BULLARD REPEATING RIFLES.

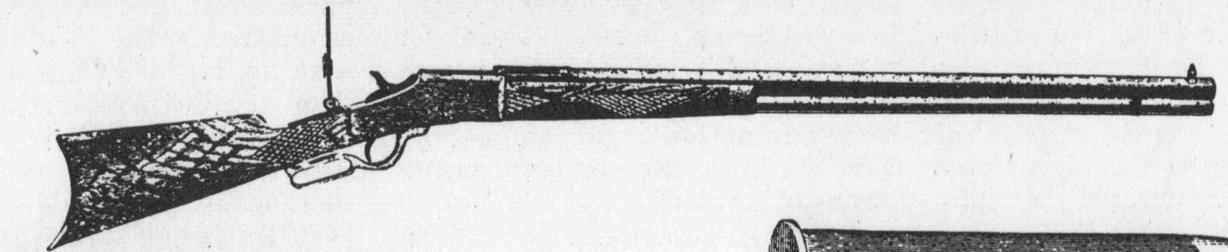

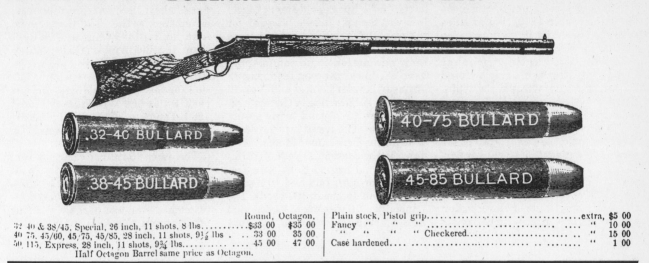

	Round,	Octagon,
32 40 & 38/45, Special, 26 inch, 11 shots, 8 lbs.	$33 00	$35 00
40 75, 45/60, 45/75, 45/85, 28 inch, 11 shots, 9½ lbs	33 00	35 00
50 115, Express, 28 inch, 11 shots, 9¾ lbs.	45 00	47 00

Half Octagon Barrel same price as Octagon.

Plain stock, Pistol grip	extra,	$5 00
Fancy " " "	"	10 00
" " " " Checkered	"	15 00
Case hardened	"	1 00

While the Bullard was a well-made rifle, it was a bit unusual, and seldom seen in the West. Yes, several Eastern hunters wrote about successfully using the Bullard lever-action in the West.

At this juncture, some 110 years later, the prices quoted for these Winchester '76s, seem ridiculously reasonable. At the time, however, the cost was not cheap. (This page from an 1883 Winchester catalog, is promoting that outfit's "centennial Model 1876" in 45-75 caliber. Looks like Winchester had a pretty good handle on the "commemorative" market, even way back then.

Winchester Rifles.

Centennial Model 1876, 45 Calibre, 75 Grains, Bottle Neck Shell.

The success attending the sale and use of Model 1873 and the constant calls from many sources, and particularly from the regions in which the grizzly bear and other large game are found, as well as from the plains where the absence of cover and the shyness of the game require the hunter to make his shots at long range, made it desirable for the Company to build a still more powerful gun.

Retaining all the essential mechanical elements of the former model, and adding such improvements as seemed possible, the result has been a gun carrying a central-fire cartridge, capable of reloading, calibre 45/100, with 75 grains of powder and 350 grains of lead, being nearly double the charge used in Model 1873, about the same as that adopted by the U. S. Government, and giving an initial velocity of 1,450 feet.

The materials used in the construction of the gun are the same in kind and quality as in the Model 1873.

Both Set and Plain Trigger Rifles are made, and all guns with a plain trigger are provided with an attachment which renders a premature explosion of the cartridge, even from carelessness, absolutely impossible.

Sporting Rifles may be had with Pistol Grip Stocks, Vernier and Wind-Gauge Sights, if ordered.

Sporting Rifle, Octagon Barrel, 45-75.

Price List.

NO.	ROUND BARREL.	EACH.
1808	28 inch Round Barrel, Plain Trigger (Regular Length), 12 Shot, Weight 9¼ lbs.,	$27 00
1818	28 inch " " " " " " Case Hardened. " 9¼ "	28 00
1838	28 inch " " Set Trigger, " " " " " 9¼ "	32 00

NO.	OCTAGON BARREL.	EACH.
1908	28 inch Octagon Barrel, Plain Trigger (Regular Length), 12 Shot, Weight 9¾ lbs.,	$29 00
1918	28 inch " " " " " " Case Hardened, " 9¾ "	30 00
1938	28 inch " " Set Trigger, " " " " 9¾ "	34 00

NO.	HALF OCTAGON, AND HALF MAGAZINE RIFLES.	EACH.
3908	28 inch Half Octagon Barrel, Plain Trigger, 12 Shot, - - -	$29 00
4908	28 inch Full " " " " Half Magazine, 7 Shot, - -	29 00

Fancy Pistol Grip Stock, 45-75 Rifle.

NO.	FANCY OCTAGON RIFLES.	EACH.
1978	28 inch Octagon Barrels, Plain Trigger, Case Hardened, Fancy Checked Pistol Grip Stock, - - - - - - - - -	$45 00
1998	28 inch Octagon Barrels, Set Trigger, Case Hardened, Fancy Checked Pistol Grip Stock, - - - - - - - - -	49 00

Carbine, 45-75 Calibre.

This cut illustrates full size and form of Cartridge of the Model 1876, 45-75, Bottle-Necked, as used in the Rifles listed on this page.

NO.	CARBINE, MODEL 1876, 45/75.	EACH.
1802	22 inch Round Barrel, Plain Trigger, 9 Shot, 8¼ lbs., -	$25 00

CONTENTS.		
Powder,	- -	75 Grains.
Lead,	- -	350 Grains.

had to watch their pack weight. Most of their working horses were only asked to carry a load of some 225 to 250 pounds—a quarter of their own weight—including rider, saddle, and anything else, so the number of items the hunter carried was kept to a minimum. The hunters preferred to use rifles weighing 8 to 10 pounds with a barrel length of 24 to 26 inches. This was too light a rifle for the 44-2⅝-inch loads, but it was just about perfect for the shorter 44-2¼-inch chamberings.

Many westerners, therefore, favored the 44-2¼-inch, which was listed as the 44-77 Sharps and Remington necked. A large number of single-shot rifles, including the Sharps, Remington rolling block and Hepburn, Winchester-Browning and reworked Army trapdoor Springfields, fired it. It was effective on any game up to the grizzly bear, but it was far from the most popular caliber in the wild West. Few repeating rifles were chambered for that round.

The 45-Caliber Cartridges

Without doubt, the most popular all-round big-bore black powder cali-

ber used in the West was the 45, and more specifically the U.S. Army's 45-70 rifle cartridge. From the time the 45-70 came out in 1873, civilian rifles were chambered for it. Its importance can't be questioned since a lot of civilians were still hunting with that round long after the Army adopted smokeless powder rifles in the 1890s. There were both single shot and repeating 45-70s, and the ammunition was available nearly anywhere.

There were, however, two other very highly regarded 45-caliber cartridges used in the West—the 45-75 and the 45-90.

The 45-75 Winchester was the cartridge the Winchester '76 lever-action was designed to fire. Winchester set

out to make a lever-action repeater which fired a load about as powerful as the 45-70, but the old Henry toggle lock was thought to be a bit weak for the powerful Army load. After some calculating, the engineers figured their new action could comfortably handle a 45-caliber load featuring 75 grains of powder behind a 350-grain bullet and get practically the same results as the 45-70 load firing a 405-grain bullet. The result was the 45-75 Winchester Centennial Model introduced in the centennial year of 1876.

This round proved to be an excellent one for big game and was quite accurate out to about 300 yards. The Winchester '76 was the most common rifle chambered for it and was very

popular in the West. Then, about 1879 or 1880, Whitney and Marlin introduced their lever-action repeaters chambered for the 45-70 Government load, and a lot of hunters bought them. In order to retain their popularity, Winchester hired John M. Browning to design a new lever-action for the 45-70 cartridge, and the result was the Winchester Model 1886. The new '86 was well accepted by the western hunters, especially in the 45-70 chambering.

The other 45-caliber cartridge that had a popular following in the West was the 45-90. Back as early as 1874, the Sharps rifle was chambered for "stretched" versions of the U.S. Army 45-70 round, the Army using a 2.1-

The Sharps 1874 was built for the West, but most of the Sharps rifles used by Westerners were converted Civil War carbines which looked almost exactly like this model. Note the prices.

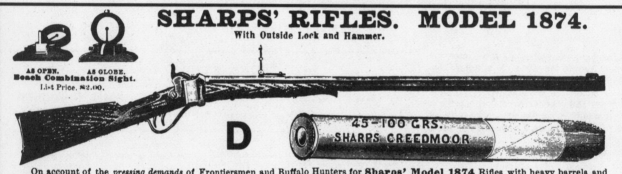

SHARPS' RIFLES. MODEL 1874.
With Outside Lock and Hammer.

AS OPEN.   AS GLOBE.
Beach Combination Sight.
List Price. $2.00.

D

**45-100 GRS.
SHARPS CREEDMOOR**

On account of the *pressing demands* of Frontiersmen and Buffalo Hunters for **Sharps' Model 1874** Rifles with heavy barrels and double triggers, we were induced to change a *limited number* at considerable expense to conform to their requirements. The barrels are of *best quality* and *workmanship*, and equal to Sharps' high standard of excellence in *every particular*. These Arms are all being completed, therefore orders varying from the following descriptions cannot be filled.

STYLE OF RIFLE.	Caliber.	STYLE OF BARREL.	LENGTH OF BARREL.	CHAMBER.		TRIGGER.	WEIGHT.	LIST.
Business.	45	Round.	28 inch.	2¹/₁₀/70 to 75	Grains.	Double.	10½ to 12	$20 00
Sporting.	45	Octagon.	30 "	2¹/₁₀/70 to 75	"	"	10½ to 12	22 00
"	45	"	30 "	2⅞ /90 to 120	"	"	13 to 14	24 00
"	45	"	30 "	2⅞ /90 to 120	"	"	14 to 16	26 67
"	40	"	30 "	2½ /65 straight	"	"	10½ to 11	22 00
"	40	"	30 "	2⅝ /90 necked	"	"	13 to 14	24 00
"	40	"	30 "	2⅝ /90 "	"	"	14 to 16	26 67

Sharp's Long Range Creedmoor Guns, 45-105, complete sights, pistol grip, horn butt plate, wgt 10, len'th 32 { List, 125 00 / Net, 35 00

This is the "Sporting" (hunting) version of the U.S. Army Allen trap-door 45-70 Springfield as sold circa 1880. (Note the specifications and prices.)

Springfield Sporting Breech Loading Rifle.

in. Octagon Barrel, Double Trigger, 45-70, 10½ to 11 lbs. 25 00
ringfield Breech Loading Musket, 32 in. Round Barrel, 45-70 .... 17 00
" " " " 32 in. " " 50-70 .... 15 00

(Right) This Winchester advertisement appeared circa 1888, about 2 years after the introduction of the featured 1886 lever-action. It wasn't cheap at the time, but western hunters took to the Winchester Model '86, quickly. (The cartridge seen as part of the ad is a 45-90 W.C.F.)

Back in 1886, John P. Lower & Sons was one of the largest sporting rifle houses catering to the needs of Rocky Mountain residents. (The rifle being held by the shooter is a Sharps-Borchardt.)

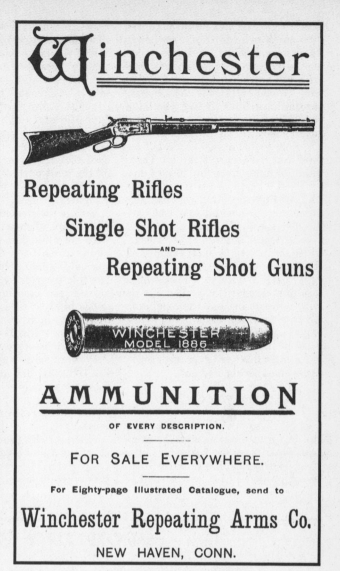

inch-long case. However, Sharps found that a 2.4-inch case firing a 300- to 350-grain bullet worked better and from the mid-1870s until the mid-1890s this load came to be considered about the best American big game sporting rifle cartridge around. It was as accurate as any big-bore black powder load ever used for hunting, and it had much better accuracy than most of the newer rounds. The 45-90 was easy to shoot well because its trajectory was flatter than most heavy black powder loads, and it had plenty of stopping power. It was not uncomfortable to shoot because its lighter bullets kept the recoil well within acceptable limits. When either more powder or heavier bullets, (or both) were used in the 45, 2-inch case, the results in anything but long-range, heavy target rifles were both uncomfortable and disappointing from an accuracy point of view. The regular 45-90 was very possibly the best of all

the big-bore, black powder sporting calibers, and it remained in wide use in the West long after black powder was obsolete.

The 50-Caliber Cartridges

The biggest, and first, of the heavy American black powder calibers was the 50. The 50s got their start when the Army adopted metallic cartridge, breech-loading arms at the end of the Civil War. In 1866 the Army adopted the new 50-70 Allen trapdoor Springfield rifle. The 50-70 trapdoors were a great improvement over the old muzzleloaders they replaced. In fact, they were such an improvement that most everybody overlooked their one drawback—the 50-70 wasn't very accurate.

Early on, in the 1860s, it didn't matter much as long as the new cartridge could be counted on to fire reliably in a rugged rifle. Certainly the 50-70 trapdoor Springfield met this

test. Hunters found the 50-70 could deal with any western game, and men like Buffalo Bill Cody used it with great success. A lot of the old combustible-cartridge Sharps were converted to fire the 50-70, and Remington even chambered their new rolling block rifle to fire that cartridge almost as soon as the Army began using it. Westerners were eager to buy rifles in this latest caliber, and these new guns earned a great reputation in the game fields. Their effect was pretty devastating on anything they hit—the only problem was that they didn't hit much of anything beyond 100 or so yards. After the Army replaced the 50-70 with the 45-70 in 1873 (to get a more accurate rifle), many Westerners hung on to their old 50-70s. However, by the 1880s they had pretty much gone out of use. Not a few of the higher quality 50-70 rifles were rebarreled to better shooting smaller calibers.

In 1879 the Winchester '76 lever-action repeater was adapted to fire the new Winchester 50-95 cartridge which soon earned a reputation for being the most accurate of the very powerful big bore, black powder "magnum" (if you will) loads. As a matter of record, the 50-95 firing a bullet of 300-325 grains was not too unpleasant to shoot. It was as accurate as a 45-70 out to 200 or 300 yards, but beyond that the accuracy fell off. There was a lot more game and fewer hunters back then, and the ranges at which game was shot were usually short enough that this load could get the job done.

Winchester created a 50-110 cartridge for its improved Model 1886 lever-action, but it never worked out very well. While it would stop a charging elephant, it kicked like an army mule. It also had the reputation for poor accuracy beyond 100 yards, and westerners never took a fancy to it. As for the old Army 50-70, very few repeating rifles were ever made for it, so the chambering died out.

Which One Was the Best?

Of all these big bore, black powder hunting rifles there is some question as to which were most popular in the West. The best bet has to be the 45-70 Government, which was issued to

troops from 1873 until about 1900. In addition to Army rifles (a large number of which passed into civilian hands), there were excellent commercial rifles chambered for the 45-70 sold in the West. There seems to be little question that, except for the days of buffalo hide hunting, more game was taken with the 45-70 than any other caliber. The hide hunters used a lot of the older 50 calibers, but for the most part switched to the 45-70 for the last few years of their slaughter.

Most of the westerners' 45-70 rifles were single shots as Army trapdoors were surplussed on the open market and priced quite reasonably. There were also a lot of old Civil War combustible-cartridge Sharps rifles converted into excellent metallic cartridge hunting rifles, and they didn't cost much more than the trapdoors. While new guns like the Remington rolling block were well thought of, they were still expensive, and this limited their use in the West. Thus the trapdoor rifle should probably top the list as the most popular big bore black powder hunting rifle of the West.

When it came to repeating rifles, it is both fact and legend that westerners preferred lever-actions. The one they liked best was the Winchester.

New Winchesters cost about a third more than new single shots, and several times as much as sporterized trapdoors, so they weren't as common as the less expensive single shots. Other makes such as Marlin, Whitney, Kennedy, and Bullard were highly regarded by some, but they were pretty scarce in comparison to Winchesters. The Winchester habit was a hard one to break.

Other big bore, black powder repeaters like the pump-action Colt Lightning, bolt-action Remingtons and Winchesters and such were oddities in the West. It would appear that most of the hunters who used them were visiting Easterners who carried them West. The Browning-Winchester single shot was a westerner's invention *for westerners,* and enjoyed some popularity despite being rather expensive.

Westerners knew from experience that rifles like the trapdoor Springfield and Winchester lever-action could take any game they were likely to run up against, so they stuck with those guns. It wasn't until around World War I that the new breed of smokeless powder rifles finally put the big bore, black powder hunting rifles of the West out of use. It had, indeed, been quite an era. An era now left to the pages of history. •

Guns, Ammo, and Optics for Deer

by LAYNE SIMPSON

Choosing the right rifle and accessories is one of the keys to successful deer hunting. Read what the author has to say — his recommendations are based on experience.

DEER ARE OUR most important big game animal, and I'm not saying this simply because I enjoy hunting them. If it weren't for such a generous availability of deer, thousands of American sportsmen would never taste the thrill of big game hunting. The reason they do experience that thrill is because a deer hunt will economically squeeze into more family budgets than will a hunt for most any other big game animal. For this reason deer are hunted by the multitudes and I mean *hunted hard!*

Deer are pursued by experts, beginners and thousands of other hunters who fall somewhere in between. In some places deer are chased by hounds and hunters with shotguns full of buckshot. He is hunted both legally and illegally (unfortunately) during all hours of the day. He is killed at close range in brush so thick you can't see anything over 15 yards

away and across plains and valleys at distances that take your breath away.

Name a rifle cartridge, and you can bet deer have felt its spiteful bark and painful stab. In one particular state deer are hunted from August 15 to January 1 with several counties having no bag limit on his kind. In another state the bag limit is one-per-day during a rather lengthy season. Some states have bow seasons, muzzle-loading rifle seasons, handgun seasons, shotgun seasons and modern rifle seasons. Very few have no season at all.

Typically, the average deer hunter has several hunting methods from which to choose. He can still-hunt, or as some prefer to call it, stalk, in wooded country. There's hunting from a tree stand in wooded country and hunting from a stand or tower in open country. Still-hunting in open country is popular as is doing the same in

steep, mountainous terrain. First let's look at what I consider to be rifles and cartridges suitable for each method of hunting. Further on we'll look at a few other things, too.

Rifles for Still-Hunting Wooded Country

Still-hunting (or stalking) in thick, brushy country is one of my favorite ways to bag a buck. In fact, I have taken close to half of my whitetails by easing along trails, old logging roads and small streams. Sadly enough though, still-hunting has become somewhat of a dying art simply because few of our younger hunters seem to have the patience to practice it successfully. In addition, some of our public hunting areas are so crowded with hunters that still-hunting can be rather hazardous to one's health. Nevertheless, in my opinion, this is the most challenging and satisfying way to hunt deer.

I judge the suitability of a rifle for still-hunting by how quickly it handles, how it fits, its accuracy and the cartridge it is chambered for. Quite often, success is dependent on how quickly one can center a buck's ribs in the sights; a heavy, poorly-fitting rifle won't cut the mustard. Ideally, the stalking rifle should be light and relatively short. When the shot one has been waiting for finally comes along, the rifle must spring to the shoulder as quick as a flash.

The best way to determine how well a rifle fits the individual hunter is simple enough. It can be done in a gunshop, your home or backyard, with the rifle unloaded of course. Simply concentrate on a small object for a second or two, close your eyes, quickly bring the rifle to your shoulder as if you're about to take a shot and then open your eyes. If your eye and sights (or sight) are (is) closely aligned and on target, the rifle/sight combination fits you.

Since it has been written that accuracy from a woods rifle is of secondary importance, you may wonder why I have included it. I have a reason. A very good one. A still-hunter who knows his business will enjoy many opportunities to shoot a buck that is either unaware of the hunter's presence or aware of the hunter but hasn't decided if he is dangerous. (In the case of a wise old buck, he's aware of both but decides that keeping still behind a screen of brush is his best bet for sur-

Although the Remington slide-action rifles vary a bit in accuracy from rifle to rifle, this particular 30-06 Remington pump is extremely accurate.

vival.) In other words, if you play the game as it should be played, all shots at bucks will not be of the "damn-the-torpedoes" or "slap-leather" variety. For this reason I prefer a rifle capable of threading a bullet twixt twig and limb and into whatever vital area I can make out. Now let's look at woods cartridges.

When the subject of woods hunting comes up, most hunters think of such traditional rounds as the 30-30 and 35 Remington. No doubt about it, cartridges of the so-called 30-30 class have killed a whale of a lot of deer over the years and will continue to do

so for as long as deer are there to be hunted. I have taken a number of deer with such cartridges as the 25 Remington, 30-30, 375 Winchester, 35 Remington 303 Savage and even the ancient Savage 22 Hi-Power. *All* will kill deer. I even used an old Springfield trapdoor carbine in 45-70 and a Winchester Model 94 in 32 Special to bag my first four deer. But, I do not consider any cartridge in this class as *ideal* for woods hunting. My reasons are twofold:

First of all, most of the areas I hunt are a mixture of terrains. In addition to thick brush, semi-open hardwoods and hellish swamps, there are huge cultivated fields, long power line right-of-ways and cutover areas of many acres. Shots at deer can range from muzzle-close to barrel-straining distances. One of the most helpless feelings a deer hunter will ever experience is to ease to the edge of an open area, spot a big buck several hundred yards away and have a rifle with rainbow-like trajectory in hand. Secondly, a big buck can be a tough customer to put down for keeps, and the farther he runs in thick country after being shot, the tougher that buck will be to find. I prefer a cartridge with enough flexibility to get the job done under several kinds of hunting conditions. A number of cartridges fill the bill including the 300 Savage, 308 Winchester, 7mm-08 Remington, 7x57mm Mauser, 280 Remington, 284 Winchester, 270 Winchester and 30-06. Now let's go back to the rifles.

As to the type of rifle to be used for still-hunting, well, it's a matter of shooters-choice, providing the choice meets my criteria. If its bolt is cycled

A rifle for still-hunting in thick country should be light, short, quick handling, powerful and accurate. This Ruger Model 77 International, in 308, fills that bill quite nicely.

My custom Ruger Number 1 in 45-70 is a fine tree-stand gun and works quite well for still-hunting too. However, some hunters might find its recoil a bit punishing when used with max handloads.

that I have more reasons for those choices. In my opinion, the need for fast follow-up shots for woods hunting is one of the most misleading of old wives' tales. Far more important is the ability to place the *first* shot where it counts. Follow-up shots made on a buck crashing through thick timber only serve to keep our ammunition makers happy. If your jaw just dropped in disbelief at such a statement, think back over the deer you've killed. How many were hit with a second, third, fourth or even fifth shot?

Rifles for Woods Hunting from a Tree Stand

For those hunters who have the patience to keep still for hours on end, sitting in a portable tree stand is one of the more productive ways of bagging a buck. The reason is quite simple. A hunter who *doesn't move around* is less likely to make mistakes. My choice in woods rifles for tree-stand hunting is often dependent on the type of stand I use and the type of tree it is used in.

Most any rifle will suffice *some times,* but not for other times. For example when sitting in one particular model of the so-called self-climbing stands, the hunter will find himself facing the tree. A rifle with a long barrel pointed to the left side of the tree trunk is a bit less than handy when a deer approaches from the opposite side. Another situation where a

by a quick flick of the wrist, I'd just as soon have the Savage Model 99. The Browning BLR is also a nice woods rifle, and quite accurate to boot. The Browning and Savage rifles are also available in excellent calibers. (The 7mm-08 and 308 come to mind.) The Remington slide-action and autoloading rifles are chambered for several excellent cartridges, but I find accuracy to vary considerably from rifle to rifle. Some will rival the precision of a good bolt-action, others leave a bit to be desired in the accuracy department. Between the two, I prefer the slide-action because it is lighter than the autoloader. I always found the carbine versions of both rifles to be more accurate and much handier in the woods, but they are no longer available except from used gun racks.

Actually, if backed into a tight corner and pressed for a single choice, I would have to pick a bolt-action rifle for woods hunting. Generally, bolt-action rifles are more accurate than lever-actions, pumps and autoloaders. Secondly, a number of the bolt-actions now available are quicker-handling than any other type of rifle, with one exception. (A few of the bolt-actions we have to choose from are the Remington Model Seven, Weatherby Vanguard VGL, Winchester Model 70 carbine, Alpha Grand Slam, Ruger Model 77 Ultralight and Ruger Model 77 International.) My second choice,

and the one exception, is Ruger's Number 1A single shot. Properly tuned, it will shoot with the best bolt-action hunting rifles, and it handles like greased lightning.

In case you're wondering why the above action-type choices are low on the firepower totem pole, be assured

The Marlin 1894 in 44 Magnum is not a *bad* tree stand rifle but why buy it when the Model 336 is available in such calibers as 356 Winchester, 444 Marlin and 45-70?

long-barreled rifle is less than ideal is when one's movement is restricted by tree limbs close to the stand. With the exception of these two examples, I find most any rifle suitable for tree-stand hunting.

Fit, handling and accuracy are less important for a tree-stand rifle than for a rifle used to still-hunt. Most often one has plenty of time for the shot which, fortunately, tends to rule out the necessity for perfect rifle fit and handling. Also of less importance is gilt-edged accuracy. Why? Simply because a hunter sitting in a tree can usually *wait* for a clear shot. However, good accuracy never hurt a thing.

I tend to use one of my still-hunting rifles when sitting in a tree stand, most often spending my mornings and evenings in the tree, the remainder of the day being devoted to still-hunting. However, for those who do not still-hunt, we can add a few more rifles to the list. They would include the Marlin Model 336 in 356 Winchester, 444 Marlin or 45-70 and the Winchester Model 94 in 307 or 356 Winchester. I own two rifles in 45-70, a Marlin and a Ruger Number 1. With handloads both are deadly deer rifles, but recoil is a bit much for some hunters. Both are also fine stalking rifles due to their custom stocks, but shooting at distant game with either is a lot like lobbing a mortar round.

Rifles for Deer at Long Range

All deer are *not* shot at close to medium ranges. For years hunters in the Northeast have sat with huge war surplus binoculars and heavy, flat-shooting rifles and sniped deer from one mountain side to the other. Years ago, for example, I hunted for several seasons in the Sherwood National Forest of North Carolina. Sometime after World War II a forest fire raged over thousands of acres of that beautiful mountain country. As a result, one could spot deer at ranges running from a few feet on up to a point where *any* shoulder-fired rifle would be totally ineffective. Shots were pretty tough, though. By the time I got around to hunting the Sherwood, the brush had grown quite thick and tall. In that area, most hunters used the 270 Winchester or one of Roy Weatherby's magnums in 270-, 7mm or 300-caliber. The 264 Winchester Magnum was also popular, and the Remington 7mm Magnum was just beginning to catch on. Mostly, I used a wildcat 25-06 which, by the way, was several years before Remington decided to domesticate it.

In some of our western states hunters shoot across valleys, meadows and wheat fields. In south Texas the popular thing to do is sit above the thick brush, in a tower, and shoot down long *senderos*.* Farther north, Texas hunters sit in blinds and shoot across pastures. In the southeast portion of the U.S., towers are built beside vast cultivated fields and hunters wait patiently for a buck to come out and nibble on corn or soy beans.

Given the above, it's obvious that it takes a special rifle to bag a deer at these long ranges. It must shoot flat, hit hard, ignore the wind as much as is ballistically possible and it must be accurate. Fact is, there are a good number of rifles around that meet the aforementioned criteria. I'll drop a few names: the Remington Model 700, Weatherby Mark V, Ruger Model 77 and a host of other rifles from our smaller companies (such as Kimber, Alpha Arms, Robert Kleinguenther and Ultra Light Arms).

Cartridges for long-range shooting are as abundant as fleas on a stray coon dog. Personally, I'd as soon have one of the several standard capacity cartridges and wouldn't spit twice for the difference between the 25-06, 6.5 Remington Magnum, 270 Winchester, 280 Remington, 284 Winchester and 30-06. When loaded with the right bullet, any of those rounds will do the job—so long as the owner of the rifle does his part. However, there's certainly no law against using magnum cartridges on deer for extremely long-range shooting. A Weatherby Mark V in 270 Magnum with 26-inch barrel has my attention at the moment. It is accurate (as Weatherby rifles usually are) and seems to deliver its bullet to a distant target a bit quicker than instantly. Other magnum cartridges worthy of mention are the 257, 270 and 7mm Weatherby, 7mm Remington and 264 Winchester.

When choosing a long-range rifle for mountain hunting, I become a bit more choosy. In addition to the requirements already mentioned, the selected rifle must also be reasonably light of weight. On the other hand, since a heavy rifle is easier to shoot accurately at long range, that's exactly what I use—but only when I'm hunting from a tower. In fact, under those "stationary" conditions, I often use what most would consider a benchrest rifle. One of the best I have ever used is a custom rifle built by Kenny Jarrett. A 280 Ackley Im-

---

**Natural or man-made path/trail through brush.*

proved, it has a Remington 700 action and Hart barrel with the receiver pillar bedded into a fiberglass stock. From the bench it consistently averages under ½-inch (for three-shot groups) with a maximum charge of IMR-4831 behind the Nosler 140-grain Ballistic Tip. Anytime a buck appears within 400 yards of this rifle, he is destined for that great soy bean field in the sky!

Bullets for Deer

There are two schools of thought on bullet performance. One side opts for lightweight, thin-jacketed bullets that go to pieces and shed all their energy inside a buck's body cavity without complete penetration. Generally, this is not a bad game plan. Compared to many big game animals, even the biggest of whitetail bucks is relative-

The tower the author is climbing into overlooks a huge cultivated field. For such hunting one of his favorite rifles is the one slung over his shoulder, a Kenny Jarrett custom job in 280 Ackley Improved with Remington Model 700 action, Hart barrel and fiberglass stock. The big 2.5-10x scope is a Schmidt & Bender, the author's favorite when hunting from a tower.

A Nosler 140-grain Partition bullet fired from this Remington Model Seven, 7mm-08 totally devastated this buck's lungs. He ran about 20 yards, leaving a generous blood trail.

construction, yet penetrate an incredible amount of hide, meat and bone. Additionally, both bullets absolutely refuse to fly to pieces on close-range shots.

For long-range shooting I prefer to use medium-weight bullets in standard capacity cartridges of 6.5mm and larger. Good examples are the 125-grain 6.5mm, the 130-grain 270, the 140-grain 7mm and the 150-grain 30-caliber. For smaller calibers I prefer the heaviest bullets available for them: like a 120-grain in the 25-06 and 100- to 105-grain in the 6mm class.

For close-to-medium-range shooting I prefer to use the Nosler Partition or Remington Core-Lokt in the medium weight range or a heavier bullet if its construction is more conventional. For example, were I to use the 30-06

ly fragile of body structure. Smack him in the lungs with a high-velocity, thinly-constructed bullet (of most any caliber) and he dies rather quickly. Such bullets work fine for open country shooting.

I see two shortcomings with this concept. First, big game animals very seldom offer a hunter the so-called broadside, picture book shot. A bullet that literally explodes within the chest cavity of a buck (on a broadside shot) may not reach his vitals on a quartering shot. Secondly, an *entrance* hole made by an expanding bullet seldom allows blood to escape the body cavity while an *exit* hole made by an expanding bullet most often does. This is especially important to remember when hunting in thick wooded country where a fatally wounded buck, that leaves no blood trail to follow, can be most difficult to find.

Two bullets that perform dependably and consistently are the Nosler Partition (available to handloaders as well as being loaded in Federal Premium ammo) and Remington Core-Lokt. They open up at long range as well as bullets of more conventional

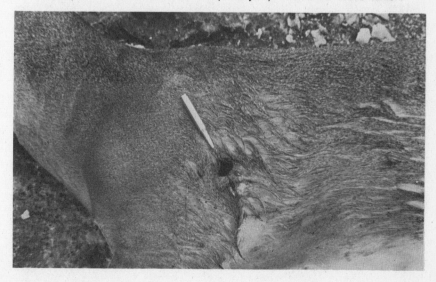

This is ideal performance from the 280 Remington cartridge on a whitetail buck. At top the bullet's entrance hole is just at the end of the cartridge. At bottom is the exit hole. The buck ran about 40 yards, leaving a blood trail anyone could follow. Bullet performance such as this is especially important to the woods hunter.

for woods hunting, a 150-grain bullet of premium construction would be the ticket. But, if I used a bullet such as the Sierra or Speer it would weigh 180 grains.

When hunting deer with a rifle chambered for one of the magnum cartridges I usually move up a notch in bullet weight to avoid excessive damage to the edible parts. For the 6.5mm, 270, 7mm and 300 Magnums, my pick would be 140-, 150-, 160- and 180-grain bullets respectively.

Open Sights and Deer Rifles

Few kind words are said about open sights these days. Few hunters still use them. But, if truth be known, woods hunters would probably kill the same number of deer if they all left their scopes at home. Actually, a rifle with iron sights has certain ad-

(Above) This is a good example why I like a powerful rifle and a bullet that blasts on through a deer from any reasonable angle. I shot this buck at about 20 yards with a Alpha Grand Slam in 243 Winchester. He ran into the swamp about 50 yards without leaving any sign of a blood trail. I was lucky I found him.

A bullet that performs perfectly on an animal standing broadside to the hunter as shown above may not perform as well on the buck shown below. For all-around use I prefer a bullet that will perform under the worst of conditions.

vantages over another with a glass sight. An iron-sighted rifle is lighter, feels better, handles faster and is more comfortable to carry with one hand. It's also less expensive.

I have a modest collection of old deer rifles with open sights. Most have never been drilled and tapped for scopes. And they'll probably stay that way as long as I own them. Every season I hunt with one or two for old-time sake. As I look at my rack, I can see a Sedgley 1903 Springfield in 30-06, a Remington Model 81 in 300 Savage, a Savage Model 99 in 300 Savage, a Remington Model 14 in 35 Remington and two rather scarce Savage Model 20 bolt-actions, one in 250-3000, the other chambered for the 300 Savage. None of those rifles are wearing glass. If I had to use any of them for the rest of my woods hunting for deer, I'd probably complain for a few days, and then go about the business of killing deer.

The best front sight blades are those with the "sourdough" or large round bead. The flat rear surface of the sourdough angles forward and picks up more light than the bead. (Replacement sights of this type are available from Burris, the company that also makes scopes.) Most beads are, unfortunately, too small for woods hunting. Ideally, a bead should measure about 0.080-inch in diameter (like the bead on the front sight of my old Remington model 600 carbine in 350 Magnum). Even better than the commonly seen gold bead is one made of ivory or white composition material. (Some say that a white bead is no good for snow-country hunting because it is difficult to see against a white background. I won't argue. Choose your bead accordingly.)

No factory rifle that I have examined lately has a decent rear sight. All cover too much of the target. So, while you're replacing the front sight, you may as well do likewise at the rear. For your money, the Williams Gun Sight Company makes the best rear sight available. It's the express-type with a wide, shallow V leaf. For quick shooting it's tough to beat.

about 40 yards from where I stood. He was really burning the wind. Try as I did, I was unable to see the front sight. I have seldom used the aperture sight for hunting since.

Scopes for Deer Rifles

When I first started pestering Southeastern whitetails in the 1950s, rifle scopes were only a little more common in my neck-of-woods than Cape buffalo. Those few hunters who used the scope suffered the brunt of campfire jokes and suspicious stares from other hunters. As a youngster I was often invited to hunt with a group of old-timers who had hunted together for many years. Most used Savage 99s, Winchester 94s, Marlin 336s and Remington 141s. One chap even used

negative side, it adds considerable cost to the rifle, and it makes the rifle feel top heavy. A rifle with a scope riding on top is also less comfortable to carry with one hand. Also, even though today's scopes are remarkably weatherproof, one can fog up or go haywire at the worst of times. We hear the occasional horror story about scopes, but I suppose I've been lucky. I have used them in every kind of weather condition imaginable—rain, snow, dust, heat and cold. And it has been about 25 years since I have had a major problem with any scope. Why? I only use *top quality scopes*.

From where I sit, the advantages of using a rifle scope far outweigh the disadvantages. A scope allows the hunter to better see his target in the

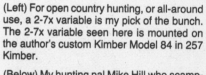

(Left) For open country hunting, or all-around use, a 2-7x variable is my pick of the bunch. The 2-7x variable seen here is mounted on the author's custom Kimber Model 84 in 257 Kimber.

(Below) My hunting pal Mike Hill who scampers about the alpine areas of Oregon and Washington thought my Bausch & Lomb Armored Compact Binocular was just the ticket for mountain hunting. So do I.

The aperture, or peep sight as it is often called, is a bit more precise than the open sight and, if the aperture is quite large, it is even quicker for fast shooting. Before the scope sight became as common as the house fly, the peep sight was touted highly by those who hunted in open country. But for woods hunting this type of sight is, in my opinion, less than ideal. Problem is, regardless of the size of the aperture, the front sight is often impossible to see in dim, deep-woods light.

Years ago I hunted black bear with dogs a great deal. Until I switched to a handgun, my favorite bear medicine was a Marlin Model 336 in 35 Remington with its barrel chopped back to 16½ inches. One year, for reasons I have yet to understand, I decided the rifle needed a receiver sight. At dawn on the very first day of the following season the hounds pushed a big blackie through thick, black timber

a chopped off 30-40 Krag. And let's not forget the doctor in our party who hunted with a Model 70 Super Grade in 30-06. He wore a wool coat and pants made by Filson, drove the biggest car I'd ever seen and wore boots that cost more than my deer rifle. His Model 70 wore a Lyman Alaskan 4x scope.

Everybody had a ball kidding ole' Doc about his "crutch" (probably out of jealousy more than anything else). But, anytime a shot rang out at the crack of dawn, you could safely bet egg money that it was Doc and his '06. From then on for the remainder of the hunt nobody kidded Doc about anything. I knew why Doc killed deer when the rest of us could hardly see our hands 2 feet from our collective noses. He could *see* his deer—long before we could see ours.

A rifle scope comes with both advantages and disadvantages. On the dim lights of dawn and dusk—those times when deer are most active. A scope also offers a margin of safety not provided by open sights. Simply put, the possibility of an inexperienced hunter mistaking another hunter for game is less likely when a scope is used. The scope is also much quicker to use than open sights.

I own a number of scopes and have definite preferences when it comes to selecting one for the various types of hunting and hunting conditions I normally encounter. For woods hunting I occasionally use a 1½x fixed power. I do, however, actually prefer a 1.5-4x variable. Brand? Probably, the king of woods scopes is the 1.5-4x Schmidt & Bender. At the low end of its power range the field of view is a whopping

when I'm walking, I personally prefer a minimal amount of weight and bulk, hence my comment about the 2-7x being "ideal." On the other hand, anytime I sit in a tower or tree stand, and survey a good chunk of open country, I'm likely to opt for even more power. My all-time favorite? It's the 2½-10x Schmidt & Bender. The S&B's huge 56mm objective lense sucks up light like you wouldn't believe, and when cranked up to 10x, that scope will reach into thick brush fringing an open field and zoom a buck right into my lap! This scope, along with the 8x56mm fixed-power Schmidt & Bender are the most popular scopes used by hunters who hunt deer from towers in my part of the country.

The smaller binoculars usually come in 7x and, for all-around use, they are ideal. In 1968 my sweet wife gave me the Bushnell. I've used it for years without a single complaint. It is as tough as a blacksmith's anvil, has excellent optics and is light enough for mountain hunting.

My favorite binocular though, is the Bausch & Lomb 10x50mm. Its light transmission borders on the incredible, and its optics are absolutely flawless. I can stare into that binocular for hours, days and weeks on end and never suffer the first trace of eye strain. For open-country hunting I don't believe they can be beat for the money. I even use them for woods hunting when sitting in a tree stand. Don't laugh at me (like my pals did with Doc and his scope) until you try it. Admittedly though, they are a bit heavy for still-hunting. That's why I own more than one binocular.

Without doubt, the most important advice I can give on binoculars is to cut corners somewhere else. You'll never regret it. If you don't believe what I'm saying here, just read on.

Last year one of our optics vendors sent me a binocular for testing. It arrived the day before I was to leave for a week's hunt so I didn't have time to try it before departing. It certainly looked nice. Optically it was a complete disaster. After 2 hours of using that binocular, my eyes felt like they would pop out at any minute from strain. Lucky for me the fellow I hunted with had a spare. *A good spare.* The other went back to its maker along with a bill for a bottle of aspirin!

The Perfect Deer Rifle

It would be awfully tough to find a better outfit for hunting deer in semi-open country than my Bausch & Lomb 10x50mm binocular, Searcy Alpiner rifle in 270 Winchester topped with a Schmidt & Bender 1.5-6x scope.

96 feet at 100 yards, and its light transmission of over 90 percent makes it the *brightest* scope I have ever gazed through. Another "brilliant" woods scope, in my opinion, is the Bushnell Scope Chief 1.5-4.5x.

I prefer a variable scope on my woods rifle for the reasons already mentioned—it has a wide field of view for close, quick shots and yet enough magnification for tagging a buck on yon side of a soy bean field.

For open country deer hunting a 2-7x variable is ideal. It has plenty of power for long-range shooting and yet adequate field of view at the low end in case I decide to go in and dig a buck out of the thickets. And, yes, I see nothing wrong in using a 3-9x or 4-12x for open country hunting; but

Binoculars for Deer Hunting

A good binocular is second only in importance to the deer rifle. Fact is, if I were, for some odd reason, forced to choose between the binocular and rifle scope, the latter would gather all the dust. When hunting open country, top quality optics are essential for sizing up a trophy or spotting a bedded buck. Most often overlooked by most hunters is the fact that binoculars are just as useful for woods hunting. Woods hunters who first use a binocular are amazed at how they can reach into thick brush and spot deer.

The best binoculars I have ever used are the Bushnell Custom Compact, Bausch & Lomb Armored Compact and Bausch & Lomb 10x50mm.

The fact that the all-round deer rifle does not exist bothers me not in the least. Fact is, I'm glad it doesn't. I enjoy using different rifles as the occasion might dictate. However, several rifles do represent an excellent compromise. If for some horrid reason I could own but one rifle for hunting deer all over this great country of ours, I would first look at the type of deer hunting I do *most,* not the type I *might* do at some foggy point in the future. The choice? It would be a rifle that would be reasonably acceptable for *all* types of deer hunting. A tall order? You bet. But not impossible.

Most often I hunt deer in country that has both wooded and open terrain. But I also occasionally hunt in mountains and plains country. If I had to pick just one deer gun I would look long and hard at two rifles: the Remington Model 700 Mountain rifle or Winchester Model 70 Feather-

This is probably the ultimate in long-range deer rifles. It's a 280 Ackley Improved with Remington Model 700 action, Hart barrel, fiberglass stock and 8x56mm Schmidt & Bender scope. With IMR-4831 behind the Nosler 140-grain bullet it reaches 3100 fps and always puts three into less than a ½-inch at 100 yards. Gunsmith Kenny Jarrett built it.

The Rem. Model 700 Mountain Rifle in 280 Rem. comes awfully close to meeting my criteria for the all-around deer rifle.

(Right) For consideration as an all-around deer rifle, this Weatherby Fiberguard in 270 Weath. Mag. deserves a close look. Its fiberglass stock is tougher than wood — and weatherproof!

weight. If the old budget could stand the additional strain I would add two other rifles to my list of possibilities— the Alpha Arms Grand Slam and the Ultra Light Arms Model 24. All of those rifles are balanced well enough for quick handling when woods hunting. In the proper chambering (we'll discuss that in a moment) they'll shoot flat enough for plains hunting and are light enough for hunting in steeper country. They are also available chambered for cartridges with more than enough power to down the biggest of bucks with great authority.

Although I consider the 30-06 to be the single most useful cartridge for the average hunter's use on big game up to elk, and consider the 25-06 to be one of our finest cartridges for shooting deer in open country, I doubt that I would choose either for my all-round deer cartridge. My choice? It would have to be either the 280 Remington or 270 Winchester, cartridges which are available in the guns just mentioned above. If I chose to shoot factory loads I would go with the Remington 130-grain Core-Lokt load for the 270 and the 150-grain Core-Lokt for the 280. Remington's Core-Lokt bullets really hold together for deep penetration on close shots and yet open up quite nicely at long range. For strictly open country hunting, I would pick the 270, 130-grain Rem-

ington Bronze Point or the 140-grain Soft Point 280 load.

If I were using handloads, I'd opt for the Nosler 130-grain Partition for the 270, and the 140-grain Partition for the 280. These would be my *all-round* loads. For open country shooting with home brewed fodder the 270 would be fed Nosler's 130-grain Ballistic Tip or Sierra's 130-grain boat-tail. The 280 would get along quite nicely with Speer's 130-grain boat-tail or the Nosler 140-grain Ballistic Tip.

Mount a good variable scope with 1.5x to 2x on the low end and 6x or 7x on the high and you've got a rifle that will bring home the venison about anywhere you choose to take it. •

THE BEATERS ARE already lining out as I reach my shooting butt, remove my shotguns from their canvas covers, place the safety sticks on my right and left, and organize my shooting paraphernalia. The beaters begin the drive a mile in front of the butts. They are still ¾-mile out when two adult grouse barrel over the butt to my right. A single shot and the first grouse of the drive is in the bag. I can see the beaters now, still over ½-mile away swinging sticks with plastic flags attached in order to flush grouse from the thick heather. More shooting on both sides heightens the tension as I scan the area in front of my butt in search of approaching birds. Out of nowhere comes a covey of six grouse. Two hurried shots, one bird down. A second covey follows, two more shots, switch guns, and fire again. A single bird curls high overhead just as a covey skims diagonally across the front of my butt. The barrels of my shotguns are hot when the horn signals the end of the drive. The beaters are within 300 yards of the butts and no more shooting forward is allowed. Hot barrels in the hands and dead birds in the heather . . . a wonderful combination indeed.

This is the glorious 12th of August,

the start of grouse shooting in Scotland. Not far from here, late in the summer of AD 83, Argicola defeated the Caledonians in the great battle of Mons Graupius, thus completing the Roman conquest of Britain. No doubt grouse were being killed for food by Scottish crofters in those days, but the era of shooting grouse for sport began in northern England and Scotland in the late 1800s with the emergence of the breech-loading shotgun and the steam locomotive.

Birth of Grouse Shooting

Several gunsmiths in Paris can take some credit for the unfolding of sporting grouse shooting as we know it today for they developed breech-loading guns. English and Scottish gunmakers followed quickly in the creation of reliable and well-balanced, breech-loading, double-barreled shotguns. Hammer guns gave way to hammerless models, choke-boring was perfected, and in the late 1870s, ejectors were patented. As the shotgun evolved, so did gun powder, from the dirty slow burning "black

by **R.J. ROBEL**

stuff" to the faster and cleaner burning smokeless powders. By the late 1880s, highly effective double-barreled shotguns were available to shoot multiple birds flying toward, away from, or past an English or a Scottish gentleman.

Coincident with the perfecting of efficient shotguns, the British railway companies recognized that there was a need to build luxurious trains for the transportation of the aristocracy. When Sandringham House in Norfolk was bought by the Prince of Wales in the 1860s, he had a railway station constructed nearby to bring his guests as conveniently near the house as possible. The Duke's actions showed that the railway, that dubious invention of a generation before, was now respectable. Aristocratic disapproval evaporated and the railway provided fast and convenient passage for the gentry living in London to the grouse moors of southern Scotland. Grouse shooting in northern Scotland was slow to develop because railways were slow to penetrate into that part of Britain. Sportsmen wanting to shoot grouse in northern Scotland had to take a train to Blackpool, then a steamer that crawled up the west coast of Scotland in very much the same way as all

"the Glorious 12th"

GROUSE HUNTING IN SCOTLAND

Shooters, loaders and dogs walk across beautiful heather on their way to the butts on the "Glorious 12th." Walking sticks help maintain one's balance as you make your way across the uneven terrain.

small craft had done for centuries. Grouse moors of southern Scotland were only 16 hours away from London's Euston Station whereas it took at least 48 hours to reach the northern grouse moors of the Scottish Highlands. Now, a century later, the cares of the world vanish each year as I ride the Night Aberdonian from London's Kings Cross Station north to Scotland in August. The *clickaty-click, clickaty-click* from the wheels of the comfortable sleeper lulls me into dreamland while I look forward to a pleasant week of shooting on the fabulous grouse moors of Scotland.

Social Acceptance of Grouse Shooting

Crucial though they were, the development of the modern shotgun and the availability of reliable rail transportation did not make grouse shooting socially acceptable or desirable. A social impetus was needed, and that was provided primarily by the Prince of Wales and his entourage of the upper classes.

Queen Victoria became isolated from her subjects following the death of her husband, the Prince Consort. The British society sensed a change forthcoming as the Prince of Wales

grew to manhood. When the Prince and Princess of Wales were married in 1864, the ascendancy of the Prince of Wales over society was complete until his death 50 years later. His personal tastes, particularly his love of shooting, became the tastes of his smarter and richer subjects. His father had introduced him to the sport of stag stalking and grouse shooting on the royal Balmoral Estate in Scotland during his youth. When the Prince of Wales became King Edward VII, his passion for shooting was well developed.

It was no coincidence, then, that the vast property King Edward VII purchased at Sandringham was the best shooting country in England. A good day of shooting for King Edward VII was second in pleasure to nothing else in the world. What he pioneered at Sandringham was copied on numerous other estates in Britain. It was an era when the monarch could do *no* wrong. He enjoyed driven grouse shooting and became an excellent shot. King Edward's second son, who was later to become King George V, also loved shooting. Thus, the sport of driven grouse shooting had royal approval. This endorsement, during the reigns of two highly admired mon-

archs, made driven grouse shooting an acceptable and highly preferred sport in Britain. An invitation to a Scottish estate for a week of driven grouse shooting was jealously cherished and coveted by the gentry of London. Grouse shooting became intertwined with business activity, political maneuvering, and social functions. Thus, grouse shooting experienced a great surge in popularity during the late 1800s and early 1900s.

Although some grouse shooting was done over dogs, the most revered type of shooting was at driven birds. After all, driven birds could be shot by the portly, those in poor physical condition, and the elderly, yet provide a challenge for even the best of shots.

Red Grouse

The red grouse of Scotland is a close relative of the willow ptarmigan of Alaska and northern Canada. As with our ptarmigan, the feet are feathered so birds can walk across deep snow during winter. Red grouse are rusty hazel to chestnut in color, the male being more rufous than the female. Ptarmigan turn white in the winter, red grouse don't. In the spring the scarlet comb above the eyes of the male red easily distinguishes it from the female. Adult male reds weigh 1½ to 1¾ pounds while females are ¼-pound lighter.

Red grouse inhabit heather moors in Britain, primarily from Wales to Yorkshire and north to Scotland, Ireland, the Orkneys and the Hebrides. Their preferred habitat is the open heather moor well away from trees. Several attempts have been made to introduce red grouse into North America. All have failed. Extensive studies in Scotland have shown that a heather diet is required by these birds, and their survival and breeding success is directly related to the quality of the heather eaten.

Red grouse populations are cyclical, that is, they fluctuate up and down over periods ranging from 3 to 10 years. The cause of these population fluctuations is not known. Some believe the fluctuation is due to changes in predation and disease while others postulate that changes in behavior cause population cycles. The causative factors probably are multiple and interrelated.

Red grouse do not move long distances like some other ptarmigan. While ptarmigan in the USSR may migrate up to 175 miles to better feeding areas during winter, red grouse seldom move over a mile during their lifetime.

During the breeding season, pairs defend their individual nesting territories. When walking across a Scottish moor in late winter and early spring, one is constantly challenged by territorial grouse. Their *kohway* and *ko-ko-ko* calls from atop a small hillock or stone warns intruders of their presence. Territorial males of-

An aggressive male red grouse perches on a rock as he defends his territory. His feathered feet allow him to traverse snow-covered expanses in the winter.

ten fly steeply upward for 30 feet or more while becking an *aa, ka-ka-ka* call. Other grouse and even foxes and sheep respect the territorial boundaries of aggressive red grouse during the spring nesting season.

The female produces a clutch of 6 to 7 eggs, and the male remains with the female during incubation. Hatching success is high for the eggs, but chick survival is low and variable from year to year, depending primarily on the physical condition of the female and weather conditions during the first couple of weeks after hatching. If the 2 weeks immediately following hatching are cold and wet, chick survival is very low, whereas cool and dry weather results in good chick survival. Normally, high chick survival produces good grouse populations the ensuing fall.

Grouse Management

There are no state game biologists in Scotland as we know them in North America. That is because the game belongs to the landowner, and that landowner is responsible for the management of the game populations on his property. Instead of state game biologists, almost every large estate has its own biologist or team of biologists. These estate biologists are known as "gamekeepers."

They are responsible for maintaining shootable populations of game on the estate. Although they do not have formal academic training, they serve a 7- to 10-year apprenticeship under an experienced gamekeeper before they take command. Most Scottish gamekeepers are highly knowledgeable individuals with commonsense

Variegated patterns on a moor reflect good heather management. The patchiness represents different age stands of heather, a result of a long-term burning program to provide food and cover for red grouse.

This female red grouse is walking across a patch of heather that was burned over, 2 years previously. Naked stems are remains of old, rank, heather growth. Grouse have a taste for, and prefer, new (as opposed to old) heather growth.

Scottish holiday. Even schools delay opening so that students can participate in the activities on the moor. Grouse are either driven over a line of shooters or walked-up behind pointing or flushing dogs. In areas with good grouse stocks, the birds are driven; on moors with lower grouse stocks or with terrain too broken for driving, the birds are walked-up, behind dogs.

Driven grouse provide superlative sport. During the 19th century heather-burning to benefit sheep grazing increased the stocks of grouse also. With the higher grouse stocks some pioneers tried driving grouse over a line of shooters. Their success led to improved systems of moor burning for grouse and the development of more effective drive strategies. The result was the finest and most sought-after sport shooting in the world. Because it was cherished and practiced by the monarchs on their well-managed moors, driven grouse shooting quickly became known as the "Sport of Kings."

Land Rovers and an old military vehicle overlook the shooters as they relax at lunch time. The large truck served to transport the beaters while the shooters and loaders rode in the Land Rovers.

management skills. They are field trained, extremely dedicated to their profession, and are esteemed by the Scottish community in which they live.

It is the responsibility of the estate gamekeeper to keep the moor in a condition that is favorable to grouse populations. Because red grouse live on the moors and depend primarily on heather for food and cover, *grouse* management is *heather* management. Heather is similar in appearance to buckbrush and reaches a maximum height of 3 feet in about 10 to 12 years. After the first 6 to 7 years heather growth slows, and its nutritional value begins to decline. Older heather shoots become rank and unpalatable to grouse; shoots of young heather are highly nutritious and palatable.

A well-managed grouse moor has a good mix of young and old heather. Young heather provides an adequate supply of food, and old heather provides nesting cover and protection against adverse weather. This important balance of young and old heather stands is maintained through a program of burning. Small fires (3 to 10 acres) are preferred to maximize the heterogeneity of the habitat and maximize the carrying capacity of the

moor. A well-managed moor is a patchwork of different age stands of heather.

Predator control is also an important part of a gamekeeper's responsibilities. High populations of avian and mammalian predators can take an incredible toll on the adult and juvenile grouse population. Therefore, gamekeepers work hard to reduce predator populations.

Shooting Grouse

The "Glorious 12th" (August 12) has long been the traditional beginning day of grouse shooting in Scotland, except when that date falls on a Sunday when no shooting is permitted. The Glorious 12th is almost a

The success of grouse driving lies primarily in one habit the grouse has—it flys along the contours of hills. Thus, "butts" (concealing structures for shooters) are placed across those contours so that the main flight pattern of driven birds is at right angles to the line of butts. Farmers, students and foresters act as beaters to flush the grouse and drive them toward the concealed shooters. A line of beaters will fan out ½-mile or more and traverse a mile or two toward the line of butts. The butts are so placed that the birds are funneled across them. A well-executed drive will push hundreds of birds over the butts, offering some of the most challenging shooting in the world.

Until the 1870s, all grouse shooting

was over dogs. Heather management increased grouse populations in the late 1800s and grouse driving replaced walked-up shooting on most Scottish moors. The current demand for driven grouse shooting exceeds the supply, so areas with lower grouse populations are experiencing a resurgence in the popularity of walked-up shooting. While walked-up shooting does not provide the challenge of driven birds, it does offer an exhilarating outing on the moor.

Walked-up shooting is done behind black and yellow Labrador retrievers, English and springer spaniels, or pointing dogs such as English pointers and setters. Seldom is shooting done without dogs because wounded grouse are easily lost in the thick heather. Even birds that fall stone dead are near impossible to find. Obviously, American hunters are quite at home walking up grouse on a Scottish moor because it is so similar to the traditional hunting of game birds in this country.

Shotguns for Driven Grouse

Autoloading and pump shotguns are simply not seen on grouse moors where birds are driven. In addition, you seldom see such guns on moors that are walked up. In fact, autoloaders or pump guns are not permitted on most grouse moors. Why? Because it's simply a matter of *tradition*. Grouse shooting is steeped in tradition and tradition dictates shooting grouse with a side-by-side double. I have shot driven grouse, on Scottish estates for 20 years and I have yet to see the use of a pump or auto permitted.

Generally the guns used on a grouse butt line are best quality English doubles. As you walk down a line of butts, you will be most likely to see Boss, Holland & Holland, Purdey, Churchill, Grant, and products of other well-known London gunmakers. Some members of my American shooting party have used Browning over/unders, or Winchester 21s, but after shooting driven grouse for a few years, they eventually arrive with a pair of Holland's or Boss' and swear by them. Because of the high cost of best quality English doubles ($10,000 to $20,000 each in 1985), a few of the higher grade Spanish guns are making their appearance on the Scottish grouse moors, especially on the moors catering to American and/or continental parties.

The most widely used gauge is the 12. A few 20s are seen, but they are rare. Even though the 16-gauge is *the*

Land Rovers are the typical means of transporting grouse shooters to and from shooting areas on the moor. Here the shooting party is getting ready to head for the grouse butts.

choice in mainland Europe, it is seldom seen on a Scottish grouse moor. For several years I used a pair of 16-gauge Lang and Hussey Imperial Ejector guns for driven grouse. They were very fast and extremely effective. I switched to 12-bores because it was difficult to obtain 16-bore cartridges in Scotland. So why fight it? When in Scotland, do as the Scottish do! Use a 12.

Because driven grouse are shot at 40 yards or less, open choked guns are preferred. The Improved Cylinder and Modified choke combination is the most popular. A shooter who concentrates solely on driven grouse will sometimes have both barrels of his grouse guns bored Improved Cylinder. The standard 12-gauge load for driven grouse is $1\frac{1}{16}$ ounces of shot pushed by 3 drams equivalent of powder. British shot sizes are different than those in North America. No. 6

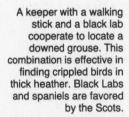

A keeper with a walking stick and a black lab cooperate to locate a downed grouse. This combination is effective in finding crippled birds in thick heather. Black Labs and spaniels are favored by the Scots.

This shooter is taking an incoming bird while the loader stands ready to exchange the empty gun for a loaded one.

the brow of a hill. A typical butt is a shallow excavated area with a low wall of peat in front. Butts are located 45 or 50 yards apart so you can safely shoot within a 120-degree arc in front of your butt. Safety markers are commonly erected to delineate the safe shooting zone for each butt. Butts are numbered from the bottom to the top of the hill and shooters draw for butts each morning.

Tips and Hints

Concealment is important. Grouse have good eyesight. If they see you move in your shooting butt, they will swerve away out of range. You *must* wear drab-colored clothing, and a hat that shadows the highlights of your forehead. I wear a tweed outfit and remain perfectly still until the birds are in range, then raise my gun and fire.

Red grouse coast at 35 to 40 mph, and move at 50 mph when they need to. Add a tail wind and the shooting really gets sporty. The position of most of the butts prevents you from spotting approaching grouse until they are 30 or 40 yards in front of you. Thus you must be alert during the entire drive or you will miss several opportunities to shoot birds in front of your butt. Quickness is essential. Although shots can be taken at birds in the rear going away from the butts, shooting birds as they approach you is much more exciting and challenging.

shot (270 per ounce) is the preferred shot size for grouse in Scotland, the British No. 6 being comparable to the American No. 7. Although high-base and magnum loads are available in Britain, they are seldom used. Recoil is excessive when high-power loads are shot in lightweight guns. The $1\frac{1}{16}$-ounce load in my $6\frac{1}{4}$-pound 12-bore Holland & Holland double is a joy to shoot and produces a beautifully even 50 percent pattern at 40 yards. It is a grouse killer when I do my part.

associated with that many people is a test of a gamekeeper's ability. With that many people, gun safety is always of first concern. Safety can never be compromised under any circumstances.

Grouse butts are located in a straight line across the contours of a hill, at right angles to the direction of the drive. They are designed to conceal the shooters from approaching birds and are often situated just over

A Day in the Butts

There is no question that driven grouse shooting combines some of the most exciting and difficult bird shooting you'll ever experience with some of the most magnificent scenery in the world. In mid-August, the heather is just coming into full bloom in Scotland. The rolling moorland is vivid with the light and dark purple of bell and ling heather. Their colors are even more vibrant under blue skies and puffy white clouds. Superimpose on that vision, the rocky crags of the Grampian Mountains in the distance, and you have a spectacular panorama. Much of the thrill of driven grouse shooting is associated with the splendor of the Scottish landscape.

A grouse shooting party consists of 8 or 9 shooters. Normally each shooter has a companion to load his/her gun if the shooter is using a pair of guns. When you add to that number, approximately 24 beaters and 4 or 5 associated individuals, a couple dog handlers and gamekeepers, you end up with 45 to 50 people on the hill for the day. Just handling the logistics

Safety sticks in place, this grouse shooter is in his "shooting butt," ready to swing on approaching grouse. Note the shooting butts just under and over the shooter's left hand. They're approximately 50 yards apart, for maximum shooting safety.

This old keeper carefully counts the grouse at the end of the drive, and places them in the bird box mounted on the front of the Land Rover.

Even the most experienced grouse shooters will expend two cartridges per bird in the bag. On windy days, or later in the season when grouse fly faster and reverse themselves in mid-air, the best of shots will often empty three or four cartridges for every dead grouse in the heather. I become elated and very confident when I manage to kill a pair of birds from a covey with my double (called a "right and left"). Reality quickly returns when I miss the next bird with two shots as it curls overhead. Shooting driven grouse is a humbling experience for any shooter.

Generally a day of driven grouse shooting includes four or five drives. Different butts are used for each drive, or on occasion, reverse drives are conducted. A reverse drive sweeps birds in to the butts from one direction followed by a second drive that brings the birds in from the opposite direction. Instead of staying in the same numbered butt for the entire day, you move up two butts each drive. This provides the fairest distribution of shooting among the shooters.

The number of grouse bagged by a shooting party in Scotland ranges from few to 400 per day. The bag depends on: (1.) the inherent quality of the moor; (2.) the success or failure of the breeding season; (3.) the standard of shooting; and (4.) the weather conditions. I do not measure the quality

of a day on the moor by the number of birds killed. Such a measure is a shallow index of the sport. I use the number of shots fired as a crude reflection of the sport of the day. We have shot on an above average grouse moor in Scotland for the last 16 years. My shooting party averages 45 to 55 shots per day each. If the weather conditions are good and the shooters are doing their job, my 8-shooter group will bag between 60 and 80 brace (120 and 160 birds) per day. A few of the best Scottish moors produce bags of 200 brace (400 birds) per day when shot by experienced grouse shooters. Such moors are the exceptions, and the country average is more like 30 or 40 brace per day.

Costs

As one would expect, driven grouse shooting is *not* inexpensive. Heather management is labor-intensive and costly. Expenses associated with predator control must also be covered. Likewise, the cost of beaters, loaders, gamekeepers, vehicle maintenance, and government-imposed taxes must be recovered by the estate. Grouse shooting in Scotland is not as expensive as shooting partridges in Spain or shooting pheasants in England. But that is a relative matter only.

Driven grouse shooting is normally let by the week, with driving conduct-

ed on at least 4 of the 5 days. This provides a spare day for rest, or an extra day if one is canceled because of inclement weather. For moors with expected bags of 40 to 80 brace per day, the going rate for a party of 8 or 9 shooters was around $3,200 per shooter. For moors with expected bags of 100 to 150 brace per day, the cost is appreciably higher. The least one should expect to pay for a week of driven grouse shooting would be approximately $2,500 on a moor that has an expected bag of 20 to 40 brace of grouse per day. Those prices do not include cartridges, gratuities, lodging or local transportation.

A quick analysis of my grouse shooting costs over the last 5 years is scary, but then on a comparative basis, not too bad. We have been shooting on the same grouse moor for the last 16 years. Our week of shooting is not booked through a commercial agent which saves us approximately 15 percent. My average cost for a week of driven grouse shooting over the past 5 years has been $2,680 including local transportation, cartridges, and all gratuities. To many that may seem very expensive. But compare that cost to $10,000 for a 7-day Dall sheep hunt in Alaska where you have a 40 percent chance of getting a nice ram, or a $7,000 elk hunt on a ranch in New Mexico where your

At the end of the day, the keeper hangs the grouse on hooks to cool in the larder. The birds will be purchased by the local game dealer the next day and be off to market soon thereafter.

chance of killing a bull is about 60 percent. Some grown people have difficulty rationalizing the expenditure of $2,680 for a week of spectacular bird shooting, but they don't bat an eye when they pay $12,000 for a new car, or $18,000 for a customized van. One year's depreciation on either of those vehicles plus the associated insurance premium exceeds the total cost of a week of driven grouse shooting in Scotland. It all depends on what you value most in life—I drive an old 1968 Ford so I can enjoy the excitement of shooting driven grouse in Scotland each year. When I'm too old to shoot grouse, I might purchase a new vehicle, but not before.

Additional information on Scottish estates that have grouse shooting available can be found in *The Scottish Sporting Gazette*. That publication can be obtained for $5 (postpaid) from John Ormiston, 22 Market Brae, Inverness, IV2 3AB, Scotland. Because of the great demand, you will need to book at least a year in advance to secure a week of driven grouse shooting in Scotland. If you have difficulty locating a place to shoot driven grouse, contact me via this publication and I might be able to steer you to something worthwhile. If you are an ardent bird shooter, haste ye to bonny Scotland for an unforgettable experience—the Sport of Kings. ●

Cleaning and oiling guns at the end of each day is almost a ritual. Drying high-quality guns is especially important after shooting in the rain or mist.

ELK

America's Premier Big Game

by FRANK PETRINI

IF THE WHITETAIL is America's favorite big-game animal, then the elk is its classiest. Why? First, let's consider the animal's unique and irresistible majesty. Truly there are few hunting trophies that'll compare with a mature Royal or Imperial bull elk. Seeing one in the pristine, rugged wilderness is awe-inspiring, breath-taking.

Elk don't *use* the wilderness; they actually *own* it. If you don't believe me just take this challenge: steal into elk country to either hunt or photograph these majestic animals and see if you don't feel like a trespasser, an interloper.

Last winter I skied through the southern part of Yellowstone Park on a trail seldom used. Coming out of a pine forest, I happened on a meadow where two large bull elk lazed in the afternoon sun. One was lying in a deep depression in the snow, the other stood on the edge of the melted snow of a thermal area. The second one had obviously been feeding—but not at that moment. Both had their eyes on me.

The mercury hovered at about the zero mark but the windless, dry, Wyoming air and bright midday sun combined to make it feel warmer than it really was. Puffs of steamy breath shot from their nostrils.

Elk are nobody's fools. If this hadn't been a national park both bulls would have been long gone before I ever made it to the meadow. They *knew* they were safe. Yet, instinctively they watched my every movement.

From my daypack I withdrew my cameras and lenses and began to work. I started first with a 500 millimeter lens, using a tree limb as a temporary tripod. After getting a few black and white and, then, color shots, I switched to a zoom telephoto and began to break trail out onto the open meadow.

Both bulls showed a lot of tolerance. I didn't get too close because my telephoto lens allowed me to work some distance off and I didn't want to spook them. During the ½-hour that I worked, the bulls went about business-as-usual unless I got too close to their comfort zone—which was about 40 yards. The bedded elk got up during this time and stepped down into the low-lying thermal bog with its partner.

Both were Royal bulls—six points on each side. Between 700 and 800 pounds of muscle and bone per bull. I guessed each at about 5 or 6 years old. Their chocolate-brown manes were thick and rich looking. Their necks were massive although nowhere near as thick as they get during the rut in the fall of the year.

Then I noticed their eyes through my camera lens. They were steady, examining—no, condescending is a better word. Actually, *fearless* is still better. I've studied the eyes of white-tails and mule deer in a similar fashion and always saw a sense of wariness touched with fear. But not with elk. In my opinion, within the species of deer, *Cervis,* the bull elk is the king.

Another reason why elk are America's classiest big-game animals is their moderate level of availability. There's enough of them to make hunting, for the serious-minded, a real possibility with a measurable level of success, but they're few enough in number to make the bagging of a trophy something to be proud of.

During the westward expansion, explorers found elk throughout the North American continent. Naturalists estimate there were as many as 10 million in North America prior to the arrival of the Europeans. There were elk in the eastern woodlands of New England, throughout what are now the Plains states, and all over the West and Southwest portions of what is the lower-48 today. They were also found in great numbers across the lower provinces of Canada.

The only places that were unique in their lack of these great game animals were the Southeast and the deserts of the West. This has led researchers to conclude that elk have no affinity for wet, swampy, humid areas or for hot, arid, wastelands.

Today, many hunters think of the elk as a mountain critter but plainly, history shows that, for many years, tremendous numbers of elk inhabited the plains areas of this country and co-mingled readily with bison and antelope in these wide-open spaces. To earn a new identification as predominantly a mountain animal, the elk had to go through almost total decimation much like the American bison or buffalo.

In the mid-1800s elk skins were as equally coveted as buffalo robes, and the meat was sought after. Anyone who has ever feasted on elk will conclude it's a prime cut of meat. Indians, mountain men, and other pioneers, plus meat hunters working for the railroads, pursued elk as hard or harder than they did the bison. Within a half-century elk all but disappeared from the plains areas.

By the end of the 1800s the elk population had dropped to well under 100,000 throughout the entire continent. The low was reached around 1930 when approximately 90,000 elk remained, more than a third of which resided in the safety of Yellowstone National Park, or in less populated areas like the Tetons, and portions of Canada.

During the slaughter, we lost a number of elk subspecies. Gone forever are both the eastern and plains varieties. Same story with the Merriam elk of the Southwest. What remains today are the Tule elk of California, the Roosevelt elk of the Pacific Northwest, and Manitoban variety in Canada, and by far, the largest group, the Rocky Mountain elk found throughout the western mountain states. (Transplants from the Rocky Mountain herds have been made to parts of eastern Canada and the Northeast and Southwest United States.)

Through careful game management and regulated hunting the elk population has been on the upswing for the last 50 years to where, today, there are more than 500,000 throughout North America. These free-ranging animals are now found in 15 states and five Canadian provinces, but not all areas have sufficient numbers to interest the serious hunter.

Where to Hunt

In alphabetical order the states with elk populations worth noting are: Alaska, Arizona, California, Colorado, Idaho, Montana, Nevada, New Mexico, Oklahoma, Oregon, South Dakota, Texas, Utah, Washington, and Wyoming. The Canadian provinces are Alberta, British Columbia, Manitoba and Saskatchewan.

The Rocky Mountain elk is America's top trophy. It's that which the tired-of-whitetail hunter usually decides on when it comes time for a real big-game hunt.

This "backpacked" elk camp is located at 9,000 feet in the Montana wilderness—dead in the middle of elk country. Utah, Colorado, Wyo-ming, Arizona, Oregon, Washington, New Mexico, Idaho are among a select group of states offering good elk hunting.

All of these have had at least some elk-hunting activity in the last 10 years, although in the case of some, like California, there have been periods of 5 or more years between seasons. If you're a resident of one of the "lesser" states, you might want to give it a try when your game department calls for a season of some sort, whether it's a "general" or "restricted" type of hunting opportunity. But it's hardly recommended for a nonresident to plan such a venture in those states that have comparatively small elk populations. It's not worth the time, effort and expense. In addition, a number of the states that do have huntable elk populations don't always allow nonresident hunting, or if they do, it's on a permit basis with only a handful available for out-of-staters.

The areas with the biggest populations are states like Arizona, Colorado, Idaho, New Mexico, Oregon, Utah, Washington, and Wyoming. Up north, the Canadian provinces of Alberta and British Columbia are good bets. It should also be noted that for nonresident trophy hunters, the "big" elk states are *Montana, Wyoming, Colorado* and *Idaho*. Of the two big Canadian provinces, *British Columbia* is the best bet, although none of the Canadian provinces have elk herds the size of those found in our own northern mountain states.

All the top elk-hunting areas in the North American continent are in the U.S. and are the home of the Rocky Mountain elk. The Rocky Mountain elk dominates the trophy lists and is *the* animal most serious elk hunters concentrate on.

If there's one thing all these elk-hunting states and provinces have in common, it's the fact that the hunting is normally *tough,* particularly if you're looking for a decent trophy bull. Much of the reason for this is simply due to the rough terrain these creatures inhabit—the Rocky Mountains in all its craggy splendor, with high peaks, rocky passes, and wide ravines. The hunter usually must be part mountain goat with the physique of a long-distance runner—or at least the leg muscles—to not only get into prime hunting territory but also to stalk the critters once there.

Getting Into Shape

Sure, most serious hunters get into prime hunting country on horseback, but the horse only gets you there (which I don't mean to take lightly, but it is just part of the job). Depending on the nature of the country, once you get there you might comb the terrain for elk concentrations. In the highest, upended country, where the biggest bulls hang out, you'll most likely rely on leg power, at least for your final stalks. And this requires the hunter to be in *top physical condition.*

Indeed, if you're office-bound most of the time, you'll need to get into pretty good shape just to survive the horseback riding, which, in itself, can be a grueling experience for the uninitiated.

On my last hunt in the Bob Marshal Wilderness of western Montana we spent a full day packing into the spike camp from which we were to hunt. After 12 hours in the saddle everyone in our party suffered leg cramps and knee aches that, for one companion, lasted the entire 8-day hunt. The morning after we hit camp we left the horses with a wrangler and started climbing, on foot. It was 8 days and 12 pounds later (I always lose weight on elk hunts) before I mounted my horse again, for the ride out.

Between horse rides we climbed more than 5,000 feet in elevation (many times up and down) and circumvented and crisscrossed an area of 25 square miles of some of the craggiest, most unforgiving terrain I'd ever seen. All of it on foot, climbing up and down drainages looking for elk presence or sign. Seldom did we come across any trails, and those that we

In the summer and fall months elk live in the high mountain meadows.

When the snow becomes deep enough, the elk migrate down to their winter range. During migration, usually in November, the wise hunter will often place himself along those well-traveled migration paths.

When they're in their winter range, elk tend to "yard up" and stick more closely together than they do at any other time of the year.

did were game trails that were virtually impassable to horses. So get those lungs and legs in shape for thin air and 80-degree slopes.

Habits and Habitat

If the *first* commandment for elk hunting is to get into top physical condition, the *second* is to learn everything possible about these animals. Just knowing that elk inhabit the high country in the early fall is not good enough. First, it's important to know that elk habits vary with the territory.

To read about or study the habits of elk residing in our western states' national parks will tell you very little about free-ranging elk in those areas open to general hunting. Most of the elk's habits have been developed to ward off predators; in the parks there are few, if any, life-threatening predators. In Yellowstone, in the midst of winter, for example, you can find large numbers of six-, seven-, and eight-point bulls within skiing distance of Old Faithful lodge if you've

got the energy and motivation to go out looking for them. But you *can't* hunt them.

On the other hand, to find a willing subject in the six-point class, or above, in, say, the nearby Teton or Shoshone national forests during the fall-winter season takes the utmost in determination, physical endurance, and hunting skill.

Elk, however, are creatures of habit. In the warm summer and early fall months, they live in the highest, most inaccessible areas where they can find plenty of grass and forbs* to eat and stay away from people and other disturbances. They come down from these high haunts only when the winter snows pile up on the grasses and their mobility and food-gathering abilities are impaired. Then they drop down to lower altitudes, which biologists call *winter range*.

Fine, you say, if the heavy winter snows have yet to arrive all you have

———————————
**herbs other than grass*

to do is climb up to the highest peaks and meadows to find your elk. Better said than done, for elk, unlike whitetails, *don't* stay within a 2-mile radius of where they were born. They'll range for miles in these high regions. Just knowing that a herd inhabits a 25- to 40-square mile range doesn't help to pinpoint the herd's whereabouts by a long shot.

Planning Ahead

Because of the above factors, it pays to know the country where you're hunting. My advice? Get in some preseason scouting. Otherwise it might be wise to engage a reputable guide who has the equivalent of this scouting experience behind him. The latter approach may be expensive, but it can save you much time and may mean the difference between success and failure.

Some states, like Wyoming, require non-resident hunters to engage a licensed guide for elk hunting. Many complain that such practices border on featherbedding; however, the facts clearly indicate that nonresident hunter success is greater on guided hunts. On guided hunts, of course, the outfitter or guide will make all the arrangements for getting you into the backcountry and, especially, for carting your elk out should you shoot one.

(Right) Those who (wisely) do some preseason scouting, are best advised to pour over topographical ("topo") maps of the area(s) they'll hunt in later on. State conservation agencies can direct you to sources for those maps.

The would-be elk hunter is best advised to do some serious preseason scouting. If you spot droppings like these, you can be sure you're on the right track.

If you go out alone, it would be wise to consider such things beforehand. If backpacking, as many lone groups of hunters do, be prepared to quarter your game and pack it out. Look over topographical maps *beforehand* and determine the nearest jeep trails where you can park a 4-wheel vehicle.

You can sometimes work a deal with a local outfitter to pack your elk out on horseback for a fee, even if you aren't using his outfitting services for your hunt. Don't be shy to ask; outfitters are businessmen, and if getting as big a return as possible on their capital investment means renting you a horse to pack your meat, they'll do it.

Those elk hunters who don't use a guide, and hunt the same areas, year after year, will certainly get to know the common elk haunts in those areas. While they may not score in the early years, their chances for success will proportionately increase with each passing season.

While on the subject of hunter success, let's embellish a bit further, since it helps to develop a realistic expectation when elk hunting. In the big four elk states, Wyoming consistently holds the record with success percentages running as high as 45 percent in some years, although elk hunting here is done strictly on a permit basis, with a limited number available to nonresidents each year. (In recent years this nonresident limit had been set at 6,000, which is small indeed compared to the approximately 70,000 total licenses issued.)

Idaho limits nonresidents to 10 percent of the total number of elk permits available. Hunter success here usual-

First-time nonresident elk hunters would do well to engage the services of a *reputable* guide. Statistics indicate that a guided elk hunt can, indeed, be a successful hunt. Also, when it comes time to pack-out your elk, you can be sure the job will be made easier by your guide's pack horses.

ly runs between 10 and 20 percent. Colorado is the top choice of many nonresident elk hunters because they get about 30 percent of that state's 160,000 to 170,000 elk licenses. And with its 17-20 percent hunter success, Colorado offers the nonresident elk hunter a good opportunity.

When making final plans consider closely the time of the year you'll be hunting. Many hunters like early season hunts. At this time of the year, late September and early October, the elk are still in the high country. It's gruelling work at those altitudes, but it's also a beautiful experience, often with warmish temperatures at midday, and spectacular scenery. If you happen to hit the rut, you'll be rewarded with a good chance at a trophy when the bulls are sex-crazed and less wary. At that time you'll also experi-

ence the eeriness and enchantment of bulls bugling in the wilderness. This offers the additonal opportunity of being able to bugle up bulls during their rutting frenzy, although it requires some expertise to do so successfully.

When the heavy snows accumulate, usually in mid-November, the elk usually migrate to lower altitudes. The cows start the migration, the bulls usually lingering in the high country a while longer. The oldest and biggest bulls usually keep to the relative safety of the mountains as long as possible. But once the snow depth reaches 2 feet (or more) even these holdouts begin their descent.

The elk are easier to find at this time of the year since they herd-up more in the snow. Also, their migration routes are pretty well set from year-to-year. As a result many hunt-

The big bulls stay in their high summer range longer than the cows and calves. Eventually, when the snow gets *above* the 2-foot mark, the elk will head down to the winter range.

A favorite elk cartridge, among the experts, is the big 300 Winchester Magnum. With the proper bullet the 300 Mag. provides plenty of penetration and knock-down power.

At the "minor" end of the elk-killing spectrum are rounds like the 7mm-08 Remington. In the author's opinion, the 7mm-08 and others should be considered minimal for elk. When rounds such as this are used for elk, bullet weight, bullet construction and bullet placement are of utmost concern.

ers connect at this time by simply hunting along those migration routes. Of course, at these lower elevations it's also easier to get a vehicle in for retreiving your kill. Though late season hunting will be colder and less exciting, you'll find it a bit easier to bag an elk, perhaps a real trophy.

Ordnance

The optimum elk rifle is in the 30-06 to 338 Magnum class. Why? Primarily because elk can go 1,000 pounds or more on the hoof. Probably the most popular cartridge is the 30-06 with the 180-grain soft point bullet, although there are some who swear by the 220-grain weight.

Minimum cartridges? To my mind they include the 270 Winchester, 7x57 Mauser, 280 Remington, 7mm-08 Remington and 308 Winchester. I personally like the little 7mm-08 in a short-action lightweight rifle like the Remington Model Seven or the easily portable Ruger M77 Ultra-Light, but I always limit my shots with these lighter calibers to those I'm certain will reach the vital organs.

With the 7mm-08 I prefer 140- to 150-grain bullets while, in 308 Winchester, the medium-weight 165-grainers are the best compromise of velocity, energy and penetration.

I, personally, can't recommend any bore size smaller than 277-inch. Yes, there are many who like the 25-caliber cartridges, like the 25-06 Remington, and even the 257 Roberts. I won't criticize another's favorite cartridge, but, in *my* opinion, any cartridge shooting a bullet under .277-inch diameter, and lighter than 130 grains, is marginal on animals the size of elk.

If they are used, extreme care must be taken to 1.) insure *precise* shot placement (preferably in the heart or lung areas) and 2.) to keep the ranges within reason. If you must use a 25-caliber on elk, then use the heavy 120-grain soft point slugs for the best penetration.

Don't, I repeat, *don't* attempt to take a bull elk with one of the 6mms, even if it's a magnum. The entire 6mm class of cartridges are barely adequate for whitetail-sized game. They simply don't have the stopping power required for game the size and strength of elk.

While the elk is not the long-range animal that the pronghorn is, he inhabits country that's equally wide and almost as open. Three-hundred-yard shots are not unheard of, although I usually try to stay well under that if I can. Don't limit yourself by using a whitetail cartridge, like the 30-30 Winchester or 35 Reming-

ton. At best, those rounds are barely adequate for elk, and then at the shortest ranges. Most resident hunters know this already, perhaps from being closer to the game to begin with; but, nonresidents frequently spend thousands of dollars to go on an elk hunt and then try to make do with their old brush rifles.

One thing to remember about elk is that when you spook one, or superficially wound it, it'll most probably run for 5 miles or more. And seldom will it circle back or even remotely stay within the same area, as it is common with deer. Elk can cover country fast when they want to — you gain little by chasing after them unless one is wounded and you suspect he'll eventually lie down.

In short, "use enough gun" — the job will be easier.

The elk is a high class animal and it deserves to be pursued with some class. ●

SOME WRITERS would have you believe that it's criminal to shoot a grouse unless: 1.) you do it with a side-by-side double; 2.) it's over an English setter's point; 3.) you're not breathing hard (nor have sweat on the brow); 4.) your wardrobe consists of the most expensive Orvis finery; and 5.) unless a Kaywoodie pipe is tightly clenched between the teeth. I suppose there's not a thing wrong with developing one's own standards for the hunt, and restricting one's self to a classic double gun I'm sure has merit to many.

The Gun

The sportsman who has been hunting ruffed grouse for 10 years or so is going to have firm convictions on what might be called the "ideal" grouse gun. Newcomers are always joining the grouse-chasing ranks, however, and it's these tyros who are looking for advice. They want to know how *they* can come up with *their* ideal grouse gun. You know, the one that points and carries itself—the one that *seldom* misses.

Of course, few ideals exist in anything. Accordingly, the lack of perfection in three of the things closest to my heart quickly come to mind—*women, bird dogs,* and *grouse guns.* As my buddy Rich Drury puts it, "

Ruffed Grouse

by Nick Sisley

Photo by Leonard Lee Rue III

get a new gun that I think is going to be great, but it always needs a piece of moleskin on the comb, the recoil pad shaved a bit on one side, the barrel bobbed a mite. It's always something." That's the way I feel about women, bird dogs and grouse guns. None of them are perfect. They all need that figurative "piece of moleskin," somewhere.

The earliest and first serious grouse-gun treatise of which I'm aware was espoused by Bill Foster in his now classic book *New England Grouse Shooting.* The title of the first chapter in this wonderful work is titled "The Little Gun." The "little gun" refers to a 16-gauge Parker that Bill's grandfather, Everel Harnden, had purchased for fox hunting in the 1890s. It weighed 6½ pounds—with

(Opposite page) Ohio grouse expert and top shotgunner Dick Nobbs with his Drahtharr, named "Poker," and Dick's glass barreled Winchester Model 59 auto. (In the text, note the author's comments on this long-discontinued grouse gun.)

(Right) It was Bill Foster in *New England Grouse Shooting* who first penned words about grouse-gun qualities. In that book's very first chapter, "The Little Gun," Foster addressed the light, fast-handling qualities which make for the best in grouse guns. The side-by-side double at the bottom is Sisley's Richland 707 20-bore.

(Below) Sisley happens to like the Franchi 12-gauge 48/AL autoloader. It's quite light under normal circumstances, however, the author went a step further by cutting back the magazine tube and shortening the fore-end.

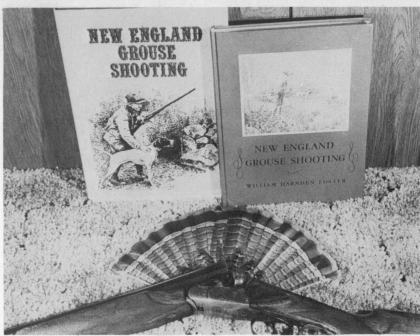

hammers. Bill Foster killed his first and many other grouse with it. The guns that market hunters carried for grouse in those days probably weighed 1½ to 2½ more pounds. Thus the age of lightness, quickness and fast-handling qualities, was introduced to enthusiasts who strove to carry, shoot and find the mythical, "perfect grouse gun."

Frank Woolner, in his *Grouse and Grouse Hunting*, made the glass-barreled Model 59 Winchester forever famous. The 59 was an extremely light, sweet swinging autoloader right from the factory, but by the time Woolner was through experimenting, he turned the 59 into a far superior grouse gun by reducing the weight to a scanty 5 pounds 11 ounces. He even added moleskin, if you will!

Because of its alloy receiver and fiberglass barrel (actually glass wrapped around a thin steel core), the 59 was light up front to begin with. The enterprising Woolner, however, had the magazine tube and fore-end cut back appreciably. This reduced "out-front weight" even more. The barrel was bobbed to 23½ inches, thereby eliminating all choke, but Frank had a second barrel (a 25-incher) with interchangeable screw-in chokes. Sound familiar? One might say they were the first Winchokes. Frank also used a low-density walnut stock with straight grip, which dropped a bit more from his grouse gun's overall weight. The end result was one of the fastest handling, best heavy cover 12 bores any grouse hunter ever one-handed. On one of his 59s Woolner even found a way to eliminate the wood fore-end, his forward hand grasping the 59's metal magazine tube when shooting. This is the 59 Frank was able to trim to 5 pounds 11 ounces—and we're talking about a 12 bore mind you!

I've never carried one of these revamped 59s in a grouse woods, though I have shot several of them at pitchdiscs. Taking Woolner's lead, I prescribed similar surgery for my Franchi 12-gauge 48/AL autoloader. Darrell Reed (Clinton River Gun Company, 30016 S. River Rd., Mt. Clemens, MI 48045) said he'd be able to accomplish what I suggested.

It was, basically, the same deal as Woolner's. Darrell cut my Franchi's magazine tube back, then rethreaded the end of it to accept the fore-end screw cap. (The magazine tube was cut back as far as possible—and still be able to fit the barrel ring over the magazine tube and tighten the fore-end screw.) Of course, the fore-end wood also had to be appropriately shortened. Prior to Dr. Reed's scalpel job (more moleskin??) that Franchi weighed 6 pounds 8 ounces. Upon its return, the needle on my baby scale swung to 6 pounds with the re-moleskinned Franchi atop.

This winter, after the grouse season, I'm going to carve off the pistol grip on this one, the carve-job serving to trim an ounce or two and provide a straight-grip stock to boot. When I finally get this revamped 12 bore Franchi the way I want it, the total heft will be under 6 pounds.

Do we need a gun that light for grouse? Is a gun so trimmed going to need even another dab of moleskin? I have a 20-gauge Franchi with a 23-inch cylinder-bore barrel. It weighs 5 pounds even. I've killed a lot of grouse with that gun, but I've come to do better with a smoothbore that weighs a tad more. For me a 6-pounder, in 12-gauge, comes close to needing very little moleskin, when we're talking about ideal grouse-gun weight. Conversely, if "specialized" grouse ordnance hefts over 6½ pounds I begin to lose interest.

I don't limit myself to shooting only over points. Those who do should carry a gun that weighs 7, maybe 7¼ pounds. To get off a shot at every ruff that gets up within range, however, one has to carry his gun at port arms—24 hours a day, so to speak. If a

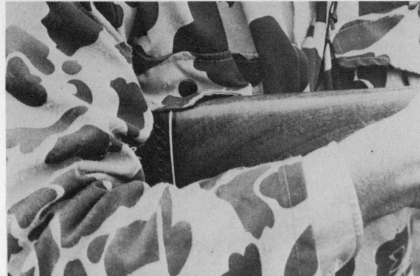

(Above) Note how rubber recoil pad hangs up on this hunter's clothing during quick mounting. Such hang-ups can occur often with that type of pad.

(Left) The author regularly takes both grouse and woodcock with his highly modified 12-bore Franchi autoloader.

(Right) A plastic buttplate like this will not hang up on clothing during ultra-fast gun mounting. Avoid rubber butt pads if at all possible.

gun weighs much more than 6½ pounds, I can't carry it for 3, 4, 5 and 6 hours at a time—all that time with both hands clutching the gun firmly—immediately ready for winged action. Of course, my main physical exercise most days is beating the tar out of a word processor keyboard. Those who throw around sacks of feed, bales of hay, move pianos, run jack-hammers and swing picks for their daily bread may look at a 6-pound 12-ounce smoothbore as little more than a feather!

Weight isn't the only factor that contributes to the over-all perfect grouse gun. Barrel length is important to both quickness and muzzle lightness. If we're talking about a magazine gun, a pump or an autoloader, my opinion is that 23 to 24 inches comes close to needing no moleskin. In a double gun, without the long receiver, a 25- to 26-inch barrel length approaches perfection.

My Franchi 12 has a 24-inch barrel. Originally it was bored true cylinder, but Darrell Reed doctored that with a set of his interchangeable, screw-in Reed Chokes. (Made of stainless steel,

they screw in flush with the end of the barrel. Also, there are no wrench notches in Reed Chokes; they look good—aesthetically clean. Reed Chokes are changed via a friction-fit tool. It's an ingenious idea.) Now, for late season hunting, when shots at grouse can be fairly long, I have the option of installing maybe a Modified or even tighter-choked Reed screw-in tube.

No perfect grouse gun should, in my opinion, ever wear a recoil pad. In the first place, rubber weighs more than light walnut. (We've already discussed weight enough.) In the second place, rubber grabs at clothing during super-fast gun mounting. The butt of the ideal grouse gun should be fairly smooth, though not totally. You want the butt to come up without catching on clothing, but once it slaps into place, it should stay put like a well-broke grouse dog. Most plastic butt plates accomplish this very well, and inexpensively. Checkered steel butt plates are fine, and perhaps more classic. A checkered walnut butt is even more classic, but it's easy to chip the heel or toe of the butt when set-

ting such a gun down.

A rib isn't essential—unless you're accustomed to shooting hundreds, perhaps thousands of rounds a year with guns possessing ribs. That's my problem. I shoot between 10,000 and 20,000 shotshells per annum—most every one of them through a gun with a rib atop the barrel. If I try to shoot grouse, *sans* rib, the sight picture is too different to what I'm accustomed to seeing all year long. So I have a rib atop my 12-bore Franchi.

I've never liked the safety that's on the Browning Superposed and many other over/unders. I'm referring to the

3¾-dram 1¼-ounce of coppered 7½s in the chamber. If the shot is at a hard driving ruff crossing at 42 yards, you can bet the shell inserted will be 1-ounce of No. 9s! It's the moleskin syndrome again. Nothing's perfect.

Hunting with Terry Moore, game biologist with the New York Conservation Department, this past fall, I noted that he shot a 12-gauge Skeet bored over/under stuffed with reloads consisting of 1¼-ounce No. 9s. John Schoen of Freeport, PA, shoots a 12-bore Franchi, among other guns for grouse, and he's a firm believer in big loads—3¾-dram, 1¼-ounce of extra-hard or coppered 7½s. He prefers a barrel with an open choke, too. The basic philosophy of both these excellent grouse shots is simple—throw a lot of shot out over as wide an area as possible. There's no question, this is the way to kill grouse consistently.

Most seasons I switch back and forth between 12-bore loads a great deal. I'd be better off going with something like a 1⅛-ounce load of chilled 7½s in the early going when the leaves still cling to the flora and the shots tend to be closer, switching to a trap load of 1⅛ ounces of high antimony, extra-hard 7½s as the leaves began to tumble, finally switching to 3¾-dram 1⅛- or 1¼-ounce coppered Federal Premiums, Remington Premiers or Winchester Double X when the leaves have dropped and/or the snow has arrived. Such would be a good basic grouse load philosophy, stacking the odds much in one's favor over the course of the entire season.

The Cover

To me, one of the most satisfying aspects of grouse hunting is not so much the shooting or the right gun with the

Sisley with a brace of grouse — and his 12-gauge Franchi autoloader with lightened, shortened fore-end.

Look closely and you *might* see the grouse directly below the pointer's keen nose. The natural camouflage of the ruffed grouse is obvious. Use a dog — you won't be sorry!

sliding button-type safety, which is moved right or left for barrel selection. In my experience, too many of these safeties hang up unless the button is moved either completely left or completely right. When they do hang up, why is it always on a grouse that goes out right at my boot tops, then offers an easy straight away shot with no limbs or tree trunks in between?

The Loads

Enough about the no-moleskin grouse gun. What about loads to stuff in them? When that 16-yard shot presents itself, you're likely to have a

This type of double-barrel selector/safety, which is moved right or left for barrel selection, can hang up if not pushed completely to the left or right before shoving the safety forward (off). If this ever happens, you can bet the grouse in question will offer a straightaway shot — with no interfering limbs or trees between.

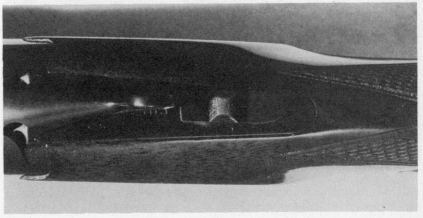

right load, but traveling to new territory and coming up with the prescription for plenty of flushes—without wasting too many hours in the quest. Each fall I like to make one or more of these exploratory out-of-state excursions, and I take pride in my track record for locating good coverts on my own. Ideal grouse cover differs over the breadth of terrain where this bird is indigenous. For instance, the ideal habitat for these birds in Washington County, Maine, is quite different from the 30 flushes a day you encounter, in Lincoln County, Wisconsin. Even in my home state of Pennsylvania, the cover varies from county to county.

The point is this: A fellow who goes searching for distant cover must not continually look for the exact type of habitat that produces for him back home. Yes, in many instances there will be habitat similarities in this context, but there will also be subtle differences. It's these subtle habitat differences which can produce a significantly higher flush rate.

One key is food. Grouse will seldom be far from a preferred food source. Just because you flush a grouse out of young aspen doesn't mean he's feeding on that trees' buds. It therefore pays to check the crop of every bird you kill, not only when you're hunting new territory, but also when hunting close to home.

Further, in some years, preferred food will be extremely limited. Sometimes you can't find any hawthorns, for example. Ditto for some other preferred foods. In my bailiwick, grouse will feed on grapes, preferring them to all other fodder. They can find grapes in plentiful supply, somewhere, every fall and winter, though in many years the supply of grapes can be restricted. When preferred foods are sparse, but you find little patches where these goodies are highly concentrated, be assured those patches will provide almost guaranteed success. Sometimes I'll find one of these "Mother Lodes" of food in the early season, but I won't flush any birds. I mentally make note, however, making certain I return to that spot a few weeks later. Generally, early in the season, foods are plentiful. With frost and snow the supply dwindles. When this happens grouse often congregate at those little corners where grapes make the vines sag, or where crab apples make the under-footing unsteady, or where thorn apples turn the ground surface crimson.

One absolute to always keep foremost in your mind as you scout for new bird territory is that grouse don't

Check the crop of every grouse taken. What's inside provides important clues to what they are eating, and subsequently, where you can find more of those challenging birds. This grouse crop was filled with thorn apples.

(Right) In thick ground cover, the author's pointer is almost lost, but the dog is locked on a grouse. Sisley is ready to put his over/under into quick action.

thrive in mature woodlands. In fact, the older a woods gets, the less likely it's going to hold birds. Farms that have been abandoned and are reverting back to a wild state tend to be excellent grouse producers—no matter where you find them. Trouble is, there aren't that many abandoned farms in grouse-land these days. Or, rather, the abandoned farms have been abandoned so many years ago that they've matured into pole timber!

Slashings and cutovers are the current-day consistent grouse producers, though a reverting farm still tends to be so much more enjoyable to hunt, for it will usually have more openings and fewer briars. Aspen cutovers result in young aspen immediately regenerating. Much of this type of timber is being harvested in the upper Midwest. Aspen grows fast, quickly choking out most briar undergrowth, so they, too, can be a pleasure to hunt. A new aspen stand can produce high-count grouse flushes within a very few seasons.

When one can find aspen that's say 8 to 14 years old, with hazel brush growing thick as the understory, it can be ideal bird cover. The grouse feed on the hazel brush catkins, during the fall, in this type of habitat, usually switching to aspen buds later in the winter season.

Where hardwoods are harvested, say in the Appalachians, the slashings which grow up immediately thereafter can be nightmares to hunt, what with horizontal slash tripping you every step. (Let's not forget canebrake briars, greenbriar and multiflora rose ripping at your skin with more fury than the cactus spines of the desert Southwest.) Still, such hells can produce birds—in spades!

The Clothes

When it comes to brush bustin' duds, the average grouse hunter would probably wear the heaviest suit

Sisley says the grouse hunter will be ideally suited with three pair of boots. On the left, for rainy weather and wet country, are 12-inch rubber boots. (He recommends 16-inch socks with an elastic top to prevent chafing the upper shin.) In the middle are 10-inch topped rubber-bottom/leather-upper paks, typified by those originated by L.L. Bean years ago. On the right are L.L. Bean leather boots with waterproof Gore-Tex between the outer leather and inner Chambrelle lining.

The author feels hunting pants could become a thing of the past. Various types of chaps, one of which he is pulling on here, could, in the future, negate the need for heavy brush busting pants.

of armor he coud find—if he could plow brush with it. I wonder if the days of even mediocre sales of duck cloth, Naugahyde, nylon-faced and other hunting pants are over. Fact is, we don't need 'em anymore. Not now that we have chaps. When one parks his vehicle next to a favorite cover these days, he can hunt in the pants of his Botany 500 suit if he merely slips a pair of Cordura or tight-weave nylon chaps over his trousers. These chaps are inexpensive, better than the toughest hunting pants, virtually indestructible, and light in weight.

A grouse hunter needs three pair of

boots. Depending upon the type of habitat he hunts most, he'll wear one of the three the majority of the time. For years I swore at rubber boots, but these days I wouldn't be without them. The most utilitarian pair I've found are those which are very light, 12 inches in height, and complete with three eyelets on top. Throw away the laces which come with them. Purchase a few pair of 16-inch socks that have strong elastic tops. With shorter socks these 12-inch boots with the three-eyelet top will rub your shin raw. When it rains, or if you're hunting flat country with wet spots galore,

you can't beat rubber boots.

The second pair of boots the ruff chaser will find necessary feature a rubber bottom and a leather upper—the type popularized for decades by L.L. Bean in Freeport, ME. For much of the hunting I do, this is the type of boot that tends to be ideal. They're great if the ground isn't too wet, if the terrain isn't too steep and rocky. They're also very light in weight.

Finally, a pair of today's waterproof leather boots are suggested. This past season I tested a pair made by L.L. Bean that featured Gore-Tex between the outer leather and inner Chambrelle lining. These waterproof boots breathe courtesy of the space-age Gore-Tex—your feet *don't* sweat. They're expensive, but they're worth it. Leather boots like this are best in steep and rocky coverts. While a Vibram lug sole is available, they pick up too much mud for me. I prefer the Vibram Evaflex sole. It offers plenty of protection from rocks and good traction, though not as good in rock-strewn country as lug soles.

Summary

If there's one absolute in grouse guns, loads, clothing, boots, and locating covers, it's that there *are* no absolutes. My figurative "moleskin" is always needed somehow, somewhere and/or on some days. The ruffed grouse is *the* gamebird in North America, and he's possibly our greatest gamebird, offering the toughest, most classic challenges of any bird on the face of the earth. ●

Always plan your day's hunt so that you'll be back at camp or at the vehicle well before dark.

LOST!

by Rick Jamison

WHEN WE THINK of getting lost, most of us think of a vast, roadless wilderness. But hunters have, unfortunately, died within a few yards of a road, or within a single mile of their own camp, simply because they didn't know the precise direction to "go in."

Getting lost could mean nothing more than getting into camp a bit late. It can mean having to spend an unpleasant night out in the woods with no lasting consequence. But if you are lost, and the weather is *severe,* and if you *aren't prepared,* you may *not* be able to survive even *one night.*

Anyone can become lost. Start now. Admit to yourself that becoming "lost" *can* happen to you. Believe me, when it does happen, it will be when you *least* expect it.

I've spent a lifetime in the woods. I grew up in the country and spent all my free time in the woods, hunting, trapping professionally and guiding other hunters. I never felt that I was in any danger as long as I didn't fall down a mountain, break through ice on a creek, or have some other misfortune. I never so much as carried a compass; I relied upon "instinct" to

get me back to the vehicle or to camp. That is, until I nearly lost my life in the woods.

I think my physical condition is what saved me. To give you an idea about the type of "condition" I'm talking about, I trained for long-distance running events with the best athletes in the world for several years. Along with this training, comes a competitive spirit, the determination to be best, and the ability to be oblivious to pain; the knowledge that you can go on when you think you can't. You're taught to mentally and physically ignore any limitations. It wasn't until I was about 32 years old that a combination of things nearly cost me my life in the woods, even though, when it happened, I was in top physical condition from running 12 to 16 miles per day in preparation for this elk hunt. I say all this not to brag, but to try to illustrate that anyone can get himself into trouble, no matter how invincible he might think he is.

Lost!

Ron Redfield and I were hunting elk out of a tent camp at the end of a road at about 10,000 feet elevation in the Colorado mountains. We were often hunting uphill from that camp at an elevation of more than 13,000 feet.

I had hunted the first day of the season without success and awoke the second day to find a foot of snow on the ground. Thinking about the easy tracking and elk-spotting conditions, I couldn't wait to grab my rifle and be off.

The sun came out, and the wet snow was melting when I spotted the tracks of what I hoped was a big bull.

I was wearing denim jeans, thermal underwear, 8-inch leather boots, a flannel shirt, and a hooded thermal sweatshirt under a fatigue jacket. I was warm and soon pulled the sweatshirt off, tying it around my waist.

Shortly, I jumped the elk I was tracking. All I could see was its tawny rump disappearing in the thick trees. I waited for ½-hour, then followed the tracks deeper into unfamiliar country, across a large canyon and several smaller ones. I didn't notice when the

Jamison is shown here in a wilderness area on a backpack trip for elk. Such a trip is rewarding but one must be in *excellent* physical condition and be prepared to survive any sudden storm.

sun disappeared behind clouds.

It started to snow about 1 o-clock, but I was so intent on tracking the elk that I didn't stop to check my watch until about 2:30. I had been walking hard in the foot-deep snow, away from camp, for 7 hours. I had only about 3½ or 4 hours of daylight left and was soaked (practically to the crotch) from the wet snow. My gloves and sleeves were also wet from climbing over blowdowns. Though I had been sweating a lot, it was getting colder, and as I rested, I began to get a chill. The wind was picking up.

I felt confident of the direction back to camp and thought that I could still make it by dark. After all, the elk had meandered a bit in the rugged country, and I thought I could take a crow's flight route, walk fast, and make it. No problem.

Thirty minutes later the wind was whipping the tops of the pine trees. When I entered a large clearing, I had to shield my eyes as icy pellets blasted my face. My denim jeans froze into a hard shell as did the cuffs around my sleeves. The wet thermal underwear was cold next to my skin, and I was getting cold hands and feet from the wet socks and gloves. I decided to stop and build a fire among some big spruce trees.

It was tough. Everything was wet and freezing, and the snowfall was getting heavier. At last, I had a fire going and fumbled at my boots and socks with stiff fingers. Finally, I had them off and set my boots near the fire, then slipped my socks over sticks. I secured the stick ends with rocks so that the socks would hang near the fire and dry faster. Then, I tried to warm my hands and bare feet.

The wind was letting up, but the snow was coming in ever-larger flakes. They melted on my jacket and hissed in the fire. The next thing I knew, the socks were smoking. I pulled them out to find that the toes had melted into a hard knot. I thought they were wool, but apparently they were partially nylon. The snowfall was putting the fire out anyway, so I decided I'd better get moving. I cut 3 or 4 inches off the toes of the socks and put them back on, such as they were.

I still wasn't worried. I would simply keep moving fast to keep warm, and I would make it back about dark. I hadn't seen the sun since 9 A.M., but I started off in the direction I thought would take me directly to camp.

I knew there was a canyon to cross, then a low range of mountains, another canyon, and then a steep uphill climb of about ½-mile, to reach the road along which we were camped. Both canyons had running water in them.

I crossed a canyon with running water and started up what I thought was the low mountain range. By now I was sinking past my knees with every step in the new-fallen snow, but I kept going as fast as I could. I thought I could hack it, but I had never worked out at 12,000 feet in knee-deep snow and didn't fully realize the effects of the elevation on both body and mind.

I climbed up the mountainside until I thought I should be at the top, but I still wasn't there. I was confronted by an old rockslide—a jumble of large boulders. I veered to the right, and climbed higher. There were more rocks, and no way around. It was either drop back down and try to find a way around the slide, or make it over the rocks. I was getting tired and didn't want to lose the precious ground I had gained on the steep mountainside. I went for the rocks.

Climbing over boulders in knee-deep snow is tough, even when you're rested; I still didn't know how close I was to exhaustion. At last I was back in the timber and had climbed at least twice as high as I thought I should have to reach the crest. My sense of direction was now shaken. I wasn't sure I was going the right way.

There was no choice but to push on. I knew I wasn't capable of getting back over the boulders I had just crossed, before dark. I climbed much higher, and finally was at the top where, on a sunny day, I could probably have regained my bearings. But in the heavy snowfall, I couldn't see more than 30 yards. There wasn't the slightest hint of sun anywhere, not even a glow to tell direction by. Now, I was almost sure that I had crossed the wrong mountain.

In trying to figure out how I had gone wrong, I only became more confused. I forced myself to believe that I was going the right way.

I half slid down the opposite slope in snow that was now practically up to my crotch. Soon, I reached the bottom of the mountain, and started across a flat. My legs began to cramp a little. Several times I thought about trying to build another fire, but everything was wet, and my hands were too cold to even get the matches out of my frozen jeans pocket. I leaned back against a pine; I was sleepy. I tried to perk up. There wasn't time to rest too long; I had to keep going if I was to make it back. Daylight was fading fast, and the storm promised a black night.

I dropped into a shallow canyon and desperately fought cramps as I climbed the opposite slope. After a long while, the cramps either didn't hurt any longer, or I blocked out the pain. But my legs just wouldn't manipulate well. My hands were no longer cold, but I could barely move my fingers.

I had an almost irresistible urge to lie down in the soft, deep snow. I no longer felt cold anywhere, and I knew I would go to sleep quickly. At the same time, I knew that if I did, I would never wake up. Temperatures dropped well below zero that night. My mind was playing tricks—resting was becoming more important than the thought of staying alive. I tried to force myself to think about the consequences of resting, but the thought of dying just didn't seem important. The thought of stopping and lying in the snow was appealing. I don't know what it was, but something made me keep placing one foot in front of the other. Darkness came, but there was no longer any worry on my part, even though I was fully aware of the facts.

Much of the mountainous West is rugged. Getting caught in country like this during a blizzard can be fatal if you aren't prepared.

Jamison is hunting in 4 feet of snow with the use of snowshoes. Snowshoes are essential when it comes to getting around in snow like this. And, a hunter should be prepared to make it out if something happened to the snowshoes. Such precautionary thinking and planning go a long way toward helping a hunter *avoid*, and if necessary, *survive* an unfortunate happening.

Long after dark I was still moving, though every step required an unbelievable amount of effort, both physical and mental. There was no importance in dying, nor in living; I was numb in both mind and body. Nothing really mattered, either way.

I was barely moving in the deep snow, wasn't even sure that I could any more, and I stopped my efforts. I just stood a minute or two, then tried to take another step. I couldn't seem to lift my leg. I hesitated, and looked to the right. Though it was dark, my eyes were well adjusted and I could distinguish outlines in the snow as much as 15 feet away. I seemed to be standing in a clearing. I managed one step to my right, toward what I thought was the center of the clearing. The clearing seemed to be long and narrow. I felt something strange underfoot and suddenly realized that I was standing in the road! A vehicle had passed by and packed down the snow. A few more steps and I would have unknowingly crossed the road, and my only chance for survival.

It was after 9 o'clock and unlikely that anyone would be traveling that dead-end road that late in a storm. Which direction was it to camp?

Something—call it instinct—moved me to the right. I shuffled a few steps in the tire track and could then see around the bend in a switchback on the road. About 100 yards down the road was a bonfire 20-feet high. It was our own camp! I had come out of the woods right on target.

Even with the bonfire in sight, and walking in the tire track where the snow was not deep, I wasn't sure I could make it . . . but I did.

Ron, my hunting partner, was doing the only thing he could—keeping a big fire burning, and hoping that I would see it. He had been periodically driving up and down the road with the big truck, chains on all four tires, keeping the road open, and hoping that I would come out. The tracks that I felt in the road were his; he said that no one else had come along the road since mid-afternoon.

To this day, no one but me knows how close I came to *not* making it back that day. What if the road had been 100 yards farther? What if I had changed direction when my confidence was shaken? What if . . .

I've related the above to give you an idea how things can go, and how *"just another hunting day"* can become a nightmare. Anyone can become lost; the seriousness of it is dependent upon how well prepared you are and how you *react* to the situation. If a person is prepared, it is less likely that he will become lost in the first place. If he does become lost, the person who is prepared, and who uses his head, will be able to survive practically any situation.

All situations are different, so there is no one answer to survival when you're lost. Getting "un-lost" may not even be a survival situation. If you begin to feel that you're turned around in the woods, don't panic. You probably aren't as lost as you think you are. You certainly aren't as lost as you will be if you throw down your equipment and run or wander aimlessly. Have confidence in the fact that if you got yourself in, you can get yourself out! It's just a matter of figuring out the best way to do it.

Use Your Head!

In your efforts to find out where you are, pay attention to where you are going. At the moment you *suddenly* determine you are lost, mark that spot clearly, always being able to return to that point, as you attempt to "work your way out." This is one point that is too often overlooked. With this in mind, the obvious and immediate solution is to climb to a high point, up a mountainside, up a hill, or even up a tree, to see if you can get your bearings. This is *usually* all it takes to determine the way you want to go.

Unfortunately, that tactic doesn't work *all* the time. You may not be able to get to a high point where you can see above the rest of the trees. An

Never go on a hunt by yourself. Even if you like to hunt alone, another person hunting out of the same camp, or the same vehicle, is insurance.

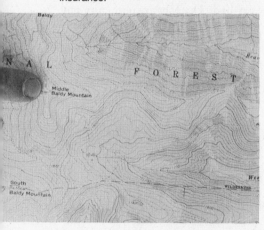

rection it runs.

If you attempt to make it back to a road in the "approximate" direction of camp, use an approach called "offset navigation." Purposely head a little toward the right or left of where you think your camp is so that when you do come out on the road, you'll know which way to walk in order to reach camp. If you try to intercept your camp directly and miss it, you won't know which way to walk when you reach the road. You could end up walking many unnecessary miles.

If the road isn't where you thought it was, don't panic. *Think things through.* Even if you can't see the sun to determine direction, there are still

There may not be a sun or stars visible to determine direction by. Take a good compass and map and know how to use them.

(Left) Learn how to read local topographic maps well by practicing with them in the outdoors *before* your hunt. After you've mastered a topo map of your home ground, buy one of the country you'll be hunting and keep it (them) with you at all times. Not only are they good insurance on a "survival" level, they are tremendously helpful when it comes to finding game.

the individual situation. Again, if you don't panic, and use common sense, you'll probably be fine. Keeping from getting lost, or the ability to survive if you do become lost, is best prepared for *before* you go hunting. Here are a few general rules that can help in any situation:

Go Prepared to Stay

Whenever you go into the wilderness, go prepared to stay for some time if you have to. Take enough emergency food and water for several days.

A sudden blizzard with heavy snowfall, high water, a vehicle breakdown, or many other situations could trap you, right where you are camped, for

alternative? Think about how long you've been walking, and what you've been doing since you left your camp or vehicle. Think about any creeks you crossed, the type of trees you were walking through, or the ground underfoot. In short, try to think through your past travels. If this gives you the confidence you need to repeat them in reverse order, go ahead, but blaze trees with a knife or axe or build a trail from rocks so you can return to where you are, if you want to later.

Try to remember any roads surrounding the area you're in, and about how far away they are. Roads, since they travel for long distances, are likely targets for interception, unlike your vehicle, or a camp, which would be little more than a dot on a map. Try to intercept a road if you *know* the direction you're traveling, the direction to the road, and the di-

ways to find your way. Which direction do the streams run? What is the prevailing wind direction? Which way was the wind blowing when you left camp? Which types of trees grow in the shaded areas of north-facing slopes, or south-facing slopes?

Be Prepared

If you use your head and think things through, you'll probably find your way in a few hours. However, if in spite of your efforts, you feel you're really lost, and darkness is approaching, you need to prepare for a survival situation. The steps to take depend upon many things: the time of year, the current weather, how you're dressed, and what you have with you. At any rate, you'll need to begin preparing a shelter well before dark. Three hours isn't too much time.

So much from here on depends upon

many days. If you take lots more food than you'll need for your planned hunt, you'll be able to survive the incident until you can get out or until help arrives.

Tell Someone

Tell someone where you are going and when you plan to return. If you change areas or move, tell someone.

If you do have a problem, you'll have the assurance that someone knows where you are and will come looking. It's up to you to make sure they know where to look. Purchase an extra map and mark your camping spot and hunting area on it, then leave it with whomever is waiting for your return. Such a map is invaluable to a search-and-rescue party.

Never Hunt Alone

Never go hunting by yourself. Even

if you like to hunt alone, having a partner who hunts from the same camp or vehicle is good insurance. If you've planned to hunt for a week and take a fall and break a leg on the first day, the folks at home might not come looking for a long time. Your partner will know much more quickly if you don't return to camp. He's also likely to know the direction you headed in on that specific day. There are an unlimited number of situations where a partner could save your life.

Use a Compass and Map

Take along a compass and map of the area and know how to use them. Many of those who carry a compass and map don't know how to use them. Others erroneously think that a compass isn't necessary because direction can be determined from the sun or the stars. What happens when a storm moves in, and you can't see either for days?

I generally purchase several maps of the area I intend to hunt; good ones are available for a small fee from the various government agencies. I usually get a "general map" illustrating a large section of area. A Forest Service map of this type illustrates creeks, rivers, roads and ponds. In addition I buy detailed topographic maps of the specific area I intend to hunt, as well as surrounding areas. Topographic maps illustrate the steepness of mountains, canyons, the location of saddles, the elevation, broad vegetation types, and other features.

The top of a map is always north, and the *scale* of the map is generally marked somewhere along the border. The scale of a Forest Service map might be ½-inch to one mile. (A distance of ½-inch on the map corresponds to 1 mile on the ground.) A more detailed map, such as a topographic map, might have a scale of something like 1:24,000, meaning that 1 inch on the map is the same as 24,000 inches on the ground, or about 2⅝ inches on the map corresponds to a mile on the ground.

Sometimes, there is a *legend* around the border of the map to indicate what the map's symbols represent. You will also find *magnetic declination* marked on the map. The needle on a compass being used in North America, points to *magnetic north*, not *true north*. The difference between magnetic north and true north is called magnetic declination, and its value is indicated in degrees on the map. Magnetic declination varies, depending upon where you are on the continent. For example, in west-

central Colorado, magnetic north lies 14 degrees east of true north. From this, you know that true north is 14 degrees west of the direction your compass needle is pointing.

Sometimes it helps to find direction by laying your compass on the map and orienting the map with compass direction. By using the map and compass in this way, and by cross-referencing landmarks, you can figure out exactly where you are, and the precise direction you need to go in order to get where you want.

Contour lines on a topographic map indicate the steepness of the terrain. These squiggly lines usually don't mean much to a person not familiar with reading them and associating them with the actual terrain they represent. An unskilled user usually can't tell an up-slope from a down-slope on a topo map. However, knowing what they mean could save your life.

You can easily determine the easiest route of travel from contour lines. You can tell whether terrain is too steep to travel easily, or at all. If you're familiar with contour lines, you can even determine whether a

longer route might be faster, just by looking at a map. You'll be able to look at a mountain and compare it with the contour lines on the map to make certain that the mountain you're looking at is the same mountain on the map.

Don't just learn what the symbols on the map are. It takes practice using them in the field. Get into rugged, familiar country where there are no trails, and try to find the easiest way from point A to point B with a compass and a topographical map. You can do this whenever you're in the field—the benefits are great, whether you're lost or not.

For example, I've often used a "topo" map and compass to scout unknown country for game. When you've used the map a lot, you'll even be able to predetermine the most likely locations for game. I once used common sense in combination with a topo map and compass to find and backpack into the best elk hunting I've ever had. The topographic map not only told me how to get into the spot, but it indicated to me that it was unlikely that there would be other hunters there. Yet, from things noted in

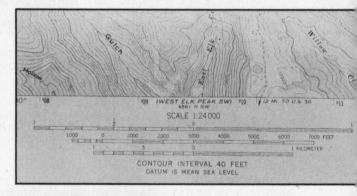

The scale of this topo map is 1:24,000 which means that 1 inch on the map equals 24,000 inches on the ground. Put another way, about 2⅝ inches on the map represents 1 mile on the ground.

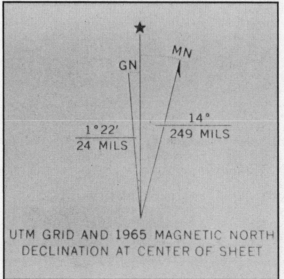

UTM GRID AND 1965 MAGNETIC NORTH DECLINATION AT CENTER OF SHEET

"Magnetic declination" is the difference between *magnetic* north (where your compass needle points), and *true* north. This deviation is noted in degrees on your topo map. Maps are laid out on grid lines and a south-to-north direction along the grid line (at the center of the map, in this instance), is called "grid north." The amount of this deviation is also noted on the map. In this instance, magnetic declination is 14 degrees and magnetic deviation from grid north is 1 degree, 22 minutes.

reading the map, it appeared that game should be there. I later found that I was on target on all counts, but I initially learned it just from reading a map.

The surrounding region was heavily hunted, but I found a huge area that was rugged; guides wouldn't even take horses there. There were no other hunters, and it was a place where the largest elk congregated once the season got underway.

The importance of using a map and compass cannot be over emphasized, and as you can see, it's productive to practice their use *before* you get lost.

Proper Clothing and Equipment

Wear proper clothing and equipment, and prepare for possible changes in the weather. It's important to keep warm and dry. If you're going to be hunting in deep snow, wear pants that don't allow melted snow to soak through to your skin. Dress in layers, and remove clothing as necessary to avoid perspiring. Add clothing as the weather gets cooler. You'll not only be safer with the proper clothing, you will be able to hunt in greater comfort.

If you're hunting in snow, wear boots and clothing that don't allow the moisture to get to your skin. A hunt that starts out warm and wet can become icy cold; when this happens it can really sap a hunter's strength.

Get "Out" Before Dark

Plan your hunt so that you arrive back at camp before dark. It can become more difficult to find your way in the dark than you think. It's also dangerous to travel on a dark night in unfamiliar country.

Once, I was hunting a brushy mountainside in Colorado late one afternoon. I was looking for bear sign and was walking up a steep mountain, thinking I was nearing the crest because I could see sky at a lower angle than before. I stepped to the edge of the thick brush and instead of standing on the crest of a ridge, I stopped no more than a step from the edge of a 1000-foot cliff. This was in broad daylight. Had I been walking in the dark, there's no question that I would have stepped off.

Build a Fire

Know how to build a fire and have the means to do it with you always. A fire can offer the advantage of warmth, dry clothing, cooking, signaling and psychological comfort.

Build any fire in a safe location. Clear dry debris from the forest floor and never build a fire under a tree. If you build a fire on snow, build it on a platform of rocks or logs. If you build it next to a large rock or wall of logs it will reflect heat into a shelter. When you need a fire most may be when it's most difficult to start one. It might be snowy and windy with everything in the immediate area also being wet and cold, including yourself; your hands might not function well. You need to be able to start a fire under these conditions, and it's a good idea to practice building a fire under poor conditions with whatever fire-starting materials you carry with you.

I generally carry matches in a waterproof container, *and* a butane lighter. A small candle is a good idea, and so is a wick, a couple of feet of heavy cotton string that has been dipped in melted paraffin. You can then cut off a couple inches of this material as it's needed. Just fray one end and light it. It burns much longer and hotter than a match.

Don't waste matches or other fire-starting materials on a poor effort. Make every effort to have plenty of dry tinder available *before* you start. Even though everything seems wet, you can sometimes find dry material under dense evergreen boughs. Though seasoned sticks may be wet on the outside, you should be able to obtain dry shavings after whittling through the outer covering. Powder

from a cartridge, sprinkled over dry tinder, can help it burn.

Steel wool, 00 or finer, makes excellent tinder, even after being wet. Water can be shaken out of it, and it will ignite from a small spark. This burns very hot, but it consumes itself rapidly so it should be used with other tinder such as pine needles or small twigs. As the fire starts, blow carefully on the flame and add tinder, then small kindling in increasingly larger sizes until the fire is large enough to burn even wood which is wet on the outside.

Carry a Survival Kit

Always carry a basic survival kit, including first-aid items. An excellent survival kit can be assembled into a tin small enough to fit into your hip pocket. It weighs little, will cost you almost nothing, and it might save your life. Put the following items in the kit:

1. At least a foot of heavy cotton string dipped in melted paraffin. Wrap it in waxed paper. Cut off a 2-inch piece, fray one end, and use it to start a fire.

2. Two or three fish hooks which can be used to catch fish for food.

3. Steel wool, 00 or finer, to be used for tinder.

4. Picture hanging wire or copper wire to be used for making snares or building a shelter. You may even include a couple of small commercially made snares (mink or marten-size) which are ideal for catching squirrel and rabbit-size animals. A coyote-size snare will catch and hold a deer.

5. Water purification tablets.

6. A small tube of antibiotic cream.

7. Wooden matches. These can be dipped in paraffin to make them waterproof.

8. Safety pins for replacing buttons or repairing torn clothing.

9. A small whistle to be used for signaling. Three blasts are a recognized distress signal, and the whistle can save your voice.

10. Adhesive bandages for small cuts.

11. Fishing line (15-pound test or better), for fishing, sewing clothing, lashing a shelter together, or making a snare.

12. A needle with a large eye to be used for sewing clothing or for any other necessary purpose.

13. Multiple vitamin pills can be used to maintain health on an inadequate diet.

14. Lastly, if you have any unusual

Maps, compass and survival gear fit nicely into a fanny pack, along with a sandwich or other food for the day. Be sure to include a knife and a canteen of water. Jamison is shown here with all of the above. It's hardly noticed while hunting.

medical condition that requires special medicine(s) on a daily basis, include a week's supply. Be sure that supply is fresh every time you go out on a hunt.

Get a metal container for all this and glue a mirror into the lid for signaling. A round, flat metal can of the type that salve comes in works fine, the bigger the better. Then, in a pinch, the can could be used for cooking food or boiling water.

Wrap the seam of the container with 5 or 6 feet of plastic electrician's tape to seal it. The tape can then be used to build a shelter, fasten splints to a broken limb, etc.

Place the tin inside a plastic bag and carry it in a fanny pack with your map and compass. The fanny pack should also contain a space blanket and a sheet of plastic, measuring at least 10 feet by 10 feet. A wire saw is handy to include and doesn't take up much space. A length of surgical (rubber) tubing can be used for many things such as a tourniquet, or for making a slingshot. Don't forget a canteen of water, and always carry a knife.

If you do get lost in a wilderness situation, remember to keep calm and think everything through carefully, *before* you act. Your own common sense is the best way to get yourself out of a tough situation. Keep all your belongings with you; don't throw anything away.

The first thing to do in any survival situation is to care for any physical injury. Next, protect yourself from the elements by building a shelter. Third, acquire food and water. Lastly, prepare for rescue.

Pain or loss of blood can reduce your efficiency so it's important to care for any injury you might have. Frostbite is the biggest problem in cold, damp weather so keep your hands, feet and any exposed area warm and dry. If you get wet, build a fire to dry your clothes.

When you build a shelter, make it (as best you can) to withstand all the elements. You will probably be strongest when you first determine your "lost" status. As a result, it's wise to remember to build a good shelter while you're still capable.

Choose the site for your shelter with care. For example, avoid building it near a dead tree that might topple in the wind; avoid avalanche or flood areas.

If you need a quick shelter, look for a natural one. A cave or even overhanging rock can offer some protection. If you're in snow, take shelter under the dense branches of a spruce tree. Just remove the snow, if possible, and the overhanging branches and piled-up snow can form an excellent temporary shelter.

Use whatever materials occur naturally to help make your shelter-building easier. For example, build a lean-to in a timbered area facing a large rock, if possible. The lean-to can be constructed of evergreen boughs interwoven over a wooden framework built of branches. A fire can be built between the rock and lean-to to reflect heat into the shelter.

A shelter can even be made in a large snow drift if it becomes necessary. Just dig out a room and make a 6-inch hole through the roof for ventilation. Arch the sides and top so that water will not drip from the roof but will run down the sides. This type of shelter is less desirable than other types because you'll get wet digging in snow. There are usually better alternatives than snow caves.

Once you have a shelter constructed, you're ready to see to your supply of food and water. Water is the more important of the two. You can survive for 2 weeks or more without food, if you have plenty of water. However, you can survive only a few days without water. You should drink 2 to 4 quarts of water daily in a survival situation, whether you are thirsty or not.

Be sure to purify all water unless you are sure of its source. It can be purified by using the water purification tablets in your survival kit or by boiling. Water usually isn't difficult to find in hunting country. If you purify it by boiling, boil it for at least 1 full minute at sea level and add a minute for every 1000 feet of elevation.

Your firearm is generally the best source of food in the wilderness. However, be sure to conserve your ammunition by making every shot count. Deadfalls and snares can provide food with little expenditure of energy on your part, once they're made, and they can be used repeatedly. They have the advantage of working 24 hours a day. A fishing line is much the same way; a hook can be baited and left unattended—any fish that's caught can be removed later. This ability to catch food with little effort can become an important factor.

Be sure to cook meat well and avoid any birds or animals that appear to be sick, unwary or lazy. They might have some disease which could be transmitted to man.

Most nuts and berries that are eaten by birds and animals are safe. It's a good idea to study books on edible plants to learn what's safe and nutritious in the area you intend to hunt.

Once you have the basic necessities of life, you're ready to think about getting *out* or getting *found*. Be ready to get the attention of any possible help because you never know when someone or something might come along. Be prepared to signal distant vehicles or aircraft if they should appear. Make a permanent ground signal in an open area that someone could see from an aircraft at a distance. A simple "SOS" stomped out in the snow could help, or the same signal arranged with rocks might get the attention of those in the air.

Three of anything is also a universal distress signal. Three shots, fired evenly apart is an example. Three fires, arranged in a triangle is another signal, as are three blasts on a whistle. Green wood on a fire will produce lots of smoke which can be seen for miles.

The alternatives are practically unlimited once you think about it, and each situation demands something different. Again, it's a matter of matching common sense to the situation to survive long enough to walk out, or be found.

Practice using a map and a compass in the field, *practice* building a fire under the worst conditions, assemble a survival kit, don't take chances, and use common sense whenever you're in the woods. I hope you never put yourself and your partner through an ordeal like the one I opened this article with. ●

THE MOST popular varmint with hunters might well be the woodchuck. But even with a mature size of 12 to 16 pounds, a woodchuck is a very small target when he is some 300 or more yards distant. And should only the head be visible, peering from some far-off den, then "tough" doesn't begin to describe the shooting chore.

One type of long-range woodchucking scenario sees the hunter going afield with great hopes. After missing 20 or 30 shots in the course of the day, at ranges from 275 to 400 yards, our nimrod becomes convinced that stories about killing woodchucks at great ranges are the result of a writer's imagination, without any connection to reality.

Yet, there are shooters who, each time they venture afield, routinely connect on 300- to 400-yard shots.

Conversely, there are hunters who routinely miss any shot past 150 yards, except for a rare accident where bullet and target are brought together. The best way for the shooter who habitually misses to become aware of what can be accomplished, is to team up with an experienced varmint hunter who makes the long shots look easy.

Long-range woodchucking is not difficult if approached correctly. The hunter needs a properly tuned, top-notch rifle, a superior scope sight, a suitable cartridge, a portable shooting rest, a good pair of binoculars and plenty of know-how, not to mention

the ability to load some highly accurate ammunition. While this is no small order, it certainly is not beyond the reach of most shooters who would like the thrill of making 300- to 400-yard instant kills, several times each day they are afield. And make no mistake about it, a nearly ¼-mile distant woodchuck killed cleanly, as it views its domain from a burrow, can bring as much satisfaction as a big bull moose cleanly dumped in some distant swamp. In fact, for some, the varmint hunting experience is even *more* satisfying due to the high level of expertise and skill required to hit tiny targets at extreme ranges. And I need

Long-Range
WOODCHUCKS

by ED MATUNAS

"Firing" at a distant chuck is a lot different than "hitting" it. That's what separates the men from the boys when it comes to long-range chucking.

not suggest that a skilled varmint shooter will prove to be a highly effective big game shot; it has always been so.

The Rifle

Not any rifle will do for long-range varmint shooting. The rifle chosen must be accurate. And this does not mean that it will put *three* shots into 1½ inches or even a ½-inch group at 100 yards. A rifle that will enable you to achieve some consistency in your long-range efforts must be able to group *all* of its shots into about 1 inch at 100 yards. This does not mean a single 5-shot group measuring 1 inch or less. Nor does it mean five 5-shot groups that will each measure 1 inch or less. More accurately, it means that five different groups fired at *one* specific target, at different times, will result in a total grouping, for the 25 shots, of 1 inch or less. The hard part here is finding a rifle that has a consistent point of impact.

As it pertains to individual group size, accuracy is not nearly as important as the rifle's ability to always shoot where it is pointed. If the stock absorbs moisture during periods of high humidity, it will swell and change the forearm pressure against the barrel. The bullet's point of impact will then vary. If you sight in with "x" stock pressure on the barrel and later shoot with "x+" or "x−" fore-end pressure, the point of impact might well vary up to 2 inches at 100 yards. This variation could be high, low, left or right, or some combination thereof. Or, if, as the barrel heats up from shooting and expands, as it will, the pressure changes created on the hot barrel will cause the shots to string up and down on the target. In some instances, in a 5-shot group, the vertical dispersion could be 2 to 3 inches between the lowest and highest shot, at 100 yards. At 400 yards this will convert to a spread of 8 to 12 inches. That's no way to hit a tiny target, let alone a distant one.

Replacing a wooden stock with a fiberglass one will cure the change of impact caused by moisture absorption or drying out. But such an expense is not necessary. Savvy varminters have been killing distant varmints for a great many years, using rifles with wooden stocks. Their secret to success is to free the barrel of any contact with the fore-end; *free-floating* it's called. With the barrel channel carefully enlarged to leave sufficient space so that the wood doesn't contact the barrel as it absorbs or loses moisture, or as the barrel expands with the heat of shooting, a common point of impact will become a reality.

With a free-floating barrel your rifle will shoot to the same point of impact in rainy weather, in dry weather, with a cold barrel or a hot one, so long as your ammunition remains constant. A good varminter will check his sights at the range at the beginning of each session, and perhaps several

(Above) The author's wife has her own pet long-range varmint rifle. It's a Remington 700 Classic, featuring a fully floated barrel and a 2¼-pound crisp trigger pull. This 700 is capable of consistently putting 10 shots into ⅞-inch or less.

(Above left) A well tuned rifle will quickly prove itself, as shown by master gunsmith, Rick Dotzenrod's trophy taken at 300 yards.

(Left) Varmint rifles that work are not always visibly different from ones that do not. Careful tuning is required to come up with a rifle than can consistently take woodchucks at ranges up to 400 yards or so. The pictured Remington 700 is obviously a winner.

times throughout if he experiences any unexplained misses. But, unless the rifle's scope has had a serious jar or extreme temperatures have affected ammo performance, a sight adjustment will seldom be necessary.

On rare occasions a shooter may discover that free-floating a rifle's barrel results in the rifle losing its ability to tightly group five shots. Such occurrences usually happen with barrels that have internal stresses. Yes, reapplying some fore-end pressure, via glass bedding or a cardboard shim, may temporarily restore accuracy. But such rifles will not be useful, over the long run, because their points of impact *will* vary with the inevitable pressure changes of the stock against the forearm.

Happily, free-floating a barrel most often results in (1) a shrinking of group size, or (2) the elimination of a rifle's tendency to walk each shot higher as the barrel heats. In fact, during 12 years of extensive gunsmithing, barrel floating proved to be the most efficient way to bring out the best accuracy of a specific rifle.

But do not be misled into thinking that barrel floating alone is a panacea for all the difficulties encountered in long-range woodchucking. A good trigger pull is essential. What's a good trigger pull? Well, it's one with no discernible movement, that breaks as crisply as a thin glass wand, and has no after-travel. And all this at about a 1½-pound let-off. Variations on the 2½-pound let-off occur with shooter preference, but most successful long-range hits on a consistent basis simply are not possible with a creepy, spongy, heavy trigger pull. With an accurate rifle, a good trigger pull, as opposed to a bad one, can shrink

groups from the 1½-inch range to the ½- to ⅞-inch range. Remember, positive trigger control is also essential to long-range accuracy.

When selecting a long-range woodchuck rifle, it's my opinion that only bolt-actions will do. It is wise to select from popular makes and models which have gained reputations for high levels of accuracy. Among my favorites are the various Remington 700 models and the Winchester Model 70. The triggers of both these models are readily adjustable (by a good gunsmith only, please) and both lend themselves to easy barrel floating. A good gunsmith should be able to adjust a Remington 700 or Model 70 trigger as well as float the barrel and reseal its channel with a suitable finish, in less than 2 hours. So, getting a rifle properly tuned should not be excessively expensive.

Finally, if you want perfection in tuning your rifle, have the action glass-bedded. Today's rifles are usually bedded well, but a good glassing can marry the action and stock into one single unit. The resulting difference in accuracy will vary depending upon the original fit of metal to wood. But a glass-bedded action never shoots worse, and any gain in accura-

cy, however small, is worthwhile for a long-range varmint rifle.

Sights and Mounts

Long-range hitting requires long-range seeing. The precision of placing a tiny bullet into the right portions of the anatomy of a very distant woodchuck requires considerable magnification. Some shooters who possess very keen eyesight get along nicely with an 8x scope. However, most of us, of normal visual acuity, do best with a 10x or a 12x scope. Yet, some hunters use scopes of 20x or greater.

Actually, once you exceed 10x, there are scope attributes that are more important than magnification. After all, a 10x scope will make a 400-yard distant woodchuck appear as though it is but 40 yards away. The desired (read "required") features are sharpness of image, color correction, ruggedness, ease of adjustment and the ability to be adjusted for the shooter's eyesight.

Obviously, a greatly magnified blur that is barely distinguishable from surrounding terrain is not much at which to aim. Yet, the variations in a high-powered scope's ability to clearly define the image and separate it from similar colored backgrounds are in-

This shooter's choice for a long-range varmint rifle has obviously been a wise one based on the quantity of woodchucks at his side. The rifle is a Remington 700 BDL in 22-250 with a floated barrel and glass-bedded action.

deed great. Because of the need for exacting accuracy, a scope must be point-of-impact adjustable in ¼-inch or less increments. (Additionally, be sure to purchase a scope that can be sharply focused if you happen to require moderate sight correction glasses.) Too, once sighted in, your scope should hold its zero through the normal use and abuse it will see in the field. Table One lists those scopes that, in my experience, meet the criteria for a long-range chuck scope.

Variable power scopes are usually poor choices for serious long-range varminting. This is because, by design, variables are simply not as sharp as fixed power scopes. Also, the minor changes that occur in point-of-impact when the power ring is turned will detract, even if only slightly, from a constant point of impact. Although none of this is of *major* consequence in the big game arena, all of those little things can add up to misses in the chuck field.

For beginning long-range woodchucking, a variable with a range finding setup might prove useful in range estimations. But as the shooter gains experience, he will be able to estimate ranges better visually than when using a range finding scope that

40 yards to infinity, depending on the maker. Simply turn the ring on the objective bell so that the range at which you are shooting aligns with the index mark on the scope tube—all parallax error will be eliminated.

Scope mounts need to be sturdy. If any movement of the scope and mount system occurs, long-range hits will be simply random luck. Mounts using the system originally offered in the Redfield Jr. style are superb. Today such mounts are available from not only Redfield, but Leupold and Millet as well.

Important is the use of a mount that will keep the cross hairs fairly close to their optical and mechanical centers. A scope setup that sights in only after almost all of the windage and/or elevation adjustment has been used will deprive the owner of some of the optical quality of his scope despite claims to the contrary. For this reason any windage adjustment in the scope mount system should be used to bring the point of impact quite close to where it should be, before the scope adjustments are used.

The Conetrol mount system, different than the Redfield type, also allows for easy windage adjustment at the front and rear base. Too, the projec-

A scope can serve as a source for vital reminders as to trajectory (t) and wind drift (w) peculiarities of the load being used at various ranges (y). A simple press-on label can be prepared to supply such vital info and the label can then be affixed to the scope's eyepiece.

Table One

Some Suggested Long-Range Woodchuck Scopes

Brand	Model	Power	Application	Comments
Leupold	M8	8x	to 320 yds.	very bright scope for late evening shooting
Zeiss	Diatal C	10x	to 400 yds.	superb and accurate ¼" click type adjustments
Leupold	M8	12x	400+ yds.	the ideal power for most shooters
Leupold	M8	24x	400+ yds.	difficult to control for shooting without a rest

The author's choice for a scope is either a 12x Leupold M8 (shown) or a 10x Zeiss. Both will do yeomanly service for long-range chucks.

depends upon the use of a fixed-height object, i.e., a woodchuck that stands 18 inches tall. Such exactness of measure seldom exists in nature. Thus, it might be wise to start with an optically superior fixed-power scope and learn to judge ranges more accurately by visually looking across the terrain.

Scopes that have an adjustable objective lens are very desirable. This adjustment allows the scope to be parallax-free at any range from, perhaps,

tionless rings of the Conetrol system make for the best looking setup available anywhere.

If for some reason your chosen mount and rings require that extreme elevation adjustments be made in the scope, it's best to get a different set of bases and/or rings. Naturally, all scope mount bases and rings should be *securely* tightened. Any looseness will drive you batty with unexplained misses and point of impact shifts.

Suitable Cartridges

Long-range varmint cartridges have been the subject of debate almost since the inception of fixed ammunition. The debate rages over such factors as accuracy, lack of recoil and trajectory. The fact is that for long-range woodchucking, accuracy is king. Yet, if accuracy alone is all that's required, the 222 Remington would be the very best possible choice. However, due to modest energy levels, this round is a crippler when the ranges get to 250 yards or more. Ample energy out at 300 and 400 yards is required to insure the necessary bullet expansion, which in turn transfers the bullet's "power" to the quarry. Yet, if accuracy and power are the only requirements, then the 264 Winchester Magnum would be a great woodchuck cartridge. But the heavy recoil of such a round makes it difficult to master during repeated shots. Further, if the attributes of accuracy, power and minimum recoil are all that are needed, cartridges like the 22-250 would never have come to be. But this type of cartridge possesses the final essential, a very flat trajectory without undue recoil. A flat trajectory makes errors in range estimation less devastating as the rise and fall of bullets is minimal, making hitting easier.

Thus, a suitable cartridge for long-range chucking must be one which is capable of a very high level of accuracy; which produces no undue accuracy-destroying recoil; which will provide sufficient energy to insure rapid bullet expansion at maximum ranges; and which offers as flat a trajectory as possible. It's not necessary to get into a lengthy discussion based on personal likes and dislikes with respect to such cartridges. Time and usage by many, many shooters has proven that there are but seven cartridges which possess all of the required attributes. Even within these selections, there are but three that will prove ideal for most shooters.

Those calibers that fit the requirements are the: 224 Weatherby Magnum, 22-250 Remington, 220 Swift, 243 Winchester, 6mm Remington, 240 Weatherby Magnum and 25-06 Remington. But let's take a closer look at the attributes and drawbacks of each to see why all would not prove ideal for every shooter.

224 Weatherby Magnum

This is as small a cartridge as you can select and still maintain enough velocity to provide the necessary flatness of trajectory. Lesser rounds, such as the 223 Remington, come up short in the trajectory department. The drawbacks of this round are that it is available only in the comparatively expensive Weatherby rifle, and brass (or ammo) is available only through Weatherby. Accuracy is superb, as is trajectory. Factory ammo shoots very well with the available 55-grain bullet, leaving the muzzle of my 24-inch Weatherby Varmintmaster at 3638 fps. The 224 Weatherby is best handloaded with a 50-grain bullet. Best accuracy with handloads comes at 3475 fps in my rifle. Recoil is negligible.

The 224 Weatherby Magnum is a fine choice so long as you can live with the difficulty of finding brass or ammo.

22-250 Remington

This round possesses a unique quality. Simply stated, that quality is, "no drawbacks." It is very accurate, shooting well with specific factory loads and handloads alike. Recoil is negligible and energy, as well as trajectory, are just dandy.

Today, the 22-250 Remington is our most popular long-range woodchuck cartridge, and its acceptance is well deserved. The superb accuracy of 55-grain Remington Power Lokt loads provide a measured 3591 fps from a 24-inch barrel. Reloads with the same weight bullet normally crank out from 3550 to 3600 fps, nicely duplicating factory velocities. This is perhaps the preferred long-range woodchuck cartridge for almost everyone.

220 Swift

This cartridge leaves me in a difficult spot. To not suggest it is to ignore its many attributes. Nonetheless, its troublesome characteristics for the reloader makes it a far from ideal cartridge for any purpose. So, my suggestion is to bypass the 220 Swift for the nearly similar performance of the 22-250 Remington. You will not only avoid reloading difficulties but will gain an increase in barrel life and, I believe, a slight edge in accuracy.

243 Winchester and 6mm Remington

Superb accuracy and easy reloadability, as well as flat trajectory and plenty of downrange energy are all characteristics of both these fine cartridges. The only disadvantage is some slight, noticeable recoil. However, I wish to point out that most experienced shooters find that any present

Clearly shown on the author's son's rifle are the projectionless and very attractive rings used with Conetrol scope mounts. These rugged mounts are not only the prettiest but also offer plenty of windage adjustment, a plus for varminting. This lad's choice of cartridges? The 243 Winchester.

(Right) Range finding scopes such as this Redfield Illuminator can be of help to the novice long-range woodchuck hunter. However, the author prefers, and recommends, a fixed-power scope for long-range chuck shooting.

When selecting a long-range woodchuck cartridge, your choice, according to the author, should be from one of these seven calibers. From left to right they are the 224 Weath. Mag., the 22-250 Rem., the 220 Swift, the 243 Win., the 6mm Rem., the 240 Weath. Mag. or the 25-06 Rem.

In the author's opinion, the best of the 22 caliber long-range ground hog cartridges are the 224 Weatherby Magnum and the ubiquitous 22-250 Remington (right).

The 220 Swift (left) and the 240 Weatherby Magnum have reputations for relatively short barrel life and are, thus, in the author's opinion, the least desirable of the long-range woodchuck cartridges. But they are *very* effective, nonetheless.

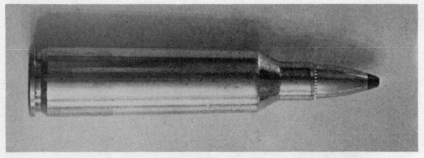

The ultimate long-range woodchuck cartridge is the 22-250 Remington. But the author points out that the selection of a 224 Weatherby, a 243 Winchester or 6mm Remington would not be disappointing.

recoil is of no consequence. Still, a few recoil-sensitive shooters might prefer a 22-caliber cartridge. These two 6mm rounds are ideal selections for a great many hunters. If you are undecided between the two, I have found the Remington round just a tad more accurate.

240 Weatherby Magnum

Comparatively short barrel life is the main drawback to this cartridge. Too, its loud muzzle blast and noticeable, albeit reasonable, recoil makes it less than a perfect woodchuck cartridge. Brass and ammo are available only from Weatherby. In my opinion, the 240 Weatherby joins the 220 Swift as being one of the least desirable rounds for a long-range varmint cartridge, although it will provide yeomanly service in the field.

25-06 Remington

This is as big as one can go without leaving the realm of ideal, long-range woodchuck calibers. The 25-06 Rem. is accurate and will provide the best trajectory of all the selected cartridges when 87-grain bullets are used. The 100-grain bullets are usually more accurate, but recoil is more obvious with this weight projectile. The 25-06 simply is not the cartridge for any shooter who is even slightly recoil shy. Muzzle blast is also quite noticeable. Yet, some shooters do so well with this round that it would be difficult to seriously imply that the 25-06 has any real disadvantage. Nonetheless, it is one of two of the seven qualifying cartridges that I do not use extensively. Why? I feel no need to burn the extra powder, to tolerate a bit more muzzle blast or to try to ignore its light, but eventually fatiguing, recoil. Still, I fault no man who opines that the 25-06 is the best of the long-range rounds.

Handloading

Is handloading a necessity? A few factory loads will provide better accuracy than many would expect. My experience with the Remington Power Lokt loadings in the 22-250, 243, 6mm and 25-06 have all been favorable with plenty of less-than-m.o.a. (minute of angle) groups. But, in honesty, there have been a few groups in the 1- to 1½-inch range. Thus, if we count every shot, as indeed we should, these fine factory loads qualify for a maximum of 300-yard shooting.

If you want every shot to stay within that magic 1 m.o.a. or less, then reloading is a necessary part of hitting, especially at 300 to 400 yards. But,

(Left) The big bores of long-range woodchuck cartridges include the 243 Win. (left) and the 6mm Remington and the 25-06 Remington (right). Both 6mms are nearly ideal cartridges for long-range ground hogs but the 25-06's recoil is a bit more than some can tolerate for truly superb accuracy.

The author believes that is unnecessary to experiment with various propellants in the search for accuracy. Simply select the one best manual-recommended powder for your cartridge, and if you must try different loads, vary the bullet rather than the propellant.

with the increased accuracy of reloads comes a few bullets that will fail to expand properly at the ranges they are capable of scoring hits. If you encounter more than but a few rare instances of a chuck escaping after being hit, I strongly suggest your bullet, regardless of accuracy level, is unsuitable for the purpose. Table Two, Long-Range Woodchuck Handloads lists bullets that have proven satisfactory for me and others. You may have another favorite and, so long as you do not lose

crippled game, your choice is just fine. But, if you are unsure of where to begin, or if you have had difficulty with a prior choice, the bullets listed in the table will prove, I believe, excellent for the applications suggested.

For most load development the handloader would do well to stick with the powder listed. Results can be better improved upon by experimenting with brand or type of bullets rather than by varying propellants. Hodgdon H335 is simply the single best

powder for the 224 W.M., as is Hodgdon 380 the best propellant for the 22-250 Remington. And DuPont's IMR 4350 is best in all three 6mms as well as the 25-06 Remington. No loading data is shown for the 220 Swift as reloading this cartridge can in my opinion, be difficult for all but the very, very experienced reloader. A second choice powder, IMR 4064, is shown for the 22-250 as its performance is mighty fine in some rifles.

There are a great many other pro-

Table Two
Long-Range Woodchuck Handloads

Caliber	Bullet Wt. Grs.	Bullet Make and Style	Powder Charge Wt. Grs.	Muzzle Vel. fps	Trajectory in Inches (to nearest ¼")				Average[1] Accuracy in inches
					100 yds.	200 yds.	300 yds.	400 yds.	
224 W.M.	50	Nosler Expander	30.0 - H335	3475	+2	+1¾	−3¼	−15	¾
22-250 Rem.	52	Nosler Match HP	38.0 - H380	3325	+2	+1¼	−5½	−20	¾
22-250 Rem.	52	Nosler Match HP	40.0 - H380	3625	+2	+2	−3	−14	⅞
22-250 Rem.	52	Nosler Match HP	35.5 - IMR 4064	3675	+2	+2	−2½	−13	⅞
22-250 Rem.	55	Speer Spitzer	38.0 - H380	3375	+2	+1½	−4	−16	½
22-250 Rem.	55	Speer Spitzer	39.5 - H380	3550	+2	+1¾	−3¼	−16	⅝
22-250 Rem.	55	Speer Spitzer	35.5 - IMR 4064	3600	+2	+1¾	−3¼	−15	⅞
243 Win.	70	Nosler	47.0 - IMR 4350	3400	+2	+1½	−3¾	−16	1
243 Win.	80	Speer Spitzer	45.0 - IMR 4350	3250	+2	+1½	−4	−16	⅞
243 Win.	85	Sierra Spitzer	44.0 - IMR 4350	3200	+2	+1½	−4¼	−18	⅞
6mm Rem.	70	Nosler	47.0 - IMR 4350	3425	+2	+1½	−3¾	−16	¾
6mm Rem.	80	Speer Spitzer	46.0 - IMR 4350	3300	+2	+1½	−3½	−15	⅞
6mm Rem.	85	Sierra Spitzer	45.0 - IMR 4350	3225	+2	+1½	−4¼	−18	¾
240 W.M.	85	Sierra Spitzer	50.0 - IMR 4350	3350	+2	+1½	−3½	−14	1
25-06 Rem.	87	Speer Spitzer	56.0 - IMR 4350	3525	+2	+2	−2½	−12	1
25-06 Rem.	100	Speer HP	53.0 - IMR 4350	3300	+2	+1½	−4¾	−18	⅞

[1]Based on a minimum of five 5-shot groups, but generally the indicated group sizes are based on a great many 5-shot groups in a number of different rifles.

Premium die sets such as these RCBS Competition dies are necessary if you want the best possible accuracy.

pellants that will work some of the time in some guns; in fact, so well so, that specific shooters will state their choice to be best. Such propellants include 748, ReLoder 7, IMR 4198 and Hodgdon H322, to name just a few. But as a whole, the powders in our table will provide the best accuracy in the greatest number of rifles.

(Please note that the loads shown are at, or very near, maximum. Thus, each load should be approached from a 10 percent reduced powder charge.

In that any load might prove excessive or even dangerous in a different firearm, or with a different lot of components, or with different assembly methods, no responsibility for the safety or use of the data is expressed or implied by this author or by the publisher.)

Use the best reloading dies you can find. RCBS Competition die sets are my unqualified favorites for getting the best from my ammo assembly efforts. And do refer to a number of re-

loading and ammo reference sources to check your ammo assembly methods against those proven satisfactory by the experts.

And while you are checking, jot down the trajectory of your favorite load as well as its wind drift. Then make up a table showing 100-, 200-, 300- and 400-yard ranges with the point of impact and the wind drift of your bullets for a 10 mph crossing wind. (A wind-drift table Table Three for the accompanying suggested loads is nearby.) If you tape the resulting table on the rear of your scope tube you will avoid a lot of misses due to guessing at hold-over or windage. It's easy to interpolate for in-between ranges or varying wind speeds if you have a ready reference to some hard numbers.

Not enough can be said about field testing your chosen load. The accompanying target photos show the results of firing five shots each at 50, 100, 200 and 300 yards from a field position using a bipod. A one-hole group was obtained at 50 yards and a 1¼-inch group was recorded at 100 yards. At 200 yards the shooter managed only a 3½-inch group while the 300-yard group was 6 inches. The moral is don't simply expect 100-yard groups to double at 200, triple at 300 or quadruple at 400 yards. The shooter's aiming error does not translate into such over-simplification.

By the way, if the "bullet holes" in the target photo appear cookie cut and larger than they should be, you are correct. The target was soaked during a downpour at the range and as a re-

Checking various loading manuals for the best methods of assembly as well as the downrange performance will pay big dividends.

Table Three
Wind Drift Tables[1] For Loads In Table Two

Bullet Wt. Grs.	Bullet Dia. and Style	Muzzle Velocity fps	Drift[2] in 10 mph wind in inches at:			
			100 yds.	200 yds.	300 yds.	400 yds.
50	.224 Spt.	3400	1.0	4.5	11.0	21.0
52	.224 HP	3300	1.0	5.5	13.0	25.0
52	.224 HP	3600	1.0	4.5	11.5	22.0
52	.224 HP	3700	1.0	4.5	11.0	21.0
55	.224 Spt.	3400	1.0	4.0	9.5	17.5
55	.224 Spt.	3600	1.0	3.5	8.5	16.0
70	.243 HP	3400	1.0	4.5	10.5	19.5
80	.243 Spt.	3300	1.0	4.5	10.5	20.0
85	.243 Spt.	3200	0.5	3.0	7.5	13.5
85	.243 Spt.	3300	0.5	3.0	7.0	13.0
87	.257 Spt.	3500	1.0	3.5	8.0	15.5
100	.257 HP	3300	1.0	4.5	10.0	18.5

[1] round your actual velocity to nearest 100 fps
[2] to nearest ½-inch

If your loads won't shoot into 1 inch or less, then you are not ready for 300- to 400 yard shots. This 22-250 Rem. group is typical of the type of groups you should be able to obtain. It measures .691-inch center-to-center.

Gunsmith Rick Dotzenrod likes his binoculars to be 9x or more. Be sure to buy a *quality* pair of binoculars — you won't be sorry!

This target was fired in the rain. When it dried, the bullet holes were less than photogenic, so they were cookie cut to 30-caliber for photo clarity. There are groups of five shots fired at 50, 100, 200 and 300 yards, all using the superb Harris bipod from a prone position. The results were a one-hole group at 50 yards, a 1¼-inch group at 100 yards (2 inches high), a 3½-inch group at 200 yards (about dead-on vertically), and a 6-inch group at 300 yards. This clearly shows that a load producing 1¼-inch groups at 100 yards might not be suitable for long-range efforts. In the field 1¼-inch, 100-yard groups do not simply scale to 3¾ inches at 300 yards. In practice, at least in this test, the 1¼-inch, 100-yard groups resulted in 6-inch groups at 300 yards, hardly acceptable for a head shot on a woodchuck at that range.

sult the bullet holes photographed poorly. So I cookie cut the target when dry with a 30-06 case centering it as well as I could over the 22-caliber holes. Thus, while not life-size with respect to bullet holes, the target nonetheless is very informative as to what can happen to accuracy in the field. I strongly suggest every would-be long-range woodchuck hunter obtain a supply of the pictured Rocky Mountain trajectory targets (#TRJ-123). Then fire at a single target, one group of five shots over varying ranges. It can be an eye-opener as to why you miss in the field. You will need to be able to hold 1½ m.o.a. groups at 400 yards if you want to score consistently on chucks at those ranges. And if all you have is a head sticking out of a hole at that range, you will have to shave it to 1 m.o.a. to score hits on a regular basis.

Hitting Them

Before 300- and 400-yard shots become more than random chances, a steady field rest is essential. The best way to accomplish this is not to hope for a handy rock, fence post, or bale of hay, but rather to attach the needed support directly to the rifle.

The Harris Bi-Pod, in its improved form is, in my opinion, as essential to long-range shooting as a good rifle or scope. The newest version of this popular rest allows for the legs to be adjusted to unequal lengths so that the rifle may be level when shooting from terrain that seldom is. Without this feature some canting of the scope reticule would occur and result in almost certain misses.

Of course, practice is the ultimate in the making of a long-range rifleman. Yes, you can practice on live targets in the field, if you so choose. But it makes more sense to use a paper target at each of 200, 300 and 400 yards. (Such practice eliminates the unusual sound heard when a woodchuck cracks up laughing at repeated misses.) First, shoot for group size only. When you can get a 6-inch, 400-yard group, then practice holding-over to allow for trajectory so as to put the bullet into the bull's-eye. And practice under calm and not-so-calm wind conditions. You will, I think, be disappointed at first. But with a well-tuned rifle, a good scope and a sturdy rest you will soon learn to take ammo that produces less than m.o.a. groups at the benchrest and get m.o.a. or at least 1½ m.o.a. groups in the field when shooting from a solid rest. In fact, you will discover with sufficient practice that groups become small much easier than you first thought. The problem will then become one of range estimation and doping wind.

One answer to the range-estimation problem is a range finder such as the 1000-yard model offered by Ranging. But such finders are not what they at first appear to be. It takes practice with the units to learn how to come up with a valid reading. Such practice is best accomplished at known distances. Too, it is the rare shooter who can get a reading from a

(Above) A good field rest is essential for long-range hits. The Harris Bi-Pod is the best of the lot, especially in its latest version which allows the legs to be adjusted to varying lengths so as to keep the rifle level when the terrain is not.

(Upper left) This shooter (Don Brinton) looks serious because that's how he approaches his hunting. Don combines a high level of skill and extensive experience to make 300-yard shots look ridiculously simple.

(Left) A good range finder can make learning to estimate ranges a bit easier. This Ranging Model 1000 is a favorite of the author's.

tiny woodchuck at 300 yards. More often you will need to obtain your readings from large boulders, trees, or hay bales, at positions near your quarry. A range finder can help, but you will eventually need to make the final estimate yourself. Actual field experience is not only the *best* teacher, it's the *only* teacher. Ultimately you will discover that the best range finder, one that's fully portable, is the one behind your eyes!

Wind doping takes a lot of practice. In the beginning, shoot, if possible, when the air is still. But sooner or later you will need to begin to learn how to hold into the wind. There's not much one can say to start you right, as every shooter needs to develop "feel" for wind. I learned by first being able to accurately gauge a 10 mph wind. When this was accomplished, judging wind at half that speed or twice that speed became easier.

Other Comments

You will eventually become quite adept at spotting woodchucks. But if you want the maximum in shooting opportunities, then you will need a good pair of binoculars. Once again, magnification is not the ultimate. Precision in color rendition and sharpness of image is of paramount importance. It's difficult to see a dark woodchuck sitting in an even darker den when it's shaded by a tree. And things don't get too much easier when everything is right and bright. I favor the Leupold Porro Prism binoculars but I have used Zeiss and old B&L binoculars that were just fine.

I have a hunting buddy, Don Brinton, of the Philadelphia firm of Sportsman's Emporium, who makes woodchuck shooting at 400 yards seem simple. I remember spotting for him as he prepared to take a 350-yard shot. The woodchuck was in his hillside den with only his eyeballs clearing the top of his hole, or so Don said. I was not sure it was even a chuck until, at Don's shot, I saw the woodchuck lift into the air falling dead, as later

learned, to an in-the-ear shot. Don's secret is perhaps not much of one. He simply is one *very fine shot*. It matters not if Don's task be small bore gallery shooting, Skeet, trap or long-range, in-the-field hunting. But more importantly, Don is a very *practiced* shooter. While you or I may not be quite so natural a shooter, we can duplicate the practice effort if we so choose.

A 300- to 400-yard, 12-pound ground hog can be a very rewarding trophy when taken cleanly with one shot, or even when missed for one or two shots and then killed cleanly. But if you want such a thrill on a regular basis, you will need the right rifle, properly tuned and chambered for a suitable cartridge, and loaded with carefully assembled ammunition. And you will need a quality scope to enable you to get the job done. But equally important you will need some long-range practice shooting. It often turns out that the most important ingredient to success is a few distant paper targets. Good shooting!   ●

CLAY HARVEY'S
Gun Cabinet

Clay Harvey looked at, shot and chose the best-of-breed, in all categories.

BEFORE GETTING on with it, let me lay out a few qualifiers. First, I have not hunted with—nor even fired—all the firearms on the market. I have, however, used quite a few of them. Exclusion of a specific make or model from this column should not necessarily be taken as a poor endorsement for any gun. Further, I may personally prefer the stock design or trigger action of one make over another for purely subjective reasons. I don't apologize for that; we all have preferences. I will strive to be fair and as objective as possible when making judgements, basing them as little as is feasible on arbitrary decisions.

While I plan to take monetary considerations into advisement, I do not intend to let that be the sole—or even the primary—criteria on which to base my decisions. Excellence has its price. Besides, in these days of $4000 elk hunts, I feel that the cost of a firearm is a relatively minor factor in determining its suitability for hunting. If all else is equal between two guns, I may elect to use cost as the determining factor. Otherwise, I'll go with what I view as best for the purpose, regardless of retail price.

Only *production guns* will be under scrutiny here. If you feel that only custom guns are truly worthy hunting pieces, you are fully entitled to that erroneous sentiment. Those of you with your feet on the ground may want to read on.

Hunting Handguns

Small-Game Revolver

My choice among all the revolvers out there intended for small-game hunting is the Ruger single-action, in any permutation. My first choice would be a toss-up between the Super Single-Six Convertible and the new 32 Magnum SSM version, depending upon whether I intended to handload or get by with factory ammo. For squirrel-sized game, the 22 Long Rifle cartridge or the 32 Magnum loaded with the lead semi-wadcutter would suit me fine, offering ample killing power with well-placed shots and a minimum of meat destruction. For vermin, or tougher edibles like the larger hares or raccoons, the 22 Magnum with Winchester hollow points or the jacketed hollow points in the 32 caliber would be apropos.

So why choose a Ruger when there are dozens of other six-guns out there, many of them more finely finished, some graced with much better trigger pulls and perhaps a smidgen tighter grouping capability? Because Ruger single-actions don't break down. Because their triggers are good *enough,* and a gunsmith can easily tune one whose pull isn't up to snuff. Because Ruger single-actions are affordable, and available, and come in both stainless or blued steel, and offer good adjustable sights in most models, and offer two styles of grip frames, and come in as many as four barrel lengths in some models. Because Ruger single-actions are as safe as a revolver can be, and are as tough as an anvil. Because I have *never* seen a Ruger single-action out of time. Because Ruger single-actions are more accurate than I am, except when I'm shooting from a benchrest, which I seldom carry into the hunting field.

So why not a double-action, for rapid follow-up shots? Mostly, I don't require rapid follow-ups on small game. How about when they're running? I don't like shooting at running game; too risky. Besides, if I did enjoy popping off at a fleeing bunny, I'd opt for an autoloader with its crisp single-action trigger and 10-shot capacity, not a six-shot revolver with a heavy double-action pull. Additionally, with a Ruger single-action rimfire, you get the choice of standard Long Rifle or WMR ammo. Few double-action designs offer that, and the ones that do don't have much to offer in trigger smoothness or precision accuracy. I'll stick with the Ruger, thanks.

Small-Game Autoloading Pistol

At the risk of your suspicion that I am under Ruger employ, I'll again go with the Southport firm when it comes to choosing a small-game pistol. I'll take the Ruger Standard Automatic, in either blue or stainless, preferably in the non-target version with 4¾-inch barrel. It is handy to tote, being light in weight and quite compact. The sights are nearly always "on" for me, and what little adjustment may be required can be easily handled with a nylon-tipped drift and a hammer. The specimens I've shot—and

Ruger's fine Super Single-Six in rimfire form, or the SSM 32 Magnum as shown, are the author's choices as premium small-game revolvers.

Author's pick of rimfire pistols, and his choice as a super bargain to boot, is this Ruger Standard Auto. Jim Roberts is the gunner.

there have been *many* over the years—are so accurate they produce wonder that many more expensive autos can't do the same. They have a fine subjective "feel," nice pointing characteristics, and are commonly blessed with a trigger that is acceptable if not laudable.

And they work. Any misfunctioning Ruger auto I've ever heard of could be blamed on a faulty magazine, an item that is not only inexpensive, but carried by nearly every gunshop. (Trying to find a spare magazine for other brands of autos at your neighborhood firearms emporium is usually a task akin to the building of an A-Bomb in your backyard!)

First-time handgunner Anne Pierce illustrates her form with author's Ruger Bisley 41 Mag. On Anne's first try with this well-balanced six-gun, she busted a gallon jug at 50 yards. From this position!

I'd like to claim that the Ruger is easy to clean, but alas, such is not the case. While the guns are not impossible to field-strip, they are no piece of cake. And reassembly can often be a study in frustration. Still, the little guns can be kept relatively neat without having to strip them to their underwear, so this is a minor irritant. (Even the most beautiful of women often have a wart or two!)

Incidentally, the Standard Auto is *very* affordable, even in stainless construction. There's no reason for anyone not to own one, unless said person doesn't like good guns. All things considered, no better rimfire autoloader has ever been produced than the Ruger auto.

Big-Game Revolver

For big critters, it's the Ruger Blackhawk, especially a 41 Mag. in the new Bisley style. Now you're convinced I'm on the take, right? Sorry. Let me state my case.

The Super-Blackhawk is at least as accurate, and probably more so. It's also a mite heavier to tote; the grip angle is not the best if you want to hit what you're shooting at; it's a tad more pricey than the Bisley. How about a Bisley 44 Mag? It's okay by me, only I haven't fired one, so I can't comment.

The Redhawk, then; from your perspective it's certainly as sturdy as the Blackhawk, is more accurate to boot, and it's a double-action, right? I agree that the Redhawk is as sturdy as the single-action Ruger, although I doubt it is more accurate. To the contrary, I've found the Super-Blackhawks I've tested to be more accurate than either of my Redhawks. I find scant use for a double-action design while hunting, especially in a heavy-recoiling hand-

gun. Finally, in my opinion, the Redhawk is too heavy to wear all day.

How about the big N-framed Smith & Wessons? I've played with a passel of them over the years. Most were excellent guns, with superb triggers, gorgeous finish, and generally provided precision accuracy. Unfortunately, big-bore magnums are hard on the machinery; in my opinion the Smiths have to be rejuvenated a bit more often than I like.

The Ruger Bisley 41 Mag has it all: accuracy, longevity, reliability, good trigger action (in my test sample, purchased *at retail,* thus not a selected specimen), nice finish, and plenty of punch. The Rugerized Bisley grip is so user-friendly it has converted me entirely from the old-style Colt single-action grip.

I recently taught Anne Pierce to shoot a handgun. We started with a 22 and worked up to a 38 Special in short order. Anne was doing very well. She kept eyeing my Magnum Bisley; I could tell she wanted to give it a go, but I was a little worried that the recoil would intimidate her. With some trepidation, I let her shoot the big Ruger. She hit what she aimed at on the first shot—a gallon milk jug at 50 yards. *Offhand!* I don't plan to take her back. Hate showoffs.

Obviously, the heft and grip design of the Bisley obviates the recoil. Good gun. The best big-bore hunting six-gun I've ever owned.

Big-Game Pistol

Semi-autos and big-game hunting don't often go together. However, some gunners feel that the 357 Magnum is just the ticket for certain species. Unless such critters as wild turkey, javelina, and bobcats are considered big game (which they often are), I disagree. I have no desire to hunt deer or boar with *any* 357.

For game up to 50 pounds or so, I *would* use a 357, and said magnum might as well be an auto-loading Desert Eagle as any other. I'd have the advantage of 10 shots at my disposal, assuming payload to be of import, as some do. I'd have a gun that is so heavy, felt recoil and muzzle rise would be scarcely noticeable. I'd also have a gun that offers a slight (very slight) ballistic advantage over a six-gun of identical barrel length. I'd have a gun that is, for all practical purposes, fully as accurate as most 357 revolvers I've shot. If I chose my options carefully, I'd have a gun with splendid adjustable sights.

Drawbacks? *Weight.* The Desert Eagle is so portly and cumbersome you'd best let your brother-in-law carry it for you. Trigger pull? Although my test piece had an acceptable trigger pull, a bit of detective work led me to suspect a professional had been at work. After examining several other *stock* Desert Eagles, my suspicion became conviction; those other handguns had atrocious pulls!

So why recommend the Desert Eagle? First, I consider its advantages to outweigh its drawbacks. Second, it's about the only game in town. So far as I know, there is only one other *available* magnum auto, and I've never seen one. So the Desert Eagle wins by default, right? More or less. But don't let that obscure the fact that the gun *is* accurate, built like a bank vault, and it works. *All the time.*

Single Shot Pistol

You may wonder why I didn't include the single-shot handgun in the above category, since it has but one chamber and is thus a "pistol" by definition. I chose to offer thoughts on the single shots as a separate group simply because I don't feel that a single-shot handgun is viewed as a competitive action type when compared to *any* repeating handgun. Single-shot devotees want *single-shot* handguns, not merely acceptable hunting arms. They love the *tool* more than the hunt—sort of like archers.

My experience with single shots is limited to the Thompson/Center Contender. Since I consider the single shot to be a varminting gun only, and one for use at moderate ranges, I chose the 22 Magnum chambering. My test gun, bought over the counter, has a superb trigger, excellent fit and finish, and it will group under 3 inches at 100 yards when fired from a rest. Naturally, my Contender is scoped; my groups run nearer to 6 inches with iron sights.

If I ever take up woodchuck or crow gunning to 200 yards or so with a

Brian Tennyson is shown with author's pet carryin' rimfire, the S&W Model 34 Kit Gun 22LR.

handgun, I'll likely stick a 223 barrel onto my mainframe and give it a go. I don't foresee that day any time soon.

The Ancillary Handgun

More of my hunting buddies carry a handgun as an adjunct to their primary hunting arm—usually a rifle—than do all the simon-pure handgun hunters I know of put together. Many of us deer hunt at a time when venomous snakes are still on the prowl; sometimes a buck will require a short-range *coup de grace;* or an occasional wild-dog pack roams the woods.

Additionally, many of us are not above snagging a windfall bushytail or bunny should conditions warrant, and a 30-06 is not the proper tool. A rimfire handgun is. I slew more than one tiny critter this past deer season

with my trusty Smith & Wesson Kit-Gun. My little Smith is light, handy with its 2-inch barrel, and rides at my belt, *unnoticed,* for hours at a time. A handful of 22 Long Rifle ammo doesn't create much of a bulge either, though it will garner plenty of succulent ingredients for a stew.

Although there are several other tiny rimfires in the marketplace, I would still choose the S & W Kit-Gun if I were shopping. Its trigger is better than most of them, as is its accuracy. It locks up tight, something many of its competitors do not; it sports *good* adjustable sights. Lead-spitting, so common among even high-quality rimfires, is absent in my Model 34. Think I'll keep it.

My other totin' gun is a 9mm Browning P-35 Hi-Power. It shoots 14 times (actually, 15 in my sample), is so accurate you wouldn't believe it if I mentioned group sizes, is potent enough to get through a deer's skull from any angle, is reliable as a Toyota truck, and is compact and moderate in *avoirdupois.* The only other 9mm as reliable as the P-35, in my experience, costs considerably more and is bulkier to boot. I've tested nearly every 9mm auto on the scene, and am most comfortable with the Browning.

The Browning P-35 is Harvey's pick of carryin' centerfire autos. Here his pal Mike Holloway shows how to dominate the pistol and hit what he's shootin' at.

Hunting Shotguns

The Pump-Action

My favored hunting shotgun is the pump. I grew up on it, love to work the action, have found them reliable to a fault. Nothing else will work under adverse conditions as well as a pump. *Nothing*.

My choice among the trombones is the Remington 870, in whatever guise fits the game I'm after. The 870 has sold more than 3,000,000 clones of itself since its introduction in 1955. The reasons are simple. It is moderately priced, of obvious quality, is available everywhere, and it works. *Always*. Fill it with mud; it works. Choke it with sand; it functions. Drown it with rain; it chugs along. Draw back the fore-end and those twin action bars open the bolt, kicking out whatever is in the chamber. Slide forward, a new round goes up the spout if there's one in the cupboard. Like clockwork.

That's what endears a shotgun to its user. And that's why, if reduced to one hunting arm, a 12-gauge 870 would be the most practical choice.

The Autoloader

Remington's 1100 is sort of a pump-action 870 that has been given an automatic transmission. The 1100 sells about as well as the 870, despite its higher price tag. So long as it's kept clean, it works about as well. The key word here is "clean." The auto is sturdy and reliable, though not so much so as its trombone sibling. Once a year, an 1100 needs to be given a thorough going-over. (Preferably with an aerosol can of Gumout Carb Cleaner.) Keep the gas-operated parts of the action spiffy, and don't clog the gun with a ton of dirt and grit; the 1100 will perk happily.

It's not as easy to clear a jammed 1100 as with some other guns, but if you take care of the gun it likely won't throw a stoppage at you. (An 870 is so easy to unjam, about all you have to do is stomp your foot and give it a mean look on those *rare* occasions when something does go amiss.)

I used an 1100 Special Field 12-gauge on doves this past season. The stubby 21-inch barrel was as easy to hit with as my 26-inch 870, with which I am *very* familiar. So long as my swing was uninterrupted and I didn't step in a hole, any dove that was within range usually fell. The gun hiccupped not once. The recoil-reducing effects of the gas operation pleased me mightily. Nice gun, the 1100—in any permutation.

Double, Side-By-Side

I'm not much on doubles, except perhaps as quail guns, so I've used few in recent years. The one I've spent more time with than any other is the Parker-Hale, made by Ugartechea of Spain. The little side-by-side weighs no more than a whisper in 20-gauge, and mine has double triggers, a straight-grip English-style stock, no buttplate, well-done cut checkering, and a boxlock design. Model designation is 645E-XXV English. My test gun boasts selective ejectors, bushed firing pins, a splinter fore-end, English scroll engraving, an automatic safety, and a Churchill A-shaped solid-post rib. The stock finish is said to be oil, and the receiver is steel left in-the-white. The trigger guard, trig-

Just try to pry Anson Byrd away from his Remington Model 1100, which aided considerably in piling up these ducks. But then maybe not: Anson is 6 feet, 4 inches tall, weighs 235 pounds and likes his Remington.

The author prefers the Remington 870 pump to all other scatterguns currently offered. Rumor has it he required three boxes of shells to garner this hapless dove. Author denies it.

This handsome Parker-Hale Model 645E-XXV is author's choice as a hunting side-by-side. It's made in Spain by Ugartechea, is a 20-bore and is *reasonably* priced.

gers, barrels, fore-end cap, and safety are blued steel. Action design is Anson & Deeley and the barrels are 25 inches in length, true to the ghost of Mr. Churchill.

Selling for well under $600, the Parker-Hale is a bargain considering its features and generally high level of craftsmanship. It shoulders like thistledown and swings with a mind of its own. I may have to try it on doves next season.

Double, Over/Under

This year when I sat shivering in the duck blind, my mitts were glued to a Browning Citori 12-gauge over/under. I even managed to hit a duck or two with it. The Citori Upland Special was my overall choice this year because I liked the easy weight, single

As Glenn Barnes illustrates, the Kleinguenther K-22 is a first-rate tool for gathering bushytails.

trigger, and pistol-gripless stock design. The short barrels and exiguous heft enabled me to get on fast-flushing snipe in a hurry. (I should say "get near;" I sure didn't hit many!)

The Citori was fitted up and finished as is typical of Browning arms: *excellent*. The cut checkering gave good purchase, the bluing wasn't too glossy, and functioning was up to par. There are other good stack-barrels around, but none I like better than the Citori at anywhere near the price.

Rimfire Hunting Rifles

Bolt-Action

Among turnbolt rimfire rifles, the standouts in both value, accuracy,

quality, and dependability are two: the Ruger 77/22 and the Kleinguenther K-22. There are other rimfires in the catalogues that are as handsome, well-built, and accurate, but they are uniformly more expensive, with the sole exception of the Anschutz Model 1416, which I have not tried. Let's discuss the Ruger first.

Since its introduction a couple of years ago, the 77/22 has increased steadily in price. Current retail is $364.50 with the buyer's choice of scope mounts *or* iron sights. While that is a reasonable price for the gun, it isn't the phenomenal bargain it was at its genesis, when the tariff was but $275! At that time, a representative of one of the major gunmakers told me that, "Ruger should *own* the high-quality rimfire market." With the

near-$100 increase, that no longer holds true.

Still, the 77/22 can stand on its own merit. It offers an 11-shot capacity without a grossly-protruding magazine. The action is both stout and smooth, and the safety is likely the best available, *at any price*. The trigger pull is only fair, and the metal finish naught to write mom about, but the stock is built of walnut and nicely checkered.

The bottom line is accuracy, and the Ruger has it in spades. My test gun groups .5096-inch at 50 yards with Eley Tenex ammo, for an average of five, five-shot strings. Only one rimfire sporter that I've tested this de-

cade would shade that, and then by only .0096-inch!

Aside from the fact that the iron-sighted Ruger isn't a particularly handsome rifle, it has no flies on it. So long as the price doesn't continue to escalate every time we turn around, I predict it will age well.

Which brings us to the K-22. There are two versions commonly available, a beech-stocked standard model and a walnut-clothed higher-priced spread. I am told that both are equally accurate. Since the only one I've shot was the more expensive rifle, that's the one I'll talk about.

My gun is cut-checkered, and fairly well-done. The metal finish is bright blue. There are sling swivels; the detachable box magazine protrudes a bit from the underbelly; the fore-end tip is of contrasting wood; there are no sights, although the receiver is grooved for tip-off scope mounting. Everything works; the large thumb-operated safety is slick and silent; the magazine loads as if it were oil-impregnated. A very nice gun.

And precise. My test piece groups exactly .50-inch with its pet fodder, fired from a rest at 50 yards. Since the standard gun sells for $299.95, I rate it as a bargain. If you haven't seen one, you should. Every writer I know who has tested a Kleinguenther K-22 has refused to send it back. Including me.

Rimfire, All-Purpose

You may wonder why I included a separate category for all-around 22 rimfire. After all, can't the 77/22 be considered a fine all-use 22, as adept at can-riddling as in garnering a tree-top squirrel? Strictly speaking, yes it would do equally well in both areas. However, in *my personal* shooting lexicon, rimfire turnbolts do not equate with *fun*. With precision, quality, dependability—yes. Fun? Nope.

Rimfires that hold a handful of ammo and can spit out leaden missiles at a *rapid* rate are *fun*. For most of us, hunters included, such little 22s are most often used to ventilate a pine cone or beverage can than to draw blood. Heck, it's how we keep our shootin' eye sharp. Boltguns are no fun for such shenanigans; too slow to load, too sluggish in function.

On the other hand, we hunters have no use for a rimfire rifle that leaves us wanting when we take a stand in a hardwood grove, or peer through our scope at a slippery cottontail. Our quick-shooting ordnance must offer game-taking precision along with its fun-gunning characteristics.

A lot of rifles do. My pick of the litter is the Winchester (USRAC) Model 9422. The gun is *extremely* high quality in terms of care of manufacture, very accurate, functionally as reliable as any turnbolt, and it operates as quickly as nearly anything you can name. Lever articulation is slick as spit on a doorknob; the iron sights are more than adequate, and the receiver is grooved for scope mounting; the metal parts are good old milled steel. No bent-wire extractors in this gun! The price, while not cheap, is within reach of anyone. You can look hard for years and still do no better than the 9422, be it in magnum or Long Rifle version.

Pretty Amy Pearson does nicely with the full-sized Kimber Model 82. In 22 LR, the author chooses this rifle as a top prestige gun.

Rimfire Connoisseur

The woods are full of gunners who want to own the best rimfire rifles money can buy. These worthies are sticklers for two primary details: ultimate accuracy and quality of fabrication and materials. There are two brand names spoken in hushed tones among the rimfire afficionados:

Kimber and *Anschutz*. I've shot both, like both, and have no clearcut choice between them.

The Kimber is the more handsome of the two, in my view, especially in the Custom Classic iteration. The magazine fits flush with the bottom of the gun; the stock design is both functional, gorgeous, and well executed.

My test Kimber groups .5129-inch at 50 yards with an elderly but clannish lot of Winchester Mark III match ammo. Functioning is faultless, as expected from a near-$1,000 rifle.

I've tested perhaps four Anschutz rimfires over the years. The most handsome is the current 1422D/ 1522D (magnum) Classic model, with its Americanized stock. The most accurate Anschutz I've worked with was the less-expensive M1418, which grouped an astounding .35-inch for its 50-yard average. That little Mannlicher-stocked rifle was a one-load gun; the second-best ammo more than doubled the group size! (My Kimber groups its second-place load into .535-inch, and third slot gets .6647-inch. My 77/22 goes .63- and .66-inch with its runner-up fodder. Considering this, the one-load aggregate of the Model 1418 isn't as comforting as it might be.)

Conversely, my Anshutz 1522D 22 WMR groups several lots and brands of magnum ammo under 1½ inches at *100* yards, with two-thirds of the loads tried running under 2 inches. Nothing else I've shot in that chambering will come close to that for across-the-board accuracy. Obviously, not all Anschutz rifles are fussy as to provender.

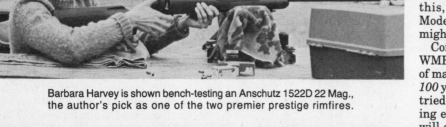

Barbara Harvey is shown bench-testing an Anschutz 1522D 22 Mag., the author's pick as one of the two premier prestige rimfires.

Harvey is shown with his choice of a 200-yard crow gun — the Krico Model 400 in 22 Hornet.

Centerfire Rifles

Varmint Moderate-Range, Bolt-Action

For woodchuck or crow hunting in heavily-settled areas, where strident muzzle blast can get you "uninvited" in a hurry, a 22 Hornet is a wise move. Up to 175-200 yards, it will do a businesslike job, and the most accurate Hornet I've spent much time with is Krico Model 400. My Krico will group good handloads under 1½ inches all day, and shoot around 1 inch on occasion. That's plenty good for the ranges involved.

Last summer, partner Jim Roberts watched me pop a cowpie-robbing crow with the Krico. Although the range was somewhat less than 100 yards, he was so impressed with the Hornet's performance, he bought one himself. Never congratulated me on my fine shot, though.

For a bit longer range, but sticking with a cartridge of mild report, I prefer my Kimber Model 84, chambered to 223 Remington. It offers a 100-yard advantage over the Hornet, and isn't all that much more sonorous. My Kimber will print under 1 inch with Federal Blitz factory loads, light barrel and all. A great walkin' varminter for shots up to 300 yards or so.

All-Around Varmint Rifle

For varmint gunning come-what-may, when you have to leave your car and walk a mile or two, I prefer a sporter-weight turnbolt in something is the Remington Model 700-V. Why? Well, I've thoroughly tested a 6mm, a 243, a 7mm-08, and a 308, and have flirted briefly with a 222 and a 22-250. *Not one of them* failed to group .80-inch or better, and the 6mm and 7mm-08 went into the 60s. The tightest group I *ever fired* with factory ammo came from the 222; Hornady Frontier soft points printed a .38-inch five-shot cluster! No other factory varminter I've *ever* shot can match that record. Or even come close!

Any complaints with 700-V? Yep. Toss out the Monte Carlo comb, stick on a soft-rubber buttpad (so the gun will stick to your shoulder when fired from prone), and satin-finish the woodwork. That's all.

Single Shot

Choosing my favorite single-shot centerfire was the toughest decision I've had to make for this column. I was tempted to make it a three-way tie between the Thompson/Center TCR '83, the Ruger Number One, and the Browning 1885. But that wouldn't be fair. There had to be a winner, right? So I made out a list of attributes, including such items as fit, finish, looks, "feel," function, trigger pull, accuracy, price and a few extra odds and ends. I ascribed five points to the best in each division, less to the others on a more-or-less graduated scale. The victor held but a one-point advantage on its runner-up. All are very fine guns.

The Oscar has to go to the TCR '83, specifically the new Hunter model. (I cannot abide double-set triggers, so the more expensive Aristocrat version wasn't even considered.) The gun is fitted up as well as either of the others (but no better); its trigger is undoubtedly the best; it offers interchangeable barrels in a myriad of calibers; its accuracy, while not quite up to the other pair in my experience, is acceptable. Lastly, and importantly in this instance, the TCR sells for $85 less

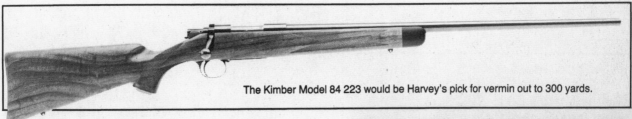

The Kimber Model 84 223 would be Harvey's pick for vermin out to 300 yards.

like 6mm Remington or 243. Specifically, my choice is the Remington Model 700 Classic, perhaps the best-feeling factory stock I know of. The one Jimmy Michael and I used on crows and groundhogs last summer was a 243. I used it to ice a crow at 260 yards, bust a chuck at 275, and Jimmy shot at all manner of critters. Might even have hit one. The Model 700 is just the right weight for a carryin' varmint rifle, and mine groups right at 1 inch with IMR 4064 and the 75-grain Speer hollow point.

A runner-up choice would be the Winchester Model 70 Featherweight, again in 243 chambering. The Featherweight has a lighter barrel contour than the Model 700 Remington, so isn't quite as accurate from a benchrest. Since most of my chuck gunning is from a field position, the slight difference in intrinsic precision is of no consequence. I do as well with one as the other.

Long-Range Varmint Rifle

While I freely admit that there are lots of very accurate heavy barrel bolt-actions out there, my first choice

Jimmy Michael, author's chuck-hunting partner, is holding the most handsome factory gun made, in Harvey's opinion. It's the Winchester (USRAC) Model 70 Featherweight.

than the Browning and $160 less than the Ruger Number One.

The TCR is not without drawbacks. It has no ejector, which I can live without but others may view it as a major omission. It is available in but one style; but then so is the 1885. The gun's subjective "feel" is a giant step behind either of its competitors, but I've found that one can become used to most anything with familiarity. The Number One is the most handsome of the single shots, but I find it hard to view that yawning price gap with indifference. The Ruger ain't *that* good-looking!

The Browning has superior wood and metal finish to either of its American-built counterparts. If it had a matte finish on the metal instead of a mirror polish, if it was offered in a wider range of calibers, and if it had a *real* adjustable trigger, it just might take the pennant back to Utah. But it doesn't, so right now the trophy is in Thompson/Center's cabinet.

Lever-Action, Classic

I decided to separate the lever-action clan into two classifications. The ones I'll refer to as "classics" are easily recognizable as to type and brand—they're either Marlins or Winchesters, or copies of same. If you need a precise definition, let's say that a classic levergun must have a tubular magazine and let it go at that.

Between the two marques—Marlin and Winchester—I have no preference except for minor esoteric considerations. For example, if one insists on a scope (which I do *not* on a traditional-style lever), I'd opt for the Winchester Model 94 AE Big Bore. Why? Because it is the *only* classic lever action truly suited to scope use. What! you scream. Either brand in any caliber will accept a scope! Correct. But *accepting* a scope and being *suited* to scope use are not necessarily synonymous. For glass-sight compatibility, a rifle must have a comb height commensurate with the scope's center;

only the Big Bore does.

Although I've tested the Model 94 carbines and rifles in most calibers, my pick is the 7x30 Waters. That combination is well-balanced, superbly accurate, has plenty of punch for deer out to 200 yards, and it doesn't kick you out from under your turban. Plus, it *looks* right.

My choice in the Marlin stable would be a toss-up between the short-barreled 356 and the bruising 444. My 356 is the most accurate Marlin I've ever shot, averaging 2.2 inches for three, five-shot strings at 100 yards with iron sights. Aside from a 7x30, no classic levergun is likely to shade that with factory ammo. (Alas, my 356 stoutly refuses to group any handload as well as the 200-grain Winchester factory stuff.)

The 444 that lives here is nearly the equal of the 356 with its pet handloads, which are numerous; the big gun groups just about any reload well. Unfortunately, factory ammo—re-

(Top left) Big Jake Barnes likes his Marlin 336 30-30 for whitetail hunting, and the author agrees. The Marlin is a fine "classic" hunting lever.

(Top right) As Wayne Warren shows, the old Winchester 94 will kill a deer or two if you give it a chance.

(Left) Browning's BLR is a fine modern lever-action, chambered to many long-ranging cartridges. This one's a 257 Roberts.

gardless of bullet weight, lot, or phase of the moon—does well to put five holes into 6¼ inches.

Actually, for hunting use the 356 Winchester cartridge is hard to beat. It hits with a 1500-1600 fpe thump way out at 200 yards with the right handloads; that's comparable to the 30-30 at the muzzle! Think about it.

Lever-Action, Modern

So what, you ask, constitutes a "modern" levergun? Simple. It *must* take "modern" high-velocity, pointed-bullet cartridges. Examples are the ancient Savage Model 99 and the up-start Browning BLR. (The fine Browning 1895 is sort of in the Twilight Zone, fitting no convenient niche.) I refuse to choose between the two brands. Both are incredibly accurate, fully as precise as many turn-bolts. I've found both to be reliable in functioning; both are reasonably priced.

The Savage 99 has a better trigger, on the average, than the BLR. The BLR offers a smoother lever throw. Each design can be accuracy "tuned" somewhat by varying the pressure on their fore-end screws. Both guns are moderately well-suited to scope use, although the M99 may be a tad better in that regard. The BLR generally boasts higher-quality woodwork, and a bit superior metal finishing and machining excellence. The M99 (in its original rotary-magazine form) has a self-contained action; the BLR utilizes a detachable-box-only arrangement that can be lost, rendering it a single shot. Both rifles are offered in good, modern chamberings, with the BLR ahead in variety at the moment. And so forth. Pick the gun *you* like; I cotton to 'em both.

Semi-Automatic

No contest here; the Browning BAR takes the raffle. Most all BARs have nice triggers; some have excellent ones. Most all BARs I've ever heard of would shoot well, say 2½ inches or less at 100 yards for five-shot groups with pet loads. Some will do *much* better. Most all BARs work; my 300 Win. Mag. has *never* malfunctioned. The BAR is affordable, though less so than the plebian versions of the Remington 742 (aka Model Four, 7400, Sportsman 74). BARs like *all* Browning sporting long arms, are *beautifully* made.

The Remington autoloader is sometimes as accurate as the BAR, but darn seldom in my experience. The Remington almost never has a trigger pull comparable to the BAR, nor does

it have the aesthetic beauty so resonant in the Browning.

The Heckler & Koch Model 770 is fully as accurate as the *best* BAR, and much more precise than the *average* Browning. It is well made, if homely. Two strikes against it: its stock absolutely precludes proper scope usage; its safety would be more inaccessible only if it were underneath the butt-plate. Accuracy *of itself* is not enough in a hunting gun.

Pump-Action

Since the demise some years ago of the neat little Savage 170 pump, Remington has had the trombone market pretty much to itself . That's okay by me; the Model Six/7600/Sportsman 76 clan is a fine (group of) rifle(s). Back when life was simpler and the slide-action from Bridgeport had but one sobriquet, I owned one chambered to 35 Remington. It shot quite well, but not astoundingly so.

A couple of years ago, I spent a few months testing, then hunting deer with, a Model Six in 6mm Remington. Now *there* was a shooter! With Remington Power-Lokt ammo, my test vehicle grouped four, five-shot strings into 1⅝ inches at 100 yards. A pet handload shot nigh as tight. Good performance.

Main complaint with the Remington pump: it's a mite portly. The trigger on my 6mm was pretty fair, although not all of the 760-series guns can lay that claim. A nice, long, heavy rifle, the 760.

Turnbolt, Woods Use

I'm certain that many hunters out there consider a bolt-action deer rifle to be a contradiction in terms, since it's relatively slow to operate compared to a semi-auto or pump. In such hunters' collective viewpoint, rapidity of follow-up shots is paramount,

(That's a heap of compost, too.) Most other whitetail hunters simply climb a tree, warm a rock, or otherwise remain still for hours at a time. Such a tactic works, if you are adept at figuring where a deer is likely to roam, can sit absolutely still for long stretches, and don't fall asleep.

A few nimrods— and I must admit to being one of them—like to combine stand hunting with still hunting, this latter being simply moving slowly and quietly through the woodlots seeking a buck. For such work, a special rifle is in order. The primary attributes are brevity of weight and a short overall length. This is pure common sense: 1) if you must carry a rifle all day in a *ready-to-fire* position, the gun must be light; 2) dodging briars or negotiating blowdowns will quickly prove the worth of an abbreviated barrel.

So, which short, light rifle is best? Easy answer. The Remington Model Seven. In my opinion, the Model 7 is *the* whitetail rifle for anyone who ever hunts on the move. It comes in several good whitetail calibers; it offers a superb adjustable trigger; it boasts a hinged floorplate, sling swivel studs, good back-up iron sights, and a near-perfect stock design. Its barrel is short (18½ inches) and its heft moderate at about 7 pounds, *scoped*. A Model 7 chambered to 7mm-08 is as fine a brush-country deer gun as can be had, and has plenty of punch for cross-right-of-way shooting to 400 yards.

A good second choice would be the Ruger Model 77 International. It is equally short, light, and accurate, and offers the identical accoutrements. Its only albatross is a too-low comb (or too-high scope rings); you have to shift your head around when shouldering an International quickly. Besides, it *doesn't* come in 7mm-08. It should.

The Ruger 77 International makes a good choice as a bolt-action for woods use, though not quite as good as the Remington Model Seven.

Weatherby's ebullient Tom Hall is at center, caressing a Fiberguard 243. Gun scribe at right is Layne Simpson, who won the privilege of being first to hunt with the Fiberguard by the toss of a coin! Author, at left, is trying, gamely, to look happy. Layne and Clay are both toting Weatherby Vanguards.

As far as the author's concerned, Weatherby put the "M" in Magnum. That's Tom Hall of Weatherby at the right, with his Mark V slung over deltoid. Mike Scearce is explaining to Tom what an antler is, since Tom has never seen one.

Turnbolt, Plains/Mountain and All Purpose

A rifle to be used on a wilderness trek should offer two primary attributes in addition to those common to other hunting rifles: zero maintenence and complete reliablity. For some gunners, complete reliablity under adverse conditions is *the* paramount consideration. For them, the action *must* be a turnbolt Mauser, for nothing else is as deadrock dependable as the old '98 when push comes to shove. The best of the current '98 derivatives is the Parker-Hale, built on the Spanish Santa Barbara action. The rifles boast an easily-regulated trigger pull, so sweet you'd think it a match unit. The inerrant "controlled feed" is there along with the faithful side-spring extractor. P-H rifles come in various stock styles and price ranges; my pick for a mountain rifle would be the light-weight Model 1100.

But how about zero maintenence, you remind me? Okay, the P-H has no advantage over any other wood-stocked rifle. If you want a warp-proof stock, you have a pair of choices: laminated wood or synthetic. Of the models on the market, I'll pick the Alpha Grand Slam. It offers an action as dependable as any other non-controlled-feed design, is light, well-balanced, and is prettier than any other no-warp gun on the shelves. It's expensive, but the workmanship is there.

If you aren't put off by the new wave of composite stocks, then have a look at the Weatherby Fiberguard. It is the most affordable synthetic item on the market as I type this, and a nice looking one. It has the same action as the other Vanguard models, and a good design it is. My test Fiberguard groups around 1⅝ inches with two different factory loads, which is pretty good for so light a barrel. At less than $600, the Weatherby is currently the leader in synthetic-stocked hunting rifles.

Turnbolt, Magnum

Let's face it, Weatherby put the "M" in magnum. Roy's Mark V has been hunted with for so long in so many exotic locales, it's tough to fault functionally. Sure, some gunners are unhappy with the stock styling and finish. Then again, others find it dashing as all get out. The bottom line is: the Mark V *works*; it is very accurate (in my experience, with *no* exceptions); the stock design does—really—reduce felt recoil, it is distinctive; it has charisma.

As for the cartridges, if Weatherby doesn't offer a belted number sufficient for your needs, perhaps you should reexamine them in the light of reason.

The author slew this six-point whitetail with his pet Alpha Grand Slam in 284. It's one of the best all-purpose/mountain rifles extant, especially if you like wood-stocked, warp-proof items.

Bargains

Although there are good solid firearms to be had in various price ranges, there are few bona fide bargains out there. However, there *are* a few.

What would you say to a nicely-built bolt-action sporting rifle with the following features: walnut stock with sling swivels, excellent cut checkering, a hinged floorplate, fully adjustable trigger, iron sights, and a steel stock throughbolt? How about if it were priced *under* $300 at retail, and available in *nine* calibers? I'd say WOW! and reach for my wallet. I did, in fact. The rifle is the Parker-Hale Midland 2100, and your dealer can get you one quick if he doesn't carry it.

Ruger's Standard Auto rimfire pistol, not to belabor the point, is so good a buy I can't pass up mentioning it again. At $180 it's almost sinful.

Guns You'll Wish You'd Bought

Finally, I can't resist digging out the ole crystal ball and taking a look down the road. There have been several models phased out of production just recently that I predict we will ultimately regret. Even if I'm proven wrong, I'll consider this a justifiable requiem.

First, there's Remington's superb Model 788 turnbolt. Although the gun was cumbersome, and homely as my Aunt Flossie, my goodness was it *accurate*! I'll slip out on a limb and opine that the 788 was the *most* accurate true *production* rifle ever built. Anywhere. For any price.

Browning's high quality BBR is history. It was derided for its unhardened receiver and excessive weight (in some opinions), but every one I ever shot was accurate. In fact, one of the *most* accurate production rifles I ever fired was a heavy-tube BBR in 22-250, which would average an honest .45-.50 MOA! The most accurate

The Savage 99 is author's pick as a modern lever gun, along with the Browning BLR.

(Below) Undoubtedly the best bargain in a hunting turnbolt is this Parker-Hale Midland 2100. It offers all the amenities, including cut checkering, walnut stock, swivels, hinged floorplate, iron sights, et al, for $299.95.

257 Roberts I have tested is my trusty BBR. Well put-together, properly finished, nice looking in the short-action permutation. . .that was Browning's BBR.

Cast adrift was the finest brush-country whitetail and boar rifle ever produced, the Ruger 44 Carbine. As offered it was short, light and quick-to-shoot, with sufficient punch to waylay the biggest buck or hog. It was embarrassed if you suprised a buck in a beanfield, say 200 steps away, nor would it group smaller than a cantelope at half that distance. But deep in the pines, with a whitetail digging turf, it was *the* rifle to toss to your shoulder.

Finally, I'll surmise that you'll rue the day you passed up a chance at a Remington 700 Classic reamed to 350 Remington Magnum. It was likely the final host for an excellent and under-rated cartridge. We may never see it offered in an affordable rifle again. That's it for '87 fellas. Concurrences or disagreements with my choices are welcome—I'm not shy. Drop me a line. In the meantime, safe shooting and good hunting! •

Author feels we let a good gun die in the Remington 788. He also thinks it's the most accurate sporter ever produced.

LAYNE SIMPSON'S

Duffel Bag

The author is the kind of hunter who has strong opinions about the gear he uses. Read on. You won't find any fluff—just fact. And it's all based on four decades of solid experience.

THERE IS OFTEN a great difference between merely looking at a product and simply describing it to the reader and reporting on a field test of same. Primarily the difference lies in the amount of time spent in developing each type of report. With general product reviews, as they are called, something that looks and feels great indoors (or as a result of limited testing) may prove to be worthless when put to its intended use.

What you are about to read is the truth, the whole truth and nothing but the truth. No skirting the fringes of honest reporting here. No indeed. If a product works, I'll say so. If it works on the whole, but has a glitch or two, I'll say that too. If it's lousy and/or doesn't do what you pay good money for, I won't include it in this opus, or next year's or the next. You'll have to read about those little goodies in other publications. Fact is, there are too many good products out there. It won't do either of us any good to waste time on the bad. Fair enough?

This year my report includes scopes, boots, broadheads and more. If you're impressed with a particular product after reading about it and want to contact the manufacturer, see the Manufacturer's Address List included in this article. Here's a taste of the cream of the crop.

Warren & Sweat Tree Stand

If dumbo awards were handed out each year, a great number would likely go to those deer hunters who drive $20,000 4x4s, wear $150 boots, shoot $1,000 rifles, take $20 steaks to camp and yet trust their fragile bodies to cheap, poorly-designed tree stands. Of course, the super dumbo award would go to those ignorant souls who pinch pennies by building their own. Each new hunting season sees an increase in the number of serious accidents and fatalities among those who seek to ambush a buck from a tree. No doubt, many can be attributed to tree stands of inferior quality and poor design.

One of the best self-climbers I have used is the Warren & Sweat Rifleman. Other models available are the Bowhunter, Shotgunner, Special and Magnum. The five models are available in standard, heavy-duty (for hunters over 250 pounds) and super heavy-duty (for hunters over 325 pounds). Optional accessories include foam cushions, bowhunter safety bar, gun rack and safety strap. Materials are the best available: marine plywood, tempered aircraft-grade aluminum and grade-five case-hardened bolts and locking nuts. Warren & Sweat stands contain *no* welds, pins or rivets. The Rifleman tree stand I have been using weighs 13 pounds.

You'd have to try hard to fall from a Warren & Sweat tree stand. I'm not saying that those hunters with Hari Kari tendencies couldn't do it, but I am saying it would have to be an intentional act. The Rifleman is by far the safest tree stand I have ever used. It is also one of the most comfortable. (It's lucky too. I have taken two bucks from mine in 1 week!)

My dad, still an active deer hunter at age 68, found the Rifleman to require little effort in gaining altitude fast. Truth is, I don't own the rifleman anymore—dad pulled seniority and confiscated it halfway through this

The Warren & Sweat self-climber is one of the safest tree stands available. My dad liked it so much he pulled seniority and confiscated it half-way through the season.

past season. If you can stand up and sit down (several times), you can climb a tree with this one.

I do have a couple nitpickers though. I do believe heavy nylon strap material would serve better than rope for the foot loops and for adjusting the back rest. Otherwise, I can think of no way to improve on this better mouse trap. A nice brochure is available.

Gott Vacuum Canteen

Did you ever lie awake nights, staring at the ceiling and wondering why vacuum bottles are mostly cylindrical in shape? Well, maybe not, but some fellow over in Japan did and decided to go against tradition's grain. You see, the evacuation process of the vacuum bottle is the key to thermal efficiency. The process is relatively easy to accomplish in a container with uniform wall surfaces—like a cylin-

During preseason scouting when the weather is hot, the GSSVC keeps your ice tea or soft drink cold all day. During summer it will keep liquid ice cold if the bottle is precooled by placing it in the deep freeze overnight. The plastic stopper is difficult to misplace because you only twist it in a half-turn to pour. And the bottle's shape is easier to squeeze into a daypack than conventionally shaped vacuum bottles. I have carried the Gott canteen in a daypack during temperatures as low as 10 degrees below zero. It will keep coffee or soup hot from dawn to dusk if it is preheated for ½-hour with boiling water.

Good job Gott.

Schmidt & Bender Scopes

There's one thing about hunting black bear that you ought to know. They're either bashful or magical.

through a jar of Carolina spring water. Their tubes measure 30mm which presents no particular problem since Jaeger offers rings this size for Redfield, Burris, Weaver and Leupold bases. Also available is the EAW quick-detach mount.

Schmidt & Bender scopes weigh a bit more than the competition (17.4 ounces for the 1½-6x) but it's not a bad price to pay for a one-piece steel tube. S&B goes to lots of trouble in making their scope tubes. After grinding and polishing, they are copper plated, then nickel plated, and finally black chromed. Lastly, the tubes are given a final coat of baked-on enamel. And there's the hitch. Once the enamel coat is scratched, it tends to flake off. I am told that a solution to the problem is just around the corner, and surely hope so.

Inside the S&B you'll find a lense

Here's the Gott vacuum canteen. It will keep your drinks hot or cold all day long and is most handy for stuffing into a day pack. It is made entirely of stainless steel.

This is the author's Schmidt & Bender 2½-10x scope. Its incredibly clear optics and massive 56mm objective lense suck up every available lumen of light. Fine scope.

der. Not so with an irregularly shaped container, like a canteen—that is until recently. The technology is Japanese, but the application in this case is American.

Latest from the Gott Company is the stainless steel vacuum canteen (GSSVC for short). In this hunter's eyes it is the best thing that's ever happened to vacuum bottles. Drop this one from the tallest tree stand, and it won't break. The GSSVC is constructed *entirely* of stainless steel. Hauling coffee to the old duck blind is no problem because the canvas carrying case (camoflauge or navy blue) has a shoulder strap.

Seems like the only time you ever see one is exactly 2.5 seconds before shooting light ends. And, there's something you should know about the way we often hunt whitetails in the Southeast. We sit in a tower or tree stand and shoot them across vast soybean fields. Only problem is, the wise old bucks like to stop near the edge of those fields and hang back just inside the woods until legal shooting time is over.

What is needed for both of the above is a rifle scope that will suck up every available lumen of available light. It's also nice to have one that will reach back into dense brush and wooded terrain and zoom the target right into your lap. I have such a scope. In fact, I have two.

My scopes are built by Schmidt & Bender. The 2½-10x has a 56mm objective lense, the 1½-6x is a 42mm. Looking through either is like gazing

system rated at over 90 percent light transmission. Some scopes barely make it past 70 percent and the real "el cheapos" transmit even less light. Yes, you *can* tell the difference. Some folks may not like having the reticle in the focal plane, as is the case with S&B variables, because its subtension is the same regardless of the magnification. I do because there is absolutely no point of impact shift through the entire magnification range.

The most popular Schmidt & Benders in my neck of the woods are the 2.5-10x56mm and the 8x56mm fixed power. The soybean field watchers are crazy about those two, and in fact, one dealer sold over a hundred to whitetail hunters during the '85 season. Woods hunters like the 1½-4x20mm and its whopping 96-foot field of view at the low end. Also available from S&B are the 1½x15mm, 4x36mm, and 12x42mm fixed powers.

You guessed it, Schmidt & Bender scopes are a bit on the expensive side. But then, have you priced a Mercedes lately?

A Weatherproof and Painless 300 Magnum

Have you ever fired a 300 Magnum rifle? If you have, you know that it caresses the shoulder right smartly and bucks skyward with each squeeze of the trigger. My 300 Weatherby Magnum doesn't act like that. When I shoot the rifle from benchrest, its forearm rises about 1 inch off the front sandbag. Practically zero muzzle jump. Recoil? I can hold the rifle with one hand and shoot it like a handgun all day long. Robert Kleinguenther, the developer of what tames the above beast, demonstrates the effectiveness of his creation by pulling the trigger on a 300 Magnum while its recoil pad rests not against his shoulder but— against his forehead.

much less than I've seen others go for.

My 300 also has Bob's Rust-Pruf finish on all its metal. It looks like a dull, matte blue. Bob says it absolutely won't rust. I'm beginning to believe him. I have swabbed the receiver and barrel with sweat, deer blood, Coke and salt water—the rifle shows *no* sign of rust! The finish is beginning to wear from the bolt body but that's to be expected—I have put over 500 rounds through the rifle.

Last but not least, Bob stocked my 300 with wood, but he didn't stop there. The stock is impregnated throughout by a process he won't discuss. What it does is stabilize the wood's moisture content so it won't twist and squirm under varying climatic conditions. Of course, his pillar bedding helps here too. All I can say here is the rifle does maintain its zero—*perfectly*.

Now you know why my 300 Magnum is both waterproof and painless to shoot.

consistently. Match shooters are also taking a hard look at this bullet. During the 1985 1,000-yard benchrest matches held in Pennsylvania, the smallest group fired at that great distance measured a mere 6.25 inches. The bullet used? The 30-caliber, 180-grain Ballistic Tip.

Now for the Ballistic Tip's performance on big game. Harold Broughton and several Texas pals loaded up their 300 Magnums and tried the 180-grain Ballistic Tip on elk—with poor results. Insufficient penetration. In my experience, as well as that of others who have used these bullets on deer-size game at close to medium ranges, they are absolutely deadly but destroy too much of the eating part. However, from all reports, the Ballistic Tip is a near perfect bullet for shooting deer and pronghorn at long range.

Bottom line? The Nosler Ballistic Tip bullet is at its best when fired

This is the author's "weather-proof, painless" 300 Weatherby Magnum. It has Bob Kleinguenther's K-RT muzzle brake, Rust-Pruf metal finish and resin impregnated wood stock. It's accurate, too.

Bob calls it the K-RT muzzle brake and claims it reduces both recoil and muzzle jump by over 80 percent. I'd say his claim is awfully close to reality. My 300 Weatherby with 180-grain bullet at 3200 fps recoils about like a 243 Winchester. Six other people have fired my rifle, and all agree with my opinion. It's amazing. What's really fun is to first let someone shoot the rifle several times with the brake, then detach it from the barrel and let them try another round.

Now for the less positive side of the picture. Like all muzzle brakes the K-RT increases muzzle blast by a considerable amount. Precisely how much is hard to say. Another thing: When shooting from the prone position, the bottom gas ports kick up dust and debris. No problem when kneeling or standing. So, the thing to do is wear good ear protection when practicing and avoid shots with the muzzle less than a foot or so from the ground. Back on the positive side, Bob will install his brake on any rifle for $80,

Nosler Ballistic Tip Bullets

Nosler has killed four birds with one little polycarbonate tip in the nose of its Ballistic Tip bullet. The results are increased ballistic coefficient, resulting in a flatter trajectory; less deformation from recoil while in a rifle magazine (which would serve to lower its BC); smoother feeding in some rifles; and good expansion at extremely low impact velocities.

After testing the Ballistic Tip bullet in several rifles, shooting three whitetails with it and talking with other hunters who have used it on game up to elk in size, here are my conclusions: First of all, the Ballistic Tip is an extremely accurate bullet. My Timber Rattler rifle in 270 will consistently put three of the 130-grainers into ¾-MOA. In another rifle, a 280 Ackley Improved with a semi-heavy Hart barrel, built by Kenny Jarrett (who also builds the Timber Rattler), three of the 140-grain Ballistic Tips grouped into 0.400-inch

The Nosler Ballistic Tip bullet (left) is designed for quick expansion, while the Nosler Partition bullet (right) is of controlled-expansion design.

from standard-capacity cartridges at deer-size game at relatively long range. It is not the ideal bullet to use for close-range shooting, but then, it wasn't intended to be. Nor is the Ballistic Tip the best choice for elk and such, which really doesn't matter since the Nosler Partition bullet has no peer in this department.

Oh, one other thing. If you shoot a 270 or 30-06, don't handload but want to give this type of bullet a try, go see your Remington dealer. In my opinion, the Remington Bronze Point and Nosler Ballistic Tip bullets are almost peas of the same pod, at least in performance.

Boots by American Waterproof and Rocky Stalker

Dear Virginia:

Yes, I know exactly how you feel. I too have been taken by companies who claim their all-leather boot to be waterproof. Morning dew proof, yes.

is Thinsulite. Other important features include removable insole, tempered steel shank, four-ply thermostatic shield between the foot and Vibram sole, brass hooks and eyelets, double skree collar and padded tongue. During independent tests, the Waterproof Plus boot was submerged and flexed 4 million times, or the equivalent of walking in water for 1500 miles. Not a single leak. The best leather boot from various competitors leaked after 25,000 flexes, or, the equivalent of a good day's hunt.

I have worn these boots while chasing hogs in the swamps and marshes. The same goes for hunting deer in melting snow and day-long downpours. I've waded creeks with them on, too. They have yet to leak a single drop. My feet say that their ideal comfort range is from 0 degrees to 45 degrees when walking and about 30 degrees minimum when sitting still for long periods of time. As a bonus, if

waterproof they are.

There's a little place I know where big whitetails go when hunting pressure gets heavy. The reason they head for that spot is because the brush is so thick that it's impossible for a man to walk without sounding like a herd of wounded buffalo. Of course, I know the secret to hunting those bucks. A little stream meanders right through the middle, and I wade down it as quiet as a mouse. Back in November I did it four times while wearing the new Rocky Stalkers. My feet *never* got wet.

The Rocky Stalker's Gore-Tex bootie is sandwiched between Cordura nylon and leather on the outside and a Cambrelle lining on the inside and Rocky Stalker boots are, absolutely, the most comfortable hunting footwear I have ever worn. (Mine are also insulated with Thinsulite.) The soles are genuine Vibram. Each boot weighs a feathery 19 ounces. As a bonus, the Stalkers can be returned to

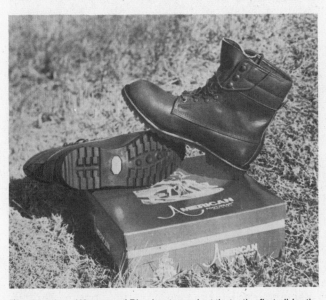
The American Waterproof Plus boots are just that—the first all-leather hunting boots that are truly waterproof. They are very well made and of top quality.

The Rocky Stalkers are absolutely the most comfortable hunting boots the author has ever worn.

Riproaring, gully washing, sloshing through the mud and snow waterproof, no. But don't lose faith in Yankee ingenuity yet. From out of the North comes the best of two worlds in hunting footwear—boots with the comfort, protection and breathability of natural leather, combined with the water shedding qualities of a synthetic.

Made by American Waterproof, the Waterproof Plus boot's secret lies in its construction. A Gore-Tex "sock" is sandwiched between a Cambrelle lining and outer leather. The insulation

these boots leak during their lifetime, you get all your money back.

I won't beat around the bush—my first pair of Rocky Stalkers leaked like a sieve. So, I wrote the company and asked why. Along with a new pair of boots (at no charge), I received an answer. The very first Stalkers were meant to be water *repellant, not waterproof*. There's a difference you know. Early Stalkers did not have a Gore-Tex bootie in their construction. They had Gore-Tex, but it didn't totally enclose the foot. The latest Stalkers do have the bootie and guaranteed

the factory for new soles and reconditioning at nominal cost.

According to my tender feet the ideal comfort range for the Stalkers is from about 20 degrees to 60 degrees when walking, and 40 degrees on the low end when sitting on a deer stand. I have worn my Stalkers over all types of terrain, from flat sandy ground to dry, steep and rocky country to slick muddy mountain sides. They haven't complained yet. Neither have I.

Yes, Virginia, there are such things as truly waterproof leather boots—

they're made by American Footwear and Rocky Boot.

Something For the Archers . . . Anderson 245 Magnum Broadhead

The fact that it took five 245 Magnum broadheads to bag a wild boar at from four to six paces is not a negative reflection on their performance. Heck no. The job at hand was complicated a bit by prevailing conditions. First of all, being knee-deep in a coastal Georgia marsh cuts down on one's mobility a tad or two. Secondly, the hog and the three hounds wouldn't stay still. Thirdly, have you ever tried to thread an arrow through finger-size marsh grass (6 feet tall), twixt three excited hounds, into the vital area of a hog doing the three-dog two-step? Try it sometime—you'll stop laughing.

Broadhead	Weight	Number Blades	Width
243 Mini Magnum	118 grs.	2 or 4	1.3 inches
245 Magnum	125 grs.	2 or 4	1.5 inches
363 Mini Magnum	105 grs.	3 or 6	1.3 inches
365 Magnum	112 grs.	3 or 6	1.5 inches

I like these broadheads for several reasons. The chisel-type tool-steel tip zips through bone without distortion, and the heavy XX8 aluminum body is built to last. The 0.027-inch stainless steel blades don't shatter on bone like some I've used, and they are easily replaced when dull. The boar's skull that I cleaned and bleached is proof of their penetration. Just as important, from my 65-pound PSE Laser and my old Bear Grizzly compounds, they fly straight and true with no tendency to

were available from Remington, 150- and 165-grain Core-Lokt. Both are fine medicine but 280 fans yearned for something with a bit flatter trajectory for open country hunting. Enter the new 140-grain soft point load. Actually, the bullet weighs 139 grains and is made by Hornady. In other words, it is a softer bullet than the 150- and 165-grain Core-Lokts. Which means, the 140-grain load is for deer-size game only. If you decide to take on moose and elk with your 280, stick with the 150-grain load for open country hunting and the 165-grain load for sneaking through thick stuff.

I know of a couple dozen big game animals that have been shot with Remington's new 280 load. On deer-size game its performance has been superb. While at the Y.O. Ranch I

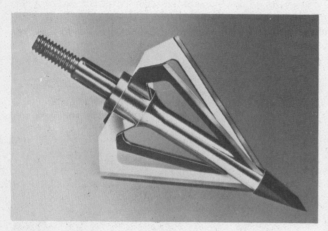

This is the Anderson 245 Magnum broadhead the author used to bag a wild boar. It comes in a variety of weights—*and works.*

(Right) Remington's new 140 grain, 280 load works great on deer-size game. (The 150 and 165 grain Core-Lokt loadings are preferred for larger game.)

First shot, broadside—clean miss (arrow deflected by marsh grass). *Second shot,* quartering away—clean miss (dog bumped against my bow). *Third shot,* head on (by now I had his attention)—head shot (missed brain pan by a gnat's eyelash) (now he was really mad). *Fourth shot,* head on—clean miss (fill in the excuse of your choice). *Fifth shot* (last arrow in bow quiver), broadside—finally hit the sweet spot, just back of the shoulder. The hog dropped to his knees and quickly expired. The 245 Magnum tipped Penetrator shaft sliced in this side and out that. For all I know it's still whizzing across a tidal flat.

The 245 Magnum broadhead is one of the popular "replaceable-blade" design. So are its mates. Here's how the four compare:

plane.

The Anderson 245 Magnum broadhead will get the job done, if you do yours!

Remington's New 280 Factory Load

One of the finest and all-round best big game cartridges available is the 280 Remington. I know because this cartridge has been one of my favorites for many years. At one time it was factory loaded with 100-grain Bronze Point and 125-, 150- and 165-grain Core-Lokt bullets. At a muzzle velocity of over 3000 fps the 125-grain load was sudden death on deer and pronghorn but unfortunately Remington dropped it some years back. The 100-grain load was also discontinued at about the same time.

Until late '85 only two 280 loads

shot a 10-point buck at 65 yards with the new load. He only ran about 25 yards before biting the dust, the exit hole measuring almost 1 inch. When used on elk-size game, the new loading left a good bit to be desired. Like I've already said, stick with the heavier loads for such game.

I bench-tested the new 140-grain offering in two rifles, a custom '98 Mauser with 24-inch barrel and the Model 700 Mountain Rifle with 22-inch barrel. Muzzle velocity from the two rifles clocked 2892 and 2933 fps, respectively. The Mauser didn't particularly care for the new load; the best it would do was 1.53 inches for three-shot groups. The Mountain Rifle averaged 1.19 inches.

I'm glad to see Remington increase the 280's versatility by offering a third loading. Now, if we only had a 160-grain pointed Core-Lokt at about 2850 fps.

Browning Down Sortie Coat

Many years ago Jack O'Connor wrote that one of the most useful items a hunter could own was a down-filled jacket. Jack didn't drop any names, but I believe he was referring to the Eddie Bauer Snap-Jac. For some reason what Jack said usually stuck in my mind. Years later, 1964 I believe it was, I accumulated enough scratch to buy a Snap-Jac.

Jack was right. And wow, did I get a lot of wear out of that jacket. I use the past tense here because in early '85 some slob in a Memphis, Tennessee, restaurant stole my treasured Snap-Jac. Immediately I called the Eddie Bauer folks but alas, the Snap-Jac had been discontinued. So, I shopped around for its replacement.

Now I'm wearing a Browning Sortie jacket and, with the exception of its slightly greater bulkiness, it is everything my old jacket was. In fact, its four pockets make it a bit more useful.

The Browning Sortie is fully insulated with down in the body and sleeves. The outer shell is a wind-breaking polyester and cotton blend. The lining is nylon. I like the two-way front zipper but kind of miss the metal snaps on my old Snap-Jac. The sleeve cuffs are nylon knit and the optional down-filled hood is nice when Mother Nature really does her thing. The colors are camoflauge, green, blue and gold. *Very good jacket.*

One thing is certain, I won't hang the Sortie on the wall of a certain Memphis restaurant.

Worthy Slug Loads

For your money, Worthy Brown's custom slug loads are some of the best available. The 12-gauge version I tested has a 1-ounce slug sitting atop a Winchester AA wad with the shot cup removed. The whole works is propelled by a charge of Green Dot from an ACTIV hull. Muzzle velocity is advertised at 1400 fps. From my 20-inch Ithaca Deer Slayer and 22-inch barreled Model 1100, the average velocity registers 1341 fps. At 50 yards the Ithaca groups 2¼ inches for five shots, the 1100 averaging a tad over 3 inches. Darned good accuracy from a shotgun.

To date, friends and I have killed two wild boar and seven deer with the Worthy 12-gauge load; performance has been excellent. With the exception of one deer, hit too far back with the first shot, all have been one-shot kills. Everyone has been impressed at the slug's awesome damage to lung tissue and its ability to punch through heavy bone without breaking up.

With lung shots on deer the slug blasts on through leaving an impressive exit hole. For this reason the Worthy slug leaves an easy-to-follow blood trail, something highly important to this old woods and swamp hunter. Brown recently introduced a 20-gauge load. While not tested, I expect its performance will prove to be a winner, too.

SSK Industries Contender Barrels

I own barrels for the T/C Contender in about every caliber you can imagine. Most are factory-made T/Cs but

J.D. Jones makes the SSK Industries custom Contender barrels. Not only does he sell them but he uses them too. He took this springbok at 290 paces with the 6.5mm JDJ. His load pushed the 125-grain Nosler Partition out the muzzle at about 2500 fps.

Here's the author wearing a Browning Sortie jacket while looking over bear and blacktail deer country in the Pacific Northwest. Jack O'Connor was right about a down jacket being so handy!

(Right) The Worthy 12 gauge slug was designed and made by Worthy Brown. The post in its center keeps wadding from being blown into the slug and destroying accuracy. Good load for woods hunting.

Daymart underwear is the original polypropylene underwear—it's still awfully tough to beat.

several are custom barrels from SSK Industries. My SSK barrels are in 45-70, 307 JDJ, 223 Remington, 17 Remington, 375 JDJ and 6.5 JDJ. All my barrels are accurate but the 223 and 6.5 are especially so. Either will consistently average under one MOA for five-shot groups. They have even won me money, twice at the range from those who didn't think a Contender could shoot so well, and once from a fellow in South Dakota who didn't believe a Contender would consistently kill prairie dogs at over 200 yards.

All SSK barrels are made from Shilen blanks and drop into a Contender frame without modification. Standard finish is SSK Khrome, a dull electroless nickel. Standard issue with heavy calibers is the T'SOB scope mount, the toughest I have ever used. Chamberings include more than 100 standard and wildcat cartridges. The quality of SSK custom barrels is superb. That and the above is why they are a bit expensive. *It's also why they are so good!*

Wishbook of the Year

Of the bushels of catalogs I receive each year, some contain mostly gimmicks and junk. Then there are those like Dunn's. No vulgar tee shirts and red-neck belt buckles here, just top-quality merchandise for the hunter, shooter and dog owner. Names like Filson, Duxbax, Carhart, Columbia, Barbour, Bob Allen, Russell, Sorel, Schmidt & Bender, and many more, can be found in a Dunn catalog.

Thinking about booking a hunt in the U.S.A., Canada, Mexico or Africa? Call Dunn's and they'll fix you right up. Need a custom rifle built for the trip? Dunn's subsidiary company, Paul Jaeger, Inc., will build a bolt-action or double rifle in any caliber up to 458 Winchester. For wing shooting Dunn's has Merkel over-unders and Bernardelli side-by-sides. Got hunting dogs? If so, about eleven pages of the current Dunn's catalog will interest you.

I could go on and on but instead, suggest that you order the catalog. *It's free.*

Tink's Penetrator Arrow Shaft

Tink Nathan is a bow hunter who believes that an arrow shaft should be rugged and heavy when shooting the larger big game. His new Penetrator should become a favorite of those who hunt such animals as bear, elk, moose and the larger African plains game. It is also a favorite of mine, and I seldom hunt anything larger than hogs, gobblers and deer with the string gun. The Penetrator is the toughest shaft I have ever used. It's a combination of compressed cedar Forgewood bonded to tough, Gordons Fiberglass. The shafts are bonded, sealed, fitted with nock and broadhead inserts and ready to fletch.

The Penetrator is available in lengths to 32-inches and spined for bows from 45 to 100 pounds. According to Tink Nathan, independent tests have shown his new Penetrator to penetrate deeper than any other commercial shaft available. He demonstrates their near indestructibility by driving over the Penetrator shafts with a truck. Tink also hangs 22 pounds of weight from a Penetrator shaft, suspended on a 26-inch center and the shaft doesn't break. Some arrow shaft!! Surprisingly inexpensive too.

Damart Thermolactyl Underwear

Five or 6 years ago an advertisement in one of the outdoor magazines caught my eye. In it were several idiots standing in snow. They were clad in nothing more than long underwear and, as the ad read, were "laughing at the cold." Obviously the ad worked on me because I ordered a set. After trying it for a week I ordered two more pair. Yep, it's *that* good. During the '85 season I ordered another pair to see if the quality is still there. It is.

Damart is, to my knowledge, the original polypropylene underwear. Now it is copied by everybody and his brother. What's so good about it? It wisks moisture away from the body so you don't freeze in your sweat when you sit a spell. This is why professional football players and mountain climbers think Damart underwear is the best thing since the wheel. One thing's for sure, it is the best I have ever used.

I have worn Damart on cool African evenings and on sub-zero Wyoming elk hunts and ice cold southern deer stands. Thus far I haven't found anything to beat it. Since I am a consultant to the construction industry I also find Damart to be most welcome during project visits in the winter.

Try Damart underwear. I bet you'll like it as much as I do.

Custom Riflesmith Kenny Jarrett

One rifle I hunted with during '85 (without success I might add) is Kenny Jarrett's Timber Rattler. (Don't ask me where he got such a wierd name for a rifle.) The old boy knows a thing or three about building accurate hunting rifles. Kenny also stays busy building expensive rifles for the benchrest shooting clan and, in fact, holds several world records himself.

A top grade Timber Rattler costs the same as his benchrest rifles, about $1400. The 280 Ackley Improved I tested averaged .400-inch for three-shot groups with Nosler 140-grain Ballistic Tips. It takes a lot to build in such accuracy, that's why a Hart barrel is part of the package.

Then we have the Timber Rattler for those who march to the beat of a lower priced drummer—like me. Mine is a Smith & Wesson Model 1500 barreled action with lapped-in locking lugs, tuned trigger and recrowned muzzle. The receiver is pillar

bedded into a fiberglass stock. A 270, it averages 0.75-inch for three-shot groups with Nosler 130-grain Ballistic tips. Its price tag reads $700. Of course, if you furnish the action, the tab will be smaller.

I also tested two other Jarrett rifles, a 220 Swift and a 220 Jay Bird, both with Hart barrels. Both averaged no more than 0.30-inch for *five-shot* groups. Not bad for a varmit rifle! The Jay Bird, by the way, is the 243 Winchester case necked down to 224-caliber. It pushes the Sierra 69-grain Match King to 3600 fps at less than half MOA accuracy.

I surely can't prove it, but it wouldn't surprise me to someday learn that Kenny Jarrett is building the most accurate hunting rifles in the world. Well, maybe in South Carolina.

Remington Model 700 Mountain Rifle

I don't plan on stuffing too many rifles into my *Duffle Bag*—that's Clay Harvey's department. However, I found a rifle I couldn't resist.

There's not a lot to say about Remington's latest rifle that hasn't already been said about the Model 700. Except it's the most handsome mass-produced rifle stock to ever come out of Ilion. Except it's the best feeling rifle stock to adorn the Model 700. Except it's the lightest Model 700 ever produced. Mine, a 280, weighs 6 pounds, 9 ounces.

Considering that I didn't lay my hands on a Mountain Rifle until mid-November of '85, I suppose I've done right well with it. One Texas whitetail with the new 140-grain 280 load and another back East with the 150-grain Core-Lokt. The 140-grain load, by the way, is intended for shooting deer-size game. If you hunt bigger stuff with a 280, stick with the 150- and 165-grain loads. The 140-grain bullet (actually a 139-grain Hornady) loaded in this cartridge by Remington opens up much too fast on the bigger animals. Don't ask questions, just take my word for it.

How does the new Mountain Rifle shoot? With factory loads mine does like this for three-shot averages; 140-grain, 1.19-inches; 150-grain, 1.21-inches; 165-grain, 1.28-inches. With handloads I have approached M.O.A. but have yet to get there. The rifle seems to prefer IMR-4350 and the 140-grain Nosler Solid Base. Muzzle velocity is a tad shy of 3,000 fps which makes me glad they went with a 22-inch barrel on this one.

Yep, the boys in green have built another winner.   •

Manufacturer's Directory

1. American Footwear Corp.
   One Oak Hill Rd.
   Fitchburg, MA 01420
   (617-342-8661)
2. Anderson Designs, Inc.
   P.O. Box 605
   Gladstone, NJ 07934
   (201-234-0123)
3. Browning
   Route 1
   Morgan, UT
   (801-876-2711)
4. Damart Thermawear
   1811 Woodbury Ave.
   Portsmouth, NH 03805
   (603-431-4700)
5. Dunn's Inc.
   P.O. Box 449
   Grand Junction, TN 38039
   (800-223-8667)
6. Gott Corporation
   P.O. Box 652
   Winfield, KS 67156
   (316-221-2230)
7. Kenny Jarrett
   Buckland Gunshop
   Rt 1 Box 411
   Cowden Plantation
   Jackson, SC 29831
   (803-471-3616)
8. Nosler Bullets
   P.O. Box 688
   Beaverton, OR 97075
   (503-382-3921)
9. Remington Arms Co.
   DuPont MCD
   2524-3 Nemours
   Wilmington, DE 19898
10. Rocky Boot Co.
    45 Canal St.
    Nelsonville, OH 45764
11. Schmidt & Bender
    Paul Jaeger, Inc.
    P.O. Box 449
    Grand Junction, TN 38039
    (901-764-6909)
12. SSK Industries
    Rt. 1 Della Dr.
    Bloomingdale, OH 43910
    (614-264-0176)
13. Tink's Hunting Corp.
    P.O. Box N.N.
    McLean, VA 22101
    (703-356-1997)
14. Warren & Sweat
    P.O. Box 446
    Grand Island, FL 32735
    (904-357-0744)
15. Worthy Products
    Box 88 Main St.
    Chippewa Bay, NY 13623
    (315-324-5298)

HILL'S SIDE

Memories Beyond The Mantel

by GENE HILL

I'VE ALWAYS been puzzled why more guns aren't sold as "works of art." I know that there is a huge market that is pure collector material, but that's not what I mean. I think the blend of art and function in certain old guns has as much or more eye and mind appeal as most prints, and the cost is about parallel. For example— an old Model 94 Winchester, or Model 97. The Remington Model 11, the Auto-5 Browning, any number of hammer guns—you have a list of your own I'm sure.

When a piece of art is outstanding, you'll find you begin to see different things in it; it will make you think differently about the everyday; it will alter your mind somewhat; it has impact, power—it is evocative.

What could you see in an old Model 97? I have one I'm going to hang on my wall, and I'll tell you why: here is the classic ideal of "form follows function." The function of the Model 97, whether intended this specifically or not, was, as it turned out, to shoot ducks—waterfowl. Here was everything the old bayman wanted: reliability, firepower and ease of handling at a reasonable price. On the bad side is the fact that the market gunner knew all this too, only better. But the old Model 97 says as much about this period of time as any print might. I can look at its tattered bluing and banged-up stock and know what it must have been like gunning over those hundreds-of-decoys rigs; I can feel the icy spray as it slops over the sides of the layout boat and I can hear the hammer click back over the rushing of the wings that are now too close to matter.

The time of the Model 97 is over—or at least the glory days of the live callers and limits of about all you'd want to carry. But I still carry one a few times every year just for the romance of it—and because my father carried one. I remember when his 97 was too heavy for me to carry very far, and I can now foresee the time when mine will be too heavy, again, and wonder where all the time went. . .I'll look into my shotgun hanging on the wall and see the beagles and the setters and the deer stands and the duck blinds and hear the names that I need a minute to fasten to a place or face.

I go now and then and pick up the old gun and swing it over a black and white pointer or slide it over a log alongside a deer trail. I can see a father smile with pride while trying not to, and feel a young boy blush with joy when his mother announces that the Sunday dinner is something *he* shot and puts her arm around my shoulders. My Model 97 keeps the pictures in my mind from fading.

Not right now, but one day not too far away I have another gun I'm going to hang next to a Model 97. They have more in common than it seems at first—one was the reason for daring to dream and the other reminds me that if you want something deeply enough it most often has a way of coming true. So under the scruffy looking pump will be my Remington 375 H&H. You probably wouldn't want to buy it if you ever saw it up for sale. The end of barrel is worn almost silver from the way I like to carry it, muzzle forward where it balances easily over my shoulder. The stock is shabby and dented from the combination of bad African roads and homemade gun racks. It may have been there and back—but it's still a shooter.

No, I haven't shot anything unusual with it. It never saved my life. It has put a few nice trophies on my wall, but that's not why I'm so fond of it.

I love the way it looks. It looks like it belongs in the tall grass where the Cape buffalo stands like a lost locomotive, his eyes the color of fire through the scope. But this is the rifle for the job, this is what it was made for. This is *the* African rifle. The day you own one you're ready to walk in the footsteps of Bell, Selous—or a Hemingway.

I bought it because I wanted one. I wanted it for the same reason I've wanted certain books or paintings—to flesh-out the dream. I had no particular plans for Africa—if you had asked me then, I'd have said "probably not, although. . . ." And then suddenly, almost without time to think about it, I was there. And I've been there again and I hope to go at least one more time. But if I don't, it won't matter all that much, I've seen the elephant and heard the lion.

Like the Model 97, the 375 H&H was easily affordable and did all that anyone asked of it—and more. At first the old-timers scoffed at it—"a fine rifle for plains game—or perhaps a lady hunter," one said back when monsters like the 4-bore were considered adequate for very dangerous game. But the 375 proved itself where it counted—in the bush country. I had to have one the way a kid has to have cowboy boots—and for the same reasons. . . someday, maybe. . . .

The 375 is a lovely combination of mass and grace. It's heavy and it looks heavy and you *want* it to be heavy. But it carries easily; it's comfortable. You pick it up and screw the scope down to 1x. You swing it around the room and the magic happens. Nothing can happen to you now, whatever—you're ready for it. You remember all the miles you walked behind the trackers, listening to Africa—the baboons cursing you, the shrikes indifferent and always the feeling of *something out there* watching you. The kid that dreamed of Africa couldn't be happier!

Having a rifle and a shotgun hanging on a wall isn't the world's most original idea but they're there for reasons other than being evocative. I'm tired of locking up all my guns—I want something out where I can see it; where everyone can see it! I'm proud that I have them, proud that I know how to use them and proud that I live in a country where I'm allowed a pretty wide latitude in their use. Not only are they symbols of their special places and times, extraordinary examples of craftmanship in their own right, they are badges of my fraternity.

When you take a moment to reflect, you'll be astounded at the impact that owning a gun has made on your life. It has given you a reason to choose certain friends and not others. It has probably influenced your choice of a wife, how you raised your children, where you live—how you vote. They allow us to go places and see things denied the person who is not a hunter. For me they have surely been the the "keys to the kingdom."

We all are familiar with the old portrayals of the frontier cabin and the gun hanging over the fireplace mantel. It was there so it was handy—a matter of practicality. But it was also there as an exhibit, a symbol, of individual freedom. That a man here could own a gun if he had the money to buy one was a drastic change from all the "old countries" where a gun was not a symbol of "everyman" but just the opposite. The very fact that having a gun could help you cope with the frontier—or make you sympathetic with those who had done so—still exists, and stongly so. Perhaps the frontier today is a social one more than geographical, or an emotional one rather than political, but it is still important—at least to me and I suspect to most of us.

Having a shotgun and a rifle on a wall says—if only to me—that there are things I need not fear and adventures I can always enjoy.

Sometimes it is the reality of a wind-whipped bay, sometimes in the softness of memory or on the limitless plains of the imagination. Whenever my eye goes to where my guns are—I am taken for some small amount of time to a place I'd rather be. ●

Loads & Reloads '87

SOME YEARS are simply more fun than others. During the past 12 months, I managed to get in more big game hunting than perhaps one man is entitled to. Yet, it can all be justified in the quest for opportunities to field-test bullets of varying kinds.

But I did come away with additional knowledge. For example, Remington's new 280 load with a 140-grain spitzer bullet is a fine cartridge for thin-skinned, light big game. For heavier game, however, I still prefer the superb 150-grain Remington Core Lokt 280 due to its ability to maintain a greater percentage of its original weight after expansion has been completed. Too, my previously used and favored 7mm diameter 140-grain component bullet had to be dropped from use (and our reloads table) due to the fact that newer lots just don't shoot well enough. (I tried five differ-ent lots with the same poor results.)

Reader input during the year has led to some final decisions on the Loads & Reloads tables; more on this later. Reader comment is not only welcome but solicited, though time constraints usually will not allow personal replies. (Address comments to: E.A. Matunas, Loads & Reloads, P.O. Box 286, Clinton, CT 06413.) Keep in mind that this is a *hunting* book and *all* our efforts are geared towards ammo and components suitable to sport hunting.

I'd like to begin this year's comments with observations on new products from various manufacturers. But before doing so, I wish to remind our readers that not every new product is discussed in these pages. Mentioned are those products that we feel are worthwhile additions. The ho-hum type products are left for other publi-cations. Too, we do mention some existing products as it is felt they would be of interest to the reader. Let's get to it!

Remington

It is this writer's opinion that Remington is the most devoted manufacturer in the shooting sports industry. Millions of new dollars are being put into keeping Remington's production facilities as modern and as efficient as possible. Though most of Remington's efforts for this year are directed toward new model firearms, and variations of existing models, as well as the reintroduction of some old favorites, they also put time and effort into new centerfire ammo loadings.

Their most notable new load is not for one of the two most popular hunting cartridges (the 30-06 Springfield and the 270 Winchester), but for a

Game bagged with the 280 Remington in its new 140-grain configuration already has included such exotic species as this aoudad sheep taken by the author — one shot at about 125 yards. The rifle is Remington's new Mountain Rifle version of their 700.

Comparative Remington Ballistics

	New 280 Rem. 140-gr.	270 Win. 130-gr.	30-06 Spring. 150-gr.
Velocity (fps)			
Muzzle	3000	3060	2910
100 yds.	2758	2776	2617
200 yds.	2528	2510	2342
300 yds.	2309	2259	2083
400 yds.	2102	2022	1843
500 yds.	1905	1801	1622
Energy (fps)			
Muzzle	2797	2702	2820
100 yds.	2363	2225	2281
200 yds.	1986	1818	1827
300 yds.	1657	1472	1445
400 yds.	1373	1180	1131
500 yds.	1128	936	876
Trajectory (inches above or below line of sight)			
Muzzle	−1.5	−1.5	−1.5
100 yds.	+2.0	+2.0	+2.0
200 yds.	+0.9	+0.4	−0.2
300 yds.	−5.5	−6.8	−8.8
400 yds.	−18.4	−20.8	−25.4
500 yds.	−38.1	−43.3	−52.3

cartridge that should share equal billing with either of those—the 280 Remington. Until now some confusion might have existed with this round as it started out in life being called a 280 Rem., then had a sexy name change to the "7mm Express Remington," and now, once again, is known by its original name. Too, listed ballistics have varied depending upon the cartridge name used. Such confusion is regrettable, as, at least to some extent, it has detracted from the attention this fine cartridge deserves.

The 280 Remington has recently been available with a 150-grain pointed soft point or 165-grain Core Lokt bullet. The 150-grain bullet, due to its spitzer shape, is the superior load, delivering considerably more velocity and energy at longer ranges than the blunter 165-grain projectile. At 400 yards, the 150-grain bullet turns in a velocity of 1975 fps and an energy level of 1300 foot pounds. The heavier 165-grain bullet has a velocity some 275 fps slower and about 240 foot pounds less energy at the same range.

The performance of the 150-grain Core Lokt bullet has been superb on light and medium big game. In fact, my favorite 270 factory load using the 130-grain Remington pointed soft point Core Lokt bullet has 120 foot pounds less energy at 400 yards, even though it has a higher velocity. But despite a similar level of delivered energy, I have preferred the somewhat

Remington's newest 280 load features a very flat shooting 140-grain bullet.

flatter trajectory of the 270 with a 130-grain bullet over the 280 with a 150-grain bullet or, for that matter, the 30-06 Springfield with a 150-grain bullet. But, in its newest (140-grain) loading for the 280, Remington has created a cartridge that is ballistically superior, in terms of trajectory, to the 130-grain 270 load—it even improves upon the 150-grain 280 Rem. load with respect to energy!

The new load uses a 140-grain spitzer bullet with a muzzle velocity of 3000 feet per second. Out at 300 yards, this bullet is still moving along at 2102 fps (about 100 feet per second faster than the 270, 130-grain bullet), and it has approximately 1375 foot pounds of energy, besting the 270, 130-grain bullet by almost 200 foot pounds and besting the 30-06, 150-grain bullet's energy by almost 250 foot pounds. Complete ballistics for this new load are shown nearby with appropriate comparisons.

One might observe that the flatter trajectory of this new 280 Rem. load is impressive, albeit no great change over the 270 Win. Nonetheless, the use of the very efficient (ballistically speaking) 140-grain weight in the 280 *has* improved its performance to the point of *surpassing* the highly touted 270 Win. 130-grain loadings. If you already have a 270 Win. or even a 30-06 Springfield that you use at long range for light to medium big game, you may not be ready to trade it in on a new 280 for a gain of only 2.4 to 7 inches in trajectory (at 400 yards) or even a 200- to 250-foot-pound energy increase. But, if you are considering a new replacement or an additional rifle that performs at this approximate ballistic level, the 280 Rem.'s newest loading is king of the hill for long-range, light, big-game applications. I, for one, will begin using it extensively despite my long love affair with the 270. I feel the flatness of trajectory to be the new 280 load's most favorable feature—and 200 extra foot pounds of energy is enough to make a detectable increase in field performance.

If I could have my druthers, I would like to see Remington put out the same bullet weight in their excellent Core Lokt design. The resulting (heavier) retained bullet weight would improve performance on game, I believe, to a notable point. However, at a recent hunt in Texas, a gang of writer types, which I had the pleasure to be part of, did indeed put a lot of stew meat into the pot with the new 140-grain 280 loading. Exotic species such as black buck antelope, axis and fallow deer, aoudad sheep and even

the much larger nilgai were taken. Too, there were a number of whitetail deer that succumbed to the same load, as well as several boar. All in all, it proved a very effective round. Handloading the 280 with a Nosler Partition 140-grain bullet should prove a dynamite combination for almost all North American big game, save really large moose, elk or bear. And for light, thin-skinned game the Nosler Ballistic Tip in the same weight should supply the flattest possible trajectory.

In conclusion, I believe Remington's effort with the 280 is a good push in getting recognition for this cartridge's obvious virtues. Combined with Remington's new lightweight Model 700 Mountain Rifle, the new 140-grain round offers most hunters everything they could ask for save Core Lokt bullet construction. I have long hoped for a slightly bigger bore diameter cartridge that could best the 270 without getting into notably heavier recoil or magnum-type loads. Now that I have it, I believe I will use the heck out of it. Proving its worth should be great fun. Perhaps next year I can tell you of more game taken and of some proven 140-grain reloads for the 280 Remington. This should easily be our third most popular hunting cartridge. It offers advantages over the 7mm Rem. Mag., i.e., lower chamber pressure, smaller (less expensive) powder charges, a tad finer accuracy and lower-cost rifles. And, it will come close, *very close,* to duplicating magnum performance.

DuPont Powder

It's no secret that handloaders have had a heck of a time trying to duplicate factory ballistics in certain cartridges. The likes of the 25-06 Remington, 264 Winchester Magnum, 7mm Remington Magnum, and the 300 Winchester Magnum have proven nearly impossible to reload to factory velocities. Most powders simply burn too fast, bringing pressures to a maximum before the desired velocity is reached. A few slower burning propellants allow the desired average velocity, but the shot-to-shot velocity/pressure uniformity is best described as "absurd."

This problem, I hope, has been forever put behind us with the introduction of a proven DuPont propellant into their canister powder line. The new propellant, IMR 7828, is just the right stuff to crank out over 3100 feet per second from the 25-06 Rem. with 117- or 120-grain bullets, or for that matter, the 264 Win. Mag. with 140-

DuPont Data for IMR 7828

Caliber	Bullet Wt. Grs.	Powder Charge Wt. Grs.	Velocity Fps	Pressure CUP
243 Win.	95-Nosler spitzer	47.0 (C)	3110	48,400
243 Win.	100-Nosler spitzer	47.0 (C)	3050	47,900
243 Win.	105-Speer spitzer	46.0 (C)	2980	48,100
6mm Rem.	100-Sierra spitzer	48.0 (C)	3040	48,000
6mm Rem.	105-Speer spitzer	47.5 (C)	2975	46,400
257 Roberts	117-Sierra spitzer BT	47.0 (C)	2720	42,700
257 Roberts	120-Speer spitzer	47.0 (C)	2745	43,900
25-06 Rem.	117-Sierra spitzer BT	55.0	3130	52,100
25-06 Rem.	120-Speer spitzer	55.0	3105	52,800
264 Win.Mag.	140-Sierra spitzer BT	65.0	3115	53,600
270 Win.	150-Hornady Spire	56.5 (C)	2860	50,600
270 Win.	160-Nosler spitzer	56.5 (C)	2780	48,400
280 Rem.	160-Sierra spitzer BT	59.0 (C)	2775	49,100
280 Rem.	175-Hornady Spire	56.0 (C)	2555	44,100
7mm Rem.Mag.	175-Nosler semi-spitzer	66.0	2910	52,000
30-06 Spring.	200-Speer spitzer	55.0 (C)	2385	44,100
30-06 Spring.	220-Hornady RN	55.0 (C)	2285	41,900
300 Win.Mag.	165-Hornady Spire	77.5	3210	53,700
300 Win.Mag.	180-Hornady Spire	74.0	3050	53,900
300 Win. Mag.	200-Nosler spitzer	71.0	2900	53,800
300 Win. Mag.	220-Hornady RN	70.0	2750	53,000
338 Win.Mag.	250-Hornady RN	74.0 (C)	2565	44,400
338 Win.Mag.	275-Speer spitzer	71.0 (C)	2430	43,400

BT = Boat-Tail; RN = Round Nose
(C) = Compressed Powder Charge

measured just barely over ½-inch. Figuring the group to be noteworthy, but probably not repeatable, I fired four more five-shot groups. The largest measured 1½ inches and still another measured as little as ¾-inch. Average accuracy was better than any handload I had ever used with this weight bullet. The average group size? It was a scant .9-inch. I repeated the test in a similar rifle equipped with a 1.5 to 5x Leupold scope. The group averaged 1.1 inches. I now had only 30 rounds left and decided to put 10 through the chronograph screens. (The temperature was a chilly 28 degrees.) The average velocity from the 22-inch barrel of a 270 Featherweight was 2809 fps with a standard deviation of 28 fps. I then repeated the test in a second 270 Featherweight and obtained an average velocity of 2818 fps with a standard deviation of 24 fps.

This load could, I'm sure, easily have made our listings for top performing factory loads, but I did not have sufficient ammo on hand to meet the minimum required 100 rounds for accuracy, plus the 40 rounds usually

grain bullets. And 2900 fps with 175-grain bullets in the 7mm Rem. Mag. is no sweat. Plus, velocities in excess of 3000 fps are achieved easily with 180-grain bullets in the 300 Win. Mag.—not shabby, to say the least.

DuPont IMR 7828 is notably slower burning than their heretofore "slowest," IMR 4831. DuPont data for this worthwhile addition is shown nearby. For complete details get a copy of the DuPont literature on this fine new propellant.

Federal Cartridge Corp.

My strong favoritism for Nosler Partition bullets is no secret to regular readers. The front half of these bullets provide rapid and reliable expansion, while the rear half stays together to continue deep penetration just so long as it has remaining velocity. These bullets will completely penetrate game on broadside shots when animal, cartridge and bullet weight are correctly matched. And on bad angles, penetration to the vitals is assured with a properly placed shot.

Federal Cartridge Corporation is the only U.S. manufacturer to incorporate the premium grade Nosler Partition bullets into factory ammo. In their Premium line of ammo, Federal has six different loads using these Nosler bullets: 150-grain 270 Win.; 160-grain 7mm Rem. Mag.; 170-grain 30-30 Win.; 180-grain 30-

Federal's Premium 270 Winchester ammo with the 150-grain Nosler bullet proved to be a very fine load during recent testing.

06 Spring.; 180-grain 300 Win. Mag. (new this year); and 210-grain 338 Win. Mag. Each of these loads will deliver the maximum possible penetration for a soft nose bullet in that caliber.

I had an opportunity recently to give some of the Federal 150-grain 270 Winchester loads, with the Nosler Partition bullet, a serious workout. From the bench, the first five-shot group (fired from a Winchester Model 70 Featherweight with a 4x Leupold)

required for velocity testing. I am, however, willing to state that if you want a top performing heavyweight bullet for your 270 Win., be it for elk or moose, the 150-grain Federal Premium Nosler Load should prove a best choice. Sighted 2.2 inches high at 100 yards, it is dead on at 200 yards, and 8.6 inches low at 300 yards. And 300-yard energy is 1470 foot pounds, just 30 pounds light of the theoretical amount needed to ideally kill elk cleanly. In other words, this load is

Federal 257 Roberts + P
117-gr. Spitzer Hi-Shok Bullet

	Muzzle	100 yds.	200 yds.	300 yds.	400 yds.
Velocity (fps)	2780	2560	2360	2160	1970
Energy (ft-lbs)	2010	1710	1445	1210	1010
Drift (10 mph wind)	—	1″	3″	8″	14″

Federal's new 257 Roberts +P load has something that factory loads in this caliber have long been without — a spitzer bullet. Improved long range ballistics will make this a very popular load.

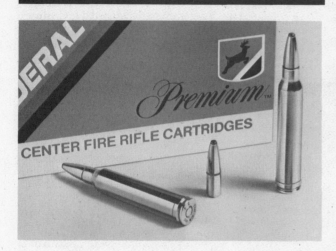

(Left) Federal's Premium 300 Win. Mag with the Nosler 180-grain Partition bullet is among the very best of factory loads for heavy game.

Also gone from the Winchester ammo line is the 22 Short standard velocity T22 round. The Short will now be available only in a high-velocity version.

perfect up to 300 yards. It's got plenty of punch as well as plenty of accuracy. I've bowled over more than a few head of game with the Nosler 150-grain Partition, enough to know that this Federal 270 load will prove a winner on big game.

One cartridge that has gone begging (in commercial-loading form) for a decent long-range deer and antelope bullet is the 257 Roberts. The blunt or semi-blunt bullets loaded by the various ammo companies in the 117-grain weight barely kept going well enough for the 257 Roberts to qualify as a 200-yard rifle on game such as deer and antelope. A few years ago, Winchester introduced a beefed-up velocity version of the 257 Roberts which stretched useful ranges to about 250 yards.

Now it's Federal's turn. They've just introduced a 257 round with the higher velocity of the so-called +P loading *and* a spitzer shaped 117-grain bullet. This combination makes the 257 Roberts useful to a full 300 yards on light big game. Indeed, energy at 300 yards is still in excess of 1000 foot pounds. Some factory loads are at that level at only half the range. A ballistics table for the new 257 Roberts load will be found nearby.

Federal has expanded its shotshell line to include No. 6 shot in the 10-gauge 3½-inch, 2¼-ounce loading, as well as a No. 2 shot load for the 12-gauge 3-inch, 1⅝-ounce shell. The

Federal 1⅜-ounce 12-gauge load is now called the "Light Magnum." A new 1¼-ounce steel shot 12-gauge 3-inch load is also now available.

Winchester Ammo

Sadly, a goodly number of loads have been dropped from Olin's ammunition line. Among the discontinued rounds are the: 87-grain 250 Savage; 256 Winchester; 100-grain 264 Win Mag.; 180-grain 307 Winchester (already?); 250-grain 356 Winchester (that didn't last long); 125-grain 308 Winchester; 220-grain *Power Point* 30-06 Springfield; 180-grain *Silvertip* 30-40 Krag; 180-grain *Silvertip* 300 Savage; and the 200-grain *Silvertip* 308 Winchester loads.

Most regrettable is the continuing

trend among ammo makers to drop the varmint loads in calibers that have dual applications for *both* big game and varmints. No longer (with factory ammunition) can the 250 Savage, 257 Roberts, 264 Winchester, 7mm Rem. Mag., and the 308 Winchester be used for that all important off-season varminting. In fact, among the original dual-purpose cartridges only the 25-06 Remington, 270 Winchester and 30-06 Springfield are now offered loaded with varmint-weight bullets. And I'd bet a nickel on the 25-06, and maybe even the 270, taking a not too distant nose dive. The ammo companies have been notorious for their less than enthusiastic support of reloading. Their actions (which literally force reloading for specific appli-

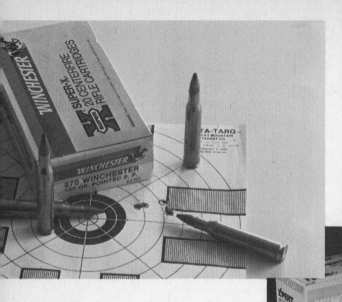

One of the few commercial Winchester varmint loads now available in big game cartridges is the 270 Win. 100-grain loading. Most of the others have gone by the wayside.

(Below) The familiar (to older shooters, that is) Xpert brand of shotshell ammo has been returned by Olin, as they discontinued the use of the Upland brand.

3600 fps. That the 22 PPC is more accurate than any other 22-caliber round, has already been established in benchrest competition. Thus, this new cartridge and the available Sako rifles should prove to be the ultimate for varmint hunting.

Just how accurate are the PPC rounds? Well, in addition to those 52 of 54 benchrest records, U.S. shooters have garnered eight gold and two silver Olympic medals thanks to the help of Dr. Palmisano. (It is of interest to note that Palmisano is a technical

cations) are surprising, but perhaps the varminters prefer to handload anyway.

Only a few years after their birth, the 307 Win. and 356 Win. have had their load offerings cut to only one in each caliber. The shooter is obviously rejecting cartridges that have long-range punch, but are chambered in short-range (accuracy-wise) rifles. This falls into the I-told-you-so-category.

The "Upland" name, which was originally selected as a great marketing ploy to enhance the sales of the old field-grade Xpert shotshells, is being dropped. The replacement name is . . . you guessed it . . . "Xpert." Several new steel shot loads are listed in the new Winchester catalog, which includes velocities for shotshell ammo, but I have misgivings about their posture of suggesting steel shot loads for upland game. A sign of the times? Perhaps, but the jury is, to my mind, still out. For additional details of other minor changes, be sure to get a copy of the newest Winchester ammo catalog.

P.P.C. Corp.

Some shooters are aware of what may well be two of the most accurate cartridges around, the 22 PPC and the 6mm PPC. These cartridges have been around for a dozen or so years and have been gaining popularity with benchrest shooters. So much popularity, that in fact these two rounds currently hold 52 of 54 benchrest shooting records. The world record aggregate for 25 shots is .145 inches—it's held by the 6mm PPC.

Dr. Lou Palmisano, one of the co-designers of these cartridges, owns and operates P.P.C. Corp., 625 East 24th St., Paterson, New Jersey, 07514. Dr.

Palmisano has informed me that factory loaded cartridges and virgin brass cases for the 6mm PPC will finally be available by the time you read this. The 22-caliber ammo and brass should be available by September. Rifles will also be available for both calibers at that time. Ammunition and guns will be manufactured for the P.P.C. Corp. by Sako.

In its factory format the 6mm PPC cartridge will use 70-grain Sierra boat-tail hollow point match bullets. As final testing of the cartridge indicates, the bullet will travel at approximately 3200 fps, give or take a few feet per second. The case will use a Small Rifle primer, and it is anticipated that the CCI benchrest primers will be selected for the task. The PPC case, based on the 220 Russian, will be improved somewhat to eliminate an inherent weak point in the head design of the original Russian round. Headstamp will read 6mm PPC-SAKO-USA.

The 22-caliber version of the PPC round will, I am sure, appeal to varmint hunters as well as benchrest fans. It will use a 52-grain Sierra boat-tail hollow point match bullet and the CCI Small Rifle benchrest primer. Currently, velocities for the factory 22 PPC are anticipated at near 22-250 velocities, i.e., 3500 to

The 6mm x 1.50-inch PPC, center, is flanked by the "tiny" 222 Rem. and the 243 Winchester. The PPC cartridges in the 1.50-, 1.75- and 2.0-inch versions are proof that good things do indeed come in little packages.

advisor for the U.S. shooting team.)

Winchester passed up the offered opportunity to produce what are perhaps the two most accurate cartridges in the world. But despite this, now, after years of effort, Dr. Palmisano, with Sako's help, will finally be in a

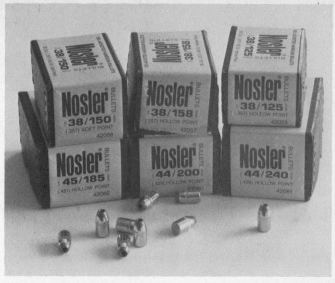

Dan/Arms 1½-ounce loads of No. 4 shot (and other sizes) should prove a favorite with semi-auto shotgun users needing a heavy, clean burning load.

Nosler's newest line-up of bullets are for the handgunner. Good expansion is insured by the ample knife cuts at the nose of the tapered jackets.

position to supply the commercial demand for these two very fine and superbly accurate cartridges.

In the works too, is a new silhouette cartridge based on a 2-inch long version of the PPC 6mm cartridge (the standard length is 1¾-inches). The 2-inch PPC round will use a 6.5mm diameter bullet of 140 grains. Preliminary tests suggest that the best silhouette round of the near future is likely to prove to be the 6.5 x 2-inch PPC.

Dan/Arms Shotshells

The acceptance of Dan/Arms shotshells continues. Indeed, this Danish firm has spent more than just a few dollars on expanding production capability. But, more importantly, their ammunition continues to perform in a top-drawer fashion, while selling at bargain-basement prices.

During the past season I had the opportunity to participate in a Dan/Arms sponsored pheasant hunt. I used a 12-gauge, 1½-ounce loading of No. 4 shot. As expected, the load performed perfectly and only one bird, out of a very large number, eluded the shot charge; my error entirely. But what was unexpected, was the condition of the shotgun's bore and action after firing two boxes of shells. None of the usual 1½-ounce load residue of unburned powder was present. Rather, the bore was nearly mirror bright and no trace of crud could be found in the action. This is, without a doubt, the cleanest burning 1½-ounce load I have ever used. But the day was a mild one with the temperature hanging at about 60 degrees. My thoughts

went to potential cold weather performance, conditions under which shotshells tend to be dirtier burning.

To determine this load's worth under more demanding circumstances, it was placed into service for some cold weather duck hunting. To date, shooting temperatures ranging from 2 degrees Fahrenheit to 24 degrees Fahrenheit have been encountered. Even under cold weather shooting conditions the Dan/Arms load still ranks as the cleanest burning 1½-ounce load I *ever* used—reloads or factory. Semi-automatic users should find this feature particularly appealing as it will, indeed, cut the needed frequency of cleaning to an absolute minimum.

Dan/Arms advises that 20-gauge shells are a-coming, and maybe 16-gauge too. For more information write: Mr. Don Brinton, Dan/Arms North America, 2900 Hamilton Blvd., Allentown, PA 18103.

Nosler Bullets

The continuing superiority of the Nosler Partition bullets over all others is made evident primarily by field performance. But the use of Nosler Partition bullets in some of Federal's Premium centerfire rifle ammo, as well as the use of these bullets in some foreign manufactured ammo, says it all. A few readers have written to complain that my efforts to let the superiority of these bullets become well known are misdirected, as Nosler Partitions are "too expensive" for the average reloader. I surely disagree. Given the right set of hunting circumstances a bullet that costs perhaps

two to three times as much as another can be a tremendous bargain. Even when considering the expense of load development and sight-in, the cost of Nosler Partition bullets is quite small compared to all the other expenses involved in a hunting trip. Too, if they save the hunter from losing an animal, then they are worth even more. For any game over 400 pounds, or for any situation where you might be tempted to take a difficult angle shot, *nothing* beats a Nosler Partition.

This year Nosler has a new line of handgun bullets. There are nine bullets in the line, two of which are full metal cased and one that is a non-expanding soft point for silhouette shooting. The remaining six bullets were very carefully designed for positive expansion. This means these bullets are well suited to the hunter's needs. Each of the expanding bullets, hollow points and soft points alike, feature a tapered jacket as well as numerous knife cuts spaced circumferentially around the bullet's nose. Limited testing to date has indicated that it's possible to get good expansion with even the 158-grain bullet at standard 38 Special velocities.

The bullets in the new line, which are of the expanding type, include 125- and 158-grain 38/357 hollow points and a 150-grain 38/357 soft point. Also, there are two 44-caliber hollow points of 200 and 240 grains and a 45-caliber 185-grain hollow point.

New, too, is a 7mm 120-grain flat nose bullet, designed for those who wish to reload for the 7x30 lever-action rifle cartridge.

Accurate Powders

I've been informed that Accurate Powders are undergoing a modification of nomenclature. These imported (from Israel) powders are having all alpha prefixes deleted from their designations and will henceforth be sold under four-digit symbols only, i.e., 2230, 5744, and 2460. One pound containers are to be available also. This will probably make it easier for dealers to more easily stock a line of Accurate Powders, and a bit less expensive for consumers.

A new loading data booklet is available from Accurate Powders. It includes revisions and additions of noteworthy consequences. Too, important information is now included with much of the data. Specific cases, style and brand of bullets, and the primers used in testing are now part of much of the data pages. New caliber listings are also included.

Steel Shot News

NTC continues to broaden their line of Eco-Shot, a soft steel shot suitable for reloading. More shot sizes, however, are just part of the news. Also new is an increase in the number of steel shot wads, as well as a sizable increase in suggested data. NTC recipe listings are now at about 40 loads, a sizable increase from their 7 loads of just one year ago. Those waterfowlers who are interested in reloading steel shot will find the NTC data booklet a must. For more info write: Jack Rench, NTC Inc., P.O. Box 4202, Port-

Hornady powder bushings for the handloading of steel shot, are now available for that outfit's Models 155 and 266 shotshell reloading presses.

land, Oregon, 97208.

Also new for steel shot fans are bushings for the non-toxic steel shot from Hornady. Designed to fit only the Hornady Models 155 and 266 shotshell reloading presses, the new bushings are available for steel payloads of 1-, 1⅛- and 1¼-ounce sizes. One bushing for shot size Nos. 4 and 6 and another for shot size Nos. 1 and 2.

And don't forget that MEC is also offering steel shot bars, as well as the necessary press conversion units for their 600 tool. Reloading of steel shot cannot be safely accomplished with lead shot bushings (or charge bars) or with tools not designed or properly converted to the use of steel shot.

Homemade Shot

Making shot at home is a comparatively new idea, but it's a good one if you get started with half-decent

equipment. I have tried several different brands of shotmakers, and the one with which I am satisfied is the Littleton Shotmaker. Yet, despite the more than 50 percent savings possible, and the more than satisfactory shot obtained when making small sizes, shot making at home has demanded more than many are willing to give.

In the past, the potential shotmaker could purchase the necessary shotmaking machine, but then had to elaborately construct, in his home workshop, stands, coolant tanks, coolant recovery troughs, bad-shot diverters, screens and graphiting tubs, etc., etc., etc. Finally, one manufacturer, again Jerry Littleton, is offering *all* of those very necessary pieces of equipment. Now the enterprising home shotmaker can get it all, from one good source.

Littleton's shotmaking kit includes such things as shot-oil separator, coolant tank, shot sorting screen, the shotmaker, shot size change drippers, stand and so on. A complete package, delivered to your door, is less than $400. For complete details write to Jerry Littleton, P.O. Box 1708, Oroville, CA 95965. Shotmaking requires a learning period, somewhat akin to casting bullets. Once learned, however, shotmaking proceeds smoothly. I passed my sample shotmaker on to a friend's son in Idaho, who at last report, had literally produced a ton of shot in a very short period of time.

Patterning Adjustments

Factory shells or reloads often do not behave exactly as we would like, some patterning too tightly and others too sparsely with our chosen shot size. The largest pellets often shoot tighter patterns from a Modified barrel rather than one with a Full choke. And steel shot certainly seems to prefer notably *less* choke for best pattern results. Shooters often wisely test different brands, shot weights and shot sizes in their pet shotguns in order to find loads that perform exactly as they like for their specific choke and hunting conditions. Yet, others do not bother to pattern guns, knowing full well that it can be a very tedious and extremely expensive process to find the ideal load for a specific hunting circumstance.

But today there is a quick, easy and inexpensive approach to adjusting patterns. Rather than trying a succession of brands, shot sizes or even shot charge weights to obtain the desired performance, smart shooters everywhere are simply screwing different choke tubes in and out of their shot-

One way to adjust patterns is not to change loads but rather to change chokes. If you own a barrel equipped with a screw-in choke, such as the new Remington offering shown here, adjustment can be a snap.

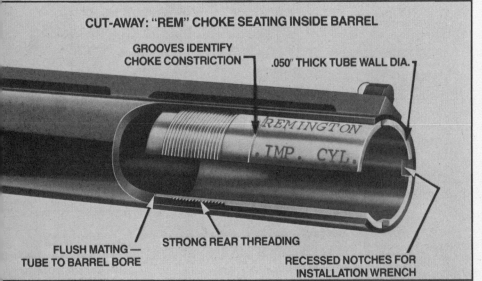

CUT-AWAY: "REM" CHOKE SEATING INSIDE BARREL

GROOVES IDENTIFY CHOKE CONSTRICTION

.050" THICK TUBE WALL DIA.

REMINGTON IMP. CYL.

FLUSH MATING — TUBE TO BARREL BORE

STRONG REAR THREADING

RECESSED NOTCHES FOR INSTALLATION WRENCH

guns. Armed with interchangeable choke tubes in Full, Modified and Improved Cylinder, it is a fairly easy task to discover which tube will make a specific load pattern as you would like.

Happily, interchangeable choke tubes are now a reality for the most popular U.S. shotguns, the Remington 870 pump and the Remington 1100 semi-automatic, and all their variations in 12-gauge. Shooters with existing fixed-choked 12-gauge Remingtons will find an accessory barrel with three choke tubes a worthwhile investment. No finer method for getting positive results from your shotshells exists.

Naturally, when wide open patterns are called for, the Improved Cylinder tube is correct. But when tight patterns are required, a Full choke is not always the answer. For Buckshot, BBs and often No. 2 shot, a Modified tube frequently provides the most uniform patterns. On some occasions even No. 4s will pattern best in a Modified tube. Steel shot performs poorly in a Full choke gun, while a Modified provides about ideal results. But, specific loads might well require a choke somewhat tighter or more open than might at first be assumed. Screw-in choke tubes, such as offered by Remington and others, are the ideal answer to pattern adjustment.

A Very Important Reloading "Tool"

Reloaders, as a whole, usually have almost all the basic tools on hand: a press, priming arm, shell holders, die sets, powder scale, case trimmer, deburring tool, vernier, and a powder measure, to mention only the more popular items.

Yet, as a whole, reloaders seem not to have perhaps one of the most important reloading "tools" required. Reloads generate different pressure levels based on the specific lots of components used and the specific assembly methods employed. These changes in pressure can take a listed load with normal ballistics down to a level where pressures are so light that cases fail to obturate properly. Equally, pressures can wind up dangerously high. But at either extreme there are visual signs that something is not what it should be. Most frequently a pressure increase might be only 2,000 to 8,000 pounds above normally acceptable levels. However, when pressures are constantly above the nominal range, yet below the level of obvious danger, the reloader might well be unaware of any problems until many, many rounds later when he

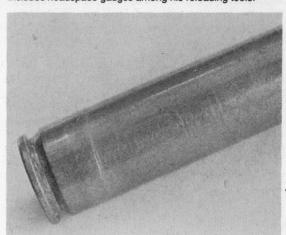

Cases which develop partial (below) or complete (left) incipient head separation can sometimes cause catastrophic firearm failures. Such occurrences can be avoided if the reloader includes headspace gauges among his reloading tools.

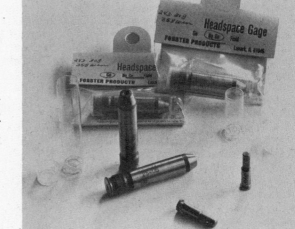

Headspace gauges, as offered by Forster Products, are available from your dealer.

suddenly notes that his cases begin to show a tendency toward incipient separation after, perhaps, several firings and full-length sizings, or maybe even after only one firing. Usually cases showing partial and, on some occasions, complete separations often do not cause catastrophic firearm failure. But on some occasions, "catastrophic" is a mild way of describing the horrendous results of case failure. Reducing a fine firearm to a useless scrap heap spattered with the shooter's blood is not my idea of what reloading is about.

The result of too much pressure—but not so much as to be obvious—is to slowly pound back the bolt lugs into their recesses until headspace increases to a dangerous level. While

there is no handy way for the reloader to measure the exact pressure of his reloads, there is a way to detect any change in headspace before such change results in a dangerous condition. This method requires a set of—you guessed it—headspace gauges.

In my opinion each reloader should have at least three gauges (a *minimum*, a *maximum* and a *too much*) for each caliber he reloads. These gauges are sometimes referred to as *go*, *no-go* and *field* size gauges. With three gauges the shooter might well find that his bolt closes easily on the minimum (go) gauge, but will not close on the maximum (no-go) gauge. When he detects that his bolt is beginning to close further down on a no-go gauge, he will be aware that his headspace is increasing, most likely due to a too-heavy load. He can then back off a few grains before any real harm is done. If he finds his rifle will close on a field ("too-much") gauge, it is too late and a competent gunsmith is needed to set the barrel and headspace right.

Fortunately, headspace gauges are comparatively inexpensive. And while they are available from several sources, I have found those from Forster Products to be particularly well machined to exacting tolerances. In my opinion, any reloading without the concomitant use of headspace gauges is asking for serious trouble.

The Trouble with the 6mm Rem.

The 6mm Remington is often touted as an identical twin (ballistically speaking) of the 243 Winchester. Too, it is sometimes suggested as a better cartridge because its longer neck and larger case capacity make it easier to reach a specific velocity level; all of which is hogwash, at least in some short-action rifles.

The 6mm Rem. has a so-called industry maximum allowable overall length of 2.825 inches, yet factory loads, even with the longest bullets (100-grain), are held to a maximum of 2.740 inches. The reason for this is that at least one popular short-action rifle allows for a maximum cartridge length of only about 2.800 inches, and then only if you are a bit nimble at getting the loaded rounds into the action. Then there is the almost zero clearance between the front end of the bullet and the magazine. Thus, the 6mm Rem. must, at least for short-action rifles, be loaded so that a 100-grain bullet is seated well past the neck, usually well down into the shoulder area. This deep seating takes up a great deal of powder space, thus reducing the cartridge's velocity potential. Even at that, because of the long jump the bullet must make to engage the rifling (when loaded to a 2.800-inch or shorter length), velocity suffers further and some accuracy potential is lost.

The net effect is that it takes about 3½ grains more propellant for the 6mm Rem. to almost obtain 243-like velocity. And it is difficult to get equal accuracy.

The 6mm Remington suffers from the same malady forced upon the 257 Roberts; too short a magazine and action and too long a throat, at least in many rifles. The 6mm Rem. is best served with a long action and magazine, long enough so that the 100-grain bullet's base will be no deeper than flush with the bottom of the case neck. Too, the throat should be such that with this combination there is only a 0.1-inch jump for the bullet to engage the rifling. The reloader can then bring this weight and all lighter bullets to the jump that proves most accurate, simply by not seating bullets as deeply into the case.

The cited shortcomings of the 6mm Rem. are, in my opinion, why it has proven to be a less popular cartridge than the 243 Winchester. It's easy to get good velocity and accuracy from a 243 short-action rifle. And while not impossible, doing so with the 6mm is far less common. No, I'm not campaigning for a change. I know the industry and its problems too well to undertake a fool's mission. Yet, with the right action, magazine and throat dimensions, the 6mm Remington would be a heck of a fine performer. Its long neck and larger case capacity would then prove to be very real advantages over the stubby-necked and shorter 243 Winchester.

To give an example of what I'm talking about, let's use two Remington Model Sevens. In one, a 243, with the bullets (100-grain Nosler Partitions) seated to an overall cartridge length of 2.765 inches, I was able to obtain 2820 fps with 40 grains of IMR 4350 from its short barrel. The same model in 6mm, with bullets seated to an identical overall cartridge length (to accommodate the approximate 2.800-inch magazine), gave only 2755 fps with components from the same lots.

It should be understood that differences existing in individual interior rifle barrel dimensions could easily account for 100 fps differences in velocity. But the example given is typical of a great many similar tests. Too, the 40-grain powder charge in the 243 was about 60 fps below the velocity obtainable with a maximum charge (41.0 grains). The 6mm was at maximum allowable charge weight. Thus, at maximum levels, the 6mm Remington was 125 fps slower than the 243 Winchester. That's not earth shaking unless two other points are considered. The 243 with the 40-grain powder charge produced an average group size of one-half that of the 6mm and did so with a 50 percent smaller standard deviation. All that at a more economical powder charge level. And it's no wonder the 243 has won the popularity contest.

The 6mm Rem. (left) is often a much harder cartridge to successfully reload than the 243 Win. (right). For details on what's "wrong" with the 6mm, see the accompanying text.

LOADS

About Our Loads & Reloads Selections

With this, the fourth edition of the GUN DIGEST HUNTING ANNUAL, we believe that the Loads & Reloads section has matured. As with any new undertaking, there was some uncertainty as to how the Loads & Reloads listings should be treated. Reader input is almost universal in that efforts should be limited so as to avoid becoming a reloading data booklet, and yet call attention to the truly outstanding loads in popular hunting cartridges. The votes have been more than 98 percent in favor of such an approach, with less than 2 percent asking for a listing of all the loads which fit our criteria.

This being a democracy, we have decided to go with the best 25 loads used each year for each category, assuming that many are found to meet the criteria. This year we easily came up with 25 reloads, but our factory load shooting turned up only 22 loads suitable for listing. No doubt there are others that qualify; we simply did not come across them in the course of our shooting. Too, as mentioned earlier, insufficient Federal ammo was on hand to do the required testing of one of their Premium 270 loads.

Our criteria for inclusion in these pages: Centerfire accuracy for listings are always based on a minimum of five, 5-shot groups in the listed firearm. However, each load must prove its worth in a number of different guns. The range for testing is 100 yards for centerfire rifles and 50 yards for handguns. Rimfire accuracy is the result of five, 10-shot groups fired at 50 yards. In all cases, no fewer than four firearms will be used for load verification, this down from the previous five units simply because coming up with five guns in some calibers is a heck of a feat.

For factory big game loads, the maximum average acceptable group size is 2 inches, with no individual group exceeding 2½ inches. Factory varmint loads must average no more than 1½ inches with no individual group exceeding 2 inches.

For reloads, big game loads must average 1½ inches or less (2 inches maximum for individual groups) and varmint loads must do at least 1¼ inches (1½ inches maximum for individual groups).

All bullets used must expand properly for the type of application suggested. Proper penetration, as appropriate, is important. There are minimum and maximum ranges applicable to bullet expansion performance. Any bullet that fails to meet our criteria will not be included in the tables.

As in the past, factory ammo will be tested at the manufacturer's request if 140 rounds of the ammunition to be tested, all from a single lot, is received.

Reader comments are solicited and should be sent to E.A. Matunas, Loads and Reloads, P.O. Box 286, Clinton, CT 06413. I regret that demands on my time do not ordinarily allow for individual replies.

This year one factory load has been deleted from the listing as subsequent tests showed less than qualifying accuracy. But three new loads have been added, in calibers 22-250 Rem., 6mm Rem., and 280 Rem. Too, the specifications of some of the previously listed loads have changed due to additional testing and, in some cases, a change in the test scope.

The Reloads Table for this year still includes one load for the 22 Hornet. But based on comments received, this cartridge will be deleted from future issues due to its low level of popularity.

Readers will also notice load additions or deletions for the following cartridges 22-250 Rem.; 6mm Rem.; 270 Win. 7mm-08 and the 30-06.

Warning: *The loads listed in the following tables were safe in the author's rifles when loaded with the author's components, with the author's assembly methods. A change in firearm, component lot, or assembly method could drastically alter the ballistic performance of any load. Therefore, in that neither the author or publisher have any control over the firearms used, the components used, or the method of ammunition assembly, no responsibility or liability of any type is either expressed or assumed for the listed loads. They are listed purely as the result of a specific test with specific components and imply no other meaning.*

Reloading or the use of factory ammunition can be dangerous if undertaken by persons not adequately instructed in all safety precautions, potential hazards, procedures and techniques applicable to the assembly and use of ammunition.

Gun Digest Hunting Annual Picks This Year's Best Factory Loads

Caliber	Brand	Bullet Wgt. and Type	Lot No.	Mfg.'s Velocity fps	Velocity fps at 10 ft.	Test Barrel Length	100 yd. Avg. Five 5-shot Groups	Test Rifle	Test Scope	Suggested Application
22 LR	CCI	40 / Comp. Green Tag	several	1138	1080	22½"	0.915"[1]	Kimber 82	1.5 to 5x Leupold	squirrel
22 LR	RWS	39 / R50	several	1070	1078	24"	0.655"[1]	Rem. 540-S	12x Leupold	squirrel
22 LR	Win.	40 / T22 Std. Vel.	several	1150	1135	20"	1.001"[1]	Ruger 77 / 22	1.5 to 5x Leupold	squirrel
22 LR	CCI	37 / Mini Mag HP	L16N11	1370	1226	22½"	1.208"[1]	Kimber 82	1.5 to 5x Leupold	varmint
22 LR	RWS	39 / Rifle Match	several	1070	1061	20"	1.067"[1]	Ruger 77 / 22	8x Leupold	squirrel
222 Rem.	Rem.	50 / Power Lokt HP	several	3140	2960	18½"	0.751"	Rem. Seven	6x Zeiss	varmint
223 Rem.	Rem.	55 / Power Lokt HP	several	3240	2855	18½"	1.008"	Rem. Seven	10x Zeiss	varmint
223 Rem.	Fed.	55 / American Eagle FMC	15B-2215	—	3014	18½"	1.009"	Rem. Seven	10x Zeiss	furbearers
22-250 Rem.	Rem.	55 / Power Lokt HP	A251.04705	3680	3591	24"	0.998"	Rem. 700 CL	12x Leupold	varmint
243 Win.	Rem.	80 / Power Lokt HP	several	3350	3004	18½"	1.399"	Rem. Seven	10x Zeiss	varmint
6mm Rem.	Rem.	100 / Core Lokt SP	D10E-B38811L	3100	2689	18½"	1.801"	Rem. Seven	12x Leupold	light big game
270 Win.	Rem.	130 / Core Lokt SP	several	3140	3060	22"	1.335"	Rem. 700 CL	4x Leupold	big game
270 Win.	Win.	130 / Power Point	several	3110	3025	22"	1.599"	Rem. 700 CL	4x Leupold	big game
270 W.M.	Wea.	100 / SP	unknown	3760	3690	24"	1.282"	Wea. Mark V	3 to 9x Redfield	varmint
7mm-08 Rem.	Rem.	140 / Pointed SP	several	2860	2675	18½"	1.442"	Rem. Seven	1.5 to 5x Leupold	light big game
280 Rem.	Rem.	150 / Core Lokt SP	several	2970	2836	22"	1.856"	Rem. 700 Mt. Rifle	6x Leupold	big game
7mm Rem.Mag.	Rem.	175 / Core Lokt PSP	several	2860	2800	24"	2.000"	Rem. 700 ADL	4x Leupold	big game
30-06 Spring.	Fed.	125 / Spitzer	several	3140	3100	22"	1.112"	Win. 70 Feath.	3 to 9x Redfield	varmint
30-06 Spring.	Win.	150 / Core Lokt PSP	several	2910	2875	22"	1.555"	Win. 70 CL	3 to 9x Redfield	light big game
30-06 Spring.	Rem.	165 / Core Lokt PSP	unknown	2800	2759	22"	1.409"	Win. 70 Feath.	3 to 9x Redfield	big game
30-06 Spring.	Rem.	220 / Core Lokt SP	several	2410	2350	22"	1.103"	Win. 70 Feath.	3 to 9x Redfield	very heavy big game
300 H&H	Rem.	180 / Core Lokt PSP	several	2880	2801	24"	1.566"	Rem. 700 CL.	4x Leupold	heavy big game

[1] Groups for rimfire cartridges measured at 50 yards. CL = Classic

RELOADS

TABLE B

Gun Digest Hunting Annual Picks This Year's Best Reloads

Caliber	Bullet Wgt.	Bullet Type	Brand	Powder Charge wgt. in grains	Velocity fps at 10 ft.	Barrel Length	Primer	Case	100 yd. Avg. 5, 5-shot groups	Test Rifle	Test Scope	Suggested Application
22 Hornet	45	SP	Nosler	11.2/IMR 4227	2612	22½"	Rem.	Rem.	1.251"	Kimber 82	6x Leupold	varmint
222 Rem.	50	Match	Nosler	23.0/H335	2921	18½"	Rem.	Rem.	0.887"	Rem.Seven	6x Zeiss	varmint
222 Rem.	50	Expander	Nosler	23.0/H335	2847	18½"	Rem.	Rem.	0.978"	Rem.Seven	6x Zeiss	varmint
223 Rem.	55	SP	Hornady	27.0/H335	3110	18½"	Win.	Fed.	1.061"	Rem.Seven	10x Zeiss	varmint
224 W.M.	50	HP	Nosler	30.0/H335	3450	24"	CCI	Wea.	0.700"	Wea.Mark V	12x Leupold	varmint
22-250 Rem.	55	spitz.	Speer	39.5/H380	3543	24"	CCI	Rem.	0.988"	Rem.700 CL.	12x Leupold	varmint
243 Win.	75	HP	Sierra	45.0/IMR 4350	2921	18½"	Win.	Rem.	1.120"	Rem.Seven	6x Leupold	varmint
243 Win.	100	Part.	Nosler	40.0/IMR 4350	2819	18½"	Win.	Win.	1.243"	Rem.Seven	6x Leupold	lgt. big game
6mm Rem.	80	spitz.	Speer	46.0/IMR 4350	2922	18½"	Rem.	Rem.	1.248"	Rem.Seven	12x Leupold	varmint
6mm Rem.	100	Part.	Nosler	43.5/IMR 4350	2753	18½"	Rem.	Rem.	1.487"	Rem.Seven	12x Leupold	lgt. big game
257 Roberts	100	HP	Speer	45.0/IMR 4350	3000	22"	CCI	Win.	1.092"	Ruger 77	6x Lyman AA	varmint
270 Win.	90	HP	Sierra	60.0/IMR 4350	3532	22"	Win.	Win.	0.995"	Rem.700 CL.	4x Leupold	varmint
270 Win.	100	spitz.	Speer	59.0/IMR 4350	3253	22"	Win.	Rem.	0.909"	Win.70 Feath.	6x Leupold	varmint
270 Win.	130	spitz.	Speer	55.0/IMR 4350	3045	22"	Win.	Win.	1.012"	Rem.700 CL.	4x Leupold	big game
270 Win.	130	Part.	Nosler	55.0/IMR 4350	3036	22"	Win.	Win.	1.018"	Ren.700 CL.	4x Leupold	big game
270 Win.	150	spitz.	Speer	52.0/IMR 4350	2800	22"	Win.	Win.	1.001"	Rem.700 CL.	4x Leupold	big game
7mm-08 Rem.	145	spitz.	Speer	42.0/IMR 4064	2550	18½"	Rem.	Rem.	1.333"	Rem.Seven	6x Zeiss	big game
280 Rem.	145	spitz.	Speer	53.0/IMR 4350	2715	22"	Win.	Rem.	1.409"	Rem.700 Mt.	10x Zeiss	big game
30-06 Spring.	110	HP	Sierra	55.0/IMR 4064	3200	22"	Rem.	Rem.	1.013"	Win.70 Feath.	3-9x Red.	varmint
30-06 Spring.	125	spitz.	Sierra	53.0/IMR 4064	3001	22"	Rem.	Rem.	1.006"	Win.70 Feath.	3-9x Red.	varmint
30-06 Spring.	165	spitz.	Nosler	50.0/IMR 4064	2662	22"	Rem.	Rem.	1.108"	Win.70 Feath.	2-7x Red.	big game
30-06 Spring.	180	Part.	Nosler	57.0/IMR 4350	2750	22"	Rem.	Rem.	1.188"	Win.70 Feath.	6x Leupold	big game
300 H&H	180	Part.	Nosler	69.0/IMR 4350	3053	24"	Win.	Rem.	1.209"	Rem.700 CL.	1.5-5x Leup.	hvy. game
9mm Luger	100	HP	Speer	5.8/231	1265	4"	Win.	Win.	2.000"(1)	S&W 59	—	varmint
9mm Luger	100	HP	Speer	5.0/Bullseye	1267	4"	Win.	S&W	2.000"(1)	S&W 59	—	varmint

(1)Groups for handgun loads measured at 50 yards (2)Standard small pistol primer   CL = Classic   Red. = Redfield

new products '87

by Robert S.L. Anderson

Scent Masking Gun Lube

It was bound to happen. Someone finally brought out a gun lube that doesn't smell like an after thought from a machine shop. It's called "Crouse's Masking Gun Lubricant" and comes in (take your pick, guys) pine or cedar scent. No, I haven't used it, but I did enjoy a nice chat with the inventor, Bob Crouse.

Obviously, Bob's excited and enthusiastic about the product. And, quite frankly, Bob's product makes sense as one can correctly assume that whitetails are well-conditioned to the presence of man and his many attendant odors.

Providing a hunter goes to reasonable length to eliminate body/clothing odors, you can presume he'll have an edge in the field. In short, the Crouse offering is like the icing on the cake. For the coming year it will probably prove quite popular with gun/bow hunters who want to eliminate as much man-carried scent as possible. Obviously, firearms and broadheads come to mind when considering the use of Crouse's; but, don't forget those ferrous-metal based accessories, i.e., knives, axes, etc.

A bottle (1¼ oz.) sells for around $4.95. You can get more info direct from Bob Crouse at Box 160, Dept. GDHA, Storrs, CT 06268.

MTM Shotshell Carrier

The MTM Molded Products Company of Dayton, Ohio, has introduced a compact, 100-round capacity shotshell carrier. Designed primarily for the hunter, shotshells are carried in two removable 50-round trays. Each shell is held securely in an upright position for easy removal.

The textured finish is dirt and stain resistant. Of prime concern to hunters is the fact that the contents of the carrier are fully protected from dust and moisture. The intregal hinge is guaranteed for one million open-close cycles.

Other features include an over-size handle designed to be used with thick gloves, and an extra-strong latch to prevent inadvertent opening. The handle folds into a recess on the top of the unit for easy stacking. Constructed of space-age polypropylene, the CASE-GARD shotshell carrier is protected by the MTM 3-year guarantee.

This MTM offering may not be for everyone, but I'll be darned surprised to hear of any *waterfowler* who'll turn his nose up at this one.

Your editor has used MTM products for years—and long before he got into the gun business. In short, anything from MTM is guaranteed "good stuff."

Those of you who have used MTM products will, I'm sure, agree with those comments.

The shotshell carrier seen here sells for around $13. Al Minneman is the guy at MTM to talk to. You can reach him at P.O. Box 14117, Dept. GDHA, Dayton, OH 45414 (Phone: 513-890-7461).

Ranging Range Finders

When the 1st Edition of the GUN DIGEST HUNTING ANNUAL hit the stands 4 years ago, we tried to attract outdoor writers who were, indeed, "real hunters." Guys like Chuck Adams, Jon Sundra and Leonard ("Lenny") Lee Rue, III, have been kind enough to supply us with the type of writing hunters have come to respect.

My point?

As I was thumbing through a pile of gun-accessory catalogs I came across one from Ranging, the folks who reinvented the rangefinding business. I tossed it aside, in the "good-stuff-to-write-about" pile. There it sat for 3 months.

When I finally looked inside that Ranging catalog I found testimonies from (you guessed it) the three writers mentioned above. I respect those guys and their opinions. If you're a hunter who owns a Rangefinder by Ranging, you probably wonder, every now and then, how you ever managed to get along without one of those "miracle" rangefinding devices.

If you're a serious big game hunter, a varmint hunter or a guy who simply hunts the "wide-open spaces," Ranging is the outfit that'll make your shooting a whole lot easier—and successful.

For a free catalog, drop Tom Hughes a note at Ranging, Dept. GDHA, Rts. 5 & 20, E. Bloomfield, NY 14443.

New Remington Hunting Clothes & Gun Cases

If you like their guns, you'll probably like the new togs as well. And they just don't have a coat or two. They've got a *complete* "Outdoor Clothing System." In fact, the press-release packet they sent out is so crammed with new types of hunting gear that it would take a whole night just to devour the info. As you know, the space here is limited. We'll give it our best shot.

First off, Remington used their parent outfit's (DuPont's) fiber technology and came up with a "system" that's supposed to keep the hunter warmer, drier and more comfortable, regardless of the weather.

Specifically, they've got upland wear and waterfowl wear. Camo this, British tan jacket that; pants here, jackets there. Let's not forget jacket features like blood proof game bag. And dare we not mention their blaze orange option? Uh, Oh! Darn near forgot to mention their gun cases made of, ". . . abrasion resistant 1000 denier cordura nylon." (That's DuPontese for, "tough stuff.") Leather trim and solid brass hardware, and much more, on the luggage.

I'll be dipped in horse pucky if I could find a single price in that press kit. So I reckon you'll have to head for a dealer to get the $ particulars. It *looks* like good gear. And I like the fact that it's got Remington's name on it. And I like the fact that Du Pont technology is an intregral part of the apparel.

Want *more* info? There's a lot available. Just drop Rick Straitman a line at Remington Outdoor Clothing, Remington Arms Company, MCD, Dept. GDHA, Wilmington, DE 19898 (Phone: 302-774-8870).

Parker-Hale Side-by-Side (GDHA Bargain of the Year!)

Go back and take a second look at what Clay Harvey has to say about these guns in his "Gun Cabinet" column. He likes 'em. You probably will, too.

Parker Hale is bringing in a nice line of 12, 16, 20, 28 and .410 doubles through Precision Sports, in Cortland, New York. (Sixteen-gauge fanciers should re-read the last sentence—'taint an error!) Features, you ask?

- Hand-checkered walnut, finished with hand-rubbed oil
- English-style scroll engraving
- Forged barrels (26″, 27″, 28″)
- Firing pins set in bushings
- Lifetime operational warranty

Let's not forget the good news! The price is a reasonable $450 to $670 for the Field Grade boxlocks, with the "Best" grade sidelocks running in the mid-$2000 range. Seen nearby are a pair of "Field Grade" boxlocks—the 645A and the 645E. (The "A" stands for "American Pistol Grip" and single trigger; the "E" denotes an "English Straight Grip" and double triggers.)

As far as I can tell, Parker-Hale has the *only* line of doubles, on these shores, available in *all* gauges. Who makes 'em? A Spanish firm by the name of Ignacio Ugartechea. Lest you think this is something totally "new," be advised that Parker-Hale has been doing a brisk business with these doubles, in England, for many years.

Contact Greg Pogson at Precision Sports, 3736 Kellogg Rd., Cortland, NY 13045-5588 (Phone: 800-847-6787).

Federal Announces Recall of Certain "Lots" of 243 Win. Ammunition

As a service to GDHA readers, we are quoting, in its entirety, a recall notice recently received from Federal Cartridge Corporation:

Federal Cartridge Company is recalling 10 lots of Premium™ brand caliber 243 Winchester cartridges. Certain cartridges in these lots have been found to produce higher than normal pressures that could cause damage to some firearms and personal injury. These cartridges may be identified by the following markings on the outside of both package end flaps:

> *Federal Premium*
> *243 Winchester*
> *85 Grain No. P243D*
> *Boat-Tail Hollow Point Bullet*

On the back panel, there is a white rectangular area in which the lot number is printed. Being recalled are lot numbers beginning with 5A or 5B and followed by any of these four digits: 4592, 4593, 4594, 4595 or 4598. (Example: 5A-4592)

Persons having Federal Premium cartridges from these lots are requested to return them to:

> *Federal Cartridge Company*
> *Att: Ronald L. Ives*
> *900 Ehlen Drive*
> *Anoka, Minnesota 55303*

Shipment is to be via United Parcel Service "collect." It is illegal to send ammunition through the U.S. Postal Service. The company will issue a refund check upon receipt of the ammunition.

Uncle Mike's Sidekick Scabbard

If you hunt on horseback or carry a rifle or shotgun on an off-road vehicle, Michaels of Oregon has come up with a brand new version of the venerable old scabbard. But instead of leather, this scabbard is made of nylon, is padded with waterproof foam and, in one version, doubles as a sturdy carry case.

The new Sidekick scabbards perform much the same as leather models, but without many of the problems inherent in leather. The nylon-foam-nylon laminate will not absorb moisture, so a rifle can be carried for days, or even stored, without danger of rust or chemical reaction to the gun's blueing.

Equipped with long, nylon web saddle straps, the new Sidekick scabbards are equally at home suspended from a horse, or fitted on an off-road motorcycle, an all-terrain vehicle or a snowmobile.

Top of the line is the Large Rifle Scabbard & Carry Case with Breakaway Hood. It will accommodate scoped or unscoped full-sized rifles, and double as a carry case as well. The large scabbard has a zippered breakaway hood that's attached to the scabbard with a quick-release buckle. The hood can be removed in two ways. (First, by unzipping the zipper, the hood falls away but remains suspended by the buckle. Second, the buckle can be released to remove the hood altogether.)

Suggested retail prices are $59.95 for the large scabbard, $49.95 for the medium model and $44.95 for the carbine scabbard. For a current catalog send $1 to Michaels of Oregon, Dept. GDHA, P.O.B. 13010, Portland, OR 97213.

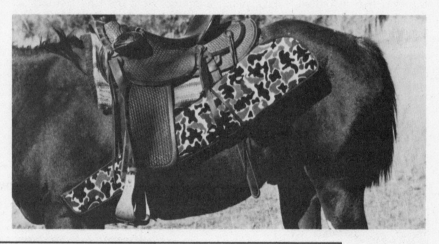

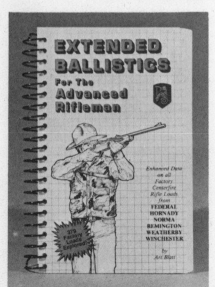

Pachmayr's *Extended Ballistics*, By Art Blatt

Art Blatt's name is, I'm sure,. well known to GDHA readers. As a hunter/reloading technician, Blatt's come up with, if you will, the non-handloader's "handloading manual."

Art has taken 379 factory-loaded cartridges (from Federal, Hornady, Norma, Remington, Winchester and Weatherby) and simplified the world of external ballistics. There are no "formulas" to stumble through, or charts that require the services of an "interpretor." It's all very straightforward.

So, what's all this got to do with the non-handloading hunter? Simple. You get a chance to (finally) understand the commercial centerfire ammo you buy across the counter. The bullet-drop aspects of Art's charts are alone worth the price of admission. But it doesn't stop there. You get projectile velocity and energy figures at enough ranges (and with enough bullet weights) to make a pronghorn turn pale.

Price: $12.95, postpaid. For more information write Art Blatt at Pachmayr Gun Works, Dept. GDHA, 1220 Grand Ave., Los Angeles, CA 90015 (Phone: 800-423-9704).

Uncle Mike's Hunter's Saw

If you're a hunter who doesn't have a camp/meat saw, listen up. This one's a gem.

As the Uncle Mike's PR release put it, they took a tip from professional meatcutters and carpenters, i.e., "Worry about the blade first, then the handle right after that." Here's what their P.R. release had to say:

Avoiding the trend toward cheap, stamped out saw blades that barely cut kindling or clog up on meat and bone, the "Uncle Mike's" crew opted for an extra thick (.045") blade of high-carbon, special alloy saw steel. The teeth are specially ground and "set" for their intended jobs . . . one side for wood, the other for meat and bone. Like any good saw, the blade

can be resharpened by an experienced saw filer.

Because situations often arise where you just can't get at the material for convenient cutting, the handle of the Sidekick Hunter's Saw can be angled by loosening a knurled knob and moving the blade. Positive

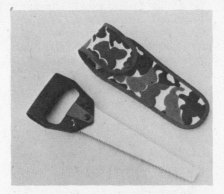

detents in the handle and "gears" in the blade keep the blade from turning once it's locked in place. The handle can be rotated a full 180 degrees for more compact packing or carrying on a belt.

The Hunter's Saw comes complete with a camouflage nylon belt scabbard with a snap-down flap. (Belt loops on the back will fit on any belt up to 2¼ inches wide.)

The saw, although adjustable, has no loose parts that can accidentally come off or get lost. The saw weighs just 7 ounces without the scabbard. Suggested retail for the Hunter's Saw is $19.95 at gun stores and sporting goods retailers.

For a catalog of "Uncle Mike's" offerings send $1 to Michaels of Oregon, Dept. GDHA, P.O. Box 13010, Portland, Oregon 97213.

New Zeiss Offering

Zeiss, the renown West German optical firm which in 1982 introduced its "C-Series" scopes to the U.S. market, has announced plans to add its European "Z-Series" to the line.

Five models will be made available: the 4x32, 6x42 and 8x56 fixed powers. Also to be made available are the 1.5-6x and 2.5-10x variables. As per the European standard, the fixed powers are based on 26mm tubes, while the

variables sport 30mm bodies, thus both require special mount systems. Although the Z-series is manufactured both with and without integral mount rails and a choice of five different reticles, only the non-rail models and one duplex-type reticle will be inventoried at Zeiss Optical, Inc., here in the U.S.

In announcing the addition of the European-style scopes, Zeiss' Bruce Cavey emphasized that the "C-Series" will remain the primary focus of the

company's marketing efforts here. "Unique features such as the Diavaris' 4-to-1 magnification ratios, superior low-light performance, and the thick, magnifying reticles of the 'Z-Series' makes them ideally suited to some specialized hunting applications," said Cavey.

For more information on the Zeiss "Z-Series" riflescopes, write Bruce Cavey at Zeiss Optical, Inc., Dept. GDHA, 1015 Commerce Street, Petersburg, VA 23803.

TECHNICAL SPECIFICATIONS: Zeiss Z-Series

Model	Length	Weight	Objective Diameter	Body Length	Tube Diameter	Maximum Internal Adjustments @ 100 yd.
Diatal 4x32	10.8"	10.6 oz	1.5"	5.47"	1.02" (26mm)	101"
Diatal 6x42	12.7"	13.4 oz	1.9"	5.47"	1.02" (26mm)	70"
Diatal 8x56	13.8"	17.6 oz	2.4"	5.47"	1.02" (26mm)	56"
Diavari 1.5-6x	12.4"	18.5 oz	1.9"	5.82"	1.18" (30mm)	72"
Diavari 2.5-10x	14.4"	22.8 oz	2.2"	5.82"	1.18" (30mm)	43"

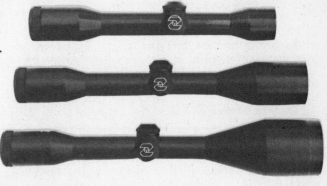

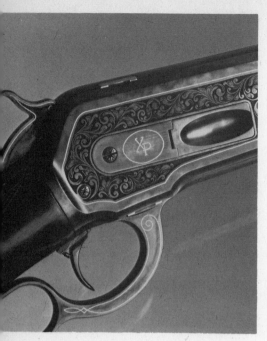

Creekside Gun Shop Custom Casehardening

I've got you guys at a bit of a disadvantage here. I've known about Creekside Gun Shop for about 25 years now—they were everything but in my backyard, in Upstate New York, when I was a teenage hunter.

About 2 years ago at the SHOT Show, I was wandering down one of the aisles when I spotted Terry Turnbull, Creekside's owner, manning his own booth! He had, displayed in front of him, some of the most beautiful casehardened guns I'd ever seen. After a lengthy chat, it was obvious Terry had a real gem on his hands. And he wouldn't (and won't) discuss the process he uses to create some of the most delicious case-colors you'll ever see.

Seen nearby in (unfortunately) "living black & white" are some examples of his work. No, you won't "get the picture," but you will get some idea of patterning and color contrast. (You've got to see his work to believe the true-to-the-art color Turnbull achieves.)

Lest you think I'm overstating my case (no pun intended), I'll add that Creekside is doing custom casehardening for the folks at Parker Reproductions.

Prices range from around $90 on up to around $300 depending on the type of firearms to be casehardened and the amount of polishing required. They specialize in original Parkers, L.C. Smiths, Fox, Winchester, Colt and others. And to quote Creekside, "This process duplicates the original colors found on these guns."

I strongly suggest you write Terry or Doug Turnbull at Creekside Gun Shop, Inc., Dept. GDHA, Main St., Holcomb, New York 14469 (Phone: 716-657-6131).

Browning Kangaroo Chukka

I was gulping down my third cup of coffee the other morning when my caffein companion Joe Dinelli looked across the table and said, "Gotta pair of new half-boots that are the most *comfortable* boots I've ever worn."

My pal went on to explain they were Brownings and lighter than a fistful of marshmallows. He continued as to how he had owned a pair of the Browning Kangaroo leather hunting boots years ago. The poor boy was in love! He went on, and on. And, again, "Oh, how comfortable!"

Well that's the way the comments go with a pair of anything "kangaroo" in the Browning boot line. And it's been that way for years.

Here's what Browning had to say about the new offering:

After an absence of 15 years, the popular, versatile, all-around sport boot is back. The Browning Kangaroo Chukka is suitable for many outdoor activities such as Skeet shooting, camping, fishing, or visiting your favorite sporting goods store.

It's not only the light, 1030 Vibram Crepe sole, or the glove leather lining, that make these boots so comfortable, but also the feather-light, foot conforming genuine kangaroo leather. This leather is extremely soft and supple, yet tougher than cowhide of equal weight. A pair of Kangaroo Chukkas weighs only 1 lb., 4 oz. (size 8D). A supportive steel shank supports your arch. Whether you'll use your Kangaroo Chukkas in your garage workshop or around the campfire, they'll probably turn out to be the most comfortable chukkas you've ever owned."

The only thing the boys from Morgan, Utah, left out was the suggested retail price—$101.50. Not cheap. But,

go out and find a pal who bought a pair of Browning Kangaroo boots years ago. They wear like iron. *Good stuff.*

For a Browning catalog, drop Paul Thompson a line at Browning Arms, Dept. GDHA, Rt. 1, Morgan, UT 84050 (Phone: 800-453-2349).

New Iver Johnson Li'l Champ Single Shot Rifle

At the heart of our hunting/shooting hobby is, in my opinion, the youngster just starting out. Fortunately, the folks at Iver Johnson think along the same line. And that's good news, especially in light of the fact that there aren't a lot of gun makers with a product for the younger crowd.

I-J's new offering is the Li'l Champ, bolt-action rimfire. It handles 22 Short, Long or Long Rifle fodder, features a durable molded stock, an abbreviated overall length of 32½ inches and tips the scales at a feather light 3 lbs. 2 oz. Any way you cut it, the Li'l Champ is ideally designed for kids who are lucky enough to have parents who want to teach their offspring the responsible aspects of the hunting/shooting sports.

There is some additional good news: The suggested retail price of the Li'l Champ is $85.95 to $99.95. (Shop around.)

For more information write Jay Connors at Iver Johnson Arms, Inc., Dept. GDHA, 2202 Redmond Rd., Jacksonville, AR 72076 (Phone: 501-982-9491).

Kimber 223 Centerfire

If I lived in "varmint" country, had a kid about 16 years of age, and wanted to introduce that lad to the world of centerfire shooting and reloading, I'd sacrifice what I had to in an effort to get that youngster a Model 84 Kimber in 223 Rem.

There's only one problem with the above approach—I'd probably never get the gun out of the kid's hands long enough to shoot it myself. To my eye, it's the most beautiful small-action bolt gun ever offered to American shooters. And, as an American shooter/hunter I'm proud to say that every nut, bolt, action, barrel and stock (of every Kimber product) is made in the U.S.A.

Like other Kimber rifles, the Model 84 comes in a number of permutations. The gun seen here is a Model 84, 223 Custom Classic complete with varmint-weight barrel. In our neck of the woods (the Midwest) 84s sell like hot cakes. For those who may have not had a closer look at an 84, in 223, I've included a close-up photo of the action. Take a good look at that photo, and you'll see the Mauser-type claw extractor. Yes, it's a true, controlled-round feed action—something that has not been made in the U.S. (on a production basis) since 1963.

You're right. It's *not* cheap. But, then again, nothing *good* is. The Custom Classic seen here will lighten your wallet to the tune of about $800—and it's worth every penny. For more info, drop Greg Warne or Ted Curtis a line at Kimber of Oregon, 9039 S.E. Jannsen Rd., Dept. GDHA, Clackamas, OR 97015 (Phone: 503-656-1704).

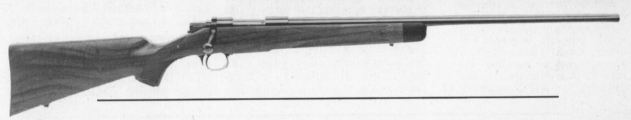

Buck Knives D.U. Collector Set

Take a look at the inside covers of this year's GDHA. Those "ads" are there for two reasons: 1) The duck population took a horrible beating last year; and 2) We (like you) want to support D.U.'s efforts—in good times, as well as bad.

Buck Knives deserves a round of thanks from all of GDHA's waterfowlers. They've created a set of two etched-blade collector's knives, with presentation box, for Ducks Unlimited.

The larger knife is an adaptation of Buck's famous Folding Hunter, dressed with rich woodgrain handles, and the official Ducks Unlimited emblem embedded. The 3¾-inch clip blade has a 22k gold overlay acid etching by Aurum, with a scene portraying ducks coming in to a marshland setting. The brown leather sheath has a gold imprint of D.U.'s duck head logo on the flap.

The second knife is based on the Knight model from Buck's "Slimline" series of folding lockblades. It has the same gold-etched duck scene on the 2-inch drop-point blade, and the DU shield embedded in the handle.

This presentation set was created especially for Ducks Unlimited, for distribution through their chapters at fund-raising dinners and other activities dedicated to conserving wetland habitat for waterfowl and other wildlife.

For further information about this limited edition set of collector's knives, contact Ducks Unlimited, Dept. GDHA, One Waterfowl Way, Long Grove, IL 60047 (Phone: 312-438-4300).

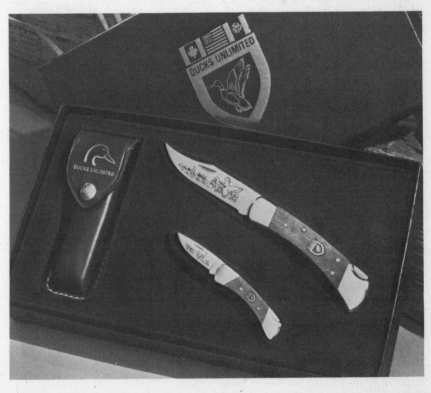

Barbour Outdoor Clothing

I've been meaning to tell you about the Brit's Barbour Line of outdoor clothing for 2 years now. My fault.

Barbour has had a booth at the annual SHOT Show for the past couple of years. And every time I walk into that booth, I find it hard to leave. Their clothing is *that* good. Those GDHA readers who've had a chance to travel, may be familiar with this 100-year old firm's offerings. They have a superb reputation, world wide. And now they've come to the U.S.

Seen nearby is a Barbour Beaufort Shooting Jacket done up in that firm's "Thornproof" fabric. In a minute I'll address the Beaufort Jacket. But, for now, I feel I should talk about the Thornproof fabric—it's the heart of the Barbour legend. Let's have Barbour describe that material:

Barbour Thornproof jackets offer the ultimate in waterproofing and a distinctive functional style that the serious American Sportsman will find an unbeatable combination. These garments are made from long staple Egyptian cotton which is oiled and waxed to provide superior wa-terproofing while keeping condensation to a minimum. All snaps, studs and zippers are solid brass and made specifically to Barbour specifications. Even Barbour thread is specially made to order. The care taken in producing a Barbour jacket makes it easy to see why a coat can still be usable after 40 years or why one was worn again after being submerged for 8 months in Lake Windermere.

You'll have to see one of Barbour's Jackets to really "experience" and "feel" that Thornproof fabric. If you're a hunter, and you get a chance to see one, it'll stop you cold. The fabric's texture, the impregnated wax, even the pleasant odor of the fabric all say "guns."

Let's get back to that Beaufort jacket. Features include a full-width game pocket with wipe-clean nylon lining and zipper on each end. There is storage aplenty: two large waist bellows pockets, a zip-up wallet pocket and two hand-warmer pockets that are ideal for cradling a gun. It also has a corduroy collar, snap-shut throat flap, storm cuffs and solid brass two-way zip. It's available in either

green or brown. Price: $180—and worth every penny.

For more information write John Bennett at Taftco, Dept. GDHA, 212 Welsh Pool Rd., Lionville, PA 19353 (Phone: 215-363-5554).

RIG #44 Bore Cleaner

Last year, as some of you may remember, I waxed enthusiastic about another brand of bore cleaner. This year I'm going to do it again.

Quite frankly, our hobby has needed, if you will, a "new generation" of bore cleaners for some time. Fortunately, the last few years has, in my opinion, seen the introduction of some of the finest bore solvents to ever hit the American shooting market. This year it's time to talk about a new bore cleaner from an old, legendary outfit—RIG Products.

The new product is called RIG #44 Bore Cleaner. And boy, that stuff *works*! No, I can't sit here and tell you about all the "fancy" chemical compounds in #44 Bore Cleaner. I wouldn't know what I was talking about. And you guys probably wouldn't care. What I do know is that RIG #44 removes bore fouling, built up carbon and goo in about as long as

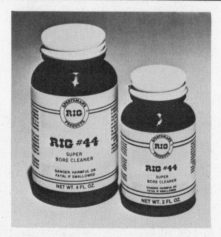

it takes to put some on a patch and run it down a barrel.

Got a dirty (and I mean *filthy*) semi-auto pistol or shotgun kicking around? Get a bottle of RIG #44 and have at it. You'll be amazed. I was. There's also an additional benefit with this product that other bore cleaners don't possess. It leaves behind a slightly dull (non-reflective) film that's beautifully water-resistant. And that, my friends, is a bonus worth having if you hunt in foul-weather territory or are looking for short-term storage protection. As an example, if I were out after ducks in *bad* weather, I'd even coat the exterior metal of the shotgun I was using. Also, if I had a high-powered rifle with a high-gloss, reflective metal finish, I'd wipe down the exterior of the barrel and action with #44 in an effort to cut down "hunter presence."

As you can see, RIG #44's got some good things going for it. To my way of thinking, the best news about RIG #44 is the price. At $2.15 per 2 oz. bottle, the stuff is close to being a give away. And it's available in 2 oz., 4 oz., 16 oz., and 1 gallon bottles. For more information, drop Al Selleck a line at RIG Products Co., Dept. GDHA, 87 Coney Island Dr., Sparks, NV 89431 (Phone: 702-331-5666).

Lyman Sportsman's Tool Kit

This one strikes me as being *very* sensible. It's something the average hunter/shooter *should* have.

The new Sportsman's Tool Kit consists of a shooter's hammer with three interchangeable heads and a knurled drift punch; a full size screwdriver set with seven bits; and a screwdriver set with five bits. All twelve bits are specially hardened, industrial grade, (blade-type, Phillips head, Allen head and Torx). The entire outfit is packaged in a sturdy, positive-locking plastic box. If you go to the range frequently, this item should be permanently placed in your shooting box. The suggested retail price is $33.95.

Write Lyman Products Corp., Dept. GDHA, Rt. 147, Middlefield, CT 06455 (Phone: 203-349-3421). Ask for it, and Ken will be happy to send you a *free* Lyman catalog.

Zeiss 8x20 "Kompact" Binoculars

Sometimes it's tough to get "quality" into things "small"—especially when those "small" things are binoculars. Zeiss, as most of you guys know, has never had that problem.

Here's what Zeiss has to say about their new 8x20 BGA Dialyt Kompact:

For maximum durability and weatherproofing, this 8x20 features an internal-focusing mechanism. Image focus is via a centrally-located wheel at the rear of the bridge, while the diopter adjustment is at the front where it is least likely to be moved inadvertently. Outside, the black rubber armoring protects the instrument against the hard knocks

of field use, plus offering the added advantage of silence so that no game-spooking noise occurs if the dangling binocular should contact one's rifle or scope. The 8x20 BGA Dialyt Kompact is supplied with a zippered field pouch and rubber rain guard to protect the eyepieces from rain and snow.

Eyeglass wearers will see the full 345 foot field of view (at 1000 yards), thanks to Zeiss' exclusive B-type eyepiece. Non-eyeglass wearers simply extend the rubber eyecups for the same, full-field viewing. Color fidelity, image contrast and definition are what you expect of Zeiss' T-coated lenses—sharp and bright right out to the edge of the field.

Weighing in at a mere 8.3 ounces and measuring just 3.5 inches wide

by 3.8 inches high (eyecups folded), this new binocular is small and light enough to please the most weight-conscious sportsman."

Drop Bruce Clavey a line at Zeiss Optical, Dept., GDHA, 1015 Commerce St., Petersburg, VA 23803 (Phone: 804-861-0033).

Colt Stainless King Cobra

Hunters and shooters who practice their hobby in humid climes, or those looking for a good handgun that can take a lot of abuse, will like this one.

Colt's new 357 Mag. King Cobra comes with a bunch of "features"—one of which is the reasonable price, $389.95 (and you might be able to beat that nicely if you shop around). Additional features include: solid rib, full-length ejector housing, red-ramp front and fully adjustable white-outline rear sight, new Colt "gripper" neoprene grips and a 4-inch or 6-inch barrel option at *no* extra cost. (The 4-inch version is seen nearby.) Accord-

ing to the guys at Colt, the "King" should hit the dealer's shelves in July/August '86.

While the new King Cobra was designed for the law enforcement market, any outdoorsman can quickly see the hunter-oriented benefits in a revolver of this type. In short, it's the kind of handgun that'll hold up under tough use. And the name "Colt" is on the barrel. Enough said.

For more information, drop this outfit a line at Colt Industries, Fire-

arms Div., Dept. GDHA, P.O. Box 1868, Hartford, CT 06101 (Phone: 203-236-6311).

Parker Reproductions (GDHA Cover Gun)

It was around 1910 when your Editor's grandfather was a very successful salesman for the Brown Shoe Company. He was an *avid* shotgunner, according to the family; and he loved setters. Living in the Midwest at the time, my granddad had, in addition to his successful "Buster Brown" shoe business, a large farm, several "hands" and more than one good setter.

It happened one afternoon. One of the farm hands came running out of the large bean field located near the family home. The farm hand was carrying the near-lifeless body of his favorite setter. A rattler had done the work. And according to the hand, there was an "infestation" of the snakes out in the field.

According to the family, it was with *tremendous* anger, and tears in his eyes, that my grandfather grabbed his D-grade Parker 12-gauge, several boxes of black powder shells and

headed for the bean field.

Along the way he stopped at the barn to cut loose the farm's entire hog population, directly into the bean field. (Rattlesnakes "had little effect" on the hog's thick hides according to my family; a bunch of hogs around a passel of rattlers is akin to a troop of Cub Scouts at a free-weenie roast—they can't eat 'em fast enough!)

When it was all over, the Parker was red hot, the entire bean field nearly destroyed.

And the stories about Parker Shotguns go on. It's *the* American double around which legends have been made.

Fortunately, the legend continues, thanks to the Skeuse family of Parker Reproductions, a division of Reagent Chemical. Absent from the gun-scene for almost a half-century, the Parker (and all it has been) is now back in 20, 28 and (soon to be available) 12.

More accurately called the "Parker Reproduction," every gun is true to its original in *every* detail. No, the "new"

gun isn't just close to original specs, they are the *same as* original specs. And yes, the "new" parts are interchangeable with the old.

I've seen Parker Reproductions in both 20 and 28 gauge. They are beautiful in every detail. The precision tooling and craftsmanship really has to be seen to be believed. The price is $2800 (single barrel set), or $3400 (two barrel set). For more information, we urge our readers to contact Jack Skeuse at Parker Reproductions, Dept. GDHA, 124 River Rd., Middlesex, NJ 08846 (Phone: 201-469-0100).

Again, take a look at our front or back cover. The Parker Reproduction is on the right—it's a 28. To the left? My friends, that's an original Parker A-1 Special in 20 gauge. The price of the A-1? Well, a collector would be happy to build you a nifty little hunting camp, in the location of your choice, just to get his hands on it.

That's just the way it is with those Parkers.

GDHA Hunting License Directory '87

As customary, GUN DIGEST HUNTING ANNUAL has solicited basic information regarding licenses and other fees routinely encountered by the resident and non-resident hunter. Each state and Canadian province is contacted annually for an update of the previous year's listing. The states and provinces have 3 months to respond to the questionnaire. The information received is condensed or expanded, as appropriate, to fit our format. Because of an early deadline we cannot guarantee that changes will not occur prior to the hunting season.

Game laws in the states and provinces vary from simple to profoundly complex. Therefore, it is impossible to list game laws in detail. Many game departments have accepted that good game management must be quite regionalized. The results are that many states have been broken into a number of smaller game management units, each with its own specific set of regulations. Sometimes a state will have more than 20 such subdivisions. Obviously, game law listings then become extremely extensive; sometimes requiring more than 50 pages of a state or provincial publication to adequately describe and detail all the pertinent information. To include all of this information from a single state would quickly exhaust our available space. Therefore, the interested hunter should contact the state or province of interest for specific details. In any event, it is hoped that the included information is useful past the point of fees and charges that the hunter might incur.

To assist you in obtaining all of the available information, one or more department name and address is included with the information from each state and province. Take the time to write each source, as the information available is often extensive and quite useful. But do write early in the year. Many states have permit regulations that are difficult to comply with if applications are not filed early in the year. For example, a hunter may have to apply for a permit by March or April in order to be able to participate in much of the available fall hunting. For many persons such regulations are, of course, difficult to comply with, but perhaps they are necessary from the game department's viewpoint. Nonetheless, such requirements do drastically reduce the number of recreational man hours that might otherwise be enjoyed by hunters who are unable to determine (6 or 9 months in advance) as to when or where they might be able to hunt.

The fees shown have been presented, where possible, in a manner that separates small game fees from big game fees, habitat stamps and other applicable charges—for resident and non-resident alike. Keep in mind that you may require a small game license or general hunting license before being able to purchase any big game tags. Too, some states offer combined licenses that may include all birds, small game, deer, bear and turkey.

The states and provinces that are keenly aware of the revenue generated by hunters often supply a great deal of information, while a few act as though it is an imposition to even receive an inquiry about potential hunting regulations or seasons. But sometimes a state or province that supplies extensive information one year will be hard pressed to supply even the briefest assistance in the following year. Budgets and personnel changes can be part of the problem. Obviously, limited information does not necessarily mean limited hunting. But a scarcity of info can make it difficult, if not impossible, for the hunter to become aware of potential opportunities, especially if he is a non-resident.

One very worthwhile method of gaining insight into the hunting opportunities within a state is to subscribe to the various state conservation magazines, when so available. I have listed those of which I am aware, along with the subscription price and the necessary address. A wise hunter will find the few dollars involved very well spent.

Many states (and all Canadian provinces—if you are a U.S. citizen) expressly prohibit the non-resident hunter from transporting or using handguns for hunting. Finally, if you are a U.S. citizen and plan to hunt in Canada, remember that you fit into their "alien-hunter" classification, not that of a non-resident, except in the province of Québec. Conversely, Canadian hunters will find that only a few U.S. states have an "alien-hunter" distinction from the non-resident hunter. And don't forget to declare your firearms with U.S. customs before leaving the states or you may find some over-zealous customs agent confiscating your firearms upon your re-entry into the states. A single, "Show me your firearms registration," can cause a lot of grief if you have not done so.

Some jurisdictions have reciprocal hunting fees. That is, they charge the non-resident the same amount that his home state would charge a non-resident from that state to hunt. However, there are often minimum fees and, quite frankly, I have no idea what happens when a resident from a state that does not allow non-resident hunting applies for a license in a state that uses reciprocal charges. Best investigate carefully if your hunting trip will put you in this position. Too, some states specifically prohibit non-resident big game hunting. Check before you go.

This year I have also included any state or provincial requirement for Hunter (safety) Orange clothing. If no mention of Hunter Orange requirements is made for a particular state or province, it means that the jurisdiction involved has expressed no official position on the matter. But laws do change. Check before you go.

States are grouped alphabetically within geographic regions, starting in the Northeast and finishing in the West. Next, the Canadian provinces are listed alphabetically.

New England States

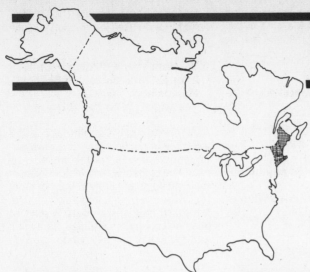

CONNECTICUT

Residents pay $9 for a basic small game firearms hunting license and non-residents spend $27. Spring turkey permits are $10, while fall (archery only) turkey permits are $5. Spring turkey permit applications for state lands must be postmarked no later than February 1st. Depending upon the place you wish to hunt and the type of firearm you will use, specific deer permits must be obtained. Some deer permit applications must be made on or before March 15th (state land). Deer permits are $10 each for residents; non-residents will pay $30 each. Archery deer hunting permits are $5 for resident and non-resident alike.

The license year runs from January 1 to December 31. For specific details write for the annual *Connecticut Abstract of Hunting and Trapping Field Guide* and the *Waterfowl Guide* (September). Address your inquiry to:

Dept. of Environmental Protection
Wildlife Unit
State Office Building
165 Capital Avenue
Hartford, CT 06106
Telephone: 203-566-4683

Pheasant tags are required and the hunter will receive 10 tags for his $5. These are available at all town clerk offices. No Sunday hunting is permitted in Connecticut.

Offshore duck hunting continues to be good, even during the low general duck population through the 1985-86 season. However, scaup were somewhat scarce during this past season, but there were more than the usual amounts of bufflehead and goldeneye available.

Questions concerning hunting, camping, recreational use of state park and forest land may be directed to one of the following field offices between 8:30 a.m. and 4:00 p.m. EST:

Eastern District HQ: 203-295-9523
Western District HQ: 203-485-0226

Hunter Orange: 200 square inches *must be shown* in outer, above-waist garment and be visible from all sides. Exceptions include bowhunters, waterfowl hunters in boats or blinds, and landowners on their own land.

MAINE

Residents pay $14 for a hunting license that is good for small and big game. Non-residents pay $46 for small game privileges and $76 for big game and small game combined. As with most states, a number of combination and specialty licenses are available. A special $5 stamp is required for all pheasant hunters. Maine does have an alien hunting license distinction and the cost is $61 for small game and $116 for big game. Licensing year is from January 1st to December 31st. Some moose hunting is allowed during a brief season running from October 20 to October 25 during the 1986 season. Moose hunting permits are by lottery only (1000 available). For more information write to:

Maine Dept. of Inland Fisheries
& Wildlife
284 State St.
State House Station 41
Augusta, ME 04333
Telephone: 207-289-2043
(licenses)
207-289-2175 (hunting info)

Maine is a large state and non-residents have a choice of hunting in farm/woodland situations in southern areas with high deer populations and hunting pressure, or in big woods, semi-wilderness settings with lower deer populations but less hunting pressure. The area surrounding Patton (on Route 11) is a good choice for bear hunting.

The 1985 harvest included 21,300 deer, 1,350 black bear and 881 moose.

A doe permit or, more accurately, a "hunter's-choice permit," will be in effect for 1986 and will allow the taking of an antlerless deer in a specified district, with the application period being June 1 to August 14, 1986. A lottery will determine who gets the permits.

Hunter Orange: All firearm hunters *must wear* an article of Hunter-Orange clothing visible from all sides. *Some* waterfowl hunters are exempt. Camouflage orange *must be supplemented* with an article of *solid* Hunter Orange.

MASSACHUSETTS

The *Massachusetts Wildlife* magazine is available at $6 annually from the Westboro address listed below.

Residents of the Bay State pay $12.50 for a combination small and big game license. However, the following fees are also applicable: $1.25 waterfowl stamp; $5 permit for each of antlerless deer, bear or turkey. Non-residents will spend $23.50 for small game or $48.50 for a combination small and big game license. The state waterfowl, antlerless deer, bear and turkey permit fees also apply to non-residents. Detailed information can be had in the Massachusetts Abstracts of Fish and Wildlife Laws. Write to:

Div. of Fisheries & Wildlife
Leverett Saltonstall Building
Government Center
100 Cambridge St.
Boston, MA 02202
Telephone: 617-727-3151
or
Division of Fisheries & Wildlife
Field Headquarters
Route 135
Westboro, MA 01581
Telephone: 617-366-4470

Massachusetts restricts deer hunting to shotguns *only*—no rifle hunting for deer is permitted. No Sunday hunting is allowed. The western counties of Berkshire, Franklin, Hampden and Hampshire offer the best deer hunting. A short spring turkey season is available, as well as special archery and primitive weapon seasons. Archery and primitive weapon stamps are $5.10 each for residents and non-residents alike. License year runs January 1 to December 31.

Hunter Orange: During shotgun deer season all hunters *must wear* 500 square inches on chest, back and head. Waterfowl hunters in a boat or blind are excepted. All hunters on wildlife management areas during pheasant and quail season *must wear* a hat of Hunter Orange.

NEW HAMPSHIRE

Currently the resident license fee of $11.25 covers both small and big game hunting. A $10 pheasant stamp is required for residents and non-residents alike, as is a state waterfowl stamp ($4). A turkey fee permit of $5 is applicable. Non-residents pay $31 for small game only or $59 for a combination small and big game license. Short term small game non-resident licenses are available. The license year corresponds to the calendar year. A fee increase is being considered. For additional information write to:

New Hampshire Fish & Game Dept.
34 Bridge St.
Concord, NH 03301

Preliminary 1985 harvest reports show a take of 90 bear and 5,658 deer. Bear hunting was permitted only in the three most northern counties.

A state conservation bulletin, currently entitled *Field Note,* and a twice-a-year magazine entitled *New Hampshire Natural Resources,* are available at a subscription rate of $6, annually. Send check to the above address.

Hunter Orange: Not required, but *strongly* recommended.

RHODE ISLAND

Residents pay $6.50 for a hunting license plus $7.50 for a deer tag. Non-residents spend $15.50 and $20 respectively for the same privileges. The license year runs from March 1 to the last day of February. Licenses are issued by:

License Section
Dept. of Environmental Management
22 Hayes St.
Providence, RI 02903
Telephone: 401-277-3576

Additional information can be obtained from:
Rhode Island Div. of Fish & Wildlife
Government Center
Tower Hill Road
Wakefield, RI 02879
Telephone: 401-789-3094

Shotguns and bows are the *only* legal methods for taking deer in Rhode Island.

Hunter Orange: All deer hunters *must wear* 500 square inches of solid Hunter Orange on head, chest and back. All hunters in game management areas *must also wear* 500 square inches. Must be visible in all directions. Waterfowl hunters are exempted.

VERMONT

Vermont hunters can hunt on Sunday, a comparative rarity in New England. Residents spend $8 for a basic game license (all game), while non-residents spend $60. A turkey stamp ($5) is vaild for two spring (must be bearded) and two fall (either sex) turkeys. Turkey hunting is with shotgun or bow only. Deer hunting with a bow is $6 additional for residents and $10 for non-residents. Non-residents may obtain a small-game only license, with certain restrictions, for $30. But remember that turkey are considered big game.

License year is January 1 to December 31. For detailed information you can write to:

Vermont Fish & Wildlife Dept.
Information & Education Section
Montpelier, VT 05602
Telephone: 802-828-3371

As appropriate, Vermont offers antlerless deer hunting. Residents are given first preference for the limited permits. The biggest deer are often killed in the mountains of northern Vermont, but the largest number are taken in the southern half of the state. Vermont boasts of a very large turkey population and the turkey hunting is indeed excellent.

1985 VERMONT DEER, BEAR & TURKEY TOTALS

County	Archery	Bucks	Antlerless	Bear
Addison	36	454	332	17
Bennington	98	807	650	23
Caledonia	31	440	351	19
Chittenden	15	282	122	6
Essex	0	219	145	27
Franklin	16	318	156	5
Grand Isle	3	23	0	0
Lamoille	13	323	240	10
Orange	83	747	601	1
Orleans	11	289	238	19
Rutland	110	1,186	878	16
Washington	95	664	622	4
Windham	119	741	512	14
Windsor	97	1,001	718	9
State Totals	**727**	**7,494**	**5,565**	**170**

1985 Turkey Seasons
Spring gobbler season total - 415 (new record). Fall either-sex season total - 887 (third highest record).

Hunter Orange: Not required, but *strongly* recommended.

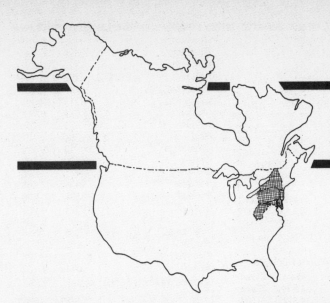

Mid-Atlantic States

DELAWARE
The license year in Delaware begins on July 1st and ends on June 30th. Residents pay $12.50 for a basic hunting license, $3.50 for a trapping license and $5.00 for a state waterfowl stamp. Non-residents pay $45 for a basic license, $25 for a combination deer/trapping permit and $5 for a state waterfowl stamp. Write to:

Division of Fish & Wildlife
P.O. Box 1401
Dover, DE 19903

The best deer hunting in Delaware is in Kent and Sussex counties. A substantial amount of public land is available for hunting. A pre-season lottery is held for reserved opportunities to hunt deer and waterfowl at specific locations on state lands. Approximately 2,500 deer are taken annually in Delaware.

Hunter Orange: All hunters must wear a total of 400 square inches of Hunter Orange on head, chest and back during the big game season.

MARYLAND
Tracks 'N Trails is the Maryland conservation magazine and is available at $3 annually from the Forest, Park & Wildlife Service at the address below.

The Maryland license year starts August 1st and concludes on July 31st. A resident pays $10 for a basic hunting license plus an additional $5.50 for a deer tag. Non-residents pay $45 or the reciprocal rate charged by their home state for a small game license. The deer tag fee is also $5.50 for non-residents. A state waterfowl stamp sells for $6. Licenses can be obtained from:

Dept. of Natural Resources
Div. of Licensing & Consumer Services
580 Taylor Ave.
Tawes State Office Building B-1
Annapolis, MD 21401
Telephone: 301-269-3216

For general information write to:
Steve Schneider
Dept. of Natural Resources
MD Forest, Park & Wildlife Service
580 Taylor Ave.
Tawes State Office Building B-2
Annapolis, MD 21401
Telephone: 301-269-3195

Dorchester, Allegany, Worchester, and Garret counties usually produce the greatest number of deer. Sitka deer are also hunted in parts of Maryland. Over 500 sitkas are annually harvested in Dorchester county.

Some especially fine Canada goose hunting can be found on Maryland's eastern shore.

Hunter Orange: Hunter Orange *must be worn* by all deer hunters and persons accompanying deer hunters, in the form of a cap and vest or jacket. Archers hunting during the archery-only season and persons hunting their own property (without a license) are excepted.

NEW JERSEY
A combination small and big game license sells for $18.50 to residents and $61 to non-residents. The license year runs from January 1 to December 31. A $9.75 license is available to juniors (ages 14 and 15) and seniors (65 years and older). A resident all-around sportsman's license is available at $47.50. Other variations are encountered and a $1, 2-year rifle permit fee is applicable.

A pheasant and quail stamp is required of all such hunters using wildlife management areas and sells for $16.50. A short term non-resident small game license is available. A state woodcock stamp is also required, as is a state waterfowl stamp. Additionally, a canvasback hunting permit is required. For details write to:

Division of Fish, Game & Wildlife
363 Pennington Ave.
C.N. 400
Trenton, NJ 08625
Telephone: 609-292-2965

Open land for hunting in New Jersey is limited. However, there are almost 400,000 acres of public land, statewide, in the form of wildlife management areas, state forests and federal lands.

The best counties for deer hunting are Hunterdon, Sussex and Warren. In addition to the regular firearm and bow seasons, there are special permit seasons for black powder and shotgun.

New Jersey Outdoors is available on a bi-monthly basis with an annual subscription rate of $6.50. Checks should be made payable to *New Jersey Outdoors* and should be sent to: N.J.O., C.N. 402, Trenton, NJ 08625.

Hunter Orange: All deer, rabbit, hare, squirrel, fox, rail or other game bird hunters *must wear* a cap or outer garment with a minimum 200 square inches of Hunter Orange, visible from 360 degrees. Waterfowl, turkey and deer hunters using a bow are excepted.

NEW YORK
One of the best conservation magazines printed is New York's *The Conservationist*. Those who hunt in New York will find the magazine very informative, and sportsmen in general will find it rewarding reading. A 1-year subscription (six issues) is available for $5. Make your checks payable to: *The Conservationist*, P.O. Box 1500, Latham, NY 12110.

New York State's 1986 pre-hunting season deer population is expected to be over the 600,000 mark. The success rate on Deer Management Permits, which allow the holder to take an additional deer of either sex, was lower than expected in 1985. Therefore, considerably more permits will be available in 1986. The number of big game hunters

NORTHERN REGION

County	Male Adult	Total Take
Clinton	305*	313**
Essex	875	909
Franklin	781	827
Fulton	272*	288**
Hamilton	1,016	1,098
Herkimer	1,040	1,339
Jefferson	410*	423**
Lewis	921*	936
Oneida	1,193*	1,733**
Oswego	773*	792**
St. Lawrence	2,646	2,720
Saratoga	799*	1,139**
Warren	441	458
Washington	1,365*	2,447**
Northern Totals:	**12,837**	**15,422**

DEER TAKE NEW YORK STATE 1985

County	Male Adult	Total Take
Greene	1,865	3,315
Montgomery	405*	816
Orange	1,990*	3,904**
Otsego	2,760	6,126
Putnam	505	556
Rensselaer	1,189*	1,480**
Rockland	40	48
Schenectady	216*	393
Schoharie	1,533	2,963
Sullivan	3,965	7,581
Ulster	2,723*	4,372**
Westchester	99	566
Southern Totals:	**27,847**	**54,034**

SOUTHERN REGION

County	Male Adult	Total Take
Albany	950	1,779
Columbia	1,918	4,217
Delaware	5,292	11,530
Dutchess	2,397	4,388

CENTRAL/WESTERN REGION

County	Male Adult	Total Take
Allegany	4,526	9,319
Broome	1,619	2,922
Cattaraugus	4,468	9,122
Cayuga	1,083	2,286
Chautauqua	2,952	6,080
Chemung	1,173	1,788
Chenango	2,599	5,346
Cortland	1,326	2,582
Erie	1,299*	2,458**
Genesee	754	1,473
Livingston	1,318	2,559
Madison	1,673	3,781
Monroe	651	1,199
Niagra	284	481
Onondaga	1,113*	2,312
Ontario	1,320	2,558
Orleans	471	878
Schuyler	804	1,683
Seneca	397	678
Steuben	4,071	6,855
Tioga	1,492	3,126
Tompkins	1,568	3,510
Wayne	583	942
Wyoming	1,167*	2,598
Yates	1,071	2,402
Central/Western Totals:	**39,782**	**78,938**
Long Island-Suffolk Cty.	127*	326**
Special Hunts	139	363
Statewide Totals:	**80,732**	**149,083**

* Record County Buck Taken 1985
** Record County Total Deer Take 1985

is approximately 780,000. A total of 149,083 deer were harvested during the 1985 season. This represents a 12 percent decrease from the 170,310 taken in 1984, reflecting the lower number of permits that were issued and the lower success rates. The top counties for total deer harvest were: Delaware (11,530), Allegany (9,319), Cattaraugus (9,122), Sullivan (7,581), and Steuben (6,855). Big game hunters also took 422 black bears during the 1985 season, down from 663 for the previous year. (The Conservation Department would like to see 700 to 800 bears taken annually.)

The license year in New York begins on October 1 and ends on September 30. Residents pay $8.50 each for small or big game hunting licenses. Non-residents pay $35.50 and $55.50 for the same licenses. Short period (3-day) non-resident small game licenses are also available.

Deer and bear are the big game animals. Turkey is considered small game, but an additional $2 permit is required. Some real wilderness-style hunting is available in the Adirondack Mountains in upstate New York. For specific details write to:

New York State Dept. of Environmental Con.
50 Wolf Road
Albany, NY 12233
Telephone: 518-457-5400
518-457-4480 (Bureau of Wildlife)
518-439-0098 Deer Management Program)

New York offers several informative booklets. Order the ones that are of specific interest to you. The available booklets include:

Annual Big Game Guide
Deer Sections of New York State
Application Booklet for Deer Management Permit System (antlerless deer permits)
I Love NY Small Game Hunting

Hunter Orange: Hunter Orange is not required, but *strongly* recommended.

PENNSYLVANIA

License year in Pennsylvania begins September 1 and ends on August 31st. Residents pay $12.50 for a hunting license, junior residents $5.50; non-residents spend $80.50 for the same rights and junior non-residents $40.50. Special archery licenses as well as antlerless and muzzleloader permits sell for $5.50 to residents and non-residents alike. A muzzleloader permit must be purchased before September 30th. Non-residents of Pennsylvania cannot apply for an antlerless permit until 30 days prior to antlerless season. Residents spend $10 for a bear tag while non-residents pay $25 for the same tag. For more specific details write to:

Pennsylvania Game Commission
P.O. Box 1567
Harrisburg, PA 17105-1567
Telephone: 717-787-2084

Antlerless deer hunting permits are issued for specific dates. It is not uncommon for the deer harvest to exceed 120,000 annually. The bear season is restricted to a proposed 3 days in November. Special archery and flintlock seasons are available.

A fur-taker license is now in effect. The prices are the same as regualr hunting licenses for residents and non-residents.

An annual subscription to *Pennsylvania Game News* is available for $6. Send check to the Pennsylvania Game Commission at the foregoing address.

Hunter Orange: Bear and deer hunters, during the firearms season, and all woodchuck hunters *must* wear 100 square inches. Woodchuck hunters must display the required Hunter Orange on the head while deer and bear hunters must display Hunter Orange on head, chest, and back.

WEST VIRGINIA

Residents pay $8 for a hunting license. Non-residents pay $50 and are not allowed to take bear. A national forest stamp is applicable and costs $1.

An antlerless deer license (residents only) costs $8 and is issued by random selection. Bear stamps are $4 and a boar permit, for residents only, sells for $5. A non-resident bear license is $100 in addition to the $4 bear stamp. Non-residents may also purchase a 6-day small game license for $10. A boar permit is available by lottery.

The license year is January 1 to December 31. An issuing fee of 50¢ is charged when purchasing licenses or stamps. For license information write to:

**Dept. of Natural Resources
Hunting & Fishing License Section
1800 Washington St. East
Charleston, WV 25305
Telephone: 308-348-2758**

For general information write to:
**Dept. of Natural Resources
Div. of Wildlife Resources
1800 Washington St. East, Rm. 812
Charleston, WV 25305
Telephone: 304-348-2771**

Over 90,000 deer are harvested each hunting season. Deer hunting is good statewide except for southwestern counties. An additional antlerless deer may be taken during both bow and fire-arm seasons with appropriate license; residents $10 each, non-residents $25 each.

The Division manages 42 public hunting areas that include approximately 250,000 acres. Public hunting is also available on 900,000 acres of National Forest land on which the Wildlife Division conducts wildlife management ac-

tivities. A big game bulletin is available in March and a small game bulletin is available in October. These provide a summary of the previous year's harvest data. The small game bulletin furnishes a forecast for both small and big game for the coming season. These publications are available *free* by writing the address given above for general information.

Hunter Orange: All deer hunters *must display* a minimum of 400 square inches of Hunter Orange.

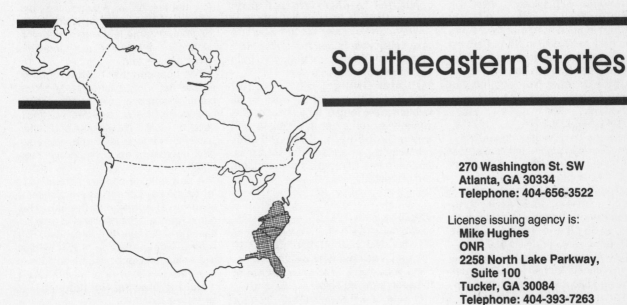

Southeastern States

270 Washington St. SW
Atlanta, GA 30334
Telephone: 404-656-3522

License issuing agency is:
**Mike Hughes
ONR
2258 North Lake Parkway,
Suite 100
Tucker, GA 30084
Telephone: 404-393-7263**

Hunter Orange: Hunter Orange is *required to be worn* in an amount of 500 square inches or more and *must be visible* from all sides by all persons hunting big game or accompanying big game hunters. The requirement is for an outer garment(s) worn above the waist.

NORTH CAROLINA

The license year for North Carolina extends from July 1 to June 30. The resident annual hunting license fee is $11.50 with a county-of-residence-only license available for $6. A big game resident license is $8. *Lifetime resident hunting licenses* are available for $150 as well as several combination and short term licenses. A small game license is required to purchase a big game license. Special "Sportsman" licenses are also available.

Non-residents pay $41 for a basic small game hunting license and $30 for a big game license. Other fees for residents and non-residents alike are: primitive weapons—$8, and game lands—$9.

Deer, bear, turkey and wild boar are available to the big game hunter. For

FLORIDA

The state conservation magazine is *Florida Wildlife* and is available at $7 annually from the Fish & Game Commission.

Residents pay $12 for a general hunting license. A non-resident pays $51 for hunting privileges. A wildlife management area fee of $11 and a state duck stamp fee of $4 are applicable. A $6 muzzle-loading stamp and a $6 archery stamp are also levied where applicable. A turkey stamp ($6) is now required. The license year runs from July 1 to June 30. Specific details can be obtained from:

**Office of Information & Services
Florida Game & Fresh Water Fish
Comm.
620 South Meridian St.
Tallahassee, FL 32301
Telephone: 904-488-4676**

The best deer hunting in Florida is in the central northeast and northwest regions of the state. Antlerless deer hunting is available to landowners with more than 150 acres. Bear may be taken in

Baker, Columbia, Gulf, and Osceola counties. A permit is required to take a bear on Wildlife Management areas.

In some wildlife management areas wild hogs, which are normally the legal domestic animals of landowners, can be hunted. Wild hogs can also be hunted in certain counties or portions thereof.

Hunter Orange: Hunter Orange is not required, but *strongly* recommended.

GEORGIA

Residents will spend $6.50 for a small game license and $5.50 for a big game license. A non-resident pays $36 for the small game license and $64 for the big game. The license year is April 1 to March 31.

A wildlife management area stamp at $10.25 is applicable to both residents and non-residents. Additional information can be obtained from:

**Joe Kurz
Dept. of Natural Resources
Game Management - Room 713**

more details contact:

North Carolina Wildlife Resources Comm.
Archdale Building
512 North Salisbury St.
Raleigh, NC 27611
Telephone: 919-733-3391

For additional information:
Travel and Tourism Division
N.C. Dept. of Commerce
Raleigh, NC 27611

An informative publication, *Wildlife in North Carolina,* is available at $5 per year and is published monthly. Send your check to Wildlife in North Carolina at the above listed address for the Wildlife Resources Commission.

Hunter Orange: Not required, but *strongly* recommended.

SOUTH CAROLINA

The state conservation magazine is *South Carolina Wildlife* and is available at $7.95 per year. Write the Circulation Dept. at the address listed below.

Residents pay $9.50 for a statewide hunting license or $3.50 for a county (of-residence) license. A state duck stamp is $5.50 and a resident game management area permit is $10.25.

The non-resident pays $46.50 for his hunting license, $25.50 for a big game permit and $25.25 for a game management area permit.

The license year runs from July 1 to June 30. For specific details write to:

S.C. Wildlife & Marine Resources Dept.
P.O. Box 167
Columbia, SC 29202
Telephone: 803-734-3888 (general information)

Short term, non-resident licenses are available for either 3- or 10-day periods. Hunting seasons are set individually for each of the 11 different state game zones. *The deer herd is large enough to permit a no-limit bag on antlered deer in some areas. Over 40,000 deer are taken each year in South Carolina.* Turkey hunting is also available to both residents and non-residents.

Hunter Orange: Blaze, Hunter Orange clothing *must be worn* by all hunters in the form of a hat, coat or vest while deer hunts are in progress with any type of firearm. Dove and duck hunters on game management areas, and all game hunters on private land, are exempted.

VIRGINIA

Virginia offers a fine outdoors magazine that is published monthly. For $5 you can receive a year's subscription. Send your check to *Virginia Wildlife* at the address listed below.

Residents will spend $7.50 each for

big game or small game licenses. Non-residents pay $30 each for these same licenses. Also, a $2 National Forest Stamp may be required. The license year runs from July 1 to June 30. A copy of *Virginia's Hunters Guide* will prove very informative. For more information write to:

Comm. of Game & Inland Fisheries
P.O. Box 11104
Richmond, VA 23230-1104

Virginia is divided into 13 different deer hunting areas. Prospective hunters should be sure to carefully review the annual game law summary before hunting. Antlerless deer are hunted to a rather large extent.

The best counties for deer hunting are, perhaps, Southhampton and York, but access to available land is severely limited. Public access to deer hunting is good in George Washington and Jefferson National forests. The average annual harvest of deer is approximately 75,000.

A new special archery license ($10 for residents, $20 for non-residents) is required in addition to the usual big game license if the hunter is to take advantage of the special bow season. This license will enable the holder to take two Archer's-License deer in addition to two firearms deer.

Hunter Orange: Not required, but *strongly* suggested.

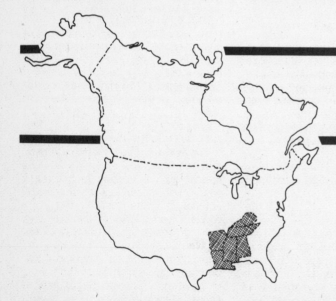

South Central States

ALABAMA

Alabama law dictates that residents of states not covered by reciprocal agreements are required to pay a specific fee to an *authorized guide* to hunt deer after December 31. Non-residents should also keep in mind that all private land in Alabama is *posted by law.* Hunt-

ing on private land is by written landowner permission *only.* Any landowner or his agent may impose restrictions.

The license year in Alabama begins October 1 and ends September 30. Resident license fees for combination small and big game are $6 for county and $11 for statewide. A state waterfowl

stamp sells for $6.

Non-resident fees can vary as reciprocal agreements have been made with *Tennessee, Mississippi, Florida, Georgia,* and *Louisiana.* Residents of states *not* having a reciprocal agreement with Alabama will pay $177 for an all-game license. A 7-day non-resident license is available for $52. For specific information contact:

Dept. of Conservation & Natural Resources
Game & Fish Division
64 North Union St.
Montgomery, AL 36130-1901
Telephone: 205-261-3260

Alabama's *one-per-day limit on deer* makes it possible for a hunter to enjoy deer hunting in a manner not generally available elsewhere. Special antlerless deer seasons are also available.

Turkey hunting is permitted and this state offers some very fine hunting for a wide variety of game.

Hunter Orange: Hunter Orange clothing is required of all firearms deer hunters during antlerless deer season when on Wildlife Management areas, and of all deer hunters on land open to public hunting. A minimum of 144 square inches of *solid* Hunter Orange is to be displayed on cap, hat, vest or jacket and must be visible from all angles. *Camouflage* Hunter Orange *does not* meet this requirement.

ARKANSAS

The state publication, *Arkansas Game and Fish,* is available free from the address listed below.

Residents pay $10.50 for a hunting license that includes a deer tag for the firearms hunter. The all-game license is $17.75. Non-residents pay $38.50 for a small-game only license and $115 for the annual all-game license. A 5-day, non-resident, all-game license sells for $78. The license year is from July 1 to June 30. Two deer are permitted during the gun-deer season. Arkansas is one of the *few* states that permits able-bodied hunters to use a cross bow (125-pound minimum pull) for hunting. A $5.50 state waterfowl stamp is required.

A number of license variations do exist and turkey hunting is permitted. For specific details contact:

Arkansas Game & Fish Commission
#2 Natural Resources Drive
Little Rock, AR 72205
Telephone: 501-223-6300

The best deer hunting appears to be in the wildlife management areas, the national forest and the southern and western parts of the state. Harvests exceeding 40,000 deer annually are not uncommon.

Hunter Orange: All hunters and persons accompanying hunters during firearms seasons for deer and bear must wear 400 square inches above the waist—and must include a Hunter Orange hat. Waterfowl hunters are exempted.

KENTUCKY

Kentucky—Happy Hunting Ground is the Department of Fish and Wildlife Resources' official publication. A 1-year subscription to this colorful and informative magazine (published six times

yearly) is a *super* bargain at only $3.

A statewide hunting license sells for $7.50 to residents and $40 to non-residents. Deer permits are $11.50 for residents and non-residents alike. Turkey permits are $6.50. The basic hunting license is required in order to obtain deer and turkey permits. The license year is January 1 to December 31. The Kentucky waterfowl stamp is $5.25.

The 1986 deer (firearms) season will begin on November 8 and will close on varying dates depending upon zone. Two deer permits may be purchased and filled. For specific details write to:

Kentucky Dept. of Fish & Wildlife Resources
Wildlife Division
1 Game Farm Road
Frankfort, KY 40601
Telephone: 502-564-4224

Antlerless deer may be taken in certain counties during a brief season, usually 1-day long. The best deer hunting occurs west of Interstate 75 to the Missouri state line. The annual harvest is usually about 16,000 deer.

Hunter Orange: Hunter Orange clothing *must be worn* by all hunters during deer seasons and must include at least 500 square inches of *solid* orange. Camouflage hunter orange *does not* fulfill the requirement. Garments to be included are hat, coat or vest.

LOUISIANA

Residents pay $5.50 for the basic hunting license and another $5.50 for a big game hunting license that includes deer, turkey and bear. Non-residents pay $25.50 and $20.50 respectively for the same hunting rights. Excepted are residents of Alabama, Arkansas, Florida, Mississippi and Texas, who pay reciprocal fees. The license year runs from July 1 to June 30. For complete details write to:

Louisiana Dept. of Wildlife & Fisheries
P.O. Box 15570
Baton Rouge, LA 70895
Telephone:504-925-4445
Telephone:504-925-3988

The chambers of commerce in the larger communities can often supply additional information on local hunting and accommodations.

The state's conservation publication is available *free* from the above address.

The legal limit is *one deer per day* (six per season), offering a fine opportunity for the serious hunter to gain invaluable experience. Under certain condi-

tions antlerless deer may be legal quarry. Seasons are broken down individually into six different areas. A copy of the *Louisiana Hunting, Fishing and Motorboat Regulations* will explain all the various laws in detail.

The best areas for public hunting are in the parishes of Clairborne, Bienville, De Soto, Red River, Natchitoches, Winn, Vernon, and the southern portions of La Salle and Catahoula.

Hunter Orange: All hunters (including archers) on wildlife management areas, and all deer hunters elsewhere (except archers when no gun season for deer is in progress) *must wear* a minimum of 400 square inches on head, chest or back. Exceptions are hunters on privately owned and legally posted land.

MISSISSIPPI

Mississippi Outdoors is the state conservation effort and is available from P.O. Box 451, Jackson, MS 39205, on a *gratis* basis.

A resident will pay $6 for a small game license or $25 for a sportsman's license. Non-residents pay $60 for an all-game license or $30 for a small game license. Other fees are applicable and a state waterfowl stamp is $2. License year runs from July 1 to June 30.

Listed costs for non-resident licenses are minimum with actual fees up to that charged by the state of residence; in other words, fees are reciprocal or minimum base, whichever is higher. Details can be obtained from:

Mississippi Dept. of Wildlife Conservation
Information/Education
P.O. Box 451
Jackson, MS 39205
Telephone: 601-961-5347

Over 200,000 deer were taken during a recent hunting season. Considering the size of Mississippi, this number makes the state prime deer hunting country. A one-antlered-deer and one-antlerless-deer per day limit has not caused any decline in Mississippi's deer herd. A maximum of three antlerless deer and five antlered deer is imposed for the year. Mississippi also has a spring turkey season.

Hunter Orange: 500 square inches of unbroken Hunter Orange, visible from all sides, must be worn by all deer hunters during firearms season for deer and must include a cap, hat or vest.

TENNESSEE

Residents pay $10.50 each for small and big game licenses. Non-residents pay $30.50 and $70.50 respectively for the same hunting rights. A 7-day waterfowl and small game only non-resident license is available at $15.50. A 7-day big game license is $50.50. The license year runs from March 1st to the last day of February.

A wildlife management area permit is required of all those using these regions. The permit is $8.50 for small game and $10.50 for big game. Hunting licenses for big game are required for each type of weapon used, i.e., rifle, bow or muzzleloader. The license issuing agency is:

**Tennessee Wildlife Resources
Agency
P.O. Box 40747**

Nashville, TN 37204
Telephone: 615-360-0500

Additional information:
**Ms. Paulette Hooper-Fugua
Information Section
Tennessee Wildlife Resources
Agency
P.O. Box 40747
Nashville, TN 37204
Telephone: 615-360-0500**

Tennessee offers deer, wild boar, turkey and bear for big game hunting. In Cumberland, Fentress, Morgan and Scott counties, boar populations are low, but liberal hunting is permitted due to crop damage. Deer limits are gener-

ous with up to four bucks being legal in deer unit A.

A late deer season (January) for either sex is held with a special permit being required. For the 1985-86 season this hunt was held in all or parts of 40 counties. Permit applications must be mailed by early October.

The *Tennessee Wildlife* magazine is available at $5 per year. Send your check and mailing address to the address listed previously.

Hunter Orange: Big game hunters using firearms *must wear* at least one outer garment above the waist, and on the head, that are visible from front and back, consisting of at least 500 square inches of Hunter Orange.

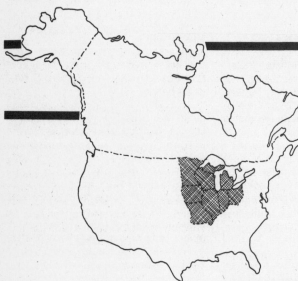

North Central States

ILLINOIS

The small game fee is $7.50 and deer tags are $15 for residents. The visitor will pay from $15.75 to $100.75 for small game privileges. Non-resident deer tag fees are reciprocal. If your home state does not allow non-resident big game hunting, then you will pay the minimum license fee of $15 and an additional $15 for a permit to hunt the county your license is issued by. The license year runs from April 1 to March 31st. Information is available from:

**Hal Davis (license issuing)
Dept. of Conservation
Room 210
Lincoln Tower Plaza
524 So. 2nd St.
Springfield, IL 62701-1787
Telephone: 217-782-2964**
or
**Dave Klinedenst (public hunting
   areas)
Dept. of Conservation
Division of Wildlife Resources**

**600 North Grand Avenue West
Springfield, IL 62706
Telephone: 217-782-6384**

Approximately 25,000 deer are taken annually in this state.

Outdoor Highlights is the official state conservation magazine and is published bi-monthly. A subscription is $8 annually. Checks should be made out to the Dept. of Conservation and sent to the Division of Information and Education at the 2nd St. address listed above.

Hunter Orange: During firearms deer season all hunters and trappers *must wear* a cap and upper outer garment of at least 400 square inches of solid orange. Camouflage orange *does not* fulfill the requirement. Migratory waterfowl hunters are exempted.

INDIANA

Residents are charged $6 for a small game license and $10 for a big game license. A turkey hunting permit will cost the resident $12. Non-residents spend $37 for a small game license and $75

for a deer license. A separate license is required for each of *archery, shotgun* or *muzzle-loading rifle* deer hunting. Non-residents *are not* allowed to turkey hunt in Indiana. A game bird habitat stamp ($3) and a state waterfowl stamp are applicable. No centerfire rifles are permitted for deer.

The license year runs from March 1 to the last day of February. No deer hunting with rifles (except muzzleloaders). For more information contact the:

**Dept. of Natural Resources
Division of Fish & Wildlife
Room 607
State Office Building
Indianapolis, IN 46204
Telephone: 317-232-4080**

Special deer hunts are held in specific areas. Consult the annual deer hunting guide for particulars. The total deer harvest has been approximately 32,000 annually. Zone 6 has been the most productive in recent years. Zones 5, 7, and 1 are also good producers and, if based on size, these three are equally as good as Zone 6.

Outdoor Indiana is the official state conservation magazine. It is available at $7.50 per year from Outdoor Indiana, 612 State Office Building, Indianapolis, IN 46204.

A *free monthly newsletter* is available by sending your name and address to the preceding address. Ask to receive "Focus."

Extensive revisions to the deer-hunting regulations are anticipated for the 1986 seasons. Please update yourself.

Hunter Orange: All deer (including archery), rabbit, grouse, pheasant and quail hunters *must wear* at least *one* of the following: vest, coat, jacket, coveralls, hat or cap. This garment *must be of solid Hunter Orange* (camo orange does *not* qualify).

IOWA

Iowa hunting licenses are valid from date of issue to January 10 of the succeeding calendar year. Licenses for a following year can be issued on December 15 and are valid for the remaining days in December. For instance, a license issued on December 15, 1985 is valid immediately, and all through 1986 as well as the first 9 days of 1987.

Hunting licenses are not valid for hunting furbearers, except coyote or groundhog. A fur-harvester license is required for all other furbearers, whether to be taken by hunting or trapping. Furbearers include: beaver, badger, mink, otter, muskrat, raccoon, skunk, opossum, spotted skunk (civet cat), weasel, wolf, red and gray fox.

Non-resident raccoon and pheasant stamps are no longer required. Duck (state) and habitat stamps are required at $5 and $3 respectively. Residents pay $8.50 for a hunting license while non-residents will spend $47.50. Non-residents may purchase a shooting-preserve-only license for $5. Resident furbearer licenses cost $15.50—non-residents will pay $150.50. Deer and turkey permits are available to residents only at $20 each.

For further information write to:
Iowa Conservation Commission
Wallace State Office Building
Des Moines, IA 50319-0034
Telephone: 515-281-5145

The best areas for deer hunting continue to be the southern sections of the state. Approximately 40,000 deer are harvested annually.

A good source of information is the *Iowa Conservationist,* the official state conservation magazine. It is published monthly and subscriptions are $6 annually. Address subscriptions to *Iowa Conservationist* at the above address.

Hunter Orange: Firearms deer hunters *must wear* at least of one the following in solid Hunter Orange: cap, hat, vest, coat or jacket. Camouflage orange *does not* meet the requirement.

MICHIGAN

Michigan Natural Resources is the state conservation publication and is available at $9.97 annually (six issues). Send checks to Michigan Natural Resources Magazine, Box 30034, Lansing MI 48909.

The resident will spend $7.25 for a small game license and $9.75 for deer hunting fees. This latter price tag can go to $28.25 if the resident wishes to hunt bear and turkey, in addition to deer. The non-resident pays $35.25 for a small game license and $75.25 to $195.75 for big game fees. The license year runs from April 1st to March 31st.

The public-access stamp has been discontinued. A passbook for the various stamps is required at $1. A fur-harvester permit is required for the trapping or hunting of fur-bearing animals. Some elk hunting is available *for residents only.* For more information contact:

Michigan Dept. of Natural Resources
Information Center
Box 30028
Lansing, MI 48909
Telephone: 517-373-1220

Additional information:
Michigan Travel Bureau
Box 30226
Lansing MI 48909

Sunday hunting on private land is prohibited in some counties. Antlerless deer hunting is permitted—check for restrictions and permits.

Hunter Orange: During daylight hours all firearms hunters must wear a hat, cap, vest, jacket, rainwear or other outerwear of Hunter Orange. Camo orange *is legal* providing 50 percent of its surface is Hunter Orange. During the firearms deer season *even archers must comply.* Exempted are waterfowl, bobcat, crow, turkey and bowhunters (during bow season for deer and bear).

MINNESOTA

A small game resident license sells for $11 and a deer tag is $15. Non-residents pay $50 and $100 respectively. License year runs from March 1st to the end of February.

Bear tags (by drawing) are available to residents at $25, and to non-residents at $150. A state duck stamp is required for waterfowl ($5) and a pheasant stamp is also available ($5). A non-resident fee of $100 is charged for raccoon, fox, bobcat, lynx, and coyote. For additional information write to:

Dept. of Natural Resources
License Bureau
500 Lafayette
St. Paul, MN 55146
Telephone: 612-296-3344

For additional hunting information:
Dept. of Natural Resources
Division of Wildlife
500 Lafayette
St. Paul, MN 55146

Approximately 45 percent of Minnesota's deer hunters fill their tags each year, resulting in a harvest of over 140,000 deer. Antlerless deer permits are readily available.

The state conservation bulletin is available *free* by writing to *The Volunteer,* Box 46, DNR, 500 Lafayette, St. Paul, MN 55146

Hunter Orange: All hunters, trappers or persons accompanying them *must wear* 50 percent bright red or blaze orange, of outer garments during the firearms season for deer. Camouflage patterns of Hunter Orange *are* included.

MISSOURI

The state conservation magazine is *Missouri Conservationist,* which is available *free to residents* and at *$3 per year to non-residents.* Address inquiries to the Missouri Dept. of Conservation at the address listed below.

The license year is January 1 to December 31. Residents spend $6 for a small game license and non-residents spend $40 for the same privileges. Resident tags are $8 for firearms deer hunting, $8 for archery hunting and $8 each for spring or fall turkey. Non-residents pay $75 for a deer tag and $55 each for a spring turkey tag, fall turkey tag and archery permits.

A state waterfowl stamp is required at $3. For additional information write to:

Public Affairs
Missouri Dept. of Conservation
P.O. Box 180
Jefferson City, MO 65102
Telephone: 314-751-4115

Information is also available from:
Missouri Division of Tourism
308 East High St.
Jefferson City, MO 65101

Hunter Orange: All firearms deer hunters *must wear* a garment of at least 500 square inches of solid Hunter Orange, a part of which *must be above the shoulders.*

OHIO

A small game license sells for $7.75 to residents, with a deer and turkey license selling for $10.75. Non-residents pay $30.75 for the basic small game license and an additional $10.75 for a deer and turkey permit.

A wetlands habitat stamp is applicable at $5.75. The small game license *is* a *prerequisite* to obtaining big game tags. The license year is September 1 to August 31. For additional information contact:

Ohio Division of Wildlife
1500 Dublin Road
Columbus, OH 43215
Telephone: 614-481-6300

For a copy of the Ohio regulations write:
Ohio Dept. of Natural Resources
Publications Section
Fountain Square
Columbus, OH 43224

Antlerless deer permits are available to residents and non-residents on a reciprocal basis. Rifles are not legal for deer in Ohio. Shotguns and muzzleloading rifles are permitted.

Hunter Orange: Hunter Orange clothing *must be* worn by all firearms deer hunters in the form of a hat, cap, vest or coat and it *must be solid orange*. Camo patterns *do not* satisfy the requirement.

WISCONSIN

Pending legislation may change bear-hunting regulations and license fees. Resident bear hunting licenses are $5.50, non-resident $20.50, and are valid for pursuit only. To take a bear an additional harvest permit is required and costs a resident $25.50 and a non-resident $100.50. These harvest permits are required to shoot, shoot at, kill or possess black bear. Deer tags are $13 each. Archery hunters spend $12.50 for a license. A turkey stamp for residents sells for $11.75. The hunting license period is September 1 to August 31.

Non-residents pay $61.50 for a small game license with a lower cost, short-term license available. The non-resident deer hunter pays $86.50. Out-of-state archers will spend $66.50 for a deer permit.

A state waterfowl stamp ($3.25) and a parks admission sticker ($12 per year) is applicable to residents. Non-residents pay the same $3.25 for the waterfowl stamp, but $20 annually for the parks admission sticker. For more details write to:

Wisconsin Dept. of Natural Resources
License Section
Box 7924
Madison, WI 53707
Telephone: 608-266-2105

For additional information:
Wisconsin Dept. of Natural Resources
Bureau of Wildlife Management
Box 7921
Madison, WI 53707
Telephone: 608-266-1877

Annual harvests of 200,000 or more deer are not uncommon in this state. Antlerless deer hunting is permitted in certain areas.

Low landowner tolerance of hunters prevails in the southern and central portions of the state. Ask before you go! Burnett and Polk counties in the north have a good deal of county forest land open to public hunting.

A bi-monthly publication is available from the Dept. of Natural Resources at $6.97 annually. Send your check to: Wisconsin Natural Resources, P.O. Box 7191, Madison, WI 53707.

Hunter Orange: Hunters in areas open to firearms deer hunting *must have* 50 percent of their above-the-waist outer clothing (excluding sleeves) in Hunter Orange, and 50 percent of any hat worn must also be Hunter Orange. Waterfowl hunters are exempted from this rule.

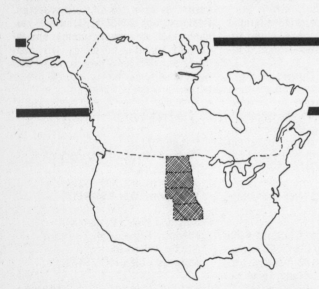

Plains States

Hunter Orange: Firearms deer hunters must wear 200 square inches of Hunter Orange or red clothing above the waist. Further, that clothing *must be* visible from the back. A similar, Hunter Orange or red hat is also required.

NEBRASKA

Nebraska charges residents $8.50 for a small game license, $20 for deer or antelope tags and $15 for a turkey permit. Non-residents pay $40 for a basic license, $100 for antelope or deer tags and $35 for a turkey permit. Additionally, a $7.50 habitat stamp *is required* for each hunter.

The license year runs from January 1st to December 31st. For specific details write to:

Tom Keith - Information Specialist
Nebraska Game & Parks Comm.
P.O. Box 30370
Lincoln, NE 68503
Telephone: 402-464-0641

KANSAS

Residents pay $9.50 for a small game license, "landowners" spend $20.50 for a deer tag and "general residents $30.50" for a deer tag. Resident turkey permits are $20.50. Resident deer hunters are 68 percent successful when firearms are used and 31 percent successful when hunting with a bow.

Non-residents pay $50.50 for a small game hunting license but are *not allowed* to hunt big game (deer, turkey and antelope). License year is January 1 to December 31. For additional information contact:

Information and Education Division
Kansas Fish & Game Commission
Box 54A R.R. 2
Pratt, KS 67124
Telephone: 316-672-5911

The *Kansas Wildlife* magazine is available for $6 per year (published six times, annually) from the foregoing address.

Antlerless deer hunting is allowed under certain restrictions.

Hunter Orange: All firearms deer hunters must wear 400 square inches of Hunter Orange on head, back and chest.

NORTH DAKOTA

North Dakota offers the hunter opportunities for deer, antelope, sheep, turkey, moose, elk and bobcats, as well as a variety of small game. Non-residents will spend $101 for firearms deer hunting, $100 for bow hunting of deer or antelope and $53 for small game. Resident small game fees are $9, a big game license $19—a furbearer license is $7. For specific information you can write to:

North Dakota Game & Fish Dept.
100 North Bismark Expressway
Bismark, ND 58501-5095
Telephone: 701-221-6300

For general tourism information write:
Tourism Promotion
Liberty Memorial Bldg.
State Capital Grounds
Bismark, ND 50505
Telephone: 701-224-2525

Excellent hunting and waterfowl maps may be obtained by writing:
Northwest Mapping Co.
P.O. Box 1234
Bismark, ND 58502

North Dakota Outdoors, the official publication of the Game and Fish Dept., is published 10 times annually. Send $7 for an annual subscription to: *North Dakota Outdoors* at the above Game and Fish Dept. address.

Hunter Orange: Hunter Orange *must be* worn by big game hunters and *must include* head covering and outer garments above the waist with a minimum of 400 square inches of solid Hunter Orange. Thus the so-called "camouflage orange" *does not* meet state requirements.

SOUTH DAKOTA

A basic, general license ($2) is required for both residents and non-residents. A small game stamp costs residents $6 and a pheasant stamp is $5. A state waterfowl restoration stamp is $2 for residents and non-residents alike. A big game resident license is $15 and a turkey stamp is $4. A furbearer stamp sells for $8. The resident can hunt a wide variety of big game that includes antelope, bighorn sheep, deer, elk and turkey.

Non-residents *are not permitted* to hunt bighorn sheep or elk. Additionally, some deer hunting locations, and seasons, are not available to the non-resident hunter. Non-resident waterfowl licenses *are limited in number,* and available through a drawing, usually held in September. Any left-over licenses are then available on a first-

come-first-served basis. The actual breakdown of non-resident hunting fees is as follows:

General Hunting	$ 2
Small Game Licenses	$50
Pheasant Restoration Stamp	$ 5
Deer	$75
Antelope	$75
Waterfowl	$50
Turkey	$25
Predators	$25

The *South Dakota Conservation Digest* is available from the Dept. of Game at the listed address for $5 annually.

The license year is January 1 to December 31. For specific information write to:

Information Officer
Dept. of Game, Fish & Parks
Anderson Bldg.
445 E. Capitol
Pierre, SD 57501
Telephone: 605-773-3485

For license applications write:
Licensing
Game, Fish & Parks
412 W. Missouri
Pierre, SD 57501

Hunter Orange: One above-the-waist garment of Hunter Orange *is required* of all firearms big game hunters in South Dakota.

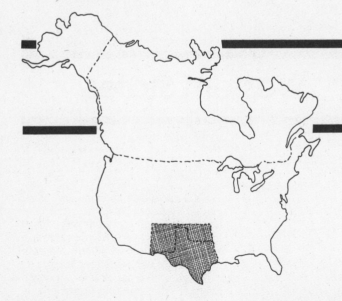

Southwestern States

NEW MEXICO

The resident pays $19 for a deer license and a non-resident pays $146. For $22.50 the resident can obtain a general hunting license that includes small game and deer.

Turkey tags are $13.75 for the resi-

dent and $54.25 for the non-resident. A separate tag is required for the spring season ($10.50 and $76). A turkey stamp for $3.50 is also required. Bear tags will cost the resident $10.50 while the non-resident must ante up $76. Antelope, elk, bighorn sheep, Barbary

sheep, cougar, oryx, ibex, and javelina licenses are also available for residents, with prices ranging from $10.50 to $48 depending upon species. The non-resident will spend from $51 to $503 for each of these tags. Small-game-only licenses are available for $9.50 and $51 respectively for resident and non-resident.

The license year runs from April 1 to March 31. License information can be obtained by writing to:

New Mexico Dept. of Game & Fish
Villagra Building
Santa Fe, NM 87501
Telephone: 505-827-7880

For other hunting information:
Byron R. Donaldson
Villagra Building
Santa Fe, NM 87501

New Mexico Wildlife, the state conservation magazine, is available at $5 annually (6 issues). Send check to New Mexico Wildlife at the Department of Fish and Game address found above.

Hunter Orange: Not required but *strongly* recommended.

OKLAHOMA

A state conservation publication, *Outdoor Oklahoma* (six issues annually) is available at $8 per year from the Dept. of Wildlife Conservation at the address shown below.

Residents will spend $10 for a hunting license and non-residents pay $68.75. Turkey tags sell for $7.50 for both groups of hunters. Deer tags are $14.50 and $137.75 for resident and non-resident, respectively. The bonus deer tags sell for the same price. Elk tags are $35 and $205.75 for the resident and non-resident. A state stamp is required for waterfowl and sells for $4.

A short-term non-resident small game license is available. Seasons are set by areas and a copy of the annual *Oklahoma Hunting Regulations* is a must. For licenses or information write:

License Section or Information & Education Div.

Dept. of Wildlife Conservation
1801 North Lincoln
P.O. Box 53465
Oklahoma City, OK 73105
Telephone: 405-521-3851 (licenses)
Telephone: 405-521-3855 (information)

More than 200,000 deer are harvested annually during bow, muzzleloader and regular firearms seasons. In several regions the last day, or last two days, of gun season are open to antlerless deer harvest. Applications for special deer hunts, chosen by random drawing, *must* be received by early August. Applications are available from license vendors or the Conservation Department.

Hunter Orange: Deer hunters must have a head covering and an outer above-the-waist garment with a minimum of 400 square inches of solid Hunter Orange. An additional 100 square inches is also required, and that may be of the camouflage orange type.

TEXAS

Texas residents pay $10 for a resident hunting license which entitles the holder to hunt all types of game birds and game animals except furbearers. Non-residents pay $75 for a small game license which entitles the holder to hunt all game birds except turkey and all small game animals except furbearers. A non-resident general hunting license

is $200 and entitles the holder to hunt all game birds and all game animals except furbearers. The license year runs from September 1 to August 31. A dove hunting stamp ($6) and a state waterfowl stamp ($5) are applicable. For detailed information contact:

Brady Mayo
Director, Information & Education Div.
Texas Parks & Wildlife Dept.
4200 Smith School Road
Austin, TX 78744
Telephone: 512-479-4992 (information)
Telephone: 512-479-4817 (licenses)

Antlerless deer permits are available to landowners. The best areas are Edwards Plateau and the southern portion of the state. *Very little public land is available.* As a result, Texas is a *poor choice* for the non-resident hunter who does *not* have access to private land. Over 300,000 deer are harvested annually.

The *Texas Parks and Wildlife* magazine is available at $8 per year from the address listed above.

Hunter Orange: 400 square inches of Hunter Orange, above the waist, are required on *all* wildlife management areas. Other areas require a minimum of 144 square inches of Hunter Orange clothing visible from front, back and sides.

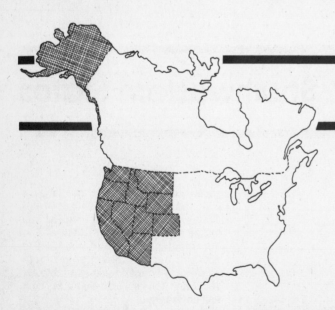

Western States

ALASKA

Alaska Fish & Game, the Alaskan conservation magazine, is available at $9 per year (six issues) by sending your check to the Dept. of Fish and Game (address listed below). It's well-worthwhile.

Alaska is considered by many to be the *last* hunting paradise. License year is from January 1st to December 31st. Residents pay $12 for a hunting license. Those residents 60 years or older may *not* have to purchase a hunting license. Resident fees for musk ox are from $25

to $500 depending upon the area to be hunted. Resident brown or grizzly bear tags are $25, but are *not required* for *all* areas. A $5 waterfowl conservation stamp is required of all non-resident and most resident waterfowl hunters.

Non-residents pay $60 for a hunting license. When hunting brown/grizzly bear or Dall sheep, non-residents must employ the services of a guide or be in the accompaniment of an Alaskan resident at least 19 years of age and within the second degree of kinship (i.e., your grandparent, parent, offspring or grandchild). Non-resident game tags are as follows:

Black Bear	$ 200
Brown, grizzly bear	350
Bison	350
Caribou	300
Deer	135
Elk	250
Mountain Goat	250
Moose	300
Dall Sheep	400
Walrus	500
Wolf	150
Musk Ox	1,100

Non-resident *aliens* (neither a citizen nor a resident of the U.S.) *are required* to be accompanied by a guide when big game hunting.

For general hunting info write to:
Dept. of Fish & Game
Public Communications Center
P.O. Box 3-2000
Juneau, AK 99802
Telephone: 907-465-2376

For license information write to:
Alaska Dept. of Revenue
Fish & Game Licensing Section
Box 5A
Juneau, AK 99811
Telephone: 907-465-4112

For more information on guides or a current guide register (available for $5) contact:

Alaska Dept. of Commerce & Economic Dev.
Guide Licensing & Control Board
Box D
Juneau, AK 99811
Telephone: 907-465-2542

Hunter Orange: Hunter Orange clothing is not required, but is *strongly* recommended.

ARIZONA
Arizona hunting licenses are valid from January 1st to December 31st of the calendar year. Non-residents should request a copy of the list of Arizona licensed guides. For more details contact:

Arizona Game & Fish Dept.
222 West Greenway Rd.
P.O. Box 9099
Phoenix, AZ 85023
Telephone: 602-942-3000

Arizona hunting fees are as follows (includes $3 application fee):

Species	Residents	Non-Residents
Buffalo Bull	$753.00	N.A.
Buffalo Cow or Yearling	453.00	N.A.
Antelope Tag	53.00	$253.00
Spring Bear Tag	10.50	53.50

Deer Tag -		
General Season	14.50	78.50
Deer Tag - Archery	17.50	78.50
Elk Tag	63.00	303.00
Javelina Tag -		
General Season	12.50	53.50
Javeline Tag - Archery	12.50	53.50
Mountain Lion Tag	4.50	53.50
Spring Turkey Tag	11.50	53.50
Turkey Tag - Archery	11.50	53.50
Bighorn Sheep Tag	153.00	753.00
General Hunting	12.50	58.50

Cross bows *are* now *legal* during the firearms and handgun/archery/muzzle-loader hunts—subject to certain restrictions.

Hunter Orange: Hunter Orange clothing is not required but *strongly* recommended.

CALIFORNIA
Residents will spend $18.50 for a basic hunting license while non-residents spend $59.50 for the same privileges. Bear tags are $15 (resident) and $105.00 (non-resident). Deer tags are $10 and $100 respectively for resident and non-resident. The two-deer tag costs residents $22.50 and non-residents $200. A state duck stamp is $7.50. Antelope and elk permits are *for resident only*. Feral pigs may also be hunted.

California is broken into more than two dozen game-management areas, and seasons, as well as bag limits—they all vary, depending on the area being hunted. For a detailed copy of the annual hunting regulations you can write to:

Dept. of Fish & Game
3211 S St.
Sacramento, CA 95816
Telephone: 916-739-3380

Additional information may be obtained from:

Dept. of Fish & Game
Wildlife Management
1416 Ninth St.
Sacramento, CA 95814
Telephone: 916-324-0769

COLORADO
Each year the state conservation magazine lists the anticipated "hot spots" for hunting. *Colorado Outdoors* is available at $5 annually with the May/June or July/August issue being the one to look for to find the "hot spots." Send check made out to *Colorado Outdoors*, to the listed address for the Dept. of Wildlife.

Residents pay $7.50 for a small game hunting license, while non-residents spend $32.50. Big game fees are as follows:

Species	Resident	Non-Resident
Antelope	$ 17	$120
Bear (spring)	25	100
Bear (fall)	25	210
Bighorn Sheep	100	500
Goat	100	500
Deer	17	120
Elk	25	210
Moose	200	Not Allowed
Mountain Goat	100	500
Mountain Lion	32	185
Turkey	7.50	50

For more information write to:
Division of Wildlife
Dept. of Natural Resources
6060 Broadway
Denver, CO 80216
Telephone: 303-297-1192

For additional information:
Colorado Guides & Outfitters Assoc.
Box 78AA
Loma, CO 81524

Colorado regulations are complex and hunters should request the annual big game season and application brochure.

The best deer hunting areas are the Eagle area, Uncompaghre Plateau, the sage brush country north and northwest of Craig, Grand Mesa, White River National Forest and the upper reaches of the Yampa River drainage (Oak Creek to headwaters).

The season structure provides a wide variety of hunting opportunities including archery, muzzleloading, early high country deer season and quality elk areas. Better than 50,000 deer are harvested during most seasons. Non-residents are limited to 10 percent of the sheep and goat licenses. The statewide population of deer is in excess of 550,000, while elk number more than 160,000 with over 17,000 bagged annually. Goat number about 800 statewide with about 50 taken each season. There are approximately 55,000 to 60,000 antelope and the annual harvest approaches 10,000 animals. Bighorn sheep number about 4,500 with an annual harvest of about 100-plus animals.

Hunter Orange: *Strongly* suggested but not required.

HAWAII
An all-game license is $7.50 for residents and $15 for non-residents. The license year runs from July 1 to June 30. The license issuing agency is:

Div. of Conservation & Resources Enforcement
1151 Punchbowl St.
Honolulu, HI 96813
Telephone: 808-548-5918

Additional information may be obtained from:

**Dept. of Land & Natural Resources
Div. of Forestry & Wildlife
1151 Punchbowl St., Room 330
Honolulu, HI 96813
Telephone: 808-548-2861**

Game mammals available in Hawaii include wild pig, blacktail deer, goat, mouflon sheep, feral sheep and axis deer. Game birds include California valley quail, Gambel's quail, Japanese quail, ringneck pheasant, Nepal Kalij pheasant, chukar, gray and black fancolin, Erckel's fancolin, turkey and two types of doves. On the six islands a total of almost 12,000 game birds were harvested in 1983, up notably from 1982. Almost 2,100 mammals were bagged during 1983, up from 1,800 during the 1982 season.

Hunter Orange: All persons, in any hunting area where firearms are permitted, must wear 144 square inches of Hunter Orange clothing above the waist, visible from front and back.

IDAHO

The state conservation magazine is *Idaho Wildlife* and is available at $10 a year from Idaho Wildlife, P.O. Box 2725, Boise, ID 85707.

Residents will spend $6.50 for a general game license. Deer tags are $8, elk are $14, mountain lion are $10.50, bear are $6.50 and turkey are $6.50. The license year runs January 1st to December 31st. Special additional fees apply to controlled hunts for deer, elk, moose, antelope, bighorn sheep and mountain goat.

Non-residents pay $85.50 for a game license and $90.50 for a deer tag, $235 for elk, $100.50 for mountain lion, $40.50 for bear and $25 for turkey. Other non-resident fees have been increased. Additional fees are applied to non-resident controlled hunts also. Quotas are established for non-resident deer and elk tags. For this reason *early purchase* of non-resident tags *is important.*

The basic game license is a prerequisite to obtaining big game tags. For additional information contact:

**Idaho Dept. of Fish & Game
600 South Walnut St.
P.O. Box 25
Boise, ID 83707
Telephone: 208-334-3700**

Idaho regulations are extensive and you will need a copy of the annual *Big Game* and *Controlled Hunt Regulations* to understand all of the opportunities. Certain controlled hunts have limited time frames for applications. There were *significant changes in hunting regulations in 1985* so be sure to get the latest info.

Hunter Orange: Not required but *strongly* suggested.

MONTANA

The license year is March 1 to February 28. Residents spend $4 for a small game license while non-residents spend $30. A $2 conservation license is a prerequisite for any license. Non-residents are restricted to approximately 17,000 big game licenses. More than 85,000 deer are harvested annually. Big game license fees are broken down as follows:

Species	Residents	Non-Residents
Black bear	$ 8	$100
Moose	52	300
Elk	10	(included in combo)
Small & big game (combo)	35	350
Sheep	52	300
Goat	52	300
Whitetail deer	9	100 and 50
Mule deer	9	100 and 50
Turkey (spring)	3	3
Antelope	8	100
Conservation license	2	2
Waterfowl stamp	5	5

Non-residents can obtain an elk tag only through the purchase of a "combination" license. Other license variations are available. The species of deer taken depends on the district hunted. For additional information contact:

**Dept. of Fish, Wildlife & Parks
1420 East Sixth St.
Helena, MT 59620
Telephone: 406-444-2951** (licenses)
Telephone: 406-444-2535 (general info)

Montana Outdoors is the state conservation magazine and is available at $7 annually from Montana Outdoors in care of the address listed above.

Hunter Orange: During the big game season all hunters must wear 400 square inches of Hunter Orange clothing above the waist. Archers, during special archery season, are exempted. Hat or cap of Hunter Orange alone is *insufficient* to fulfill the requirement.

NEVADA

The license year runs from March 1 to the last day of February. The following hunting license and big game tag fees will be in effect for non-residents July 1, 1986 - February 28, 1987.

Non-resident hunting license	$ 80
Non-resident Nelson (desert) bighorn sheep	$800

Non-resident antelope (four tags only)	$250
Non-resident mountain lion	$125
Non-resident mule deer	$130

The above are the only big game hunts open to non-residents.

The following hunting license and big game tag fees will be in effect for residents, July 1, 1986 - February 28, 1987.

Resident hunting license	$15
Resident Nelson, Rocky Mt., Calif. bighorn sheep	$75 each
Resident antelope	$30
Resident elk	$75
Resident mountain goat	$75

There is a non-refundable $3 application fee required for each big game tag applied for.

Deer season dates and quotas will be set by the State Wildlife Commission on May 10. Upland game bird, rabbit, furbearing animal (trapping) and mountain lion seasons will be set August 2. Waterfowl seasons and bag limits will be set September 6. For additional information write to:

**Nevada Dept. of Wildlife
1110 Valley Road
P.O. Box 10678
Reno, NV 89520-0022
Telephone: 702-789-0500**

Hunter Orange: *Strongly* recommended but not required by law.

OREGON

The *Oregon Wildlife* magazine is available from the listed address at no charge.

Residents pay $8 for a basic license and $6 for a deer tag. Non-residents pay $75 for a basic hunting license and $75 for a deer tag. Deer tags are sold for both blacktail and mule deer. The license year runs from January 1st to December 31st.

Besides deer, licenses are available for bear, sheep (residents only), antelope, cougars, turkey and elk. Elk tags are sold for both Roosevelt and Rocky Mountain species. Elk tags sell for $15 to residents and $112 to non-residents. Residents pay $5 for a bear tag while non-residents must spend $75. Other tags sell for $2 to $150 depending on species and status of residency. Additional information can be obtained by writing:

**Oregon Dept. of Fish & Wildlife
P.O. Box 59
Portland, OR 97207
Telephone: 503-229-5403**

Hunter Orange: Not required, but *strongly* suggested.

UTAH

Residents will pay $12 for a small game license and $15 for a big game license that includes a deer tag. Non-residents pay $40 and $150 for the same hunting rights. The license year is January 1 to December 31. For details write to:

**Information
Utah Division of Wildlife
  Resources
1596 West North Temple
Salt Lake City, UT 84116**

Elk and antlerless deer permit applications are accepted during June. Over 75,000 deer have been taken annually in past seasons. In addition, hunting is available for antelope, moose, buffalo, desert bighorn sheep, goats, bear, cougar and bobcat. (Contact the DWR in January for buffalo, desert bighorn and goat permit information.)

Hunter Orange: 400 square inches of Hunter Orange must be worn on head, chest and back when hunting big game.

A recorded hunting information message is available by calling 801-530-1297.

WASHINGTON

The state conservation magazine (unnamed in the response to our inquiry) is available from Vernon Publications, Inc., 109 West Mercer St., Seattle WA 98119, at a cost of $6.50 per year.

State residents pay $12 for a small game license and $15 for a deer tag. Non-residents pay $125 and $50 for the same privileges.

Elk, bear and turkey tags are available to residents at $20, $15 and $15 respectively. A non-resident is charged $100 for an elk tag, $150 for a bear tag and $15 for a turkey tag. Cougar tags are $20 for the resident and $300 for the non-resident.

License year is January 1 to December 31. For additional information contact:

**Dept. of Game
600 North Capitol Way
Olympia, WA 98504
Telephone: 206-753-5700**

For other information contact:
**James R. Carlin
Game License Manager
600 North Capitol Way
Olympia, WA 98504
Telephone: 206-757-5719**

There is only a small amount of non-resident hunting in Washington and no licensed guides are available. About 60,000 deer are harvested annually during a good season, along with 10,000 elk and 2,500 bear.

Hunter Orange: At this writing legislation is pending which will require hunters to wear same.

WYOMING

The official magazine of the Wyoming Game & Fish Dept., *Wyoming Wildlife,* is available at $8 per year from Wyoming Wildlife Magazine at the Game & Fish Department's address listed below.

We received only non-resident information for this year. As a result, the resident info may not be current.

Residents will spend $5 for a small game license and non-residents $25. Big game license fees vary with species as follows:

Species	Residents	Non-Residents
Deer	$15	$105
Additional deer	$7.50 to $15	$105
Elk	$25	$255
Small game	$ 5	$ 25
Archery	$ 5	$ 10
Black bear	$10	$ 55
Mountain lion	$20	$105
Wyoming game tags	$ 2	$ 2
Interstate game tags	$ 2	$ 2
Pioneer antelope	$ 2	N.A.
Pioneer deer	$ 2	N.A.
Pioneer additional deer	$ 2	N.A.
Pioneer elk	$ 5	N.A.
Antelope	$15	$105
Additional antelope	$7.50 to $15	$105
Mountain goat	$50	$505
Moose	$50	$305
Bighorn sheep	$50	$405
Spring turkey	$ 6	$ 30
Fall turkey	$ 6	$ 30
Grizzly bear	$50	closed
Game bird	$ 6	$ 30
Conservation stamp	$ 5	$ 5

License year is January 1 to December 31. Certain license applications must be made quite early in the year. *All* hunters *must purchase* the annual conservation stamp. For more detailed information write to:

**Wyoming Game & Fish Dept.
5400 Bishop Blvd.
Cheyenne, WY 82002
Telephone: 307-777-7735**

Approximately 60,000 deer are taken annually in Wyoming.

Hunter Orange: All big game hunters *must wear* one or more of hat, shirt, jacket, coat, vest or sweater (exterior garment) of solid Hunter Orange. Camouflage orange *does not* fulfill the requirement.

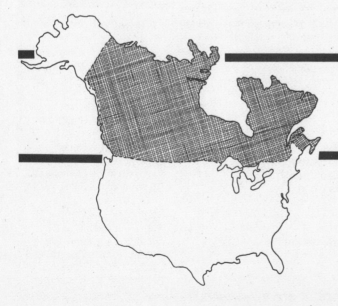

Canada
(All license fees are expressed in Canadian dollars.)

ALBERTA

A wildlife certificate and resource development stamp must be purchased ($11) before obtaining any hunting licenses. License types are many and are catalogued in part as follows:

Species	Resident	Non-resident	Alien
Black bear	$10	$ 50	$100
Grizzly bear	$20	$125	$250

Cougar	$20	$100	$200
Deer (4 types of licenses)	$10	$ 75	$150
Elk (2 types of licenses)	$10	$100	$200
Moose (3 types of licenses)	$10	$100	$200/$100
Sheep (trophy)	$20	$125	$250
Wolf	–	$ 15	$ 25
Game bird	$ 5	$ 25	$ 50

Additional information is available from:

Public Enquiries Officer
Energy & Natural Resources
Fish & Wildlife Division
Main Floor, North Tower
Petroleum Plaza
9945 - 108 Street
Edmonton, Alberta
Canada T5K 2C9
Telephone: 403-427-8580

Special licenses are available for goat, non-trophy sheep and antelope. Also there are some limitations on the number of licenses for which the hunter can apply.

BRITISH COLUMBIA

A basic hunting license costs a resident $17, a non-resident Canadian $17 and a non-resident alien is charged $43 to hunt game birds or $93 to hunt all game. The license year is April 1 to March 31.

Species licenses are required for the hunting of the following big game animals and are required in addition to the basic licenses listed above:

Licenses	B.C. Resident	Non-B.C. Res.
Black bear	$ 8	$ 50
Caribou	$20	$120
Cougar	$20	$120
Deer	$ 8	$ 60
Elk	$20	$120
Grizzly bear	$70	$320
Moose	$20	$120
Mountain goat	$30	$130
Mountain sheep	$50	$300
Wolf	not required	$ 25

For additional information write to:
Wildlife Branch
Ministry of Environment
Parliament Building
Victoria, BC
Canada V8V 1X5
Telephone: 604-387-4373

Annual big game seasons are often announced in February in a preliminary manner and are legally confirmed when annual regulations are published in July.

The 1986 season will see some change in the northeast with only large-rack caribou being allowed (and antlerless moose prohibited) in one area.

Certain regional restrictions apply and it is *important* to have a copy of the *latest regulation synopsis*.

MANITOBA

The license year in Manitoba begins April 1 and ends on March 31. Current license fees are as follows:

License	Resident	Non-resident (alien)
Wildlife certificate	$ 5	$ 5
Wildlife habitat fund	$ 5	$ 5
Game bird	$ 7	$ 85
Deer	$17	$100
Moose	$25	$300
Caribou	$30	none allowed
Elk	$30	none allowed
Turkey	$10	none allowed
Black bear	$12	$100

These fees are tentative and subject to change by the Minister of Natural Resources.

All non-residents hunting big game require the services of a licensed guide. With the exception of NR (alien) moose licenses (which are purchased by the guide or outfitter for the non-resident) licenses may be bought upon arrival in Manitoba or mailed for in advance. All checks must be made payable to the Minister of Finance, then mailed to:

A. Conyette
Cashier/Licensing
Box 42, Dept. of Natural Resources
1495 St. James St.
Winnipeg, Manitoba
Canada R3H 0W9

Migratory bird hunters must purchase Migratory Game Bird Permits from any Canadian Post Office or in care of the Winnipeg Post Office, 266 Graham Ave., Winnipeg, Manitoba R3C 0J8.

Four-day package plans are available through Travel Manitoba, 7th Floor, 155 Carlton St., Winnipeg, Manitoba, R3C 3H8. For more information write to:

Public Information Service
Dept. of Natural Resources
Box 42
1495 St. James St.
Winnipeg, Manitoba
Canada R3H 0W9
Telephone: 204-945-6784
and
Dept. of Economic Dev. & Tourism
Travel Manitoba
Dept. 3041
Winnipeg, Manitoba
Canada R3C 0V8

Antlerless deer are hunted in Manitoba.

Hunter Orange: 400 square inches of Hunter Orange clothing, including a hat of solid Hunter Orange must be worn by all hunters *except* archers and timber wolf hunters.

NEW BRUNSWICK

New Brunswick residents will spend $6 for a small game license and $16 for a deer tag. Spring and fall bear tags are $10 each, for the resident. Non-residents will spend $35 for a small game license, $60 for a deer tag and $25 for each bear tag. Moose licenses are sold to residents *only*. All non-resident hunters must employ a guide. A deer license, as long as tag is attached, is valid for ruffed grouse, spruce grouse, rabbits and migratory birds. A varmint license is $6 for residents and $15 for

---

1986-87 Manitoba Season Dates (Tentative)

Deer	
Firearms	November 10 – November 29
Muzzleloaders (residents only)	November 10 – November 15
Bowhunting	August 25 – November 29
Elk (resident only)	
Firearms	September 15 – January 30
Bowhunting	September 1 – December 13
Moose	
Firearms (residents)	September 1 – December 13
Firearms (non-residents)	September 1 – November 1
Bowhunting (residents only)	September 22 – October 25
Caribou (residents only)	September 1 – February 14
Black Bear	
Firearms	August 25 – November 15
	April 1 – June 28
Timber Wolf (residents only)	October 27 – March 28
Grouse	September 1 – December 13
Ptarmigan	September 1 – February 14
Waterfowl	September 1 – November 22

non-residents. Senior citizen licenses are available. For more information contact:

Fish & Wildlife Branch
Dept. of Forest, Mines & Energy
P.O. Box (C.P.) 6000
Fredericton, NB
Canada E3B 5H1

There is no Sunday hunting in New Brunswick. The farm country in the south and the St. John River Valley, as well as the Tobique valley are the best hunting areas for deer. During a good season, in excess of 30,000 deer will be harvested. The area around Plaster Rock is highly favored by deer hunters.

NEWFOUNDLAND (including Labrador)

There is no deer hunting in Newfoundland, but bear, moose and caribou are hunted. Residents pay $15 for bear tags and $25 each for moose and caribou tags. Canadian non-residents are charged $25 for a bear tag, $250 for a moose tag and $400 for a caribou tag. Alien (U.S. citizen) non-residents will spend $50 for a bear license, $350 for a moose tag and $600 for a caribou tag.

Non-resident big game licenses are allocated to outfitters operating licensed hunting camps within specific areas, and the number of licenses are limited. All non-residents are required to use the services of a guide. License quotas are frequently sold out early in the year so early action is required. Opening date for 1986 moose and caribou season is September 13. There will be a spring Black Bear Hunt from May 3 to June 28.

Small game licenses (rabbit, ptarmigan, ruffed and spruce grouse) are $5 for residents, $10 for non-residents.

Non-resident caribou hunting is restricted to four of nine management areas in Newfoundland. Non-residents may hunt moose in 14 of Newfoundland's 39 game management areas. There is some very fine, but relatively unexploited black bear hunting in Newfoundland. Record-book size blacks are not uncommon.

There is no Sunday hunting. For more information contact:

Wildlife Division
Dept. of Culture, Recreation &
  Youth
P.O. Box 4750
St. John's, Newfoundland
Canada A1C 5T7
Telephone: 709-576-2815

Non-residents may not hunt moose in Labrador, but they may hunt caribou and bear. A Labrador caribou tag is

$115 while a bear tag is $50. Two animals may be taken on each license. Information on these hunts may be obtained by contacting:

Tourist Services
Dept. of Development & Tourism
P.O. Box 2016
St. John's, Newfoundland
Canada A1C 5R8
Telephone: 1-800-563-6353 (toll-free)

Hunter Orange: Hunter Orange is not required but *strongly* recommended.

NOVA SCOTIA

Nova Scotion Conservation magazine is available at no charge from the Dept. of Lands and Forest at the address shown below.

It is an offense for *any* person to enter *any* forest that is unfamiliar, for the purpose of hunting, unless the following items are in possession: working compass; axe or knife; supply of waterproofed matches.

Residents will spend $10 for a small game license and $15 for a big game license. Non-residents will pay $35 and $75 respectively for the same privileges. A second deer tag is priced per the first one and allows for the taking of a total of two deer. The license year runs from April 1 to March 31 and licenses must be purchased *in person* and are *not available* through the mail. Specific information on fees, guides, statistics, etc., can be had from:

Dept. of Lands & Forests
P.O. Box 68
Truro, NS
Canada B2N 5B8
Telephone: 902-895-1591

Additional information is available from:
Dept. of Tourism
Box 130
Halifax, NS
Canada B3J 2M7
Telephone: 902-424-5000

Approximately 50,000 deer are harvested annually with a calculated success ratio of 50 percent. Antlerless deer are hunted. The northeastern counties provide the best hunting.

Hunter Orange: All hunters, trappers, or anyone accompanying them, *must wear* a cap or hat and a shirt, vest or coat that's made of Hunter Orange and is visible from all sides. Only waterfowl hunters are exempted.

ONTARIO

Landmarks, Ontario's conservation

publication, is available by writing to Landmarks, Circulation Dept., Ground Floor, 70 Bond St., Toronto, ON M5B 2J3. The current annual subscription rate (four issues) is $5 (Canadian), but is expected to increase during the summer of 1986.

Ontario residents will spend $16.50 to hunt deer, while non-residents pay $80. Moose fees are $22 for residents and $200 for non-residents. The resident spends $10 for a bear tag, the same tag costing the non-resident $25.

All small game hunters must purchase the $5.25 small game license. In addition, non-residents must purchase a $36.75 tag.

Only residents may apply for the antlerless deer tag drawings. Non-residents hunt for antlered deer *only*. Non-resident moose hunters *must be* registered guests of a licensed Ontario tourist outfitter, except under certain circumstances. Deer and bear hunters must do likewise in specific areas of the province. Export fees are charged for big game. For additional information contact:

Ministry of Natural Resources
Public Information Center
99 Wellesley St. West
Toronto, ON
Canada M7A 1W3
Telephone: 416-965-4251

PRINCE EDWARD ISLAND

Hunting licenses are $6 for residents and $25 for non-residents and are valid from September 1 to August 31. A $5 permit to hunt raccoon at night is applicable. There is no big game hunting on P.E.I. Ruffed grouse, Hungarian partridge, snowshoe rabbit, fox, raccoon and migratory birds comprise the available game. Pheasants have been proposed as a legal 1986-87 game bird. A migratory bird provincial permit, validated with a $4 habitat conservation stamp, is required at $3.50. For more information write to:

Alan Godfrey
Fish & Wildlife Division
Province of Prince Edward Island
3 Queen St.
P.O. Box 2000
Charlottetown, PEI
Canada C1A 7N8
Telephone: 902-892-0311

QUÉBEC

Two years ago changes in Quebec's regulations did away with the higher cost "alien non-resident" license fees. Now these hunters (U.S. citizens) will pay the same fees as Canadian non-residents. License fees for the 1986-87 hunting seasons are as follows:

Species	Residents	Non-Residents
Small game	$ 6.25	$ 30
Black bear	20	50
Deer	20	115
Deer on Anticosti Island	20	115
Caribou	20	115
Moose	20	115

The 1986-87 hunting season is scheduled as follows for all zones inclusive. Be sure to consult the regulations for specific opening and closing dates for specific zones. Obviously, Québec is interested in attracting U.S. sportsmen to the Province's *splendid* hunting opportunities. As a result of 1) the *excellent* hunting, and 2) the *discontinuance* of "alien non-resident" license fees, Québec is recommended for your north-country hunting. On behalf of the American sportsman, GDHA congratulates the province of Québec for this major licensing change. Hopefully, other provinces will adopt similar changes.

Moose

| Firearms | Sept. 13 to Oct. 26 |
| Archery | Aug. 30 to Oct. 5 |

Deer

| Firearms | Nov. 1 to Nov. 16 |

Archery

On Anticosti

Island	Oct. 4 to Oct. 12
Firearms	Aug. 1 to Dec. 1
Archery	Aug. 1 to Dec. 1

Caribou

| Fall season (86) | Aug. 25 to Oct. 31 |
| Spring season (87) | Feb. 15 to April 15 |

Black Bear

| Fall season (86) | Sept. 13 to Nov. 9 |
| Spring (87) | May 1 to July 4 |

Smaller game is available and includes wolf, coyote, porcupine, woodchuck, bobcat, fox, raccoon, hare, waterfowl, various grouse, ptarmigan and gray partridge. Québec publishes an annual summary of regulations for hunting and a listing of Québec outfitters. These are available from:

Gouvernement du Québec
Ministère du Loisir, de la Chasse et
de la Pêche
Direction des Communications
C.P. 2200
Québec, QC
Canada G1K 7X2

A great many moose are harvested, over 11,000 annually. It is estimated that close to 1 million man-days are devoted to moose hunting. The deer population is approximately 120,000 on the mainland and 90,000 on Anticosti Island, where the annual harvest is ap-

proximately 6,500 deer. The caribou herd on the George River area (Ungava peninsula) is the largest in the world, numbering about 600,000 animals. In some areas, the caribou take is two-per-hunter. Fall and spring seasons account for this.

Beyond doubt, at least in my mind, the *world's best deer hunting* is on Anticosti Island where a two-deer-per-hunter limit is in effect. Hunter success on Anticosti averages about 1.7 deer per hunter. Anticosti Island bucks tend to run big, and my experience is that they weigh between 140 and 150 pounds, *after* field dressing, on the average. The Island's biggest buck weighed 243 pounds. For details on Anticosti Island hunting contact:

Gaétan Hallé
Société des établissements de
plein air du Québec
Île d'Anticosti
Port Menier (Anticosti) QC
Canada G0G 2Y0
Telephone: 418-535-0231

Game populations are *very* high in Québec. Moose are estimated at 100,000 to 150,000. Bear populations are undetermined, but at established camps hunter success runs about 35 percent. There are a great many outfitters in the province and details on these can be obtained from:

André Chassé
Directeur Général
Québec Outfitters Assoc.
482, boul. St.-Cyrille ouest
Québec, QC
Canada G1S 1S4
Telephone: 418-527-1524

In this writer's opinion Québec is a hunter's paradise and a land of a million memories.

Hunter Orange: All hunters and guides *must wear* at least 500 square inches of Hunter Orange on the back, shoulder and chest, which must be visible from all angles. Exempted are crow, migratory bird, coyote, wolf, fox and archery (during archery season) hunters.

SASKATCHEWAN

There will be no woodland caribou season during 1986. Additionally, some minor changes to season dates and bag limits will occur for the 1986 season.

License types are game birds, deer, moose, elk, caribou, bear and antelope, but not all species are available to non-residents. Deer fees are $25, $100 and $200 for residents, Canadian non-resi-

dents and alien non-residents (U.S. citizens) respectively. Moose fees are $30 for residents, $150 for Canadian non-residents and $300 for alien non-residents. Elk tags are $30 for residents. Black bear fees are $15, $50 and $100 respectively.

Most other big game licenses, available only to residents on a lottery basis, are $30 each. Additional information is available from:

Parks & Renewable Resources
3211 Albert St.
Regina, Saskatchewan
Canada S4S 5W6
Telephone: 306-787-2700

Other information is available from:
Tourism & Small Business
Bank of Montreal Bldg.
2103 - 11th Ave.
Regina, Saskatchewan
Canada S4P 3V7

Approximately 35,000 deer are taken annually in this province.

Hunter Orange: Big game hunters *must wear* a complete outer suit of scarlet, bright yellow, Hunter Orange or white. Also, a hat is required (any of scarlet, bright yellow or orange, but not white). Exempted are archers during archery season.

YUKON TERRITORY

It was necessary to reprint our 1985 material as this province, once again, failed to respond to our repeated inquiries.

Residents will spend $5 for a small game and game bird license, while $10 will buy a small game, game bird and big game license.

A non-resident from Alberta or British Columbia with a valid and subsisting game bird license issued in his home province pays $5 for a small game and game bird license. Other non-residents spend $20 for the same license. Non-resident Canadians are charged $75 for a big game/small game/game bird license and aliens pay $150. Seal fees for species (purchased before hunting) range from $5 to $25. Non-resident trophy fees range from $50 for coyote to $750 for a female grizzly bear.

Other available game includes mountain sheep, moose, caribou, mountain goat, black bear, wolf and wolverine. Additional information is available from:

Renewable Resources
Wildlife & Parks Services
Box 2703
Whitehorse, Yukon
Canada Y1A 2C6